PREHISTORY AND HUMAN ECOLOGY OF THE VALLEY OF OAXACA

Kent V. Flannery and Joyce Marcus
General Editors

Volume 1 *The Use of Land and Water Resources in the Past and Present Valley of Oaxaca, Mexico*, by Anne V.T. Kirkby. Memoirs of the Museum of Anthropology, University of Michigan, No. 5. 1973.

Volume 2 *Sociopolitical Aspects of Canal Irrigation in the Valley of Oaxaca*, by Susan H. Lees. Memoirs of the Museum of Anthropology, University of Michigan, No. 6. 1973.

Volume 3 *Formative Mesoamerican Exchange Networks with Special Reference to the Valley of Oaxaca*, by Jane W. Pires-Ferreira. Memoirs of the Museum of Anthropology, University of Michigan, No. 7. 1975.

Volume 4 *Fábrica San José and Middle Formative Society in the Valley of Oaxaca*, by Robert D. Drennan. Memoirs of the Museum of Anthropology, University of Michigan, No. 8. 1976.

Volume 5 Part 1. *The Vegetational History of the Oaxaca Valley,* by C. Earle Smith, Jr. Part 2. *Zapotec Plant Knowledge: Classification, Uses and Communication about Plants in Mitla, Oaxaca, Mexico*, by Ellen Messer. Memoirs of the Museum of Anthropology, University of Michigan, No. 10. 1978.

Volume 6 *Excavations at Santo Domingo Tomaltepec: Evolution of a Formative Community in the Valley of Oaxaca, Mexico*, by Michael E. Whalen. Memoirs of the Museum of Anthropology, University of Michigan, No. 12. 1981.

Volume 7 *Monte Albán's Hinterland, Part 1: The Prehispanic Settlement Patterns of the Central and Southern Parts of the Valley of Oaxaca, Mexico,* by Richard E. Blanton, Stephen Kowalewski, Gary Feinman, and Jill Appel. Memoirs of the Museum of Anthropology, University of Michigan, No. 15. 1982.

Volume 8 *Chipped Stone Tools in Formative Oaxaca, Mexico: Their Procurement, Production and Use*, by William J. Parry. Memoirs of the Museum of Anthropology, University of Michigan, No. 20. 1987.

Volume 9 *Agricultural Intensification and Prehistoric Health in the Valley of Oaxaca, Mexico,* by Denise C. Hodges. Memoirs of the Museum of Anthropology, University of Michigan, No. 22. 1989.

Volume 10 *Early Formative Pottery of the Valley of Oaxaca,* by Kent V. Flannery and Joyce Marcus, with technical ceramic analysis by William O. Payne. Memoirs of the Museum of Anthropology, University of Michigan, No. 27. 1994.

Volume 11 *Women's Ritual in Formative Oaxaca: Figurine-making, Divination, Death and the Ancestors*, by Joyce Marcus. Memoirs of the Museum of Anthropology, University of Michigan, No. 33. 1998.

Volume 12 *The Sola Valley and the Mone Albán State: A Study of Zapotec Imperial Expansion*, by Andrew K. Balkansky. Memoirs of the Museum of Anthropology, University of Michigan, No. 36. 2002.

Related Volumes

Flannery, Kent V.
  1986 *Guilá Naquitz: Archaic Foraging and Early Agriculture in Oaxaca, Mexico.* New York: Academic Press.

Marcus, Joyce, and Kent V. Flannery
  1996 *Zapotec Civilization: How Urban Society Evolved in Mexico's Oaxaca Valley.* London: Thames and Hudson.

Museum of Anthropology, University of Michigan
Memoirs, Number 36

Prehistory and Human Ecology of the Valley of Oaxaca
Kent V. Flannery and Joyce Marcus, General Editors
Volume 12

The Sola Valley and the Monte Albán State
A Study of Zapotec Imperial Expansion

Andrew K. Balkansky

with a study of the carved stones by Joyce Marcus
and shell artifact analysis by
Linda M. Nicholas and Gary M. Feinman

Ann Arbor, Michigan
2002

©2002 by the Regents of the University of Michigan
The Museum of Anthropology
All rights reserved

Printed in the United States of America
ISBN 0-915703-53-X

Cover design by Katherine Clahassey

The University of Michigan Museum of Anthropology currently publishes three monograph series: Anthropological Papers, Memoirs, and Technical Reports, as well as an electronic series in CD-ROM form. For a complete catalog, write to Museum of Anthropology Publications, 4009 Museums Building, Ann Arbor, MI 48109-1079.

Library of Congress Cataloging-in-Publication Data

Balkansky, Andrew K., 1967-
    The Sola Valley and the Monte Albán state : a study of Zapotec imperial expansion / Andrew K. Balkansky ; with a study of the carved stones by Joyce Marcus and shell artifact analysis by Linda M. Nicholas and Gary M. Feinman.
       p. cm. -- (Prehistory and human ecology of the Valley of Oaxaca ; v. 12) (Memoirs / Museum of Anthropology, University of Michigan ; no. 36)
    Includes bibliographic references.
    ISBN 0-915703-53-X (pbk. : alk. paper)
    1. Zapotec Indians--Mexico--Sola River Valley. 2. Zapotec Indians--Antiquities. 3. Land settlement patterns, Prehistoric--Mexico--Sola River Valley. 4. Monte Albán Site (Mexico). 5. Sola River Valley (Mexico)--Antiquities. I. Title. II. Series. III. Memoirs of the Museum of Anthropology, University of Michigan ; no. 36.

GN2 .M52 no.36
[F1219.8.Z37]
306--dc21
[972.7'401]   2002038668

The paper used in this publication meets the requirements of the ANSI Standard Z39.48-1984 (Permanence of Paper)

Contents

LIST OF TABLES, *vi*
LIST OF FIGURES, *vii*
LIST OF PLATES, *ix*
INTRODUCTION TO VOLUME 12, *xiii*
ACKNOWLEDGMENTS, *xvi*
CHAPTER 1. INTRODUCTION, *1*
    What This Book Is About, *2*
    A Brief History of Oaxaca Archaeology, *4*
    A Surveyor's Guide to Ancient Oaxaca, *5*
    How Survey Sets the Agenda, *8*
    Evaluating Approaches to Social Evolution, *9*
    Monte Albán and the Evolution of Zapotec Civilization, *10*
    The Emerging Perspective: Regional Variation but Uniform Processes, *13*
    The Organization of This Book, *14*
CHAPTER 2. THE REGIONAL ARCHAEOLOGY OF THE SOLA VALLEY, *15*
    Models for the Oaxaca Macroregion, *16*
    Questions Guiding the Sola Valley Survey, *16*
    The Sola Valley Study Region, *21*
    The 1995-1996 Sola Valley Settlement Pattern Project, *25*
    Overview of the Project Results, *33*
CHAPTER 3. THE SOLA VALLEY IN THE FORMATIVE PERIOD, *35*
    The Ia Phase (Middle Formative), *35*
    The Ic Phase (Late Formative), *37*
    Period II (Terminal Formative), *45*
    The Zapotec Expansion, *49*
CHAPTER 4. THE SOLA VALLEY IN THE CLASSIC TO EARLY POSTCLASSIC PERIOD, *51*
    Period IIIa (Early Classic), *51*
    Period IIIb-IV (Late Classic–Early Postclassic), *57*
    The Territorial Limits of the Zapotec State, *65*
CHAPTER 5. THE SOLA VALLEY IN THE LATE POSTCLASSIC PERIOD, *69*
    Period V (Late Postclassic), *69*
    Sola's Historical Kingdoms, *78*
CHAPTER 6. SUMMARY AND CONCLUSIONS, *83*
    What Sola Tells Us about Monte Albán—What Monte Albán Tells Us about Sola, *84*
    Sola Valley Settlement Patterns 500 B.C.–A.D. 1521, *84*
    Answering Questions about the Sola Valley, *85*
    How the Regional Trajectories Compare, *87*
    How the Macroregion Changes Views about Monte Albán, *93*
    Implications of This Study, *94*
    Conclusions, *101*
CHAPTER 7. CARVED STONES FROM THE SOLA VALLEY, OAXACA, *by Joyce Marcus, 103*
CHAPTER 8. SHELL FROM SOLA DE VEGA, *by Linda M. Nicholas and Gary M. Feinman, 123*
CHAPTER 9. RESUMEN EN ESPAÑOL, *125*
APPENDIX A. SITE DESCRIPTIONS AND MAPS, *127*
APPENDIX B. STRUCTURE SUMMARIES, *159*
APPENDIX C. SITE SUMMARIES BY PHASE, *165*
APPENDIX D. PRODUCTIVE POTENTIALS BY PHASE, *170*
BIBLIOGRAPHY, *173*

Tables

- 2.1. Highland Oaxaca survey coverages, *21*
- 2.2. Yield ranges for land types in metric tons per hectare per year, *26*
- 2.3. Distribution of land classes (in hectares) by grid square for the Sola Valley, *26*
- 2.4. Settlement densities in the Valleys of Sola, Ejutla, and Oaxaca, *26*
- 2.5. Settlement density by phase for the Sola Valley, *26*
- 2.6. Population densities (per km^2) for the Sola Valley, the Ejutla Valley, and subregions in the Oaxaca Valley, *28*
- 2.7. Potential and archaeological population levels by phase for the Sola Valley, *28*
- 2.8. Subregional distribution of prime farmland in Oaxaca, *29*
- 2.9. Correlation coefficients for actual versus potential population by grid square in the Sola Valley, *29*
- 3.1. Sola Valley settlement by environmental zone during the Ic phase, *41*
- 3.2. Population centers in Sola, Ejutla, and the southern Oaxaca Valley during the Ic phase, *43*
- 3.3. Sola Valley settlement by environmental zone during Period II, *45*
- 3.4. Population centers in Sola, Ejutla, and the southern Oaxaca Valley during Period II, *47*
- 4.1. Sola Valley settlement by environmental zone during Period IIIa, *54*
- 4.2. Population centers in Sola, Ejutla, and the southern Oaxaca Valley during Period IIIa, *57*
- 4.3. Sola Valley settlement by environmental zone during Period IIIb-IV, *60*
- 4.4. Population centers in Sola, Ejutla, and the southern Oaxaca Valley during Period IIIb-IV, *65*
- 5.1. Sola Valley settlement by environmental zone during Period V, *72*
- 5.2. Population centers in Sola, Ejutla, and the southern Oaxaca Valley during Period V, *77*
- 8.1. Marine shell from the Sola Valley, *123*
- C.1. Ic phase sites in the Sola Valley, *165*
- C.2. Period II sites in the Sola Valley, *166*
- C.3. Period IIIa sites in the Sola Valley, *166*
- C.4. Period IIIb-IV sites in the Sola Valley, *167*
- C.5. Period V sites in the Sola Valley, *167*
- D.1. Productive potentials of occupied grid squares in the Sola Valley during the Ic phase, *170*
- D.2. Productive potentials of occupied grid squares in the Sola Valley during Period II, *170*
- D.3. Productive potentials of occupied grid squares in the Sola Valley during Period IIIa, *171*
- D.4. Productive potentials of occupied grid squares in the Sola Valley during Period IIIb-IV, *171*
- D.5. Productive potentials of occupied grid squares in the Sola Valley during Period V, *172*

Figures

1.1. Map of the State of Oaxaca showing places mentioned in the text, *3*
1.2. Chronological sequences for highland Mesoamerica, the Sola Valley, and the Valley of Oaxaca, *5*
2.1. Map of the Sola Valley survey area and other Oaxaca surveys, *18*
2.2. Prehispanic sites and modern towns in the Sola Valley, *19*
2.3. Histogram of Sola Valley site sizes in hectares, *27*
2.4. Histogram of Sola Valley population centers, *27*
2.5. Potential and archaeological population levels in the Sola Valley, *29*
3.1. Ia phase settlement pattern in the Sola Valley, *36*
3.2. Ic phase settlement pattern in the Sola Valley, *38*
3.3. Ic phase scatterplot of potential and actual population in the Sola Valley, *41*
3.4. Histogram of Sola Valley site sizes during the Ic phase, *41*
3.5. Rank-size graph for the Sola Valley during the Ic phase, *42*
3.6. Period II settlement pattern in the Sola Valley, *44*
3.7. Period II scatterplot of potential and actual population in the Sola Valley, *46*
3.8. Histogram of Sola Valley site sizes during Period II, *46*
3.9. Rank-size graph for the Sola Valley during Period II, *48*
4.1. Period IIIa settlement pattern in the Sola Valley, *52*
4.2. Period IIIa scatterplot of potential and actual population in the Sola Valley, *56*
4.3. Histogram of Sola Valley site sizes during Period IIIa, *56*
4.4. Rank-size graph for the Sola Valley during Period IIIa, *58*
4.5. Rank-size graph for Sola, Ejutla, and the southern Oaxaca Valley during Period IIIa, *58*
4.6. Period IIIb-IV settlement pattern in the Sola Valley, *59*
4.7. Period IIIb-IV scatterplot of potential and actual population in the Sola Valley, *61*
4.8. Histogram of Sola Valley site sizes during Period IIIb-IV, *61*
4.9. Rank-size graph for the Sola Valley during Period IIIb-IV, *64*
5.1. Period V settlement pattern in the Sola Valley, *70*
5.2. Scatterplot of potential and actual population in the Sola Valley, *75*
5.3. Histogram of Sola Valley site sizes during Period V, *75*
5.4. Rank-size graph for the Sola Valley during Period V, *76*
7.1. Carved lintel at San Martín Huamelulpan, Oaxaca, *104*
7.2. Carved lintel at San Martín Huamelulpan, *104*
7.3. Drawing of carved lintel at San Martín Huamelulpan, *105*
7.4. Two carved stones embedded in the wall of the church at San Francisco Sola, *105*
7.5. Two carved stones embedded in the wall of the church at San Francisco Sola, *105*
7.6. Two carved stones from Sola, evidently intended to be tenoned into a wall, *105*
7.7. Carved stone found at Reyes Etla, Valley of Oaxaca, *106*
7.8. Carved stone found in the ball court at Reyes Etla, Valley of Oaxaca, *106*
7.9. Carved stone found at Zaachila, Valley of Oaxaca, *107*
7.10. Carved stone found at Tlacochahuaya, Valley of Oaxaca, *107*
7.11. Carved stone found during excavations in the Yagul ball court, Valley of Oaxaca, *108*
7.12. Carved stone found in Tomb 7 at Mitla, Valley of Oaxaca, *109*
7.13. Ball court at Yagul, showing the location of a carved stone, *109*
7.14. General view of a Valley of Oaxaca ball court, *109*
7.15. Sola 39 ball court, showing location of a carved stone, *110*
7.16. Carved stone found in the center of the ball court at Sola 39, *110*
7.17. Carved stone found in the center of the ball court at Sola 39, *111*
7.18. Carved stone found in the center of the ball court at Sola 39, *111*

7.19. Carved stone from Sola 10 showing a human figure and a tri-lobed motif, *111*
7.20. Drawing of lintel set into the church of Santa María Sola, *112*
7.21. Lintel set into the church of Santa María Sola, *112*
7.22. Examples of the "Jaws of the Sky" motif, *113*
7.23. Photo of carved stone embedded in the church wall at Santa María Sola, *114*
7.24. Stone found embedded in the church wall at Santa María Sola, *114*
7.25. Carved stone from Sola that bears four calendar dates, *114*
7.26. Ejutla carved stone showing a Zapotec noblewoman, *115*
7.27. Ejutla carved stone showing crossed arms, *115*
7.28. Ejutla carved stone showing crossed arms, *115*
7.29. Ejutla carved stone of a crouching jaguar consuming a stylized human heart, *116*
7.30. Ejutla carved stone of a crouching jaguar consuming a stylized human heart, *116*
7.31. Painted mural at Teotihuacan, showing a jaguar consuming human hearts, *117*
7.32. A stylized human heart with blood dripping from it, from mural at Teotihuacan, *117*
A.1. San Juan Sola (S1), *127*
A.2. Detail of the civic-ceremonial core at San Juan Sola, *127*
A.3. Detail of Mound 2 at Sola 3, *128*
A.4. Detail of the civic-ceremonial core at Sola 8, *129*
A.5. San Ildefonso Sola (S10), *130*
A.6. Detail of the civic-ceremonial core at San Ildefonso, *130*
A.7. Detail of the civic-ceremonial core at Sola 16, *132*
A.8. Detail of the civic-ceremonial core at La Cumbrita (S20), *133*
A.9. Los Chilillos, Cueva Negra Group (S23), *134*
A.10. Los Chilillos, Portillo Group (S23), *135*
A.11. Detail of the civic-ceremonial core at Los Chilillos, *135*
A.12. Detail of Structures 14-15 at Los Chilillos, *135*
A.13. Detail of Structures 21-25 at Los Chilillos, *135*
A.14. Texcoco (S39), *139*
A.15. Detail of the civic-ceremonial core at Texcoco, *139*
A.16. Detail of the West Ball Court at Texcoco, *139*
A.17. Detail of Structures 27-31 at Texcoco, *139*
A.18. Detail of the civic-ceremonial core at Sola 47, *141*
A.19. Piedra de los Anticuados (S61), *144*
A.20. Detail of the civic-ceremonial core at Santo Niño Mueve Corazones (S65), *145*
A.21. La Muchacha (S67), *146*
A.21a. Detail of civic-ceremonial core at La Muchacha (S67), *146*
A.22. Detail of civic-ceremonial core at Sola 81/82, *149*
A.23. Detail of the civic-ceremonial core at Cerro Orcón (S84), *150*
A.24. Detail of the civic-ceremonial core at Shilegua (S97), *153*
A.25. Los Paderones (S111), *156*
A.26. Detail of the civic-ceremonial core at Los Paderones, *156*

Plates

2.1. The seventeenth-century church at San Miguel Sola de Vega is in the center of the valley, *20*
2.2. View of the Sola Valley looking southeast, *20*
2.3. Carmelo Aragón with men from San Juan Sola wait outside a ritually significant cave and nearby archaeological site, *23*
2.4. The church at Santa María Sola has several prehispanic carved stones set into its walls, including the rectangular tomb lintel resting above the arched entryway, *24*
2.5. Heinrich Berlin first recorded this prehispanic carved stone set into the east-facing church wall at Santa María Sola, *25*
2.6. Polished stone axes from the Sola Valley survey from a site dating to the Postclassic period, *28*
2.7. Projectile points from the Sola Valley survey, from sites with a mix of Classic and Postclassic period occupations, *28*
2.8. Surveyors working at S23 (Heinrich Berlin's "Los Chilillos" site), *30*
2.9. Carmelo Aragón, Verónica Pérez, Lázaro Aragón, and Everardo Olivera wait to meet with the municipal president at San Ildefonso Sola, *32*
3.1. Grayware and fine brownware ceramics from S39 that date to Monte Albán I, *37*
3.2. G.12s from the Sola Valley (some misfired to a yellow-orange color), including two combed bases that date to Monte Albán Ic, *39*
3.3. The town of Rancho Viejo is located near the juncture of the Sola and Atoyac rivers at the southeastern limit of the project area, looking east, *39*
3.4. S61, looking northwest toward the center of the Sola Valley, *40*
4.1. Gray eagle-claw support and G.23, *53*
4.2. Everardo Olivera and Carmelo Aragón measure a structure at S23, *55*
4.3. The ball court at S23, with a carved stone fallen in the center, *55*
4.4. Brownware urn fragments typical of IIIb-IV sites in the Sola Valley, *58*
4.5. Brownware brazier fragments from the top of the stone outcrop at S61, probably dating to late IIIb-IV, *58*
4.6. Laura Stiver surveys near Structure 1 at S39, the most monumental IIIb-IV site in the Sola Valley, *62*
4.7. The plaza and surrounding structures at S1, typical of the smaller IIIb-IV sites with architecture in the Sola Valley, *62*
4.8. Structure 1, situated on the east side of the plaza at S1, *63*
4.9. Surveyors walk through corn planted in the ball court at S1, *63*
5.1. G.3Ms (some misfired) typical of Postclassic sites in the Sola Valley, *71*
5.2. Sola Valley red-on-creamwares, dating to the Postclassic period, *71*
5.3. The fortress at S40, on the summit of a mountain near Santos Reyes, *73*
5.4. Structure 1 at S111, probably the ruler's palace, *74*
5.5. The main ball court at S111, *74*
5.6. Architectural complexes from S111, Cabo de Hacha and the passage into the Valley of Oaxaca, *79*

para
Gary M. Feinman, Stephen A. Kowalewski y Everardo Olivera Díaz
mis maestros en el recorrido arqueológico
y Fausto Olivera Mendoza
quien anda todavía en nuestra memoria

An Introduction to Volume 12 of the Series

by Kent V. Flannery and Joyce Marcus

During the last twenty years of Oaxaca archaeology, a remarkable achievement has begun to take shape: the Oaxaca highlands are becoming the setting for the largest continuous full-coverage settlement pattern survey in the New World. One by one, from north to south, the regions of Cuicatlán, Tamazulapan, Nochixtlán, Huamelulpan, Jaltepec, Peñoles, Etla, Tlacolula, Guirún, Zimatlán, Ocotlán, Ejutla, Sola de Vega, and Miahuatlán have been systematically surveyed on foot. While a few gaps between survey blocks remain to be filled in, archaeologists are already reaping the benefits of this "macroregional" data set. One cannot only see early Mixtec and Zapotec states emerging in this vast area, but also find clues to how each state put together its tributary hinterland.

This Memoir, the twelfth in our series of monographs on the prehistory and human ecology of Oaxaca, deals with changing patterns of settlement in Sola de Vega, west of Ejutla. However, the fact that so many neighboring valleys have already been surveyed allows the author, Andrew Balkansky, to see large-scale patterns that would otherwise be invisible.

At an earlier stage of the Oaxaca project, Joyce Marcus pointed out that hieroglyphic inscriptions from ca. A.D. 1-100 recorded the names of provinces that Monte Albán claimed to possess. These provinces lay some 75-150 km outside the Valley of Oaxaca, and the question was: How were they brought under Monte Albán's control? So far, two of the regions named in the inscriptions have been surveyed, and the answer to the question is different in each case.

The first province surveyed, the Cuicatlán Cañada, turns out to have been conquered by Monte Albán in late Period I or early II. The second, comprising Miahuatlán and Ejutla, appears to have been taken over peacefully, although some demographic reorganization and centralization accompanied the takeover.

Now Balkansky has added Sola de Vega, a third region assimilated by Monte Albán. It turns out that Sola was so sparsely populated in Monte Albán I that it could simply be colonized by immigration from the Valley of Oaxaca.

Balkansky's work shows us that Zapotec expansion was not a uniform process, destined to look the same in every outlying region. He concludes that when one part of their hinterland was nearly vacant, like Sola, the Zapotec expanded by simple colonization. When outlying regions were ethnically Zapotec and not overly jealous of their autonomy, like Ejutla, they could be brought under Monte Albán's hegemony by royal marriage or military alliance. Only when an outlying region was ethnically different and unwilling to be taken over, like Cuicatlán, did the Zapotec resort to outright conquest.

As Balkansky points out, the richness and diversity of Zapotec political strategy only become visible when many outlying provinces have been surveyed. It is the macroregional nature of the aforementioned full-coverage survey that has broadened our perspective on imperial expansion.

Balkansky's revision of old ideas, however, goes beyond the diversity in strategies for expansion. He also challenges the notion, popular among cultural ecologists of the 1960s, that access to good land explains the overwhelming majority of site locations. Balkansky argues that the Zapotecs' main reason for colonizing Sola was to establish a route from the temperate Valley of Oaxaca to the tropical Pacific Coast. The result is that two of Sola's early population centers were on defensible hills at either end of the valley; keeping the route open was evidently more important than living adjacent to the best farmland.

Nor is Balkansky convinced that Monte Albán's outlying provinces were part of a Zapotec "world system," however appealing that term may be to some of his fellow archaeologists. Wallerstein's original world system model was really about the penetration of Western capitalism into formerly undeveloped Third World communities. Balkansky points out that in Wallerstein's scheme, the West extracted raw materials from its colonies and sold them expensive manufactured goods. Gary Feinman and Linda Nicholas's excavations at Ejutla, however, show the reverse of this pattern: Ejutla manufactured "expensive" shell ornaments for shipment to the Valley of Oaxaca. Balkansky's conclusion that the world system model is inappropriate for Oaxaca recalls Gil Stein's reevaluation of the model's appropriateness for understanding Mesopotamia (Stein 1999).

Further Mesopotamian-Oaxacan analogies can be found in Balkansky's "chain reaction" model for state formation in the Oaxaca highlands. Our current data suggest that the Zapotec state was the first to form. San José Mogote, the paramount center for one of three rival chiefdoms, seized a defensible mountaintop at 500 B.C. and created the city of Monte Albán. Over the next 300 years, Monte Albán both (1) took over its valley-floor rivals, and (2) expanded into the Cuicatlán Cañada and Sola de Vega, creating a Zapotec state.

Monte Albán's growth and expansionist tendencies posed a threat to its Mixtec neighbors, many of whom responded by consolidating and moving to defensible hilltops. The population of the Tilantongo Valley moved to Monte Negro at a time equivalent to late Monte Albán I. Yucuita in the Nochixtlán Valley, already on a hill, increased its size. Perhaps the closest parallels to the Valley of Oaxaca can be found in Huamelulpan, a valley previously surveyed by Balkansky. There Santa Cruz Tayata, paramount center for the largest of several rival chiefdoms, moved to a defensible mountaintop at 300 B.C. and created the city of Huamelulpan. Those Mixtec polities that consolidated their population on defensible hills successfully resisted Zapotec takeover, and some created states of their own.

Analogies can be found in southern Mesopotamia, where the Uruk state had formed by 3500 B.C. For a time Uruk was unchallenged as a large, walled urban center, and "outposts" or "enclaves" with Uruk affinities could be found as far up the Euphrates as modern Turkey. By 2700 B.C., however, neighboring urban centers like Umma, Shurruppak, Zabalam, and Bad-Tibira had grown up to rival Uruk (Adams and Nissen 1972:19). We suspect that this case, too, reflects a "chain reaction" on the part of neighboring polities, following an initial case of state formation. A frequent problem in identifying such chain reactions is that one's ceramic chronology may be too coarse-grained to detect the time lag between the emergence of the region's first state and the second, the third, and so on. Serial state formations may appear simultaneous until we establish a fine-grained chronology, such as that produced by stratigraphic excavation.

Finally, Balkansky makes a contribution to our understanding of *cacicazgos*, petty kingdoms typical of the Late Postclassic. *Cacicazgos* were societies in which state-level kingship and social stratification survived, even though the polity itself might have shrunk to the size of a typical chiefdom (and might display only a three-tiered administrative hierarchy). Balkansky is convinced that *cacicazgos* have a longer history than previously thought; he believes he can see them forming on the periphery of larger states during the Classic period.

With the recent death of Gordon R. Willey—considered the father of settlement pattern survey, despite his assigning much of the credit to Julian Steward—this would seem an appropriate time to consider the future of that research method. Willey trained William T. Sanders, who trained Jeffrey R. Parsons, who trained Richard E. Blanton, who trained Gary M. Feinman and Stephen A. Kowalewski, who in turn trained Balkansky. But full-coverage survey on foot is a young scholar's job, and it is not yet clear whether there is a new generation of full-coverage surveyors on the horizon. More provinces of the early Zapotec state are still out there: Nejapa, Ocelotepec, Chiltepec, Chichicapan, Guilá, Ixtlán, Yalalag, and the Sierra Juárez. Let us hope that in addition to all his other projects, Balkansky has time to train the young legs who will survey to the limits of Monte Albán's tribute territory.

Adams, Robert McC., and Hans J. Nissen
1972   The Uruk Countryside: The Natural Setting of Urban Societies. Chicago: University of Chicago Press.

Stein, Gil
1999   Rethinking World-Systems: Diasporas, Colonies, and Interaction in Uruk Mesopotamia. Tucson: University of Arizona Press.

Acknowledgments

The Sola Valley Settlement Pattern Project originated during my doctoral studies in anthropology at the University of Wisconsin-Madison. I thank my graduate advisor, Gary M. Feinman, and Linda M. Nicholas for their supervision and assistance in starting this project. I also thank Charles S. Spencer at the American Museum of Natural History, New York, for that institution's support during the analysis and writing stage. I made the final revisions to this volume at George Washington University, Washington, D.C. I thank Joyce Marcus for reading and commenting on successive drafts of this final manuscript. Tinker-Nave and National Science Foundation grants supported the field research.

The Instituto Nacional de Antropología e Historia and the Centro Regional de Oaxaca granted necessary permits, and provided institutional support in Mexico. I am especially grateful for the assistance of Victoria Arriola, Eduardo López, Nelly Robles, and Roberto Zárate. The survey would not have been possible without the expert field assistance of Carmelo Aragón, Lázaro Aragón, Ruth R. Edelstein, Everardo Olivera, Fausto Olivera, Verónica Pérez, and Laura R. Stiver. Ronald Spores in Oaxaca, and the Olivera family in Xaaga offered retreats from the survey madness. Alejandrina Martínez was our friend and host in the field. Finally, I thank the municipal authorities and people of Sola de Vega, Oaxaca for the opportunity to study their past.

Chapter 1

Introduction

The Tropic of Cancer is a convenient dividing line between the desert north and the high civilizations of ancient southern Mexico. I was returning from my dissertation fieldwork in the southern state of Oaxaca, driving a beat-up truck with balding tires for hours turning to days of basically straight road and ceaseless desert, when it hit me. After passing the sign that demarcates the end of tropical latitudes, but long before Laredo and the borderlands, the realization flashed in my mind: "I have no paradigm!"

In science, we tend no longer to speak of epiphanies or "Eureka!" moments, but instead call them "paradigm shifts." I cannot agree with the esteemed Professor Kuhn (1962) on the nature of such occurrences, or at least those contemporary interpretations of Kuhn suggesting that worldview trumps data. I was too naive at the time to understand the politics of the discipline. And my not-so-old professors were still alive and kicking. My own Eureka! moment came entirely upon examination of the new data before me. But before returning to Madison, Wisconsin, where I would start writing my dissertation, I had a scheduled stop in New Orleans at the Society for American Archaeology meeting.

I was thinking about the paper that I was going to give on urban beginnings in the Mixteca Alta of Oaxaca (Balkansky 1998a). I had worked in the Mixteca Alta before and I would work there again. Some scholars might call this set of regions a "periphery" of Monte Albán and the Valley of Oaxaca. This despite the fact that the known Mixteca Alta is several times larger than the Valley of Oaxaca and its demographic and political development at the time of state formation was equivalent (Balkansky et al. 2000). Even if it could be regarded as peripheral, the Mixteca Alta certainly was not the same kind of periphery as the Sola Valley (the project from which I was returning). In fact, I did not think that this Mixtec region was a periphery of Monte Albán at all.

After surveying Huamelulpan and nearby sites in the Mixteca Alta, I was convinced that this place became an urban society and state at roughly the same time as Monte Albán, and that the conquest of Huamelulpan by Monte Albán was not a good explanation for the changes in this region. Even catchall phrases such as "hierarchically structured inter-group interaction" and "core domination" missed their mark. Huamelulpan and Sola—the two regions I had worked in—had completely different evolutionary trajectories. Huamelulpan urbanized rapidly and became a rival of Monte Albán. The Sola Valley was colonized or conquered by the Monte Albán state. Yet both regions evolved in the same historical setting, and both had something important to tell us about those times.

Most archaeological studies of interaction use some form of world system reasoning (e.g. Hall and Chase-Dunn 1993), such as Immanuel Wallerstein's (1974) historical explanation for the origins of capitalism. The world system according to Wallerstein is an economic zone composed of core and peripheral societies that extends beyond a single region or state. An exchange differential soon develops, with the benefit going to core states. Yet time and again, when actual (rather than assumed) archaeological and historical cases are examined, the so-called periphery fails to develop as it should under world system expectations (e.g. Stein 1998; Stern 1988). The recurring criticism is that peripheral societies are more active in structuring exchange relations, and their economic organization is more variable, than the world system model allows.

Archaeologists nevertheless use the world system to describe prehistoric societies at virtually any scale or level of social complexity; the concept is now so over-used that it has lost whatever explanatory power it once held (Stein 1998). Some scholars claim the "world system" has been in operation for the past 5000 years (Frank 1993). I have no doubt that we will soon hear of the "Paleolithic world system." Stealth world system models also abound—formulations that ignore Wallerstein but carry the same conceptual baggage. One reason that archaeologists are attracted to world system models is that the operative lingo is easily imported into the systems reasoning with which they are already familiar. Explaining culture change can then follow well-established (read "tired") patterns but with snazzy new terms.

Apart from its questionable validity in noncapitalist economies, Wallerstein's and other archaeological modifications of the world system are functional and overly focused on the core zone. This means that scholars can describe social systems but not their origins and causes of change, and that latent diffusionism is hidden within the model. As the core goes, so goes the periphery, an invariant zone of secondary importance in most world system models. Yet multistage processes, including the expansion of large-scale economic networks, cannot be articulated in this synchronic framework. The question of origins is always conflated with later functional utility in explanations of so-called prehistoric world systems.

There is one last objection to excessive and uncritical use of world system models, and it brings me back to Oaxaca. Wallerstein calls attention to scales of analysis beyond the region. An archaeologist would say "so far, so good"—but this observation alone says little. That is because there was always a notion of center and periphery in archaeology. You only have to read a bit of V. Gordon Childe to know that. Oaxaca archaeologists shared the belief that Monte Albán was the center and the periphery was something else out there and more or less the same. We now realize that each outer region (or sector of the periphery) has its own separate history, and that regional variation is the key to understanding the overall system and its sources of change (e.g. Balkansky 1998b; Feinman and Nicholas 1990a; Marcus 1992a).

As I drove along, I was thinking that the core/periphery concept breaks down when we start to document the variation in each peripheral region; I was not going to define yet another type of periphery (there are even regions called "semi-peripheries"). The proliferation of peripheries had already stretched the world system model too far from its starting point to remain coherent. I was concerned with explaining culture change: a world system (and its other systems analogues) was a good framework for describing long periods of relative stasis, but not episodes of change. It was clear that we needed a more dynamic model of social evolution to encompass the growing range of regional variation.

I entered the field thinking about how my results would fit the main but overly generalized ideas about Mesoamerican civilization. Afterwards, my confrontation with actual data forced me to rethink those ideas, and begin to see the emerging picture.

What This Book Is About

The early state in traditional social science models begins with a single urban center formed over centuries of slow evolution (e.g. Adams 1966; Flannery 1972; Renfrew 1972). As urbanization proceeds, the capital expands and restructures its subject territory and the state is formed. Other urban and state societies eventually arise from the stimulus or "civilizing influence" of the original center. Networks of states become civilizations, and our reconstructed states march onward toward their decline and fall. I argue that the traditional models for the evolution of complex societies are no longer valid. Emergent states can form in multiple locations under conditions of intensified interaction; and the rise of states and later changes are not the outcome of long-term trends alone, but also transformative events of short duration. Study of the single site or region reveals only part of the multistage process.

Archaeologists mostly do without a multiregional frame of reference. It takes decades of concerted effort to build comparative databases on the macroregional scale. Yet most social evolutionary theory dates before the era of comparative regional survey, and continues to be predicated on capital-centered notions of the ancient world. On the effects of this skewed perspective, Kowalewski (1990a:53) writes:

> In its fascination with pyramids, tombs, and inscriptions, has not archaeology contributed mightily to images of prehistoric civilization as a social engine for pyramid-building, the pyramid as reflection of the entire social order, and the view from the top of the pyramid as the best view in the ancient world?

The study of settlement patterns in some world areas is now extending beyond the single region. Archaeologists can begin to articulate urban capitals with their most distant hinterlands, and assess the variation in evolutionary trajectories over multiple regions (e.g. Billman and Feinman [eds.] 1999; Feinman and Marcus [eds.] 1998).

The subject of this book is the Monte Albán state. A few years ago I began a survey of the Sola Valley to see how this region compared to others in Oaxaca. This project is part of a shared effort that goes back more than 30 years to build comparative databases for Oaxaca's many separate regions. This work will discuss the changing views of Monte Albán that were the outcome of regional survey, and how new data from these surveys challenged older paradigms. Oaxaca archaeologists used to think that apart from Monte Albán every peripheral or subordinate region was basically the same. As regional surveys progressed, this view has proved to be wrong time and time again; even the most committed surveyors have been forced to reevaluate their ideas in the face of expanding survey coverage (e.g. Finsten and Kowalewski 1999). The challenge is to generate models of culture change that keep pace with the new results.

Monte Albán was the center of the emergent Zapotec civilization in the southern highlands of Mexico (State of Oaxaca) in the second half of the first millennium B.C. (Bernal 1965; Blanton et al. 1999; Marcus and Flannery 1996). Monte Albán had the earliest concentration of hieroglyphic writing, and was among the first urban and state societies in Mesoamerica. After the founding of Monte Albán, the Zapotec capital began an expansionist phase that eventually brought much of Oaxaca into its political sphere. Monte Albán also interacted with other autono-

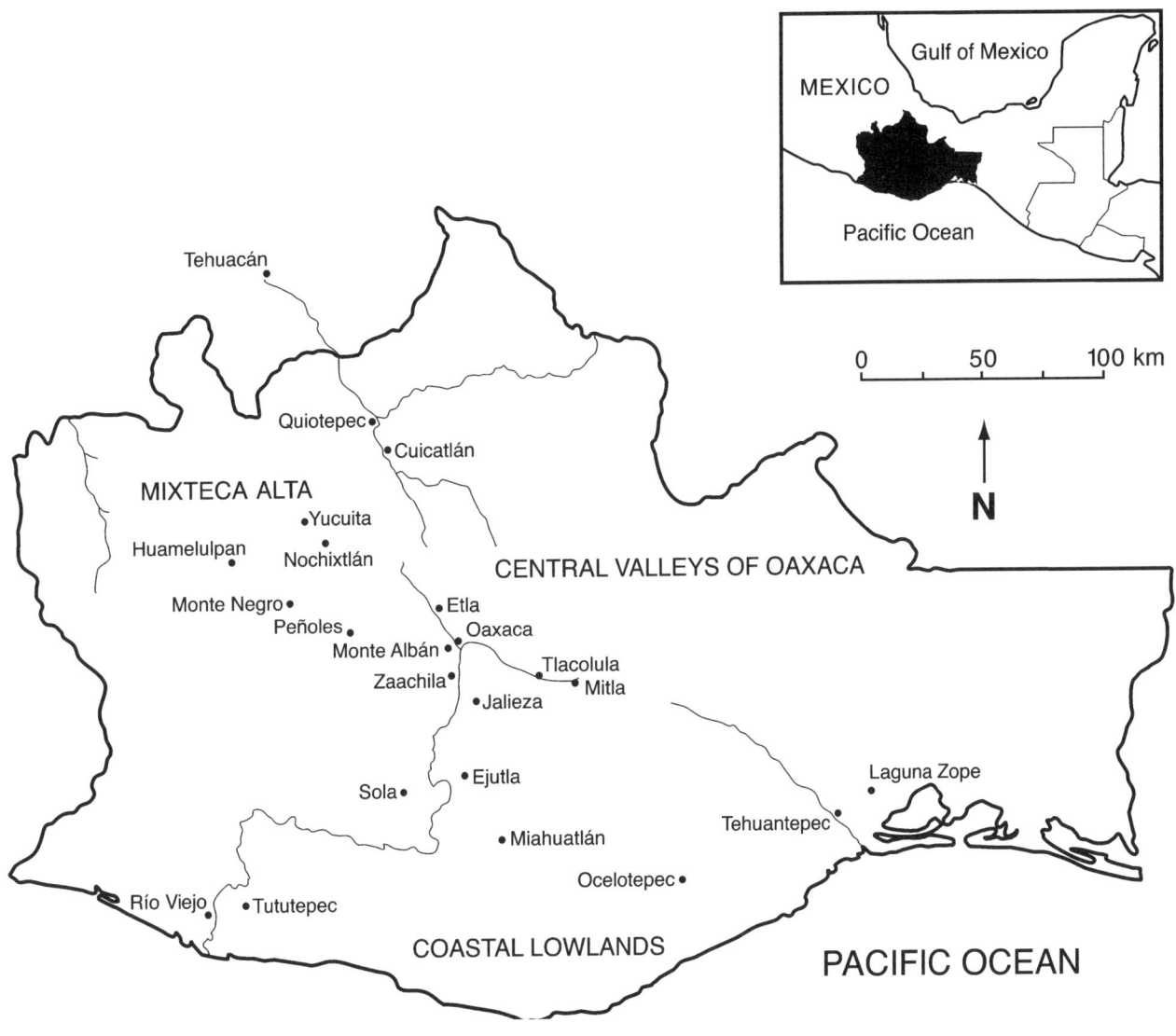

Figure 1.1. Map of the State of Oaxaca showing places mentioned in the text.

mous societies via trade, diplomacy, and warfare in more distant regions. After 30 years of systematic surveys, recurrent patterns are now visible in studies of the Valley Zapotec and their neighbors (e.g. Balkansky 1998b, 2001; Marcus and Flannery 1996:195-207). Each regional pattern is unique though evolved in the same large-scale context.

Most Oaxaca archaeologists agree that urban beginnings and state formation are the broader explanatory contexts for the early period under study (after 500 B.C.). Monte Albán's collapse is the explanatory context for the later period (after A.D. 500). After A.D. 800, Monte Albán's decline leaves a political vacuum that is eventually filled by multiple small states called *cacicazgos*. The *cacicazgo* is the basic regional political structure at the time of Spanish contact in the 1520s. The disagreements among scholars (and there are many) arise when trying to explain why these things happened the way they did, and the extent to which particular regions should be tied together in unified theories. One point I want to make at the outset is that state evolution is continuous: the Classic period and earlier polities were direct precursors for the late prehispanic form of state. First-, second-, and third-generation states in Oaxaca were not as different as is often assumed.

The approach to social evolution that I am using is less about finding trends in complex systems than in defining the nested structures within which social actors operate. I find this a more productive way to explain culture change than the systems approach. In that approach, which still influences regional models, explanations of culture change project varying sets of prime movers until reaching some threshold or other, defined after the fact. It is then assumed that the social system will return to its relative steady state or change occurs. Agency is buried in the mix.

In the transformational/historical approach that I follow (e.g. Spencer 1990), the underlying systemic structures remain important, but the explanation relies on social actors who change the system (see also Marcus and Flannery 1996:31). One consequence of this view of social evolution is that it keeps separate the events of Monte Albán's specific history from the larger-scale processes of state formation and collapse. A second consequence is that the study of evolutionary trends does not tell us everything we need to know about culture change.

In this volume are the results of my archaeological survey in the Sola Valley of Oaxaca (Balkansky 1997a, 1997b) (Figs. 1.1, 1.2). The Sola region, which borders the Valley of Oaxaca, is one passageway to the coastal lowlands of Oaxaca. It is one of several suspected Zapotec provinces (e.g. Feinman and Nicholas 1990a; Marcus and Flannery 1996:195-207; Spencer and Redmond 1997). The Sola Valley case study is relevant to questions about Monte Albán interaction and the evolution of complex societies. Are the effects of Zapotec state formation visible in regions outside the Valley of Oaxaca? What are the mechanisms of state control? How do multiregional, multi-ethnic polities form, and how long do they last? Do cycles of expansion and contraction occur in early states? How is Monte Albán's later collapse manifested in nearby regions? What do these large-scale patterns tell us about our models of social evolution? By shifting the scale of analysis into successively larger frames of reference we can begin to address these questions.

I present the Sola Valley survey results for each archaeological phase in a multiregional framework. I then summarize the results and evaluate their implications for general models of social evolution. The results of this project expand the known range of variation in Oaxaca settlement patterns, and further refine our ideas about Monte Albán.

A Brief History of Oaxaca Archaeology

Monte Albán is near the geographic center of the Valley of Oaxaca; the site is also the centerpoint of past and current archaeological work in the modern state. Excavations continue at other sites; surveys expand outward; but most projects eventually refer back to the ancient capital. Monte Albán was among the first cities and state-level societies in Mesoamerica. Our earliest evidence for hieroglyphic texts also comes from Monte Albán. As recorded on stone monuments in the city's grand plaza, Monte Albán's full territorial boundaries extend far outside the valley in certain periods. Other sites and regions can tell us much about the urban revolution in Oaxaca.

Scientific archaeology in Oaxaca began in the late nineteenth century at Monte Albán and other valley sites (Bernal 1965, 1980). The research history that I recount here (also Balkansky 1998b; Blanton et al. 1999:22-31; Marcus and Flannery 1996:27-29) began with the work of Caso and others in the 1930s. Their research anticipated the modern era in using ethnohistorical sources, regional comparisons, and the dual databases of survey and excavation. This integrated approach remains the most enduring and productive research tradition. After decades of research, we have the accumulated results from survey and excavation at Monte Albán, but also from systematic survey at over 5000 sites in the modern state and several follow-up excavations. Oaxaca is now one of the world's principal laboratories for the study of social evolution (Marcus and Flannery 1996:32).

Our understanding of Monte Albán and its origins begins with Caso et al.'s 18 field seasons (1931-1958) of excavation at the site (Bernal 1965; Caso, Bernal, and Acosta 1967). Caso's Monte Albán Project established the ceramic chronology and construction episodes of Mesoamerica's earliest city. Monte Albán was shown to have a continuous occupation from 500 B.C. until modern times. The study of urban origins continued with Caso et al.'s explorations of contemporary centers in the Mixteca Alta (Acosta and Romero 1992; Caso 1938, 1942). Caso (1928, 1947, 1965a, 1965b) also began his study of the Zapotec and Mixtec writing systems at this time.

After the Monte Albán Project, Bernal (1965) surveyed and excavated other Valley of Oaxaca sites. Bernal showed the valley to be a coherent study region with a ceramic complex similar to Monte Albán. Some of Bernal's sites turned out to be important pre-Monte Albán settlements that were excavated by Flannery and his students (e.g. Flannery [ed.] 1976). Bernal and others also established the outlines of Monte Albán's collapse with studies at Classic and Early Postclassic sites in the Valley of Oaxaca (e.g. Bernal 1958; Bernal and Gamio 1974; Paddock et al. 1968). Bernal et al. also continued to work in the Mixtec-speaking regions of Oaxaca (e.g. Bernal 1949; Paddock 1966).

Since the late 1960s, a triumvirate of long-term research projects continued the study of Zapotec civilization (Marcus and Flannery 1996:27-29). First, Flannery and Marcus's Prehistory and Human Ecology Project has systematically analyzed excavated Archaic and Formative period sites in the Valley of Oaxaca (Flannery [ed.] 1976; Flannery [ed.] 1986; Marcus and Flannery 1996). The monographs of this Michigan project contain evidence for social conditions on the eve of the urban revolution (also Drennan 1976; Whalen 1981). Second, Marcus's Zapotec Monuments Project is a catalogue of carved stones from the valley and nearby regions (Marcus 1992b). The study of Zapotec writing has recovered historical information not otherwise available to the archaeologist. The latest study of Sola carved stones is included in this volume. Third, Blanton et al.'s Settlement Pattern Project collected survey data from Monte Albán, the Valley of Oaxaca, and several nearby regions (Blanton 1978; Blanton et al. 1982, 1993, 1999; Kowalewski et al. 1989). Settlement pattern survey provides regional and macroregional perspectives critical to understanding complex societies. The work reported here continues in this tradition.

The modern synthesis is not complete without reference to the neighboring Mixtec civilization. Spores' (1967, 1972, 1984) Nochixtlán Valley Project and subsequent work in the Mixteca

YEARS	MESOAMERICA	VALLEY OF OAXACA	SOLA
A.D. 1500	HISTORIC		
1400	LATE POSTCLASSIC	MONTE ALBAN V	MONTE ALBAN V
1300			
1200			
1100			
1000	EARLY POSTCLASSIC	MONTE ALBAN IV	MONTE ALBAN IIIB - IV
900			
800			
700	LATE CLASSIC	MONTE ALBAN IIIB	
600			
500			
400	EARLY CLASSIC	MONTE ALBAN IIIA	MONTE ALBAN IIIA
300			
200			
100	LATE/TERMINAL FORMATIVE	MONTE ALBAN II	MONTE ALBAN II
100			
200		MONTE ALBAN LATE I	MONTE ALBAN LATE I
300			
400		MONTE ALBAN EARLY	MONTE ALBAN EARLY I
500	MIDDLE FORMATIVE		
600		ROSARIO	UNDOCUMENTED PRE - MONTE ALBAN FORMATIVE
700			
800		GUADALUPE	
900			
1000		SAN JOSE	
1100	EARLY FORMATIVE		
1200			
1300		TIERRAS LARGAS	
1400			
1500 B.C.		ESPIRIDION	

Figure 1.2. Chronological sequences for highland Mesoamerica, the Sola Valley, and the Valley of Oaxaca.

Alta is the counterpart to Zapotec studies. To understand Monte Albán, we must bring Mixtec and Zapotec regions into one interpretive framework. The other relevant volumes in print since the time of my fieldwork are: Blanton et al. 1999; Joyce, Winter, and Mueller 1998; Marcus and Flannery 1996; Spencer and Redmond 1997; Urcid 2001; Winter [ed.] 1994). Since the time of Caso, these projects have provided the empirical basis for ongoing debates in Oaxaca archaeology.

A Surveyor's Guide to Ancient Oaxaca

I am often asked about my field experiences. It is hard to convey what it feels like out there. "You just have to try it yourself sometime," is what I usually say. The closest approximation is visiting a site somewhere off the beaten path. Students become very animated the first time they do this with their professors.

We had a student visitor early in the Sola survey. We were working a mountain site, standing among the ruined buildings hardly touched since their abandonment and covered in centuries-old pine forest. I saw her excitement, and I remembered the first site I ever surveyed. I asked her if she was staying. I knew the answer: she could imagine finding sites like this one a hundred times more. Verónica Pérez was going to be a crewmember.

That is the basis of "survey fever" that unchecked can lead to "survey madness." This phenomenon is the oxygen-deprived state in which otherwise rational surveyors begin climbing the next hill even as the sun is setting. It is not the pure science, the discovery of lost sites, or even the altitude that makes them climb. It is all of these things and something more. And that something more is sometimes dangerous. I found this out a few months later.

It had been a brutal two-and-a-half hour climb almost straight up from the valley floor, and that was just to reach our starting point. You walk a few paces and then stop for rest while holding onto a branch. Every so often you think you see the top but it turns out to be a short flat before the next steep ascent. Eventually you get there, and you see some wise guy pretending to pull you along with an imaginary rope.

The wise guy on this day and most others was Everardo "Lalo" Olivera. He was one of the world's most experienced surveyors, having worked on every major Oaxaca survey since 1980. The others on the crew this day were the aptly named Lázaro, his son Carmelo Aragón, and Ruth Edelstein. Lázaro surveyed as he smoked and used his short cane to search for snakes; he looked somewhere between his actual age of 60 and 120 years old. But he was a tough old bird who knew the terrain. Carmelo was proving to be a major asset as well; he was a quick learner who never tired. Lalo called them "*trabajadores de oro,*" and he was right. Ruthie joined the project shortly after spraining her ankle on a beach vacation. Although this fact did not bode well for the project, her condition was improving.

After a short break we split into separate groups to cover all the fingerlike projections coming off the mountain. It was not long before we recorded our first site of the day. The terrace site was typical of others in the region: site number 55, with two small mounds, a plaza, and eight surviving terraces that encircled a narrow prominence overlooking the valley floor. Ceramics and an ax fragment were visible on the surface even though the site was not plowed. The site was nucleated and defensible to the point of paranoia—you could only approach its terraces from the narrowest saddle—and the saddle was cut by a ditch 2 m wide. It was a nearly straight drop on all other sides. And people were living up here, perhaps fifty persons or more, sometime before A.D. 500. We searched for several hours more, but only a few small sites came our way.

As the others were taking their lunches, Lalo and I stood looking into the distance toward the next hilltop. It seemed so close and looked promising. We knew that we would never come back to this place. Now was the time to survey that hill or not at all. It was 1:30 P.M. and the winter shadows were getting longer. With grim faces because we knew the risks, Lázaro, Carmelo and I moved on to the next hill. Lalo was taking Ruthie down slope to check for sites near town. Our rendezvous was scheduled for 4:30 P.M. We had caught the fever—survey fever—and it was quickly turning into survey madness. That was our critical error. After a brief historical intermission, I will explain why.

The Historical Background

What is the reason for survey? Is it to find sites to excavate? To test population pressure models? The answers are "no" and "certainly not," although survey results are useful for these purposes (and can test models beyond a narrow cultural ecology). As I see it, we survey to better understand the total range of contemporaneous sites, and the relationship of one place to the next. These objectives take us back to the beginnings of scientific archaeology in Oaxaca (Balkansky 1998b).

About the time Marshall H. Saville and Leopoldo Batres first climbed Monte Albán, the site became the focus of scientific research in Oaxaca. The migrations of peoples from distant lands figured prominently in the earliest explanations of culture change (e.g. Saville 1898). Zapotec origins were variously ascribed to Classic Maya and Postclassic Aztec, among other noncontemporary and distant sources. Subsequent researchers looked to an intermediate spatial scale to consider how contemporary urban centers such as Monte Negro might be relevant to Monte Albán (e.g. Caso 1938). Yet, even at the scale of central Oaxaca, archaeologists were still crossing vast expanses of unknown territory to compare sites.

Since the 1960s, systematic regional surveys have filled some of the gaps between major sites, and forced archaeologists to reconsider the older diffusionist notions of culture change (e.g. Balkansky et al. 2000; Blanton et al. 1999). It is now possible to consider site-to-site relationships from within a single study universe. Once these data are fit to a workable body of theory, we will have a powerful interpretive tool at our disposal. But before we turn to the emerging macroregional perspective, we must first consider its constituent parts.

Ignacio Bernal (1965), in seeking systematic large-scale information, made an inventory of Valley of Oaxaca sites (other studies that foreshadow later regional surveys include Guzmán 1934 and Berlin 1951). Bernal (1965:795) (in collaboration with Lorenzo Gamio) visited 251 sites and recalls: "I began the work by trying in all innocence to collect pottery wherever it lay and to mark the sites on the map. I soon found that it was easier to mark places where there was nothing, since the valley is literally covered with remains of all sorts, especially potsherds." This observation is still true today. Bernal (1965, 1983) showed the valley to be both a geographic and cultural region, with a widespread ceramic complex comparable to the Monte Albán sequence. Among his most significant discoveries was the existence of pre-urban Formative period sites, some of these later excavated by Flannery and his students (e.g. Drennan 1976; Flannery [ed.] 1976; Flannery and Marcus 1994; Whalen 1981).

An explicitly regional approach to Oaxaca archaeology began with the Nochixtlán Valley Project in 1966 (Spores 1972). Nochixtlán is the largest of the Mixteca Alta valleys. Work in these valleys is the basis for comparing Mixtec and Zapotec civilizations. Shortly thereafter, Richard Blanton and others started work in the Valley of Oaxaca. This project covered Monte Albán and continued to the margins of the valley. From these origins, two survey traditions emerged: first, the patchwork of mostly small-scale Mixteca Alta surveys (Balkansky 1998a; Byland 1980; Byland and Pohl 1994; Finsten 1996; Plunket 1983; Spores 1972; Stiver 2001); second, the coordinated and mostly contiguous survey projects that started in the Valley of Oaxaca (Balkansky 1997a; Blanton 1978; Blanton et al. 1982; Feinman and Nicholas 1990a, 1996; Kowalewski et al. 1989; Redmond 1983). The Mixteca Alta and Valley of Oaxaca survey blocks have since been conjoined into a single contiguous survey area (Balkansky et al. 2000; Kowalewski et al. 1999).

A funny thing happened on the way to full-coverage Nirvana: analysts at first looked inward to their own regions in seeking explanations of culture change (Feinman and Nicholas 1990a). Surveys of Monte Albán and the Valley of Oaxaca offered the regional perspective on Mesoamerica's earliest city. Marcus (1992a) noted, however, that the full extent of the early Zapotec state was ten times the size of the Valley of Oaxaca. It was a multigeneration project to collect information at a spatial scale sufficient to study Monte Albán. The noncontiguous boundaries of the prior Mixteca Alta surveys likewise placed interpretive limits on the results of those projects (Balkansky 1999). Generations before, archaeologists conceived a scale of analysis at least the size of highland Oaxaca (e.g. Bernal 1965; Paddock 1966). Yet the first surveyors for a time seemed to forget the advantages of comparing regions on this scale. As the expanding survey blocks came together, more of the earlier regional models were found in need of revision.

In every instance, expanding the survey coverage changed our view of ancient Oaxaca. Students who read this book might try a simple exercise. Tape one of the Valley of Oaxaca settlement pattern maps (Kowalewski et al. 1989) to a wall and stand with your nose touching Monte Albán. What do you see? This was the regional study universe in 1971 when Blanton and others started their survey (Blanton 1978). Now imagine that the first systematic data on Monte Albán outside the monumental precinct are available and estimates of the site's size and population have become possible. Explanations for Monte Albán's origins will focus on its residential barrios with a model that can be tested in the valley.

About 5000 persons occupied the hilltop in its founding period, and as many as 30,000 persons during its heyday centuries later. At least three distinct residential wards, possibly representing the three arms of the valley, are proposed as a model for the site's origins. A massive defensive wall was constructed at the end of Period I. Over time, several small ceremonial areas were built outside the Main Plaza, and became foci of the expanding residential wards. The city's urban growth in Classic times eventually spilled over its Formative period defensive perimeter to cover over 6 km^2.

Now take a step back, and step back again. Keep stepping backward until the entire valley fills your view. It is now 1980 and the Valley of Oaxaca survey is complete (Blanton et al. 1982; Kowalewski et al. 1989). The origins of Monte Albán and Zapotec civilization were unquestionably products of local evolutionary change. The pre-urban occupation of the valley was sufficiently dense and continuous, such that external migrations could not account for the profound changes that occur. At least three autonomous polities occupied the separate arms of the valley. The head towns of these societies have been identified and ready for further study. Eventually, the entire valley came together to form a unified regional state. The possible explanations for Monte Albán's origins gradually focus on social processes of change rather than purely environmental factors. Explanations for the Classic to Postclassic transition also narrow on a few well-conceived and testable models.

As always happens on a good survey, there are many surprises, including the size and extent of terraced sites in the valley during certain periods (Finsten and Kowalewski 1999). At the end of Period I and again in Period IIIa, the "piedmont strategy" of settlement on terraced hilltops was in full force. One of these places, the site of Jalieza, eventually grew even larger than Monte Albán. And despite the decades-long focus on Classic period Monte Albán, the surveyors found that the Postclassic period had more people living in the valley than at any time in its history. As a result of the survey, more than 2,500 newly recorded sites became candidates for future research. This overview has been an abbreviated list of these surveyors' accomplishments, to be sure.

Step back a few steps more and you can take in the Ejutla Valley (Feinman and Nicholas 1990a), then Peñoles (Finsten and Kowalewski 1991), and the Guirún area (Feinman and Nicholas 1996). You will need to tape up several extra maps by now. These latter projects start to test ideas about changing boundary conditions over time, and the extent to which neighboring regions are integrated with the Valley of Oaxaca during certain periods. Ejutla is an extension of the valley surveys to the south; Peñoles and Guirún cover mountainous regions on the margins of the valley. I would not want you to forget the important regional work in Cuicatlán (Redmond 1983) or Nochixtlán (Spores 1972) either. These are regions outside the modern Zapotec-speaking area. Their relations with the Monte Albán state are at the forefront of current debates.

This was the empirical setting for the Sola Valley survey when I started fieldwork there in 1995. There were new results, but also new questions were being asked, resulting in new outcomes of each step back as the survey coverage expanded. At each stage in the survey program, the archaeologists learned something new and sometimes really nailed down an issue or two in the literature. At a further remove, once later survey projects were complete, the surveyors soon realized that important parts of their earlier models were in need of revision. Some questions required more survey, others more refined site-intensive research. The two methodologies were not at odds, but complementary.

As a first stage of research in the Sola Valley, I designed a survey that would be comparable to prior projects (Chapter 2). Sola was not well known archaeologically, but based on prior results it would be possible to ask and answer several important questions at the regional scale. It should be obvious by now the extent to which the Sola survey rested on its antecedents. One of the strengths of the Oaxaca survey program has been its tradition of multigeneration training, and the cumulative effect of its empirical results.

Today, the era of comparative regional analysis is fast drawing to a close. As we step back once more, we find ourselves facing a map of sites on the macroregional scale. The challenge is to build models of social evolution that keep pace with the changed empirical reality.

The Perils of Survey Fever

As almost always happens, our inviting hilltop was farther away and a steeper climb than it seemed, and it was connected to a broad chain of peaks that led one into the next. We were now "off map," having hit a seam on the satellite-based images we used to navigate. Gigantic trees were all around with interlocking canopies, interspersed with patches of incredibly dense thorn bushes and the occasional maguey. It was impossible to see nearby landmarks. In Colonial times this area had been used for wheat farming, but no trails remained and the local people had no recollection of this land being used in their lifetimes. We were lost in the middle of nowhere.

Hours later, we were walking in circles (sometimes crawling through the thickest tangles). The afternoon was wasted and we had put ourselves too far out to make it to the truck before nightfall. At this point we argued, for the only time on the project, out of frustration and shame. I spoke to Lázaro with words to this effect: "*¡Rayos, solo andamos dando vueltas!*" The 60-year-old bantamweight narrowed his eyes, and in a low tone stated the inescapable truth: "*Nos hemos metido demasiado al monte.*" He was right. We had put ourselves in this place. It was the survey madness.

After a time we found a remnant trail, barely visible in the secondary growth. We stood looking down the path and hesitated. Was this our way out? Was it even a trail? Forty-five minutes later, after several times losing and then finding the ephemeral path, we were out of the thicket. Finding that trail was our salvation. We ran it and found ourselves looking out into the valley. Far from any familiar landmarks, I took a compass bearing and an educated guess about our direction home. Off we went to the next overlook, and the next, sliding down leaf-littered slopes into dry gullies, and up the next rise.

At the last overlook we made a break for it: running the long flat of the hill in desperation for the clearing at its edge, and our last chance to look into the valley and find ourselves. No signal, no discussion, we just ran with night falling fast for our last chance lookout—and still caught in the survey madness, I ran looking for sites. It was now too dark to see the surface and Carmelo hit a snag and fell in front of me. I stopped for a moment and looked around. I could at least see if there were mounds intermingled among the trees but there were none. At last we reached the edge of the clearing but still there were no familiar landmarks, and we saw the sun set and that was the last light of day.

It occurred to me that this was how people died in the field. Even the most experienced local hunters could become disoriented. The community we were working in had lost someone in this way the year before. Another day or two without water and we were done for. Our last "emergency" bottle was emptied hours before. I was almost resolved to spend the night in the field, sheltered among the rocks with a small fire kept safe from the dry tinder all around. We could survive the cold. But we could not last much longer without water, and there was no water in the gullies this time of year. Without discussion we continued walking along our last compass bearing.

About two hours earlier the wily Lázaro, in anticipation of our being caught in the mountains after dark, had cut *ocote* torches from the fallen branches of sticky burning pines. We marched onward, torches in hand, under a moonless sky with visibility reduced to six feet. We would later be told that our torches were visible hours before we reached our destination.

Of course we found our way out of the mountains, the bobbing points of light following one shepherd's path into the next, and crossing now moonlit streams to the main road and our rendezvous. Lalo and Ruthie were waiting for us, just as good surveyors should. It was 11:30 P.M. We had been in the field almost 18 hours. Over a plate of cold *tasajo* and *agua mineral* we told our war stories. Apart from frazzled nerves it had been a monster survey day. About 10 km^2 covered, plus interesting sites. We went out again at six the next morning. I cannot explain the psychic hold of this work, other than to call it madness.

A last word about the "something more" that I mentioned earlier. You cannot stay with the survey program over decades just for the thrill of finding new sites, or even the pressing scientific questions in need of regional views. About that last elemental force driving surveyors to the brink? I think it has something to do with inner fires, so that no matter the circumstance you saddle the ponies and ride. A spirit of adventure is essential to doing archaeology. That is why I dedicated this book to some of the weather-beaten and adventuresome spirits that taught me how to survey.

How Survey Sets the Agenda

A quick look through the literature shows the shifts in research priorities since the mid-1960s, the last period before surveys really began to change our views about Oaxaca (Balkansky 1998b). Articles in *The Archaeology of Southern Mesoamerica* (volume 3 in the *Handbook of Middle American Indians*) contain the best summaries of pre-survey work in Oaxaca (e.g. Acosta 1965; Bernal 1965; Caso and Bernal 1965). Since that time, some of the most interesting questions have been asked from a regional point of view. It is also the case that thinking regionally, which is all about population structures, is the opposite of the old culture history paradigms. Survey has fit well with the New Archaeology and later theoretical currents.

The Valley of Oaxaca survey is a collective effort, starting in the 1970s, to study Monte Albán in regional, and now macro-regional, perspective (e.g. Blanton et al. 1999). Site-level results from Monte Albán open new questions in need of regional-level data to answer them. Where did Monte Albán's founding population come from? When was the valley unified into a regional state? Why did these things happen as they did? Are indications of Monte Albán's later collapse visible at contemporary sites in the valley? The Monte Albán survey results become the intellectual rationale to continue surveying the rest of the valley.

On a theoretical level, the Oaxaca surveys provide an explicit test for William Sanders' (1965, 1972; see also Sanders, Parsons, and Santley 1979) view of social evolution, based on his survey in the Teotihuacan Valley and the Basin of Mexico. Sanders, Parsons, and Santley (1979:360) claim that a few key environmental variables explain 80% of the variation in regional settlement patterns. I will not belabor the theoretical issues in this section. The point is that Sanders' ecological model opened research directions not otherwise available. Members of the Oaxaca Settlement Pattern Project soon found that their methodology was relevant to more than narrow ecological relationships (Blanton 1990). Their own results provided the impetus for the subsequent twenty years of field archaeology in Oaxaca.

Examples of survey-influenced work in the past two decades abound. Feinman and Nicholas (1990a) surveyed the Ejutla Valley in 1984-1985 as a southern extension of the Valley of Oaxaca surveys. Their idea was to test Valley of Oaxaca boundary relations with a contiguous valley's settlement system. Settlement shifts occurred in both regions, phase by phase, but not in a uniform or predictable way. Feinman and Nicholas (1990a) found a Period II administrative center in Ejutla, and argued that the site formed part of Monte Albán's multiregional settlement hierarchy. But during the next period these formal political ties ended. Ejutla was not the mirror image of the Valley of Oaxaca nor its microcosm—even at a smaller scale.

One unusual feature on the surface of Ejutla Valley sites is the high density of marine shell. Prehispanic shell was a luxury item used for ornamentation and exchange. This unexpected discovery led to excavations in the 1990s at the Ejutla town site, where the goal was to understand shell production and exchange (e.g. Feinman and Nicholas 1993, 1995). Excavators found shell and other craftwork in a Classic period household (e.g. Balkansky, Feinman, and Nicholas 1997; Middleton 1998). Ejutla's Classic period shell-workers were links in a chain connecting sources on the Pacific coast to elite consumers at Monte Albán, and perhaps as far away as Teotihuacan. These results clarify both household-scale economic strategies and interregional exchange ties in Classic period Oaxaca.

Spencer and Redmond's (1994 to the present) work at the site of San Martín Tilcajete is designed to understand the rise of the state in Oaxaca. Blanton's crew first recorded the Tilcajete site located 20 km south of Monte Albán on the 1977 valley survey (Blanton et al. 1982). The survey report indicates that the site was one of the valley's autonomous pre-urban polities, and later became a second-tier center of the Monte Albán state. The site's location shifted from valley floor (Period I) to terraced hilltop (Period II) in sight of the Zapotec capital. At issue is the timing and means of Tilcajete's incorporation into the Zapotec state.

Spencer and Redmond's program of intensive site survey and excavation measures community-level changes during the Period I transition to the state (e.g. Spencer and Redmond 2001). Their detailed map and surface collections refine data on the site's size and location over time. Excavations now reaching completion show the community-scale contexts for social action. One example is the excavated plan of Oaxaca's earliest known palace. Other ceremonial areas and several lesser households are also under study. This research is yet another example of the complementary nature of survey and excavation in Oaxaca.

Surveyors provide information on the large-scale social contexts not otherwise available; just as important, they also open doors to new research. Survey results are great for generating hypotheses to be tested. But there is a difference between testable hypothesis and conclusive result. Every regional model must ultimately be tested on a site-to-site basis. The best answers usually come from integrated programs of survey and excavation. The work of Feinman, Nicholas, Redmond, and Spencer is proof enough of this maxim. The best surveyors complete their work by asking a lot of new questions. At the end of this book I will ask some new questions about the Sola Valley, and suggest ways that future work there might proceed.

Evaluating Approaches to Social Evolution

As a statement of first principles, social evolutionary models must account for directionality in sequences of historical change (Sanderson 1990). Social scientists customarily study past directional trends and instances of parallel evolution: most notably the transitions to agriculture and sedentism, states and civilization, and the capitalist world economy (e.g. Childe 1951; Flannery 1972; Lenski 1976; Steward 1955; Wallerstein 1974; White 1959). Evolutionary trends are characteristic of human societies, but distinct from evolution in the natural world; natural selection produces local adaptations only, each unique and unrepeatable (Flannery 1995; Gould 1996:219). As social scientists attempt to explain evolutionary trajectories common to more than one society, some scholars now question whether the directional trends themselves are the causes of prehistoric culture change. Are major social transformations the outcome of long-term trends and cumulative processes alone? Are unique historical factors of equal importance in transformational episodes of culture change?

Anthropological archaeologists are now reevaluating the significance of cross-cultural regularities, compared to the roles of history and the strategizing individual in processual outcomes (e.g. Blanton et al. 1996; DeMarrais, Castillo, and Earle 1996; Joyce and Winter 1996). Any number of scholars have seen fit to reject the evolutionist program altogether. The result is often nothing more than creating new typologies to replace the old, or turning social actors into reified evolutionary trends. In this section, I will first review the basic structure of evolutionary models, and then suggest ways to improve them. Evolutionary models are flexible enough with modification to allow for historical factors and agency in explanations of culture change. It is wrongheaded to throw out the evolutionary baby with the proverbial bath water in the cross-cultural program (Spencer 1990).

Since the 1950s, evolutionary anthropology has been the main influence in culture change studies. Stage-based evolution is the model for those social structures seen cross-culturally; its practitioners view culture change in terms of societies being driven to new organizational plateaus (e.g. Carneiro 1970; Fried

1967; Service 1962, 1975). It is the directional trends and critical thresholds in societies that determine when change is likely to occur. Yet the predictions of social evolutionists are confounded by emergent properties. Emergence refers to the appearance of novel forms in complex systems that cannot be predicted from their original components (e.g. Flannery 1986; Mayr 1997:19-20). As a consequence of emergence, the directional trends best reflect periods of relative stasis lasting centuries or even millennia between episodes of rapid evolution.

The evolutionist program is now under siege (see Spencer 1990). First, evolutionist explanations are criticized for being too deterministic in their focus on ecologically functional or system stress models of culture change. Second, evolutionists are accused of neglecting contingent factors and social actors in their models. Third, neoevolutionism and stage-based typologies are assumed to eliminate variation within societal types, and to carry an air of progressive inevitability (e.g. Brumfiel 1992; Cowgill 1993; Giddens 1984; Hodder 1986; Sewell 1992; Shanks and Tilley 1988). The first two objections are the subject of this review, but I take issue with the third since it suggests that evolutionism writ large is a pointless exercise.

The last point on "typological thinking" is the most common refrain in the reaction against evolutionism. The problem with this reaction is that the earlier generation of scholars never equated evolutionary stages with invariant societies. They simply never commented excessively on the obvious: terms such as "chiefdom" and "state" refer to commonly occurring forms, similar to the biologist's terms "reptile," "mammal," and so forth (Flannery 1995). The biological typologies refer to qualitatively different kinds of organisms within which exist a wide range of species. Evolutionary anthropologists likewise understand that chiefdoms are not identical, but their organizational form is qualitatively different from states. It is by no means a sterile typological exercise to identify state institutions in the archaeological record. The precise timing of state emergence has processual implications.

Other scholars now focus on episodes of transition that are historical in character, and not amenable to analysis by evolutionary trends and system functions alone. Marcus and Flannery (1996) place the long-term evolution of Zapotec civilization in an actor-based framework; the disjunctive and unpredictable historical events are key features in the process of state formation.

An action theory approach seeks to articulate specific persons and social groups with their environmental and social systems or structures. Evolutionary structures shape human action, but "aggressive actors . . . can change the system, and many of the changes they bring about can have unintended long-term consequences" (Marcus and Flannery 1996:31). Each region in Oaxaca also has a prior history whose evolutionary trajectory is determined and knowable via human agency and not by factors beyond human control.

As Marcus and Flannery (1996) note, transitional episodes vary cross-culturally (and require historical perspectives), but action theory is less useful for making broad comparisons or understanding the antecedent conditions of culture change. For this reason, Marcus and Flannery (1996:245, citing Spencer 1990) call for a "dual approach" emphasizing the contribution of history but also the common principles of social evolution. Spencer (1990) argues for the retention of our typological constructs for purposes of comparison; it is the stable periods, the evolutionary stages, which look alike cross-culturally. Archaeologists should therefore adopt a transformational (rapid and contingent) perspective on culture change, rather than maintain continued reliance on directional evolutionary (gradual and cumulative) trends in the system.

Archaeologists must continue to use evolutionary and systemic frameworks to define the social and environmental structures within which culture change occurs. But they must also explain the unique features of culture change. A perusal through the literature on early states suggests that these considerations have merit (e.g. Feinman and Marcus [eds.] 1998). The archaeology of civilizational collapse is similarly varied in its specific details (e.g. Yoffee and Cowgill [eds.] 1988). Social action theory revitalizes the older ecological-evolutionary models. However it is not a replacement for evolutionism. The objective in evolutionary studies is to identify points of transition, and then refocus our analyses on those purposeful systemic modifications that succeed because of selection.

Monte Albán and the Evolution of Zapotec Civilization

The theoretical tension between culture viewed as a functional system versus more historical forms of analysis underlies efforts to model the origins of Monte Albán and the Zapotec state. Sanders and Nichols' (1988) reanalysis of the Valley of Oaxaca survey data reignited the debate over analytical priorities and the chain of causation in the emergence of Zapotec civilization. Are early states the outcome of long-term ecological-evolutionary factors alone? If so, then which ones? How do societies change from one steady system to another?

Sanders and Nichols (1988) use population pressure as the trigger for changes in Valley of Oaxaca settlement patterns. Monte Albán is the outcome of long-term evolutionary trends—population growth exceeds carrying capacity, and the competition over resources is the catalyst for new administrative institutions. However, their ecological stress model is limited to the local scale of analysis; for example, much of the debate over Monte Albán's origins concerns estimates for the population and agricultural productivity of land within ten kilometers of the capital. This approach makes population pressure the sole evolutionary trend at work in all times and places, without regard to the unique characteristics in each case.

The response to Sanders and Nichols' (1988) environmental determinism (Marcus [ed.] 1990) reflects multicausal approaches with an emphasis on social factors operating in multiple regions. I refer to Blanton et al.'s (1993, 1999) confederation model and Marcus and Flannery's (1996) expansion model for the rise of the Zapotec state (also Blanton 1976, 1978, 1983; Blanton et al. 1981, 1982; Flannery and Marcus 1976, 1983a; Marcus 1992a; Redmond 1983; Spencer 1982; Spencer and Redmond 1997). The confederation and expansion models are at odds over the specific timing of state formation, differences that have causal implications (Balkansky 1998b).

Blanton and others (Blanton et al. 1993, 1999) conjoin the founding of Monte Albán with the origins of the state in Oaxaca. Monte Albán, these authors argue, is the capital of a confederation of chiefdoms, each representing one arm of the Valley of Oaxaca. In this view, city and state arise simultaneously at the onset of Monte Albán Period I when the valley is unified. Their model is built around cumulative evolutionary trends ranging from population growth to agricultural intensification to exchange that necessitate the rise of a coordinating center.

Marcus and Flannery (1996) consider Monte Albán's founding in Early Monte Albán I, or phase Ia, to be an event separate from Zapotec state formation, which occurred by Early Monte Albán II. They see state formation as the result of centuries-old conflict among valley chiefdoms. The Etla chiefdom at San José Mogote reestablishes itself at Monte Albán as part of this ongoing within-valley conflict. The eventual incorporation of rival valley polities and some outlying regions is the catalyst for new administrative institutions and the state. For these authors, both urbanization and state formation must be situated in their separate historical contexts.

Each model differs in the proposed timing, chain of causation, and emphasis given to evolutionary trends versus unique historical factors. The analytical scale, however, is fundamental to interpretive differences. On local and even regional scales, explanations often focus on the environment and population (the ecological stress model). On macroregional scales of analysis, social factors are more likely to enter the mix of explanations (as the distance from a center's sustaining area grows, the environment operates as a background or conditioning factor in the confederation and expansion models). An underlying subtext to these debates is the role of social actors measured against evolutionary imperatives in models of culture change.

I should make it clear at the outset that each of these models remains incompletely tested, some more incompletely tested than others. There is simply too much separation between the questions asked and the available data to declare one model to be the final answer. The growing variation in regional trajectories is testing the resilience of each model. Each new project's results contributes to refining—and sometimes rejecting—the models currently under consideration.

To resolve this theoretical impasse, research must be conducted in a wider spatial perspective to evaluate patterns of interaction with the Zapotec state. The Cuicatlán Cañada (Spencer and Redmond 1997), Ejutla (Feinman and Nicholas 1990a), Peñoles (Finsten and Kowalewski 1991), and Guirún (Feinman and Nicholas 1996) are among those regions that either border or are in close proximity to the Valley of Oaxaca. Most analysts agree that these regions are incorporated into the Zapotec state by Period II, albeit through differing mechanisms. Peñoles would be the exception, an interacting though autonomous region at this time (Finsten 1996).

Still other perspectives come from the Mixteca Alta (e.g. Balkansky et al. 2000; Spores 1972) and coastal regions in Oaxaca (e.g. Zeitlin and Joyce 1999). Analysts tend to emphasize the political autonomy of these regions, but differ in the extent to which they tie each region to others in more general explanations. Extant data nonetheless provide the intellectual context to derive a series of expectations for the long-term evolution of the Zapotec state. The Sola Valley survey provides another comparative perspective to test these expectations.

I advocate an approach to social evolution that incorporates short-term, historical events. Evolution and agency are not competitive theoretical positions, but complementary views of the culture change process. What follows is a detailed breakdown of each model to illustrate their contrasting approaches to social evolution.

Blanton et al. (1993:69-77, 1999) argue that a confederacy of chiefdoms establish Monte Albán on a prominent hilltop in the center of the valley to facilitate communication among member sites; to provide defense against external threats; and to legitimate the site's status as the regional capital. In the confederation model, Monte Albán's founding is concurrent with state formation: "[t]he founding of Monte Albán in the Early I phase capped the previous two-tier administrative system with a new hierarchical level, a regional capital" (Blanton et al. 1993:69).

Monte Albán resolves the growing systemic pressure on valley sites to process information: the level of intersite interaction crosses an undefined critical threshold, hence the state forms (e.g. Blanton et al. 1982:13-25). Monte Albán does not form an empire until Period II, however, because societies in other regions are not sufficiently complex to be incorporated into the state administrative apparatus (Blanton et al. 1993:82-87). Once frontier societies become more hierarchical, the local power structures can be manipulated as "modular units" or "subassemblies" to extract surplus production. Blanton et al. (1993) leave the causes for growth in provincial complexity unspecified, and provide no indication of where on the size-complexity continuum societies are ready for incorporation.

The confederation model presents a concatenation of causes but no real nexus of change. Blanton et al. (1982:13-25, 1993:21-23, 1999) cite long-term trends stretching from the Rosario phase through Period II as critical factors in their model. The model is essentially unchanged since Blanton's (1976) original publication on Monte Albán that predates the Valley of Oaxaca survey (Blanton et al. 1982; Kowalewski et al. 1989), and valley survey results for the Ia phase are somewhat equivocal with regard to Monte Albán's span of control (Balkansky 1998b; Marcus and Flannery 1996:160-65). Competing chiefdoms outside Etla maintain their populations in the Ia phase; they could not have been founding members of a confederacy at a new regional capital. The valley's regional settlement and administrative hierarchies are also muddled in ambiguity for the Ia phase.

In the confederation model, each of the usual suspects in models of culture change, including population pressure, agricultural intensification, trade, warfare, and other prime movers, are rounded up and put into a systems framework. Yet the distinction between evolutionary and proximate cause (Flannery 1986) is lost in the blur of systems interactions. Hidden critical thresholds lie somewhere in the system beyond the reach of human agency. Social evolution is reduced to the shift from one relatively static system-state to another; the actual processes of change cannot be observed. Monte Albán's origin is located on the threshold of long-term trends leading to state formation, and thereby conflates a shorter-term event (the founding of Monte Albán) with the longer-term process of Zapotec state formation.

Sanders and Nichols (1988) argue similarly that states are the outcome of long-term evolutionary trends, albeit a single trend, putting state formation in Period IIIb. In their model, Monte Albán's location next to irrigable farmland results in sustained population growth and a long-term demographic edge over its rivals. The population grows inexorably until a critical threshold is reached (in this case carrying capacity) and the state forms out of necessity.

Valley of Oaxaca survey results indicate that Monte Albán is located on some of the region's poorest agricultural land (e.g. Feinman and Nicholas 1990b; Nicholas 1989). Sanders and Nichols (1988) nevertheless consider the nearby valley floor land sufficiently productive to support sustained population growth and eventually state formation. As a rebuttal, the "sufficiency criterion" is not convincing, since Monte Albán could be located virtually anywhere in the southern highlands with substantial arable land. Monte Albán's founders abandoned the best agricultural lands in Etla, so factors other than proximity to the best alluvium must have shaped settlement patterns from the city's earliest times.

Sanders and Nichols (1988) use an implicit evolutionist assumption to equate Monte Albán's Period IIIb height of population and monumentality with a stage of political development and presumed territorial size. Sanders and Nichols (1988) cite Monte Albán's highest-ever population, the presence of palaces and royal tombs, its degree of social stratification, and its function as a unifying central place (and purported market center) as evidence for state formation.

Yet their proposed timing for state formation does not conform to current data on regional political structure (Balkansky 1998b). Monte Albán's Period IIIb political domain was much reduced from former times; settlement was no longer continuous even within the valley, as its subregions were becoming more autonomous (Kowalewski et al. 1989: Maps 6, 7). Monte Albán had long since withdrawn from its former provinces outside the valley (e.g. Feinman and Nicholas 1990a; Redmond 1983). Sanders and Nichols' (1988) evolutionist assumption that links center size to political territory can no longer be maintained (cf. Marcus 1992a).

Blanton, Sanders, and their collaborators are at odds over specific explanatory emphases, but both sets of scholars try to track evolutionary trends to a breaking point: Sanders and Nichols (1988) expect population pressure to exceed carrying capacity. Blanton et al. (1982, 1993, 1999) predict that multiple interacting factors ("interacting potentials") pass a critical threshold, after which the state forms. Population and carrying capacity are measurable empirical matters, but other thresholds such as interaction potential are more problematic. Blanton and others (1993:76) write: "We are not in a position to test these hypotheses or to identify what minimal levels of interaction are required for complex political and economic institutions to develop. To our knowledge, no research has been done along these lines." Thus Sanders and Nichols' (1988) model is wrong on empirical grounds, and Blanton et al.'s (1993, 1999) model cannot be tested. Yet, the ecological and confederation models share the same approach. Both models emphasize concentrated populations crossing a critical threshold that requires state institutions for their efficient organization, and both models operate entirely on the level of systemic stresses. It is simply a matter of whether you prefer one prime mover or many.

As a result of emergent properties, the system-level analysis precludes knowledge of proximate cause in processes of culture change. It is for this reason that final causes must be sought in the short-term, potentially disruptive effects that actors have on their social systems. Social evolution is more than a summation of directional trends; it is also the proximate outcome of unique and unrepeatable sequences of change.

Spencer (1988) calls for the evaluation of an expansion model in his response to Sanders and Nichols' (1988) paper. Growth of a multiregional database from continuing survey now makes it possible to study the relationship between territorial expansion and state formation. Evolutionary constructs of chiefdom and state underlie the expansion model, but it also allows for the effects of agency and specific regional trajectories of change. Monte Albán's founding was part of ongoing conflict among chiefly centers, the outcome of which could have taken centuries to resolve. Monte Albán's founding and the evolution of the state should therefore be treated as two separate research problems. The crucial test is when and in what manner Monte Albán took control of the Valley of Oaxaca and neighboring regions.

Monte Albán's Period I status as a maximal chiefdom, transitional society, or early state remains an open empirical question (Marcus and Flannery 1996). If the expansion model is correct, then scholars should find evidence for the evolution of state institutions during the time that rival polities are incorporated. Elements of the standardized grand plaza design, with its palaces, ball courts, and two-room temples should appear in nascent form. The settlement hierarchy of first-, second-, and third-tier administrative centers should crystallize with plausible links to their capital. The full criteria for identifying the Zapotec state should come together after Monte Albán Ia phase, but no later than early in Period II. This is a target window of about 200 years. The real-time transition to the state, however, could well have occurred within the lifetime of a single ruler. What factors could have motivated or triggered Monte Albán's expansion?

Ethnohistorical sources suggest that Monte Albán would attempt to control exchange corridors from the highlands to the coast (e.g. Berdan et al. 1996; Hodge 1998; Marcus 1992a; Spores 1993). Mesoamerican states of the contact period used multiple strategies to control trade routes and find new sources of revenue. These strategies included, but were not limited to, conquest, colonization, and co-option via trade, alliance, and threat of force.

Marcus and Flannery (1996:206), noting the location of conquered provinces claimed by Monte Albán, write:

> When one plots on a map all those provinces where Zapotec expansion is indicated, either by pottery changes or textual claims, it appears that Monte Albán was trying to establish a north-south "corridor of influence" between Tehuacán—the gateway to Central Mexico—and the Pacific Coast, the gateway to the tropics. At its peak in late Monte Albán II, that corridor may have included 20,000 km² of subject territory.

These are testable propositions. The expansion model links the state to territorial control, and in my view is relevant to understanding the rise of complex societies in more distant regions. Evolutionary causes converge with specific mechanisms of change in the model.

How could the expansion model be rejected with results from the Sola Valley survey? If propositions for the expansion model are correct, then Sola Valley sites should reflect contact with the Valley Zapotec—whether through colonization, conquest, or more indirect means of interaction. Analysis of settlement patterns should place the Sola Valley within Monte Albán's political sphere in the Monte Albán Ic phase or Period II. There should be state institutions at sites in the Sola region. The ceramics, settlement patterns, and site layouts should be broadly similar in both regions. Episodes of transition should be concurrent with other nearby regions. One route from Monte Albán to the coastal lowlands passes through the Sola Valley. There should be sites situated on exchange corridors. Coastal regions now under study should reveal important changes at the time of Zapotec expansion.

The Emerging Perspective: Regional Variation but Uniform Processes

The research issues in this book concern the critical social evolutionary transitions in Oaxaca's later prehistory: the rise and collapse of regional states. The specific issues include the significance of the founding of Monte Albán versus its later expansion during the rise of the Zapotec state; Monte Albán's effect on the emergence of complex societies elsewhere in Oaxaca; and the causes for Monte Albán's later collapse. Variation tests competing models of social evolution: the better the model, the wider the range of variation that it can handle. Each regional pattern is unique mostly for historical reasons, and not simply because of differences in the environment. Human agency must be built into our traditional ecological-evolutionary models, though "agency" should not be modeled as though it were another evolutionary trend.

I argue that the standard systems-based theories of culture change are inadequate to explain the successive social transformations into urban and state societies, where prevailing models emphasize evolutionary trends to greater social complexity without attention to the unique and unpredictable features of culture change. Extending the same reasoning to the collapse era in the Late Classic period, I argue for a historical explanation of the collapse based on multiple sites and regions, and not simply Monte Albán.

Monte Albán's expansion into regions outside the Valley of Oaxaca in its varied militaristic, diplomatic, and demographic dimensions best accounts for the emergence of complex societies where none existed before. Zapotec rulers used new mechanisms of territorial control to out-compete rival centers, and to gain access to more distant sources of finance. Elites outside the zone of Zapotec control opportunistically enhanced their status and defended their territories through similar mechanisms of control. Although I favor an expansion model of state formation, I would extend it to include the simultaneous rise of states in other interacting regions via mechanisms of reciprocal evolution.

Centuries later, after the collapse of first-generation states in Oaxaca, these same regions transformed themselves into *cacicazgos* (the small states of the Conquest era). Emergent centers challenged Monte Albán both within and outside the Valley of Oaxaca. Monte Albán's loss of control over the Valley of Oaxaca was the watershed moment after which the transition to petty kingdoms began. These changes were not the outcome of cumulative evolutionary trends alone. Historical contingence must be balanced against the longer-term evolutionary background in our models of culture change.

What sort of methodology could be used to detect historical factors on regional survey? As I see it, there are two general criteria by which to recognize the unique effects of social actors on settlement patterns. First, any settlement characteristic not attributable to ecological necessity might be the product of agency. These characteristics include objectively nonadaptive or "irrational" settlement decisions, at least from an ecological point of view. Moving to a mountaintop is one such example.

The site of Monte Albán was not especially well situated with respect to farmland and water resources. There must be reasons other than population pressure, or the search for quality farmland, for that site's origins. This pattern was replicated at other hilltop centers in Oaxaca. Population/resource imbalances, if present, occurred only after the fact of a strategic resettlement. Sites in the Sola region were usually found on hilltops; some of the most productive lands appear to have been left vacant during its initial period of occupation.

Second, agency might also account for the variation in regional trajectories now apparent in macroregional perspective. Variation both within and between regions must have been due to more than the environment. Monte Albán's varied strategies of incorporation (measured against local constraints) account for many regional differences in Late Formative times. Some regions were colonized (Sola), others were co-opted (Ejutla), and still others conquered (Cuicatlán). And this small sample does not exhaust the full range of possibilities.

In Classic period times, the elite in some regions stayed tied to the Monte Albán state, but others chose to go their separate ways. I suspect that this pattern of changing allegiances occurred even within the Valley of Oaxaca in the Classic period. Sites in the Sola region seem to be relatively autonomous in the Classic period, though local leaders probably used marital alliances with Valley of Oaxaca elite to boost their status. I provide the settlement pattern evidence to support these observations in the coming chapters.

It is not necessary to choose between evolutionary structures and social actors in modeling culture change. The factors of environment, population, and political structure are at the analyst's disposal. The effects of social actors are also visible in each site and region's particular history. What matters in evolutionary models is the way these complementary classes of evidence are combined.

The Organization of this Book

I evaluate models for the rise and collapse of states in Oaxaca by examining the changing relationship between the Sola Valley and the Valley of Oaxaca. In this chapter I have given the project's antecedents and theoretical background. Chapter 2 contains the research design and method, and an overview of the region. At the end of Chapter 2, I give summary results from the settlement pattern project.

Chapters 3, 4, and 5 contain the phase-by-phase project results. I argue that the Sola Valley in the Formative period provided one conduit for Monte Albán to reach the coastal lowlands. Zapotec rulers gained access to exotic preciosities via the highland-coastal exchange corridor. Elites on the Zapotec frontier also built their status in the changed circumstances brought by the first conquest states. State formation in this context was the by-product of new strategies of territorial control.

Occupation of the Sola region continued into the Monte Albán "collapse era" and beyond. As Monte Albán's political domain contracted in the Classic period, settlement patterns shifted even though the highland-coastal corridor remained the focus of regional settlement. Emergent elites in the Sola Valley used genealogical claims and other mechanisms to solidify their positions in the wake of Monte Albán's political decline. By the Postclassic period, the Sola Valley was divided into *cacicazgos* with shifting alliances to other small-scale polities in Oaxaca.

Chapter 6 contains the project summary and comparisons with other regions in Oaxaca, and I return to the research issues outlined in this chapter. An actor-based approach, targeting nonadaptive and even seemingly irrational settlement decisions, brings unique historical factors into the analysis of Sola Valley settlement patterns. Each region's history is unique in its specific details because of agency and not simply the environment, making human agency the proximate factor in episodes of culture change. This approach to regional analysis defines the broad-scale time-space structures of social action. The theoretical challenge is to build models that tie the separate regional trajectories together.

Appendices follow, with site descriptions, site maps, and much of the primary data in tabular form. Joyce Marcus, Linda Nicholas, and Gary Feinman cover specific topics and data sets. The results of this project extend the known range of variation in prehispanic settlement patterns, and lay the groundwork for future research in the Sola region.

Chapter 2

The Regional Archaeology of the Sola Valley

A famous liar once told me that the trees on the Zócalo in Oaxaca City were painted white at the base of their trunks because it rarely snowed. On those rare occasions with snowfall the people were so enchanted with the accumulation that they wanted the trees to stay whitened. None of this was true, of course. But what did I know? It was my first time in Oaxaca in 1991. That was the year I first heard about a place called "Sola."

I was working for my advisor, Gary Feinman, at his excavations in Ejutla. As I explained in the previous chapter, this project had stemmed from an earlier regional survey. Most of the crew had worked on the Ejutla Valley and before that the Valley of Oaxaca surveys. The Sola Valley was another region in Oaxaca that needed to be surveyed before sites like this one could be excavated. Sola was essentially unknown but had a bad reputation: rumors of lawlessness and danger mixed with the promise of unexplored sites. Still, some trouble with locals in western Ejutla were well remembered, and that was as close to Sola as most of the old surveyors cared to get.

We were digging every day and focused on the work, but one thing seemed out of place. I wondered why the stories told by crewmembers in the evenings were always about past survey experiences; after all, we were excavating at the time. The same famous liar was one of the storytellers. He told me that more adventures took place surveying than excavating, and that meant more survey stories. He also told me that survey work was a lot more fun. This time I believed him. We made plans for a new survey project. We were going to Sola.

By 1994, I was a veteran of several field projects in Oaxaca. I could tell my own excavation and survey stories—and the famous liar had been right after all. I also knew by now the intellectual reasons for starting a regional survey program in the Sola Valley. Sola had sites with architecture and carved stones, an ethnohistorical record of native religious practices, and the time was right to test models about the Zapotec expansion.

Heinrich Berlin (1951) visited the Sola Valley in the 1940s and found many prehispanic sites and carved stones. Three hundred years earlier, Gonzalo de Balsalobre (1988 [1656]) brought the Inquisition to San Juan Sola to eliminate the resurgence of prehispanic religious practices. It was certain that the prehispanic occupants of the region spoke a variant of Zapotec and once shared iconographic and epigraphic ties to the Valley of Oaxaca.

What was missing was the *regional context* for problem formulation. After mapping sites on the regional scale, it would be possible to compare the Sola Valley trajectory to other regions in Oaxaca, and then generate specific questions for later site intensive research. At the time, there was still an acute sense of aggravation among Oaxaca archaeologists over Sanders and Nichols' (1988) reanalysis of the Valley of Oaxaca settlement patterns. One result of the aggravation was that the lines of demarcation about Monte Albán came to be better drawn than before (e.g. Marcus [ed.] 1990; Spencer 1988). Marcus (1992a) had also published an influential paper on Monte Albán's initial expansion and later Classic period contraction. So I had a lot of ideas to work over for my dissertation proposal.

I found myself sitting on the Zócalo at the Bar Jardín and once again looking at those white tree trunks. Gary Feinman and Linda Nicholas were sitting there too. It was time to commit to a dissertation and this was the place to do it. Most projects in Oaxaca were first conceived on cocktail napkins at the Bar Jardín. You ordered *huevos a la oaxaqueña* with *café con leche* in the morning, Negra Modelo with *cacahuates* and *limones* if meeting at night. You ignored the archaeologists sitting at other tables and spoke in low tones. It was all part of the ritual.

Gary and Linda were in town analyzing their excavated materials from Ejutla; there were a lot of artifacts, especially pottery, in their collections. I was working on a survey project in the Mixteca Alta, but all this was prelude. Gary suggested that

I take one of two dissertation options; the choice would be mine, but so would the consequences. In other words, I could play it safe or go for broke. I could measure thousands of rim diameters from Ejutla to explain why the pottery was brown and misshapen, or risk everything and survey the wilds of the Sola Valley. It was an easy choice.

Models for the Oaxaca Macroregion

Ancient Oaxaca has been modeled in two distinct ways: an ecological functionalism, especially on the local scale, versus social processes operating on the macroregional scale of analysis (e.g. Sanders and Nichols 1988). If the Sola Valley's earliest occupants chose site locations based primarily on agricultural productivity, then this result would support the priority of environmental concerns or the materialist position. Over time, the better-located sites should grow differentially and remain the leading centers in the region. If factors *other* than land quality were at work, and local settlement patterns shifted in tandem with other regions, then this result would favor macroregional views with emphases on large-scale sociopolitical dynamics (e.g. Marcus [ed.] 1990; Marcus 1992a). Several specific models existed within each of these general frameworks.

Among the most contentious issues for researchers in the Valley of Oaxaca was the significance of Monte Albán's foundation versus its later expansionist phase in the process of Zapotec state formation (e.g. Blanton et al. 1993, 1999; Marcus and Flannery 1996). A related issue concerned Monte Albán's role in the emergence of complex societies outside the Valley of Oaxaca (e.g. Balkansky 1998b; Marcus 1992a; Marcus and Flannery 1996; Zeitlin and Joyce 1999). Authors debated the timing of state formation, its contrasting voluntaristic and militaristic aspects, and the relative autonomy of regions outside the valley.

Monte Albán's collapse was another issue that required macroregional perspectives for its final resolution. Sanders and Nichols (1988) argued that Zapotec state formation occurred in the Late Classic period; Marcus (1992a) considered the state already in decline by this time. Most authors assumed that Monte Albán's population history reflected its degree of political control over the Valley of Oaxaca and nearby regions. Yet the instability brought from competing centers both within and outside the Valley of Oaxaca suggested a model that had not yet been explored (Balkansky 1998b).

Human agency was an underlying theme throughout these debates. Evolutionary imperatives often masked unique historical factors in models of culture change. The trouble was in identifying agency without ignoring persistent evolutionary structures. Some scholars were beginning to suspect that variable regional trajectories were due to more than evolutionary factors (Spencer 1990). Extant data from regions throughout Oaxaca suggested a broad range of alternative possibilities.

To resolve this theoretical impasse, it was necessary to conduct research in a wider spatial perspective to find the full range of interaction with the Zapotec state. Cuicatlán (Spencer and Redmond 1997), Ejutla (Feinman and Nicholas 1990a), Peñoles (Finsten and Kowalewski 1991), and Guirún (Feinman and Nicholas 1996) were among those regions that either bordered or were in close proximity to the Valley of Oaxaca. Most analysts agreed that these regions were incorporated into the Zapotec state by Period II. Peñoles would be the exception, having grown in complexity while remaining autonomous (Finsten 1996). I suspected that the wave of colonization and conquest also swept across the Sola Valley. It was anyone's guess what happened in later periods.

Still other perspectives came from the Mixteca Alta (e.g. Balkansky et al. 2000; Spores 1972) and coastal regions in Oaxaca (e.g. Marcus and Flannery 1996; Zeitlin and Joyce 1999). Analysts tended to emphasize the political autonomy of these regions, but differed on the extent to which each region was tied to others in more general models. All of these regions taken together provided a range of expectations for modeling the Oaxaca macroregion. The Sola Valley was another case on which to test expectations for macroregional relationships involving Monte Albán.

Questions Guiding the Sola Valley Survey

This study of Monte Albán and the Zapotec state uses results from my settlement pattern project in the Sola Valley of Oaxaca, Mexico. Mountains separated the valleys of Sola and Oaxaca, and Sola had never been surveyed or studied systematically by archaeologists. A systematic regional survey was a good first step toward addressing questions about an unknown study region. Survey results would be relevant to mapping Monte Albán's changing territorial boundaries. It would also contribute to understanding the full range of regional variation in Oaxaca.

My original concern was with Zapotec state formation; I soon found that this region's occupation also figured in Monte Albán's collapse and the Postclassic transition. What persistent macroregional factors linked the valleys of Sola and Oaxaca through successive political fluctuations? How did Sola Valley settlement patterns shift over time compared to other regions in Oaxaca? These are the first of ten specific questions that I asked originally in my dissertation proposal. I will answer these and related questions in the last chapter.

In the rest of this chapter will be found the remaining research questions, the background to the study region, the analytical and field methods, and an overview of the project results. The specific questions are basic to what archaeologists need to know for each separate region in Oaxaca. Some answers come from the long-term settlement history of the Sola Valley; others come from the analyses within each phase. One common theme is that macroregional relationships operate in several directions at once and not simply from Monte Albán outward. Another theme is that no single region ever existed in a vacuum.

Systematic regional surveys had covered more than 7000 km² of highland Oaxaca by the spring of 1999 (Balkansky et al. 2000). From this large-scale perspective it was possible to chart the changing configurations of early states and their component parts. Theorists of cultural evolution have seldom had access to comparative data on this spatial scale; earlier models often required revision once the changing boundaries of early states were better understood. Sola Valley settlement patterns were now part of the emerging picture for ancient Oaxaca.

Ecological Processes

Sanders and Nichols (1988) would expect population pressure to trigger episodes of settlement reorganization. Given the higher than normal rainfall in the Sola Valley, population growth and political development might have begun earlier than in the relatively dry parts of Oaxaca. On the other hand, the Sola Valley's far smaller area of farmable alluvium might have made the region less desirable for early settlement. An ecologically functional model would predict that settlement in a marginal region would be especially constrained by environmental factors. What was the precise timing of the Sola Valley's initial occupation? How did population/resource balances affect Sola Valley settlement patterns over time?

Monte Albán's Origins

Based on the regional settlement hierarchy, scale of monumental construction at Monte Albán, and presence of public buildings at lower-order centers, Blanton and others (1993, 1999) argued that a unified regional state was in place at the onset of Period I (or urban origin was coeval with state formation). Marcus and Flannery (1996:160-65; Flannery and Marcus 1983a) considered Period I transitional and questioned whether the entire Valley of Oaxaca was unified at this time. The latter view was based on excavations at centers predating Monte Albán, and more specific criteria for identifying states archaeologically (see the Valley of Oaxaca discussion in Chapter 6).

How significant was Monte Albán's founding (the urban dimension) for understanding other social innovations (such as state formation)? Blanton and others (1993, 1999) linked urbanization to a constellation of other processes including state formation; Marcus and Flannery (1996) regarded Monte Albán's founding and Zapotec state formation as two separate research problems. Each set of propositions was contingent on the degree of valley-wide integration over the course of Period I. Yet, both sets of scholars agree that by the succeeding Period II, the Monte Albán state was conquering regions outside the Valley of Oaxaca.

The Zapotec Expansion

Marcus's (1976) study of the Building J monuments from Monte Albán identified provinces subject to the Zapotec state. Each monument whose place name has been deciphered referred to places 85-150 km from Monte Albán; early Zapotec rulers apparently delimited their territory by listing their border regions, much as their sixteenth-century descendants had done (Marcus and Flannery 1996:195-98). Marcus's analysis of the monuments indicated that rulers used variable strategies of incorporation. Not all places had inverted heads below the place or "hill sign." Those monuments with inverted heads—perhaps signifying outright conquest—include Cuicatlán. Other monuments had the "hill sign" but lacked the upside down head, for example Miahuatlán; these latter places were suspected of paying tribute, but not necessarily having been incorporated through conquest.

Archaeological and epigraphic evidence indicated that by Period II, Monte Albán controlled Cuicatlán, Miahuatlán, Ejutla, and Guirún (Feinman and Nicholas 1990a, 1996; Markman 1981; Spencer and Redmond 1997). Monte Albán first conquered Cuicatlán, and then co-opted through diplomatic means (via royal marriage alliance, trade, or military threat) Ejutla and Miahuatlán. Guirún's colonization defined the eastern limit of the Zapotec state, but its economic impact extended still further. If Monte Albán controlled a multiregional political territory, then how did processes of incorporation manifest themselves in regions outside the Valley of Oaxaca? One conclusion shared by these studies of subject provinces was that no region had a static relationship with Monte Albán; the nature of these interregional relationships changed over time—and not always in concert.

The Sola Valley fell within the geographic range of places subject to Monte Albán (Marcus 1992a; Marcus and Flannery 1996:195-207); systematic study of the Sola Valley's Formative period occupation was one means to evaluate the expansion model. What was the timing of the Zapotec expansion into the Sola Valley? Was the Sola Valley colonized to act as a buffer zone against rival powers, or to gain access to more distant provinces? The incorporation of the Sola Valley into Monte Albán's political sphere would support arguments favoring Monte Albán as an expansionist state. The expansion model would be rejected if the Sola Valley were more autonomous at this time.

Marcus's (1992a) model for Monte Albán's expansion was a general model: specific manifestations of incorporation would be unique to each study region. It had to be determined how the Sola Valley enriched the general model, and what specific strategies of incorporation were used. Valley by valley refinement of the general model will be one outcome of future work. Settlement patterns from the Sola Valley should provide some indication of its role in these broader patterns of interaction.

Emergence of Complexity on the Zapotec Frontier

At a further remove from Monte Albán, other regions felt the impact of Monte Albán expansion, but not from colonization or conquest (Balkansky 1998a, 1998b, 1999; Balkansky et al. 2000). Cerro Jazmín, Huamelulpan, Monte Negro, and

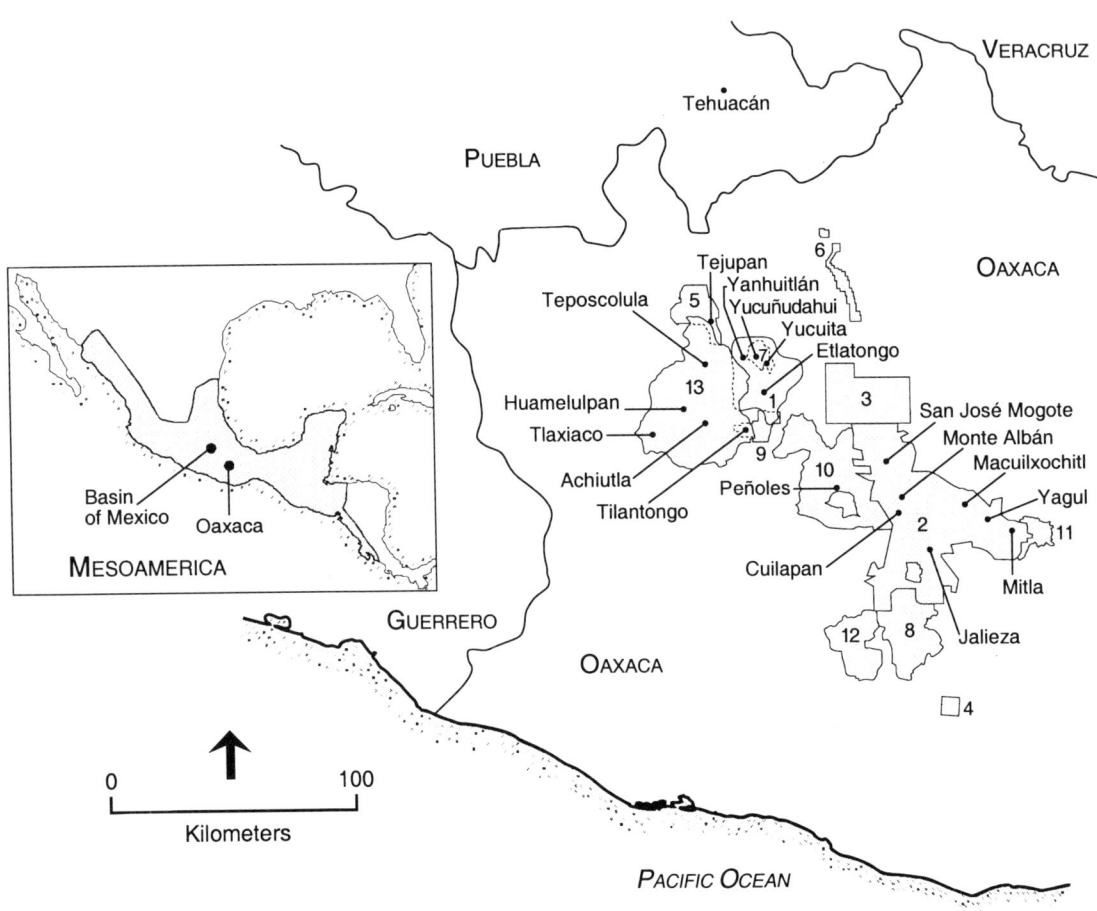

Figure 2.1. The Sola Valley survey area and other Oaxaca surveys, in order of initial fieldwork, and modern Mexican states: (1) Nochixtlán Valley; (2) Valley of Oaxaca; (3) Sierra de Oaxaca; (4) Miahuatlán Valley; (5) Tamazulapan Valley; (6) Cuicatlán Cañada; (7) Yucuita sector, Nochixtlán Valley; (8) Ejutla Valley; (9) Jaltepec and Tilantongo sectors, Nochixtlán Valley; (10) Peñoles area; (11) Guirún area; (12) Sola Valley; (13) Central Mixteca Alta.

Yucuita were walled Mixtec cities, capable of both defense and practicing their own predatory expansion. Militarism triggered a chain reaction across highland Oaxaca. Some Mixtec centers survived to form their own state-level societies; others were short-lived experiments, soon abandoned. Why did these complex societies emerge in regions outside Monte Albán's political control?

In the lower Río Verde Valley and southern Isthmus of Tehuantepec, the sites of Río Viejo and Laguna Zope became important regional centers during the Zapotec expansion (Zeitlin and Joyce 1999). Grayware ceramics similar to the Valley of Oaxaca's were common there. Monte Albán claimed the province of Tututepec near the Río Verde (e.g. Marcus 1983a; Marcus and Flannery 1996:197) but not Tehuantepec. Río Viejo was the capital of an urban and possible state-level society. Laguna Zope elites monopolized control of shell and obsidian, and possibly exchanged these items with long-distance traders from highland Oaxaca. Archaeologists working in coastal Oaxaca nevertheless rejected evidence of a Monte Albán takeover (Zeitlin and Joyce 1999). The Sola Valley results are relevant to this debate. How was Monte Albán–coastal interaction connected to the Sola Valley, and did the timing of sequential expansion fit?

Elite on the fringes of Monte Albán's political territory could have built their status in the context of the Zapotec expansion (Balkansky 1998b). The changing complexity on the Zapotec frontier could also have had reciprocal evolutionary effects at Monte Albán. Profound changes in the Mixteca Alta were tied to Monte Albán's militaristic expansion, but in the form of co-development rather than conquest (Balkansky 1998a, 1998b). Similar processes may have occurred in coastal regions as well.

Figure 2.2 (opposite). Prehispanic sites and modern towns in the Sola Valley.

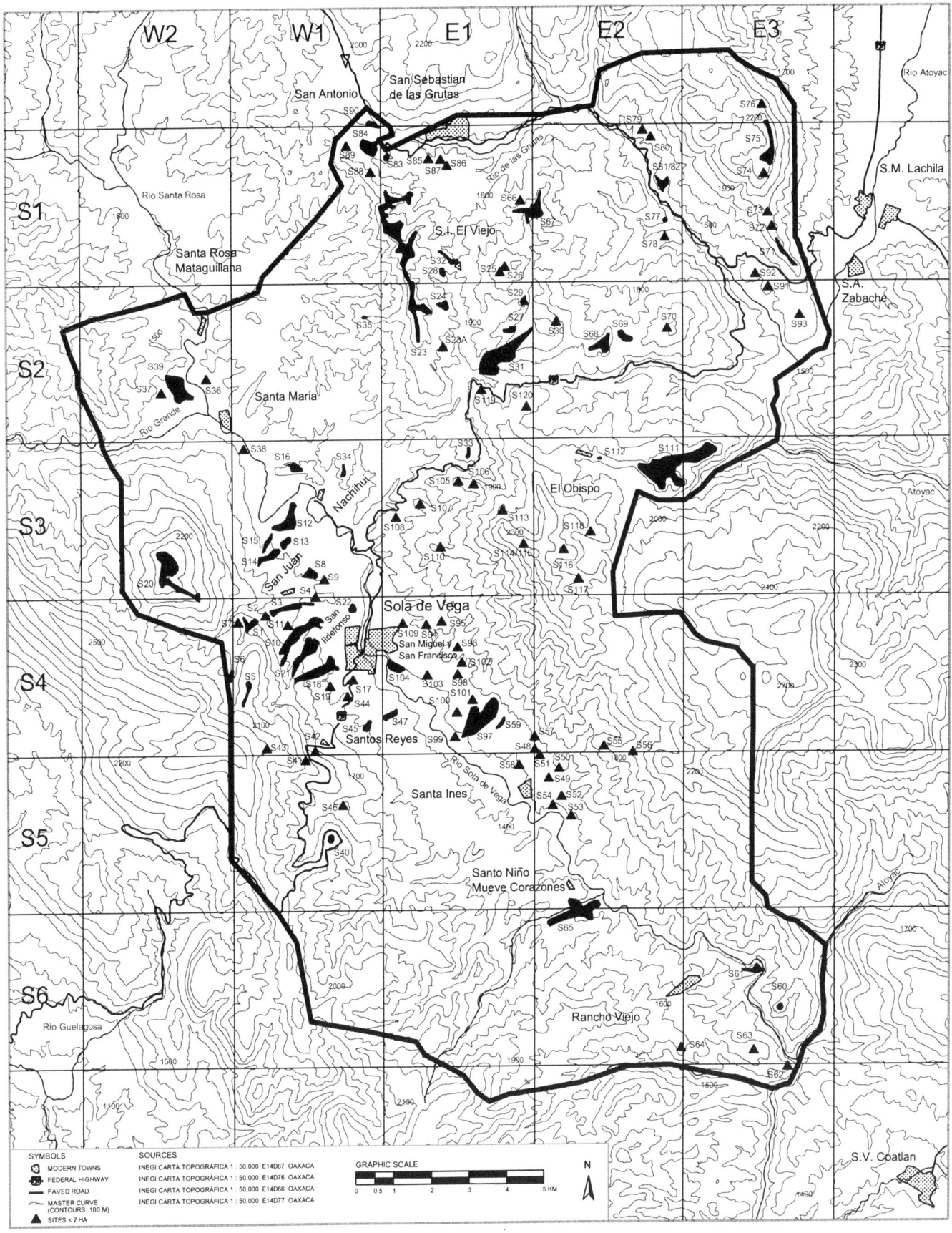

Plate 2.1. The seventeenth-century church at San Miguel Sola de Vega is in the center of the valley, looking east-northeast toward high mountains beyond which is the southern part of the Valley of Oaxaca.

Plate 2.2. View of the Sola Valley looking southeast. The church at San Miguel is visible in the center left of the frame.

TABLE 2.1. Highland Oaxaca Survey Coverages

Region	Size (km^2)	Total Sites	Coverage (%)	Main Reference
Nochixtlán Valley	450	176	100	Spores 1972
Valley of Oaxaca	2150	2700	100	Kowalewski et al. 1989
Sierra Norte	650	—	—	Drennan 1989
Miahuatlán Valley	300	65	10	Markman 1981
Tamazulapan	253	230	100	Byland 1980
Cuicatlán Cañada	52	93	100	Redmond 1983
Yucuita Sector	80	42	100	Plunket 1983
Ejutla Valley	522	423	100	Feinman and Nicholas 1990a
Jaltepec/Tilantongo	—	—	100	Byland and Pohl 1994
Peñoles Area	1000	545	100	Finsten 1996
Guirún Area	110	68	100	Feinman and Nicholas 1996
Sola Valley	370	120	100	Balkansky 1997a
Cent. Mixteca Alta	1621	1024	100	Balkansky et al. 2000

A mix of strategies and forms of interaction—from colonization, conquest, and co-option to co-evolution—remain viable working hypotheses for the change in complexity on the coast.

The location of the Sola Valley suggested that it was a corridor between the highlands and coastal Oaxaca. Modern transportation routes to the coast passed through the region. The list of conquered provinces and changes in coastal ceramic complexes suggested ties to the Zapotec capital. Monte Albán's expansion was synchronous with the emergence of complex societies on the coast. Highland-coastal links would tend to negate the coastal autonomy models. I designed my study of the Sola Valley to evaluate these alternative positions.

Sola's Later Settlement History

Sola Valley survey results also reflected the changing extent and organization of the Classic period Zapotec state. Sanders and Nichols (1988) would expect regional population to grow until a critical ceiling is reached. The state would arise when Monte Albán was at its peak population in Period IIIb (Sanders and Nichols 1988:51-52; also Sanders and Santley 1978), or 700-1000 years later than current evidence suggested (Balkansky 1998b; Blanton et al. 1993:69-77, 1999:85; Marcus and Flannery 1996:155-94). The Sola Valley might also be expected to reach its highest population and fullest political integration with Monte Albán in Period IIIb.

A related issue concerned the eventual dissolution of first-generation states in Oaxaca. Marcus (1992a) predicted the contraction of Monte Albán's political territory in Period IIIa and IIIb-IV (though the site itself was then at its greatest size and monumentality). The Valleys of Sola and Oaxaca should become more autonomous by the Late Classic period. It should not, however, be expected that the Sola Valley's later settlement history would necessarily mirror that of other regions. How did macroregional dynamics shift after Monte Albán's decline?

Regional Settlement Pattern Survey

One point on which there was substantial agreement between all investigators was the need to extend settlement pattern coverage beyond its present limits (e.g. Marcus 1992a:409; Sanders and Nichols 1988:33). The political territory of the early Zapotec state was ten times the size of the Valley of Oaxaca. Study of this early state presented a serious methodological problem in which an analytical focus on regions (the core area of Monte Albán) was inadequate to measure the phenomenon of interest: the expansion and contraction of the Zapotec state.

Settlement pattern coverage in outlying regions has better defined the fluctuating borders of the Zapotec state (e.g. Feinman and Nicholas 1990a; Redmond 1983). These studies have shown considerable variation in settlement patterns; in terms of explanation, they present nonexclusive alternatives such that the restructuring of regions was the only common feature. These results could be taken as one response to the final but frequently asked question: Have we surveyed enough by now?

The Sola Valley Study Region

The Sola Valley was located 65 km southwest of Oaxaca City, the modern capital of the State of Oaxaca, in the southern highlands of Mexico. Compared to other regions in Oaxaca, little was known of the prehispanic Sola Valley when my work began. Extant data taken from ethnohistoric, archaeological, and linguistic sources nevertheless placed the Sola Valley in potential contact with Monte Albán (Plate 2.1, 2.2).

In an intriguing parallel to these arguments, sociologists Murphy and Stepick (1991) suggest that Oaxaca City (located on the valley floor below Monte Albán) has since Colonial times experienced alternating cycles of engagement with a broader "world system." It was during periods of engagement that the Colonial capital had its greatest impact on surrounding regions.

The modern capital has so far existed in a period of strong state authority and intersocietal interaction operating on the global scale. Oaxaca City's impact on nearby regions has consequently been proportionately greater than at other times in the past.

Sola and its surrounding region were inhabited by nearly 18,000 people during the last census, two-thirds of them living in the district capital at San Miguel Sola de Vega (Región Sierra Sur 1990). Sola de Vega monopolized administrative and economic functions in its district, and provided benefits not available in the smaller towns; the entire region nonetheless depended on Oaxaca City for critical services and financing (as shown by the suppression of local markets and the importance of state-sponsored construction projects). Murphy and Stepick's (1991) model seems to hold true for the contemporary setting; the extent to which these conditions existed in times past has remained unknown.

Environmental Characteristics

Present-day environmental similarities among regions in highland Oaxaca include the interconnected river basins defined by the Río Atoyac; the environmental zones of alluvium, piedmont, and mountain zones; and the semi-arid climate with annual wet and dry seasons (Kirkby 1973; Lorenzo 1960). Still, even at the Valley of Oaxaca scale, there are significant regional and subregional variations in local environments and agricultural potential (Feinman and Nicholas 1990b; Nicholas 1989). There is some variation in altitude, rainfall, land, water tables, and human labor, each of which affect agricultural production. Wild resources are not uniformly distributed either. Sola's environmental characteristics would be expected to vary within these parameters.

In highland Oaxaca rainfall is the limiting factor (Flannery et al. 1967; Kirkby 1973). In comparison, the Sola Valley receives more precipitation than portions of the Valley of Oaxaca and exceeds the critical minimum of 700 mm yearly for reliable maize farming (Carta de Efectos Climáticos 1980). Early settlement might be expected, given the suitability of the region for rainfall farming, but the advantage of increased precipitation is offset by Sola's far smaller valley floor (20 km^2). The Valley of Oaxaca has the largest expanse of flat land in the southern highlands (over 700 km^2), and this fact explains its demographic advantage over other regions (Blanton et al. 1982:4-5). Still, Sola's valley floor land would have been sufficient to support significant occupations from earliest settled times on.

Topography accentuates the differences between the valleys of Sola and Oaxaca (INEGI 1988). High mountains separates the two regions and, in contrast to the broad alluvium of the Valley of Oaxaca, a narrow and steep V-shaped river valley defines the Sola region. Sola's valley floor measures only 1.1 km at its widest point. The landscape is deeply incised by the juncture of the Río Sola and Atoyac, leaving a narrow, sandy, and unproductive alluvium. Elevation in the Sola Valley ranges from 1300-2700 m; the steep gradient is crossed within 10 km of horizontal distance. The main farmable alluvium is located at 1400-1500 m in elevation near San Miguel Sola de Vega. A second, smaller zone of flat land is located near San Sebastián de las Grutas in the northeastern part of the project area. Modern boundary disputes (Dennis 1987) often hinge over control of Sola's limited valley floor land.

The floral pattern also varies from other nearby regions; there are more bromeliads and palmettos in the Sola Valley than usually seen in the Valley of Oaxaca, suggesting a transition from highland to coastal botanical regimes. Sola's well-watered alluvial soils also permit winter corn and bean harvests that are not always practicable elsewhere. In the alluvial shallows at the river's edge, Sola's farmers often plant fruit trees including avocado, orange, lime, banana, and grapefruit. Stands of cane and willow trees also grow along the riverbank. Other more lucrative cash crops are hidden among cornfields in the piedmont and mountain zones. Whether there were differences in agricultural production or products between the Valleys of Sola and Oaxaca in the past remained an open question at the time of the survey.

Still other environmental factors are potentially relevant to the prehispanic settlement history of the Sola Valley. Study of the surface bedrock geology (Carta Geológica 1980) suggests that lithic raw material sources might be present (e.g. Parry 1987; Whalen 1986). The numerous caves are also a notable characteristic of the region (e.g. near San Sebastián de las Grutas; see also Garzón 1994 [1777]). Caves offer the possibility of finding Archaic sites; in later periods, they were probable ritual locations, especially when associated with water sources (but since Sola's caves are wet, future excavations would be unlikely to recover plant remains).

A final consideration is the geographic location of the Sola Valley. Steep terrain and a distance of 75 km separate the Sola Valley from coastal Oaxaca; Sola is nevertheless a logical corridor between the Valley of Oaxaca and regions on the coast. The modern highway passes through the region. Historical accounts support the connection for Colonial times (Whitecotton 1992). At the time of the field project, the most intrepid pilgrims still took the footpath through the mountains to pay homage to the Virgin of Juquila. Thus, Sola's geographical placement alone made it a promising region for study.

Ethnohistoric and Linguistic Perspectives

It is regrettable that sixteenth-century Oaxaca had no Sahagún to chronicle the indigenous culture. Córdova (1578a, 1578b) must suffice for the early contact period. The earliest substantial accounts are those of Burgoa (1989 [1674]), and these were written long after Spanish contact. Although less detailed than Burgoa, Gonzalo de Balsalobre's report (1988 [1656]) focused specifically on the Sola Valley. Under the charge of "Inquisitor Ordinario" granted by the Bishop of Oaxaca, Balsalobre investigated the continuation of pre-conquest religious practices. Balsalobre (1988 [1656]:114) described the major "deities" and

Plate 2.3. Carmelo Aragón (second from left) with men from San Juan Sola wait outside a ritually significant cave and nearby archaeological site on the mountain above their town.

ritual performances, and his account reflects the ecclesiastical fixation on sacrifice:

> there are places talked about where they go to carry out their vows, as they do on a hill in my jurisdiction, called Quijaxila in the language of the natives, it being found half a league from the town of San Juan, and another half league from the head town [San Miguel Sola de Vega], [and] on whose summit appear the ruins of a building, which is widely said to have been a Temple of Idols in heathen times, and to which they go to perform sacrifices.*

The ruins that Balsalobre called the "Temple of Idols" were found on Cerro El Quialase, a hilltop archaeological site and nearby cave that overlooked modern San Juan Sola. The site (Sola 20) was important in Postclassic times. The cave has remained a focus of community ritual; one informant said it was more important than the town church (Plate 2.3).

Balsalobre's account leaves many unanswered questions about the nature of this society prior to Spanish colonization. The high degree of religious and cultural syncretism is evident in the *Relación* of 1656: this was a world that had passed through the twin crucibles of conquest and demographic collapse, and had experienced over a century of Colonial administration (Carmagnani 1988; Taylor 1972). Since the documentary record for the prehispanic Sola Valley was limited, I turned to the full corpus of Oaxaca ethnohistory to build expectations for the Sola Valley's place in ancient Oaxaca.

Gerhard's (1972) data on Colonial political jurisdictions provides further insight into Sola's late prehispanic occupation. Sola de Vega (also Tzola; Zola) was composed of twelve townships when it was congregated in 1599; by the eighteenth century, subject towns were listed as Santa María, San Juan, Santos Reyes, and Santa Inés. Santa María Lachixio (now part of Sola's district) was a sixteenth-century dependency of Tlapacoyan (sometimes listed as pertaining to Cuilapan), a head town in the southern Valley of Oaxaca. Lachixio's territory included San Sebastián de las Grutas in the northeastern part of the survey area. The modern district was thus divided into east/west administrative districts in Colonial times.

Sola may have been tributary to the Aztec, the coastal Mixtec kingdom of Tututepec, or both. Gerhard (1972:275) suggests that Sola, along with the highland Mixtec kingdom of

---

*(se) tienen lugares disputados donde ocurren a cumplir sus votos, como lo tienen en un cerro de la jurisdicción de mi beneficio, llamado en lengua vulgar de los naturales Quijaxila, que cae como media legua del pueblo de San Juan, distante de la cabecera otra media legua, en cuya eminencia parecen las ruinas de un edificio, que es constante voz común, y corriente, que fue Templo de sus Ídolos en la Gentilidad, y allí ocurren a poner en execución sus sacrificios.

Plate 2.4. The church at Santa María Sola has several prehispanic carved stones set into its walls, including the rectangular tomb lintel resting above the arched entryway.

Teozacoalco, occupied a frontier or buffer zone between tributary domains of the Aztec empire and coastal Tututepec. But there may have been a Sola/Mixtec connection. A 1565 document mentioned that Teozacoalco's population decline was due to epidemic disease and emigration to Sola (Gerhard 1972:277). The Colonial boundaries had divided the Sola region into east/west segments. I later found that the Late Postclassic settlement patterns show two probable kingdoms on the east and west sides of the valley. The western kingdom had ceramic and other ties to the Mixteca Alta. The eastern kingdom was located closer to Ayoquezco and Ejutla and was more closely tied to the Valley Zapotec (Chapter 5).

Other documentary information pertains to Late Postclassic exchange patterns. Once again the Sola region was located at the crossroads of multiple large-scale interactions. Monte Albán's decline was followed by an era of political fragmentation yet great commercial integration (e.g. Blanton et al. 1993:99-103). Those relationships that extended beyond ethnic and geographic boundaries include warfare, royal marriage alliance, and trade in cotton, shell, obsidian, quetzal feathers, and slaves (e.g. Hunt 1972; Spores 1967, 1974; Whitecotton 1977, 1992). At least two exchange networks linked highland Oaxaca to the lowland regions of coastal Oaxaca and Tehuantepec, and to more distant ports of trade in Chiapas and Guatemala (Ball and Brockington 1978).

As summarized by Whitecotton (1992:60-61), the first exchange network joined the southern Valley of Oaxaca, the Mixteca de la Costa, and the Mixteca Alta with Tehuantepec. A principal element of this trade was cotton. Raw cotton came from the lowlands by way of Tututepec and Tehuantepec, and was manufactured into textiles at the highland towns of Tlaxiaco, Coixtlahuaca, and Nochixtlán in the Mixteca Alta, and possibly Cuilapan in the Valley of Oaxaca. This network was linked to a second exchange sphere that stretched from western Mexico to the eastern lowlands, and trafficked in polychrome pottery, bronze and copper bells, copper axes, macaw and quetzal birds, hallucinogenic drugs, and textiles. Whitecotton (1992:65-69) characterizes these interactions as a "world system" whose origin likely dated from the Classic period, and centered on Monte Albán. By the Late Postclassic period, the southern highlands were incorporated into a still larger "world system" whose center of gravity lay in the Valley of Mexico (Berdan et al. 1996; Blanton and Feinman 1984).

These commercial ties over multiple regions typified highland Oaxaca in the Postclassic period and likely began in earlier times. Yet the earlier patterns of interaction were less clear, for the insights of ethnohistory can only be retrodicted so far. There is less written on the antecedents of these economic relationships, their origins and evolution, and the significance of places such as Sola in Oaxaca's prehispanic political economy.

Plate 2.5. Henrich Berlin first recorded this prehispanic carved stone set into the east-facing church wall at Santa María Sola.

Finally, modern language distributions offer a view into the past. Colonial-era native peoples in the Sola region spoke a dialect of Southern Zapotec, and were located along a linguistic frontier with four other language groups (Fernández de Miranda et al. 1960; Rendón 1975; Swadesh 1967). Rendón (1967) argues that the latest split between Zapotec speakers in highland Oaxaca occurred during the Postclassic period, although the precise timing and boundaries of earlier divergences are matters of contention (e.g. Beals 1969; Marcus 1983b; Whitecotton 1977). As the end point of a 5000-year continuum, the pattern of these modern language distributions is intriguing. Still, our understanding of the origin and specific pattern of cultural divergence in the Sola Valley has awaited the long-term perspective of a systematic archaeological research program.

Archaeology of the Sola Valley

What was known from archaeology before this study suggested the long-standing participation by the people of the Sola Valley in the cultural interplay of highland Oaxaca. The pioneering studies of Heinrich Berlin established the archaeological baseline for the Sola Valley. Berlin's (1957) study of unpublished Inquisition documents further amplifies Balsalobre's (1988 [1656]) account. Of particular concern to this project are Berlin's (1946, 1951) studies of prehistoric settlements and carved stone monuments.

Berlin identified seven sites, and inferred the existence of at least a dozen others, described by informants to be the proveniences of the carved stones and other artifacts found out of context (Plate 2.5). A series of prominent ruins known locally as El Obispo, Piedra Siempre Viva, and Los Chilillos had mounds, monumental architecture, ball courts, carved stones, and cruciform tombs—unmistakable evidence of complex cultural developments in Oaxaca. Among the artifacts that Berlin examined were several Zapotec funerary urns that date to the Classic period, and one copper ax of the type used in tribute payments in the Late Postclassic period. There were numerous carved stones similar to those from Monte Albán, which Berlin considered to be in the Zapotec tradition; other stones had a unique figure that Berlin called the "Sola God" (see Marcus, this volume).

It was clear from both ethnohistoric accounts and archaeological evidence that the Sola Valley had a significant prehispanic occupation, albeit one not well understood. In nearly fifty years since Berlin's initial explorations there had been no subsequent studies of the Sola Valley. The archaeological data were promising, but prompted more questions than could be addressed from the existing evidence.

The 1995-1996 Sola Valley Settlement Pattern Project

Berlin (1951:1) was a pioneer but even he could not foresee the eventual impact of systematic settlement pattern surveys as he was touring the Sola Valley:

[T]hough odd and antiquated, surveys have recommendations of their own: not much money is needed to be spent on costly excavations, nor does one need to secure either governmental or any other permission. An open eye and open mind combined with a certain professional curiosity are the only requisites for the job. It has, moreover, the advantage that no definite conclusions are expected of it.

Mesoamerican archaeology has changed conisderably in the last five decades.

As a method to locate and map sites on a landscape, archaeologists using settlement pattern surveys have made significant contributions to our knowledge of the prehispanic past (e.g. Kowalewski et al. 1989; Sanders, Parsons, and Santley 1979). Prior to the advent of systematic regional surveys, only a few of the most prominent sites were recorded (e.g. Bernal 1965); today, thousands of sites have been mapped in highland Mesoamerica alone (e.g. Blanton et al. 1993).

TABLE 2.2. Yield Ranges for Land Types in Metric Tons per Hectare per Year

Phase	Type I (Low/High Rainfall)	Type II (Low/High Rainfall)	Type III (Low/High Rainfall)
Present	2.0-2.8 / 2.0-2.8	0.4-2.8 / 1.2-2.8	0-1.2 / 0.4-2.0
V	1.4-1.9 / 1.4-1.9	0.3-1.9 / 0.8-1.9	0-0.8 / 0.3-1.4
IIIb-IV	1.1-1.5 / 1.1-1.5	0.2-1.5 / 0.7-1.5	0-0.7 / 0.2-1.1
IIIa	0.8-1.1 / 0.8-1.1	0.2-1.1 / 0.5-1.1	0-0.5 / 0.2-0.8
II	0.7-1.0 / 0.7-1.0	0.1-1.0 / 0.4-1.0	0-0.4 / 0.1-0.7
Ic	0.6-0.8 / 0.6-0.8	0.1-0.8 / 0.4-0.8	0-0.4 / 0.1-0.6
Ia	0.5-0.6 / 0.5-0.6	0.1-0.6 / 0.3-0.6	0-0.3 / 0.1-0.5

(After A. Kirkby 1973: Fig. 27; Kowalewski 1982: Fig. 9.3)

TABLE 2.3. Distribution of Land Class (in Hectares) by Grid Square for the Sola Valley

Grid	Type I	Type II	Type III 100%	Type III 10%
N1E2	—	4.25	15.25	470.50
N1E3	—	—	—	476.25
S1E1	116.75	22.00	553.25	926.25
S1E2	—	50.50	123.75	1425.75
S1E3	—	38.75	—	1053.50
S2E1	—	140.50	112.50	1347.00
S2E2	—	—	—	1600.00
S2E3	—	92.50	—	1157.50
S2W1	5.00	—	160.00	1395.00
S2W2	235.00	—	127.50	865.00
S3E1	—	—	20.00	1580.00
S3E2	—	—	—	1340.00
S3W1	357.50	—	785.00	457.50
S3W2	—	—	20.00	1102.50
S4E1	302.50	—	565.00	732.50
S4E2	—	—	10.00	1512.50
S4E3	—	—	—	1040.00
S4W1	120.00	—	370.00	1110.00
S4W2	—	—	—	1087.50
S5E1	157.50	—	450.00	992.50
S5E2	160.00	—	202.50	1237.50
S5E3	—	—	—	1600.00
S5W1	—	—	—	1472.50
S5W2	—	—	—	467.50
S6E1	—	—	—	1472.50
S6E2	25.00	—	152.50	1422.50
S6E3	—	—	25.00	1350.00
S6W1	—	—	—	705.00
Total	1479 (4%)	349 (1%)	3692 (10%)	31,339 (85%)

TABLE 2.4. Settlement Density in the Valleys of Sola, Ejutla, and Oaxaca.

Valley	Sola	Ejutla	Oaxaca
Area (km^2)	370	522	2150
# Sites	120	423	2700
Sites/km^2	0.32	0.81	1.25
Components	207	691	6353
Components/km^2	0.56	1.32	2.95

TABLE 2.5. Settlement Density by Phase for the Sola Valley

Phase	Components	Hectares	Density (ha/km^2)
Monte Albán V	83	378.01	1.02
Monte Albán IIIb-IV	39	341.62	0.92
Monte Albán IIIa	52	297.09	0.30
Monte Albán II	11	35.57	0.10
Monte Albán Ic	19	62.96	0.17
Monte Albán Ia	1	0.33	—
Not defined	6	0.55	—

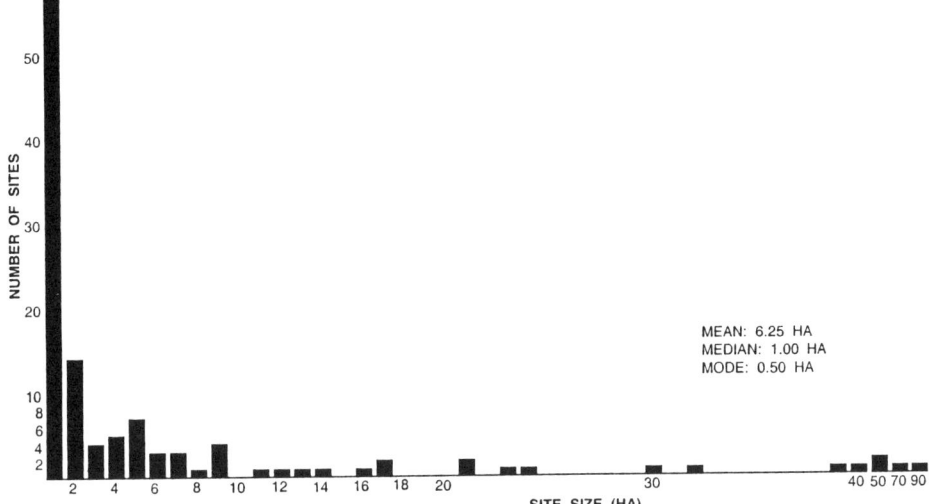

Figure 2.3. Histogram of Sola Valley site sizes in hectares.

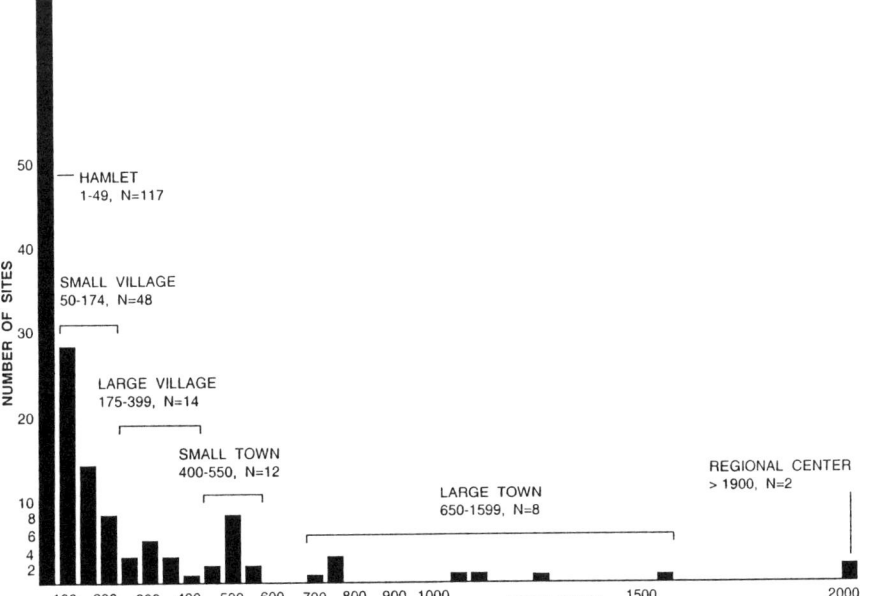

Figure 2.4. Histogram of Sola Valley population centers.

Sola and other regions in highland Oaxaca had ideal conditions for archaeological surveys (Fig. 2.1; Table 2.1). The vegetation cover was sparse, and nonmechanized farming practices continually brought archaeological materials to the surface. The modern urbanization that has affected other regions in highland Mesoamerica (e.g. the growth of Mexico City since the 1960s) was not a problem for most regions in Oaxaca, meaning that few sites have been destroyed. In highland Mesoamerica, settlement pattern survey was the least-cost solution to gather data at a spatial scale sufficient to measure the questions of interest to this study.

Field and Laboratory Procedures

I adapted the highland survey methodology pioneered in the Basin of Mexico (Sanders 1965; Sanders, Parsons, and Santley 1979) for use in the Sola Valley. The same or similar methodologies were used in the Valley of Oaxaca (Blanton 1978; Blanton et al. 1982; Kowalewski et al. 1989) and other regions in highland Mesoamerica (e.g. Feinman and Nicholas 1990a; Hirth 1980; Redmond 1983). The objective was to obtain specific regional data sets: site size over time; site plans; artifact distributions; place names; modern boundaries; ancient and

TABLE 2.6. Population Densities (per Km²) for the Sola Valley, the Ejutla Valley, and Subregions in the Oaxaca Valley

Phase	Sola	Ejutla	Valle Grande	Ocotlán	Oaxaca
Monte Albán V	24.32	38.26	58.52	67.06	76.11
Monte Albán IIIb-IV	19.10	5.80	28.39	15.18	34.65
Monte Albán IIIa	20.82	28.08	62.44	66.26	53.59
Monte Albán II	2.25	4.18	11.77	5.74	19.22
Monte Albán Ic	4.16	6.62	20.15	7.43	23.68
Monte Albán Ia	0.02	0.50	4.69	1.47	6.81
Rosario	—	0.08	0.48	0.42	0.85
Guadalupe	—	—	0.27	0.12	0.83
San José	—	0.05	0.25	0.12	0.90
Tierras Largas	—	—	0.16	0.09	0.15

TABLE 2.7. Potential and Archaeological Population Levels by Phase for the Sola Valley

Phase	Potential Population (Based on Resources)	Potential Population (Based on Labor)	Archaeological Population
V	42,257	14,005	8998
IIIb-IV	32,703	16,181	7066
IIIa	24,719	9931	7703
II	20,525	2792	833
Ic	17,625	2795	1539
Ia	—	—	8

Plate 2.6. Polished stone axes from the Sola Valley survey; these two examples are from a site dating to the Postclassic period.

Plate 2.7. Projectile points from the Sola Valley survey, from sites with a mix of Classic and Postclassic period occupations.

TABLE 2.8. Subregional Distribution of Prime Farmland in Oaxaca

Subregion	Type I (ha)	Type II (ha)	Total (ha)
Etla	5117	88	5205
Central	1261	2652	3913
Valle Grande	3345	2600	5945
Ocotlán	2003	1180	3183
W. Tlacolula	618	6118	6736
E. Tlacolula	396	1584	1980
Ejutla	1527	3702	5229
Sola	1479	349	1828

TABLE 2.9. Correlation Coefficients for Actual versus Potential Population by Grid Square in the Sola Valley

Phase	Correlation (r)	Extreme Value Removed
V ($n = 18$)	+0.045	—
IIIb-IV ($n = 13$)	+0.475	—
IIIa ($n = 17$)	+0.258	+0.107
II ($n = 7$)	-0.155	+0.244
Ic ($n = 10$)	-0.017	+0.302
Ia ($n = 1$)	—	—

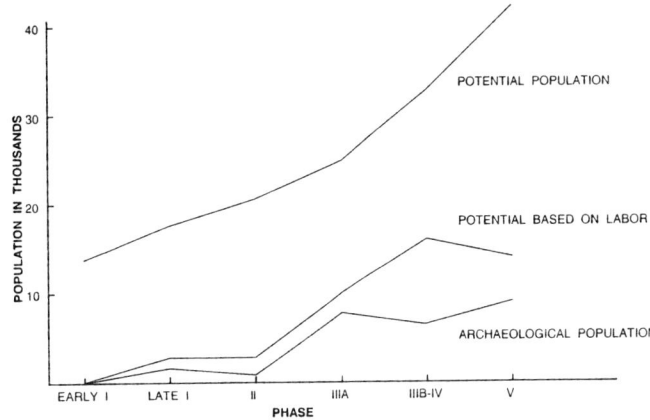

Figure 2.5. Potential and archaeological population levels in the Sola Valley.

modern agricultural features; and characteristics of the environment.

I designed the Sola Valley survey for 100% coverage (Kowalewski 1990b). A probability sampling design to locate sites was not practical in the Sola Valley; the few roads and difficult terrain would require survey crews to walk great distances just to locate sample units, while permission from local townships would still be necessary in order to cross their land. In addition, probability-sampling designs obscure the regional variability of sites (Kowalewski 1990b:37-39)—especially for the subset of larger sites—which has unfortunate consequences for data interpretation (e.g. Flannery 1976:159). A better use of probability samples would come during a second stage of research, once preliminary results were available for the Sola Valley, and more particular questions could be addressed.

A related issue concerned the intensity of survey coverage. The artifact recovery procedures were standardized, with representative collections taken from circumscribed locations shown on the site map. This was an opportunistic sampling procedure suited to regional data requirements.

On regional survey, ceramic collections were made primarily to date the occupations, and not to measure intrasite variations in style, specialization, or other characteristics. Sites were dated through field observations, and the later analysis of chronologically diagnostic ceramics in the field laboratory. I used the ceramic sequence established for the Valley of Oaxaca from excavated data (Caso et al. 1967) and subsequently adapted for use on Oaxaca surveys (Kowalewski, Spencer, and Redmond 1978). Surveyors took representative ceramic collections from most sites for later analysis in the laboratory. Surveyors also noted the location of diagnostic ceramics even in places where collections were not taken.

Other artifact classes included obsidian, shell, chert, and ground stone. Obsidian blades, for instance, would be recorded in the notebook and a few examples collected. Green or gray; blade, core, or finished tool; and remarks about the apparent surface density of the obsidian—that was the grain of the data in this instance. I often argued with obsidian enthusiasts about leaving blades in the field. I agreed that the blades were pretty. I also pointed out that we were usually at multicomponent sites, and so we could not date the nonceramic artifacts to phase. Our time was better spent gathering the kinds of data that regional surveys are best suited for.

As for the obsidian and other stone artifacts, it was best to get a few examples to make general observations valid on the regional level of analysis (Plate 2.6). In many cases the resulting study would be limited to presence or absence, but it would be better than nothing (also Kowalewski 1990c). Although I view it as inadvisable to make sweeping claims about ancient economies from these kinds of surface data, regional survey observations often do lead to significant follow-up studies at individual sites.

Shell was rare and it did not weigh very much, so we collected every example that we saw. Every projectile point and finished tool was also collected. The points were often chronologically diagnostic (and proof that you did a careful job surveying; the student should be wary of results from projects that seldom find projectile points, Plate 2.7). Characteristic tool types seemed to vary from region to region, so it was important to have examples of them too. Manos and metates, on the other hand, were noted but never collected—you would have to be pretty strong, or dumb, or both to carry bowling balls in your backpack all day. Human remains often found eroding from the surface were noted but not collected.

One last point on coverage and collection strategies: I compromised the intrasite data on purpose in favor of building

Plate 2.8. Surveyors working at S23 (Henrich Berlin's "Los Chilillos" site). Verónica Pérez is taking notes while Lázaro Aragón measures the base of the structure, and two men from San Ildefonso Sola watch the proceedings.

intersite and interregional data sets. Experiments with intensive collection strategies in regions measured in hundreds of square kilometers have proven disappointing (e.g. Kowalewski 1976; Spores 1972). In these studies, the time spent making intensive collections offered little improvement in chronological control, but placed unacceptable limits on the number of sites visited, and the total area covered. The "first law" of regional survey stated that other things being equal, more survey coverage was always better, and I followed it to the letter. As Kowalewski (1990c) explained, the methods chosen must be appropriate to the physical size of the object under study. Kowalewski (1990b), being a wise old owl, has also said that the choice of method entails a theoretical consequence. He was right about that too. It would be a mistake to turn regional surveys into intensive site surveys. It was not possible to employ intensive site survey methods in the Sola Valley and still address the present research questions.

I defined sites as being potentially interpretable vestiges of prehispanic settlement (Kowalewski et al. 1989:29-30; Plog, Plog, and Wait 1978:389; Sanders, Parsons, and Santley 1979:34). I also used the "100-m rule" to define discrete site areas. If the distance between observed surface remains exceeded 100 m, then the new material was recorded as a separate site.

Sites could always be combined later in the laboratory; it was much harder to split them apart after the fact.

Surveyors recorded sites directly onto 1:50,000 INEGI maps of the valley. Aerial photographs have proven cumbersome in forest-covered regions with high relief where sites were seldom visible from the air. As part of the standard field methodology, we mapped on graph paper each prehispanic feature visible on the surface with pace, tape, and compass at 1:1000 scale. These features included earthen mounds, stone foundations and walls, terraces, plazas, stairways, walkways, and roads. The possible effects of postdepositional events such as later occupation, erosion, and alluviation were examined at each site. Careful mapping of structures provided data on site organization. Other surface remains provided indications of activity areas, which could be studied later with more intensive collection and excavation strategies. These procedures were applied consistently throughout the project area and provided, as near as possible, a 100% sample of the variation in regional settlement (Plate 2.8).

The highland valley survey methodology was modified for the mountainous zone separating the valleys of Sola, Ejutla, and Oaxaca. These changes were consistent with other mountain surveys in the southern highlands (e.g. Drennan 1989), and reflected the changed circumstances of topography, vegetation, and possible site location. The Peñoles project (Finsten and Kowalewski 1991; Finsten et al. 1996) set the gold standard in mountain survey, and it was their procedures that were used in the more remote parts of Sola.

Surveying in the mountains required different techniques from those used in the low piedmont and valley bottoms to ensure efficient coverage. You could not spread your entire crew equidistantly and then comb the surface as was done on the valley floors. Much of the area was too steep for habitation, or for walking. Oak and pine forests extended for kilometers with only occasional clearings and made travel, transport, and communication difficult. Dense mats of leaves, pine needles, and secondary growth often limited surface visibility. These factors discouraged modern agricultural use and full coverage surveys; they nevertheless allowed for a modified and effective survey strategy.

Most modern and prehispanic settlements in the mountains were found on broad and relatively flat ridge tops, or had been terraced. Places too steep for occupation (and too steep to walk) were passed over. How steep was too steep? If you had to rappel across the surface, then it was too steep to survey; otherwise, we checked it out. Under these conditions, the best strategy was for two- to four-person survey crews to walk the principal ridge tops and obtain supplementary information on site location from local informants.

What this meant in practice was that crews climbed a mountain, and then split into two-person teams to follow the narrow ridges running off the peak. Everyone would regroup periodically at predetermined locations. It is not smart to fly solo in the mountains. This survey technique covered the full habitable area. The main limitation was that satisfactory ceramic collections could be hard to obtain; however, this limitation was balanced against the often extraordinary architectural preservation. After surveying with these methods in the mountains north of the Valley of Oaxaca, Drennan (1989) concluded that few sites went undetected (cf. Finsten and Kowalewski 1991).

My main regret about our mountain surveying in Sola was that we did not camp overnight, as was done in Peñoles (Finsten and Kowalewski 1991) and during later Mixteca Alta surveys (Balkansky et al. 2000). Several tens of kilometers of unsurveyed terrain were easily reachable from base camps in the mountains, but on the Sola survey we did not have the logistic capacity (and extra money) needed for this work.

In the field laboratory, all artifact collections were washed, analyzed, and stored under the auspices of the Centro Regional de Oaxaca (INAH). After leaving the field, I prepared topographic base maps for each phase of occupation at the University of Wisconsin and the American Museum of Natural History. I used Charles Spencer's compensating polar planimeter to measure site sizes for each occupational component. I consulted the field notes, site maps, and artifact tabulations to complete the site forms and write the site descriptions. I then wrote several early drafts of my dissertation, none of which were acceptable to my advisor. Population estimates and land use analyses are described below. The results detailed in later chapters were based on these data.

Population Estimates

An underlying assumption in population estimates is that site size varies with population, although this relationship is not the same in every case. To obtain population estimates, I measured the site and component areas in hectares and then multiplied by a density figure (persons per hectare). Population estimates were never meant to be immutable, but rather subject to modification after intensive surveys and excavation.

Sanders (1965:50) and Parsons (1971:23) calculated their population densities based on modern rural communities in highland Mexico, with density increasing from "compact ranchería" to "scattered village" to "compact low-density village" and finally to "compact high-density village," each with an upper and lower density range. They chose an appropriate population density, based on surface sherd densities at archaeological sites that could range from 2-5 persons per hectare to 50-100 persons per hectare for the highest density occupations (Sanders, Parsons, and Santley 1979:34-40).

Blanton et al. (1982:10-11) found that surface sherd densities in the Valley of Oaxaca were less than the Basin of Mexico. Sherd densities, moreover, were affected by complicating factors that included recent plowing, past erosion, past occupations, and vegetation cover. Non-terraced Valley of Oaxaca sites fit Sanders' "light-to-moderate occupation" at 10-25 persons per hectare. Most variation in Valley of Oaxaca population estimates therefore depended on site size (Feinman et al. 1985; Kowalewski et al. 1989:25). I also used the figure of 10-25 persons per hectare for non-terraced Sola Valley sites (see Redmond 1983:41). I made exceptions for isolated residences and assigned densities of 5-10 persons per house based on historic-era household sizes in rural Mexico (Sanders 1970).

On terraced sites, the number of houses was estimated for each individual terrace, based on actual house counts when possible (Blanton et al. 1982:10-11). This method generated more precise population estimates than site area alone. At multicomponent sites, however, actual house counts were problematic, since it was not always clear which houses were truly contemporary. Some terraced sites were also too damaged from plowing and erosion to map accurately; in these instances I used 25-50 persons per hectare to estimate population.

I knew that population density changed over time, but too few single component sites have been surveyed intensively, or excavated extensively, to modify population density estimates by phase with precision. I therefore chose not to deviate from using 10-25 persons per hectare for non-terraced sites and 25-50 persons per hectare for terraced sites, but the published data would allow future analysts to modify these density estimates.

In subsequent data transformations with the population estimates, I relied on mean values. For example, a 10-hectare non-terraced site with a density of 10-25 persons per hectare would

Plate 2.9. Carmelo Aragón, Verónica Pérez, Lázaro Aragón, and Everardo Olivera wait to meet with the municipal president at San Ildefonso Sola.

have an estimated population ranging from 100 to 250 people. In later analyses, however, I would use the mean value of 175 persons for this hypothetical site.

Population estimates have advantages over simply (and with far fewer assumptions) comparing site areas. First, higher density terraced sites are distinguished from less dense valley-floor sites. Measures of regional hierarchy and land use are best made with finer-grained population estimates sensitive to terraced sites. Second, population estimates also ensure comparability with prior studies (e.g. Kowalewski et al. 1989; Sanders, Parsons, and Santley 1979) that gave their principal results in population rather than site size. Third, land use studies that derive from carrying capacities require population estimates. Fourth, population estimates track relative change over time in a region, regardless of the chosen densities. The disadvantages include the fact that readers of survey volumes often become cross-eyed after reading sections on population such as this one. As an aid to the weary, population estimates and site sizes by phase are tabulated in the appendices.

Land Use Analysis

In the land use analyses, I followed the procedures outlined in Kowalewski (1982a) and Nicholas (1989). My data come from archaeological population estimates, and the estimated productivity of farmland in the Sola Valley. I placed a 4 x 4 km grid that was continuous with the Ejutla and Oaxaca Valley survey grids over the study region (e.g. Feinman and Nicholas 1990a: Fig. 6; Kowalewski et al. 1989: Map 1, Fig. 3.1). These grid squares (16 km^2 each) were the basic units of analysis. Grid square N1E3 was the "magic box" connecting the Sola, Ejutla, and Oaxaca Valley survey boundaries.

As had been done in earlier Oaxaca land use studies (Feinman and Nicholas 1990b; Kowalewski 1980; Nicholas et al. 1986), I estimated land quality and agricultural productivity using data from Kirkby's (1973) monograph on contemporary land use in the Valley of Oaxaca. Kirkby (1973) defined multiple land types based on their potential productivity, with the critical limiting factor being access to water. Kowalewski (1982a) condensed Kirkby's (1973) typology into Type I, II, and III land, each distinguished by its potential corn yield. Corn was the proxy measure for total crop yields (given its unknown crop mixes) in the prehispanic past. Type I land had the best potential yield because of the high water table and the potential for canal irrigation in the alluvium. Type II land had the potential for irrigation but with less consistent yields. Type III land had limited irrigation potential and was essentially dry-farmed. Type III land was further subdivided into those lands cultivable over 100% of their area versus those (especially mountainous) lands in which only an approximate 10% of the surface area was farmable.

I then extrapolated potential yields into the past, based on Kirkby's (1973:124-26) study of prehistoric corn from dry caves in Tehuacán whose cobs increased in size over time (Table 2.2). Kowalewski (1982a) and Nicholas (1989) used Kirkby's (1973) cob-length curve to estimate yields for each archaeological phase. Kirkby found a linear regression relationship between cob length and yield, meaning that productivity gradually increased over time. Table 2.3 is the distribution of land type by grid-square for the Sola Valley.

I also calculated yearly consumption estimates to compare potential population to the archaeologically observed population. How many people could potentially be supported on the land, based on corn consumed (as a proxy measure of all foodstuffs) per person per year? The consumption estimate is based on ethnographic data from Oaxaca (Kowalewski 1982a:158) given as a range of consumption figures (160-290 kg per person per year). As with the population estimates, I used only mean values in the analysis.

At long last, I was able to calculate potential population for each grid square and for the entire region in each phase. I then compared these figures to the archaeological population estimates to determine whether land quality was the determining factor in settlement decisions (e.g. Sanders, Parsons, and Santley 1979:360). I assure you that this work was a never-ending nightmare. In using these calculations, one assumes that land was the limiting factor.

My worries over land and water were not yet over. I still had to consider labor to estimate how much corn prehispanic populations actually (rather than ideally) could have produced. Kirkby (1973:73) estimated that with prehispanic technology one farmer could cultivate 2 ha of land. Kowalewski (1982a:157-58) used ethnographic data from the Valley of Oaxaca and assumed a work force of 50% of the archaeological population. I then recalculated potential population based on the availability of labor (50% of the archaeological population estimate) and its productive capacity (2 ha farmed per person). Potential population estimates using labor as the limiting factor are better indicators of surplus and deficit production on the archaeological landscape than those using land as the limiting factor.

Overview of the Project Results

In this section, I provide an overview of the project results with emphasis on the broad, phase-by-phase settlement patterns. This material includes project particulars, long-term population and land use trends, and comparisons to adjacent regions. Phase-by-phase settlement patterns are detailed in subsequent chapters. Project aims included study of Monte Albán's effects on hinterland regions.

Members of the Sola Valley Settlement Pattern Project surveyed an area of 370 km² over six months of fieldwork (September-October 1995 and January-April 1996). The principal crewmembers were Carmelo Aragón, Lázaro Aragón, Ruth R. Edelstein, Everardo Olivera, Fausto Olivera, Verónica Pérez, Laura R. Stiver, and myself (Plate 2.9). We worked in the modern municipalities of San Francisco Sola, San Ildefonso Sola, Santa María Sola, San Miguel Sola de Vega, and several agencias de policia (Oaxaca: Planos Distritos 1996). The project boundaries included the physiographic Sola Valley, the surrounding mountains, and parts of the mountainous corridor that separated the Valleys of Sola, Ejutla, and Oaxaca.

There were 120 prehispanic sites with 227 total components recorded in the project area. These figures represented site densities less than one-half the Ejutla Valley, and less than one-fourth the Valley of Oaxaca (Fig. 2.2; Table 2.4). A lower site density might be expected in a comparatively marginal region, marked by a narrow alluvium enclosed by precipitous heights. The region's settlement history might also be expected to mirror (albeit on a reduced scale) that of its larger neighboring valleys. Sola's settlement history was by no means static, with successive temporal phases marked by shifts in total sites, site sizes, locations, and regional organization (Table 2.5). These changes resemble settlement shifts in other regions in timing, but not always in directionality.

In studying the Sola Valley data sets, I used the region's placement adjacent to other regional surveys (e.g. Feinman and Nicholas 1990a; Kowalewski et al. 1989) to increase the analytical power by factors of ten and higher. Analysis of the survey data, therefore, was not limited to the Sola Valley, but included the contiguous Ejutla Valley and the southern Valley of Oaxaca (1500 km²), and by extension, the entire survey coverage in highland Oaxaca (7000 km²). Figures 2.3 and 2.4 give the regional hierarchies in site size and estimated population by phase for the Sola Valley. Table 2.6 gives the settlement density by phase for contiguous subregions in the Valleys of Sola, Ejutla, and Oaxaca.

Sola's settlement history began later than that of nearby regions, suggesting that initial settlement began with colonization from the Valley of Oaxaca. Sola's regional population skyrocketed in the Monte Albán Ic phase, coincident with the Monte Albán expansion into other regions. Period II population leveled off and possibly declined; most of Sola's inhabitants at that time lived in one central place. Period IIIa was another phase with significant population growth, similar to other nearby regions. The Sola Valley occupation remained less dense than the Ejutla and southern Oaxaca valleys, but the growth trend was the same. In Period IIIb-IV, Sola maintained its population even though some neighboring regions declined. Period V populations grew throughout central Oaxaca, and continuous intervalley occupations erased regional boundaries.

Phase-by-phase population trends for the Sola Valley showed episodes of growth, but these changes were at all times far below the region's potential population (Fig. 2.5; Table 2.7). Over time, the Sola Valley's archaeological population ranged from 4% to 31% of its resource potential or carrying capacity. Even in a bad year, Sola's regional population was below a hypothetical carrying capacity. The inescapable conclusion was that *factors other than population pressure must have caused the Sola Valley's settlement shifts.*

Land use analysis illustrated the Sola Valley's relative marginality compared to nearby regions (Table 2.8). Still, no significant relationship ever existed between land use and settlement in the Sola Valley (Table 2.9); indeed Sola's early settlement history showed a neutral to inverse relationship between land use and settlement. In later periods this relationship changed, but population never exceeded or even approached the regional carrying capacity. Agricultural potential was an important consideration, but land quality alone was not a good predictor of settlement decisions.

In the Sola Valley, successive temporal phases were marked by dynamic settlement shifts, prompting consideration of synchronous changes in other parts of Oaxaca. Sola, however, did not change in a uniform or predictable way—in other words, not based on population pressure models, and not based on carbon-copy changes in nearby regions.

The main general conclusions are twofold: (1) the Sola Valley survey results extend the known range of regional settlement variation in prehispanic Oaxaca; and (2) variation at this scale—all of highland Oaxaca—is the minimal unit of analysis needed to understand Monte Albán. Specific conclusions are given in the phase-by-phase project results in the next chapters.

Chapter 3

The Sola Valley in the Formative Period

In this chapter I describe the transformation of the Sola Valley from a vacant frontier region into a subject province of the Zapotec state. Sola's settlement shifts in Monte Albán Periods I and II were one manifestation of the Zapotec expansion, but the region's specific evolutionary trajectory was nonetheless unique in its details. Valley Zapotec settlers moved into the Sola Valley as part of Monte Albán's strategy to increase its territorial size via colonization and other means. Sola was one route to the Oaxaca coast. Monte Albán's apparent objective was to control Sola because it was one pathway to coastal resources.

After the founding of Monte Albán in the Ia phase, its rulers began to expand territorially in the Ic phase and Period II, bringing regions throughout Oaxaca into contact with the Valley Zapotec (Marcus and Flannery 1996:195-207). Monte Albán conquered some regions and fomented growth in others beyond its political frontier. By the Ic phase, Monte Albán expansionism had transformed the Mixteca Alta into an urbanized landscape (Balkansky 1998a, 1998b, 1999). Mixtec cities formed in response to external threats from Monte Albán and their own Mixtec neighbors. In the coastal lowlands, long-standing patterns of exchange shifted and societies became more hierarchical (Joyce, Winter, and Mueller 1998; Zeitlin 1993; Zeitlin and Joyce 1999). I would argue that these regional patterns are not unique. It is my contention that these separate cases should be linked into a single interpretive framework.

Monte Albán state expansion in its varied militaristic, diplomatic, and demographic dimensions linked Zapotec state formation to the emergence of complex societies elsewhere in Oaxaca (Balkansky 1998b). Monte Albán itself, however, was not the universal model for other sites and regions, or even for the rise of states. The founding of Monte Albán occurred long before the full range of state institutions was in place (Marcus and Flannery 1996:173-91). Monte Albán's later militaristic expansion was the context for state formation.

Evolutionary trends and systems models fail to account for these successive transitions to urbanism and the state. Action theory best accounts for the varied stratagems and diverse evolutionary trajectories in each of the regions interacting with Monte Albán. Monte Albán/Valley Zapotec colonization of the Sola Valley supports the link between territorial expansion and the rise of pristine states (e.g. Marcus 1992a; Spencer 1990, 1998).

The Ia Phase (Middle Formative)

Sola's settlement history began in the Monte Albán Ia phase (ca. 500-300 B.C.) with a single small site that measured less than 1 ha, located next to humid bottomlands at the origin of the Río Sola (Fig. 3.1). Occupation in Sola began much later than in Ejutla or the Valley of Oaxaca (Feinman and Nicholas 1990a; Kowalewski et al. 1989: Fig. 3.1). Miahuatlán likewise was not occupied before Period I, and then only in low densities during the Ia phase (Markman 1981). Monte Albán's founding had little impact on the Sola Valley. Sola as well as nearby regions in Ejutla and Miahuatlán were separate parts of an undifferentiated frontier.

Sola's Ia ceramic complex had grayware and burnished brownware outleaned-wall bowls, including some with incised designs near the rim (Plate 3.1). These vessel forms and decorative motifs resembled the Middle Formative ceramics in nearby regions (Caso, Bernal, and Acosta 1967:23-33; MacNeish, Peterson, and Flannery 1970:114-34; Spencer and Redmond 1997:93-153). Sola's Ia phase occupation was found in the vicinity of the main ball court at Site S39 (the "Texcoco" site near Santa María Sola) and constituted the oldest part of this long-lived site.

Site S39 covered 0.33 ha in the Ia phase. This figure is probably an underestimate because of the overburden of later mate-

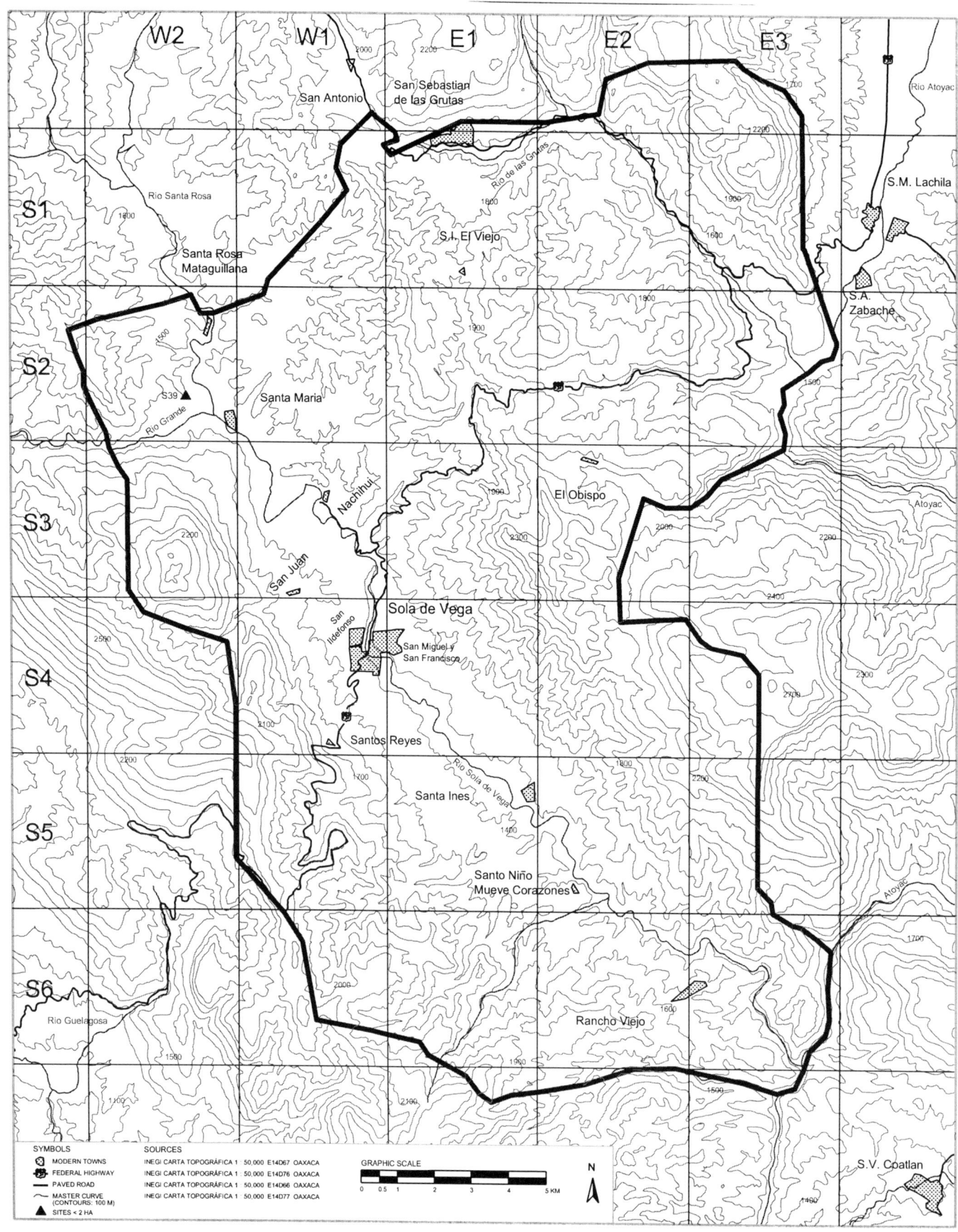

Plate 3.1. Grayware and fine brownware ceramics from S39 that date to Monte Albán I.

rials, but not too much of an underestimate. It is unlikely that this site exceeded 1-2 ha in size, based on comparable occupations in other regions. No architecture or other materials could be dated reliably to this phase. More details on S39 are available in Appendix A.

Sola's low-density occupation in the Ia phase could not have been predicted prior to the survey. Other parts of Oaxaca had high-density occupations at this time, including regions every bit as "marginal" as the Sola Valley (see the regional comparisons in Chapter 6). Sola's initial occupation was a single, isolated site. Not until the Ic phase did significant colonization begin.

Since Monte Albán Ib is a transitional moment that cannot be identified from surface remains, we now proceed to the Ic phase

The Ic Phase (Late Formative)

By the Monte Albán Ic phase (ca. 300-200 B.C.) the Sola Valley population had grown substantially, especially at four large sites (8-15 ha each) around the circumference of the valley (Fig. 3.2). S39, the lone Ia phase site, remained among the most prominent of the Ic phase sites. The other prominent sites were S61, S82, and S84. Ten new grid squares were occupied. Sola Valley population increased 192-fold over the previous phase to reach an estimated 1,539 persons. Sola's per annum growth rate of 5.26% was far in excess of the 0.6-0.7% maximum growth rate expected from natural increase alone (Cowgill

Figure 3.1 (opposite). Ia phase settlement pattern in the Sola Valley.

1975; Hassan 1981:139). The Ic phase was thus the moment of serious colonization of the Sola Valley.

The Valley of Oaxaca's population grew during the Ic phase and expanded into locations not occupied previously (Kowalewski et al. 1989:115, 150-52). Similar developments occurred in the Ejutla Valley (Feinman and Nicholas 1990a). Miahuatlán's population also grew substantially (Markman 1981). A continuous settlement system linked the valleys of Sola, Ejutla, and Oaxaca (Fig. 3.2; Feinman and Nicholas 1990a; Kowalewski et al. 1989: Map 3). One of the Ejutla Valley's largest sites was located on the pass leading into the Sola Valley (grid square S1E3 in Feinman and Nicholas 1990a: Fig. 7). Sola, Ejutla, and Miahuatlán sites were differentiated in size and monumentality for the first time. Site hierarchies were present within (but not between) these valleys.

Ceramics and Dating

Sola Valley ceramics had the characteristic attributes for the Ic phase at Monte Albán (Caso, Bernal, and Acosta 1967:23-33, 146-95; Kowalewski, Spencer, and Redmond 1978). The most distinctive vessels were the type G.12 (combed bottom) serving bowls that were the principal decorated vessel at Monte Albán. Other ceramic diagnostics included types G.5, G.17, K.3, C.2, C.4, and C.13. There were also utilitarian brownware vessels, often burnished with red paint, which resembled (but were not identical to) Period I creamwares.

Few if any sherds were true creamwares with the distinctive Atzompa clay body (Shepard 1967). Even our G.12 examples were often misfired, and could depart from pristine Caso, Bernal, and Acosta (1967) examples. To be sure, variation in ceramic

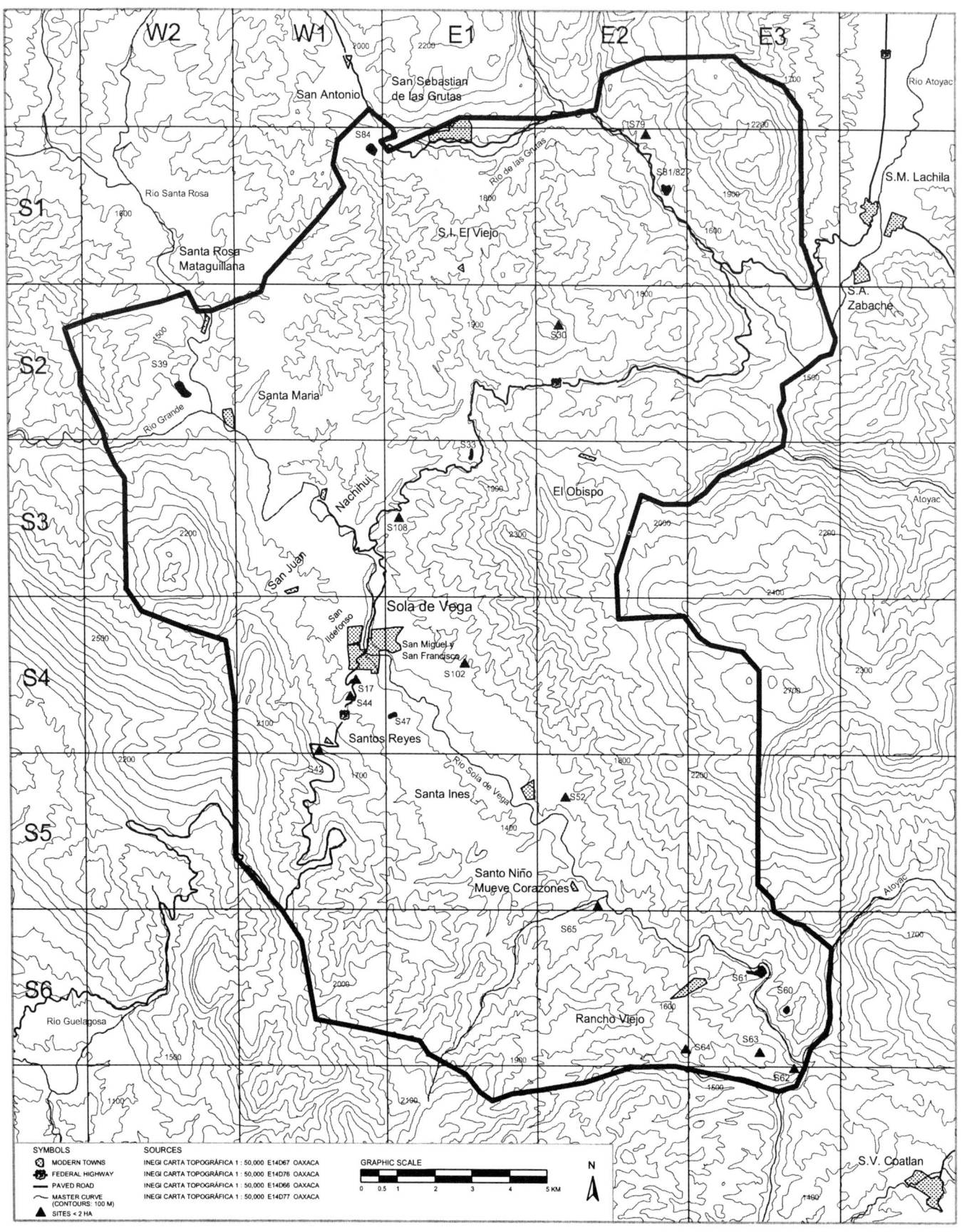

Plate 3.2. G.12s from the Sola Valley (some misfired to a yellow-orange color), including two combed bases that date to Monte Albán Ic.

Plate 3.3 (above). The town of Rancho Viejo is located near the juncture of the Sola and Atoyac rivers at the southeastern limit of the project area, looking east. The rock outcrop at center left of the frame is S61, one of the larger and most defensible Ic phase sites in the Sola Valley.

Figure 3.2 (opposite). Ic phase settlement pattern in the Sola Valley.

Plate 3.4. S61, looking northwest toward the center of the Sola Valley.

complexes on the scale of the Sola Valley examples occurred even within the Valley of Oaxaca (Kowalewski et al. 1989).

Ceramic forms included many outleaned-wall bowls with flared to everted rims, vessels with eccentric and crenellated rims, medial flanges, and composite silhouettes (Caso and Bernal 1965; Caso, Bernal, and Acosta 1967:143-210). The style of combing on the G.12 bases was true fine line; there were no examples of coarser combed bottoms that could date to the Monte Albán Ib phase (e.g. Caso, Bernal, and Acosta 1967: Fig. 6). Charles Spencer brought this last point to my attention in 1998.

One isolated find was a Zapotec-style slab tomb associated with Ic phase ceramics at Site S44. The presence of the tomb was revealed from nearby road construction and possible looting. The style of this tomb reinforced the evidence that Valley Zapotec settlers colonized the Sola Valley. Other support came from the ceramics, the synchrony of population growth and settlement expansion in the Valley of Oaxaca, and the continuities linking sites in the valleys of Sola, Ejutla, and Oaxaca. However, I also consider an alternative hypothesis—that Sola's earliest colonists came from somewhere other than the Valley of Oaxaca—in the conclusion to this chapter.

Sites and Their Characteristics

Sola's Ic phase sites were distributed throughout the valley. Among other salient features, four aspects of the regional settlement pattern stood out: (1) population and administrative centers were located on the outer margins of the valley, especially in places leading to adjacent regions; (2) a second set of smaller sites was located in the interior of the valley, on the precise route to the Oaxaca coast; (3) most sites were terraced and defensible; and (4) the estimated population was far below what the region's potential agricultural productivity could support, despite the population growth. Sites, moreover, were not always situated with respect to agricultural resources; other factors entered into site locations. Each of these points is analyzed in the following sections.

Sola Valley sites averaged 3.31 ha in size. This figure was comparable to the Valley of Oaxaca (3.03 ha) overall, but somewhat larger than Valley of Oaxaca site size averages if we remove Monte Albán (Kowalewski et al. 1989:117). Seven of nineteen Sola Valley sites had mounds associated with Ic phase ceramics, and this ratio was also slightly higher than in the Valley of Oaxaca (Kowalewski et al. 1989:116).

Sola Valley sites were located in the piedmont and mountain zones; sites averaged 1611 m in elevation. Nine sites had terraces associated with Ic phase ceramics. Sola's terraced sites were the main population centers, indicating that defense outweighed agricultural concerns, since some of the best agricultural land was left unoccupied. An analogous settlement shift to the piedmont zone occurred during the Ic phase in the Valley of Oaxaca (Kowalewski et al. 1989:123-24).

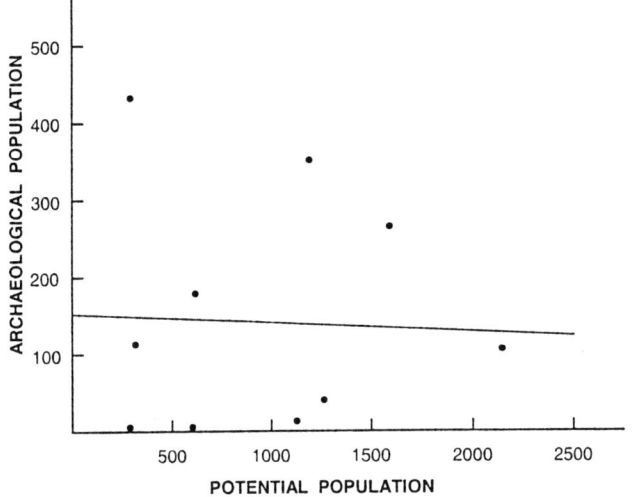

Figure 3.3. Ic phase scatterplot of potential and actual population in the Sola Valley.

TABLE 3.1. Sola Valley Settlement by Environmental Zone during the Ic Phase

Environment	Sites	Total (ha)	Population	% Population
Low Alluvium	0	—	—	—
High Alluvium	0	—	—	—
Low Piedmont	16	50.62	1,123	73%
High Piedmont	2	12.33	408	27%
Mountain	1	0.01	8	—

Sola's Ic phase occupation had four large, first-tier sites. S61 was located at the southeast limit of the project area and measured 13.22 ha in size. The site was terraced, and set against a pillar-shaped rock outcrop at the confluence of the Sola and Atoyac rivers (Plate 3.3). The site was accessible only from a narrow path connected to the piedmont shelf, requiring a steep 100-m climb from the river bottom. The site had four isolated mounds with a uniform north/south orientation that pertained to the Ic component. None of the mounds exceeded 3 m in height (Plate 3.4).

S39 near Santa María Sola in the northwest corner of the project area measured 14.81 ha in size. The site was terraced, but not as defensible as S61 (S39 was located at the base of a hill). The Ic phase architectural configuration was obscured by later construction. Several building complexes existed within the Ic component of the site and could have begun at this time. S39 provided access to points north and west of the Sola Valley.

The other key centers of the time were S82 and S84 (6-10 ha in size); each of these sites also had probable Ic phase public architecture, and was located on a hilltop with terraces on the circumference of the valley. The precise site sizes could not be obtained because of high-density later occupations, and poor surface visibility in places. S82 and S84 were nonetheless larger than most other Sola sites of the time. S82 was near the Sola-Ejutla-Oaxaca junction; S84 covered the route north to the valley of Santa María Lachixio. The overburden of later construction also obscured their Ic phase layouts.

Architectural profiles exposed from modern irrigation canals (at S39), looting (at S82), and erosion (at S84) suggest the beginnings of monumental construction at these sites. S39 and S84 also had ball courts of uncertain initial construction that were located in zones of Ic phase occupation. Sola's Ic sites were roughly equivalent in size and civic-ceremonial importance based on the surface data. Each site is also well preserved and deserves more intensive scrutiny.

S33, S47, and S60 were second-tier sites (4-5 ha each). Each of these sites had artificial mounds, above-average populations, and a defensible hilltop location. S33 and S47, moreover, were

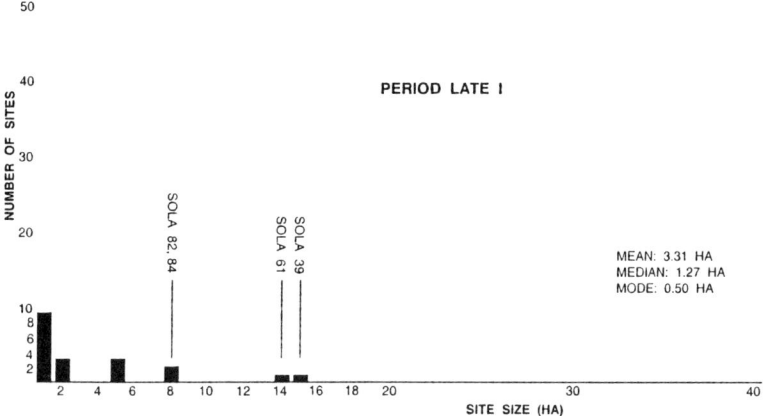

Figure 3.4. Histogram of Sola Valley site sizes during the Ic phase.

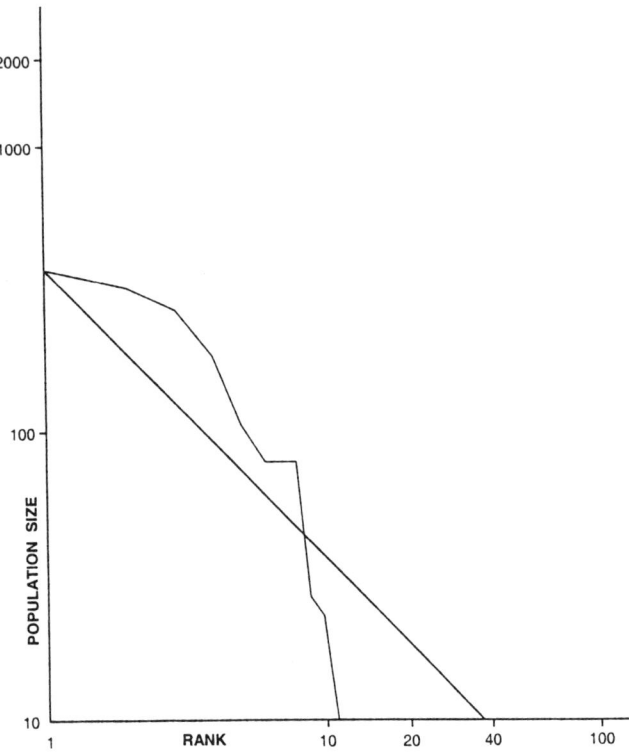

Figure 3.5. Rank-size graph for the Sola Valley during the Ic phase.

endpoints on each side of the transport route to the coast. Several smaller sites (less than 2 ha each) were also located along this route. Sola's transport corridor was followed by the modern highway, walked by pilgrims in historical and modern times, and lined with modern shrines and archaeological sites of various time periods.

The remaining sites were located near S61. There was no clear reason for this placement, except possibly that more vigilance was needed at the southern extreme of the region. S61 also had greater constraints on growth, owing to its less productive land nearby and the narrow confines of its site location. Satellites may have budded off because of these factors. Another, as yet unsurveyed, valley lies southeast of S61 in San Vicente Coatlán.

Settlement and Land Use

Ic phase sites in the Sola Valley were located in piedmont and mountain zones (Table 3.1). Seventy-three percent of the population was found in the low piedmont. These piedmont sites were often, but not always, located in highly agriculturally productive grid squares. Sola's population centers generally were within an hour's walk of quality farmland, but not necessarily the region's best land.

As with the Ia phase, there was a preference for canal-irrigable and high-water-table land. Occupied grid squares had an average potential population of 917 persons, compared to unoccupied squares that averaged only 470 persons. There were, nevertheless, many settlements on less desirable land. S39 (grid square S2W2) was near productive Type I land; S61 (grid square S6E3) was near some of the region's poorest agricultural land. These sites were the two largest population centers at the time. Their contrasting potential productivity characterized the Ic phase occupation of the valley.

In the region as a whole, the relationship between potential population (land quality/carrying capacity) and the archaeological population (estimated from survey) was negative (Fig. 3.3). The correlation coefficient ($n = 10$) between these variables was -0.017. The removal of a possible outlier (S61) improved the correlation to +0.302, yet neither value was significant at the 0.05 level. Examination of the Ic phase scatterplot suggested *no relationship* between the potential and estimated archaeological populations. Many of the region's most agriculturally productive grid squares (S1E1, S3W1, S4W1, and S5E1) had no occupation whatsoever. Sola's initial colonization, therefore, was not designed to maximize agricultural production.

Sola's negative relationship between land and settlement was not necessarily a prelude to population stress. The estimated archaeological population could have sustained itself without external food supplies, even with less than optimal site locations. Seven of ten grid squares had the potential for surplus production. Sola Valley farmers could have fed an added 1262 persons, or a total of 82% more than the estimated archaeological population.

Agricultural surplus might have offset local shortfalls via exchange or funded the region's administrative apparatus. Nicholas (1989) has argued that during dry years in the Valley of Oaxaca, 58-70% of the population depended on external food production (i.e. surplus from another grid square). Sola Valley farmers could have participated in this large-scale exchange strategy to limit bad-year risk. In this examination of surplus and deficit production, the distribution of labor, not land, was the limiting factor.

Sola's Ic population growth was evidently not from colonists in search of the best quality agricultural land. S61 and its satellites were located on marginal piedmont soils with steep slopes that showed the complexity of human/land relationships in the Sola Valley. S61 itself was located in one of the few grid squares with deficit production; the site could not have supported itself without frequent inputs from other parts of the region. Even at the scale of the Sola Valley there was considerable interdependence among centers. Other factors than land quality must account for Sola's Ic phase settlement pattern.

Regional and Macroregional Organization

The Sola Valley's Ic phase occupation was distributed widely but unevenly. Sola's main population and administrative centers (S39, S61, S82, and S84) were positioned on the region's periphery, and several smaller sites were situated along the path of the

TABLE 3.2. Population Centers in Sola, Ejutla, and the Southern Oaxaca Valley during the Ic Phase

Site	Region	Grid	Size (ha)	Population	Rank
SM Tilcajete	Valle Grande	N7E8	49.70	879	1
La Soledad	Valle Grande	N8E7	17.40	616	2
La Ciénega	Valle Grande	N8E5	33.70	606	2
Texcoco (S39)	Sola	S2W2	14.81	360	3
SN Quilana	Valle Grande	N6E6	19.60	343	3
	Ejutla			330	3
Anticuados (S61)	Sola	S6E3	13.22	320	3
OC-SMT-SMT-23	Valle Grande	N8E8	16.80	301	3
Cuilapan	Valle Grande	N10E5	10.80	289	3
Ejutla	Ejutla			274	3
	Ejutla			271	3
SB Coyotepec	Valle Grande	N9E8	34.10	263	3
Cerro Orcón (S84)	Sola	S1W1	6-10	262	3
ZA-ZA-ZA-12	Valle Grande	N9E5	4.50	260	3
Zimatlán	Valle Grande	N7E6	14.60	256	3
OC-SJT-PG-4	Ocotlán	N3E9	5.30	250	3
Yogana	Ejutla			228	3
	Ejutla			222	3
Progreso	Ocotlán	N2E8		219	3
Amatengo	Ejutla		12.50	186	3
El Vado (S82)	Sola	S1E2	6-10	178	3

(Feinman and Nicholas 1997; Kowalewski et al. 1989: Table 6.4)

modern highway that bisects the valley. Endpoints on this transport corridor at S33 and S47 were defensible sites with mounds.

Site-size histograms reveal a three-tiered settlement hierarchy, suggesting that Sola's first colonists brought considerable organizational complexity to the valley (Fig. 3.4). The first tier was composed of sites S39, S61, S82, and S84; the second-tier sites were S33, S47, and S60. S82 and S84 occupied an intermediate position in the site-size hierarchy, but their population estimates placed them among the first-order centers. Sites on the first and second tiers had mounds and probable administrative functions. No site on the third tier of Sola's settlement hierarchy had mounded architecture.

Sola's site-size hierarchy was dispersed, but relatively flat in its top ranks. Of the nineteen Sola Valley sites, five (26%) had more than 100 persons, but none of these sites dominated the valley. In this respect, Sola and Ejutla were quite similar— both regions lacked a coordinating center, and both had limited settlement hierarchies (Feinman and Nicholas 1990a: Fig. 7). It is possible that Sola and Ejutla were composed of multiple autonomous centers. In Sola, however, the smaller sites S33, S47, and their satellites were poor candidates for survival without cooperation from the larger centers.

Hierarchical distinctions among population centers in the southern (or Valle Grande) Valley of Oaxaca were much greater, but most of these sites were near San Martín Tilcajete, more than 20 km from the Sola-Ejutla-Valle Grande frontier (Kowalewski et al. 1989: Map 3). In the southernmost Valley of Oaxaca, near modern Ocotlán, the local settlement hierarchy was similar to that of Sola and Ejutla. Table 3.2 gives the interregional settlement hierarchy in adjacent portions of Sola, Ejutla, and the Valley of Oaxaca.

The absence of an obvious coordinating center in the Sola Valley is apparent from the rank-size graph that measures regional integration (Fig. 3.5). In integrated central place hierarchies, the size (or population) of the largest site is twice that of the second largest site, triple the third largest site, quadruple the fourth largest site, and continues in this fashion to the "nth" site below which no central place functions exist. This so-called "normal relationship" between rank and size is linear, and gives a slope of -1 in double logarithmic transformation.

Archaeological hierarchies commonly deviate from the idealized rank-size relationship (Johnson 1977, 1980; Kowalewski 1982b; Smith 1976). Top-heavy or "primate" distributions yield a concave rank-size curve, with secondary and tertiary centers far smaller than the log-linear model predicts. At the top of the hierarchy, primate centers monopolize regional exchange and administration, and often articulate with still larger settlement systems outside their regions. Convex rank-size curves, on the other hand, are characterized by low integration among centers. Convexity stems from having more large sites than expected. Study regions with convex rank-size graphs may be "pooled" with two or more autonomous settlement systems in the analysis, inherently open, or marginal to a larger-scale settlement system.

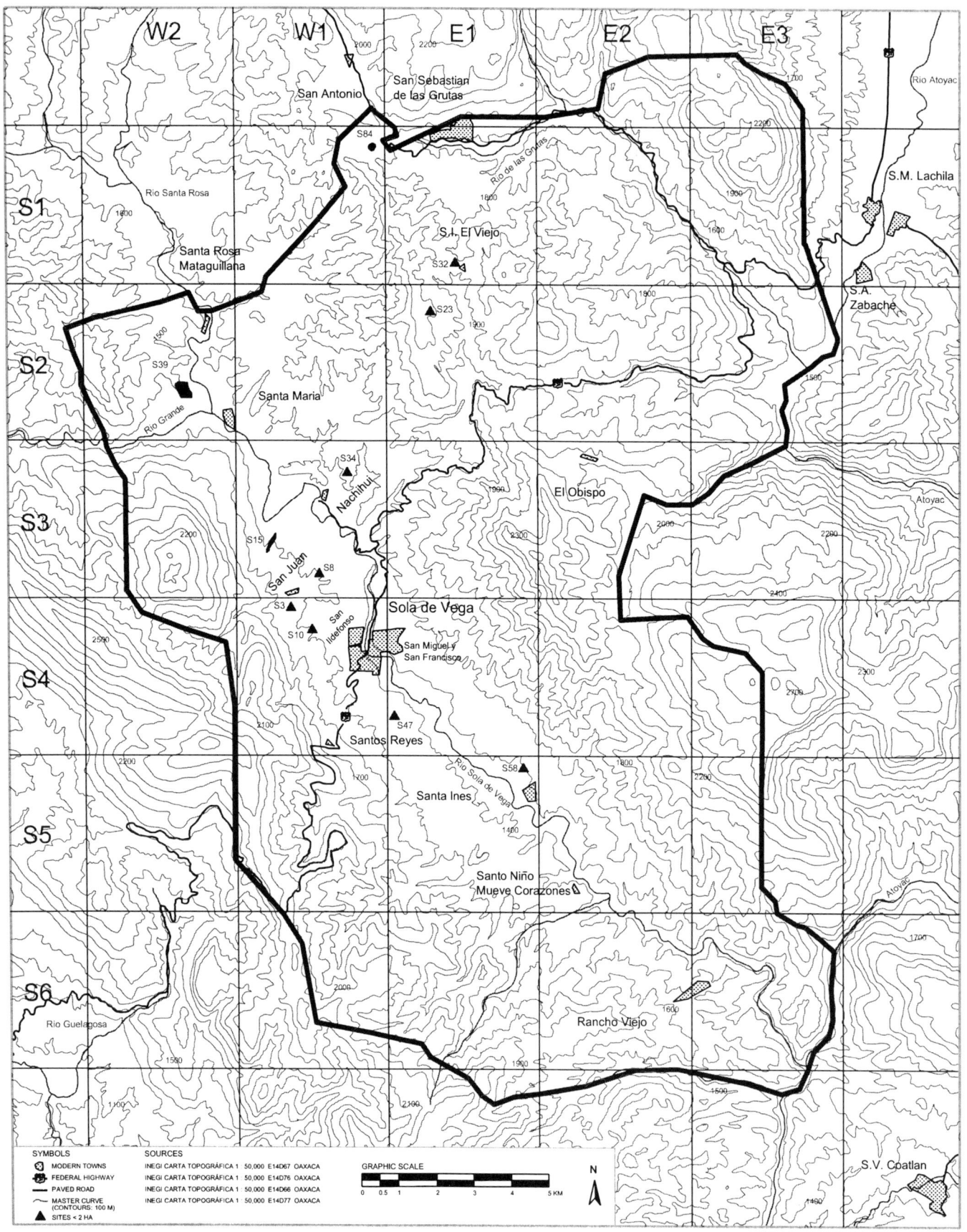

Sola's rank-size curve is convex at the top, and such convexity suggests there was poor integration among its centers. Sola's rank-size convexity possibly reflects the pooling of autonomous settlement systems (e.g., Johnson 1981). But since the size of each individual center was much smaller than central places elsewhere in Oaxaca, and most of the smaller sites were not associated with any particular center, I would suggest that the Sola sites were not pooled. Each subregion in the Valley of Oaxaca also displays a convex curve for this time period (Kowalewski et al. 1989:146-48).

Valley of Sola and Oaxaca subregions are more likely partitioned analytical units (Paynter 1983), separated from one or more primate centers. Sola's flat hierarchy is characteristic of regions on the margin of dendritic settlement systems, where individual centers are more strongly articulated with an external power than with each other. Sola's nearest major centers were San Martín Tilcajete (Valle Grande subregion) and Monte Albán. Sola's rank-size fall-off (Johnson 1987) occurs just below 100 persons; its second-tier centers were the smallest sites with probable administrative functions.

TABLE 3.3. Sola Valley Settlement by Environmental Zone during Period II

Environment	Sites	Total (ha)	Population	% Population
Low Alluvium	0	—	—	—
High Alluvium	1	0.25	8	1%
Low Piedmont	7	29.05	635	76%
High Piedmont	3	6.27	190	23%
Mountain	0	—	—	—

Summary and Conclusions

Sola's initial occupation dates from the Ia phase, but colonization did not begin in earnest until the Ic phase. Sola sites were defensible and located on passageways out of the valley. The land use data for Sola indicate that considerable interdependence was needed to distribute food surplus to less productive sites. The rate of population growth in the 100-year span of Period Ic (Drennan 1983) was too high for natural increase alone. Sola Valley sites shared ceramic and other material ties with the Valley Zapotec; the timing of Sola's early growth also coincided with the expansion of settlement in the Valley of Oaxaca (Kowalewski et al. 1989:113-52).

From the three-valley perspective of Sola, Ejutla, and the Valle Grande, the top two tiers in the macroregional hierarchy were confined to sites in the Valle Grande. In the Ocotlán subregion of the Valley of Oaxaca, as well as in Ejutla and Sola, Ic sites are relatively undifferentiated. I would question whether these frontier regions were independent entities, considering it more likely that they were articulated with the more complex nearby settlement systems. The synchronicity of changes in these "edge" regions suggests a common causal factor. Sola was more likely linked to San Martín Tilcajete, Monte Albán, or both, in the nascent Zapotec state. Colonization brought a complex settlement system to the region, most likely to control the transport route to the Oaxaca coast.

Period II (Terminal Formative)

In Period Monte Albán II (ca. 200 B.C.-A.D. 200), many of the earlier sites were abandoned or greatly reduced in size, and

Figure 3.6 (opposite). Period II settlement pattern in the Sola Valley.

settlement was focused near S39 (Texcoco), now the region's single major center (Fig. 3.6). S39 clearly grew at the expense of settlements elsewhere in Sola. The number of occupied grid squares in Sola was reduced to seven, but three grid squares were occupied for the first time. This shift in settlement location was tilted toward S39. Regional population declined to 833 persons, or 54% of the Ic phase estimate; yet higher than expected densities at S39 would make the decline in overall population more apparent than real. S39 appears to have a denser occupation than before, but comparative observations of this sort are problematic on surface survey, especially at multicomponent sites.

The emergence of regional capitals during Period II was replicated in Ejutla, Miahuatlán, and Valley of Oaxaca subregions (Feinman and Nicholas 1990a; Kowalewski 1989:158-61, 198-200; Markman 1981). In the Valleys of Ejutla and Oaxaca these changes took place in the context of overall population declines. The same pattern is replicated at contemporary sites in the Mixteca Alta (Balkansky et al. 2000). Sites and entire regions were abandoned in Period II times, even though a few sites grew to unprecedented size. The concurrent abandonment in some places, and reorganization in others, must be understood in terms of shared causality.

Ceramics and Dating

Sola ceramics, settlement patterns, and architectural evidence point to continued ties with the Valley of Oaxaca. Period II pottery diagnostics in Sola include types G.12, G.21, A.9, C.6, C.7, C.11, C.12, C.20, and brownware utilitarian vessels that fit a Period I-III identification (Caso, Bernal, and Acosta 1967:61-77). As noted above for the Ic phase, the specific character of Sola ceramics nonetheless varies from standard Valley of Oaxaca reference material.

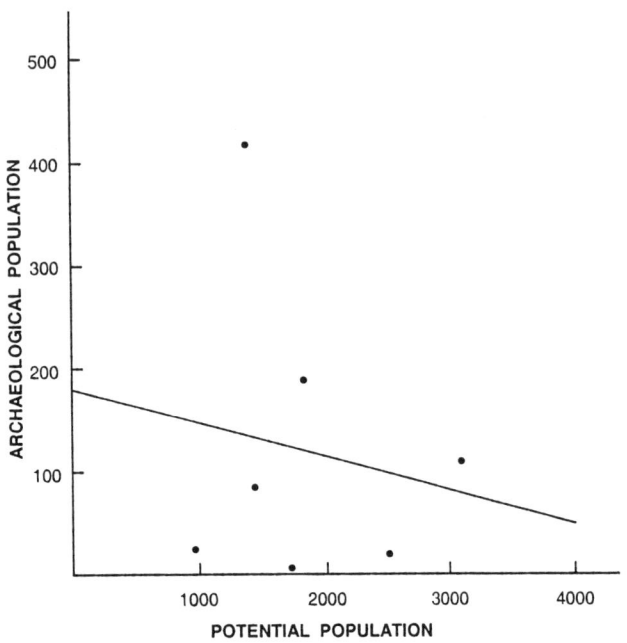

Figure 3.7. Period II scatterplot of potential and actual population in the Sola Valley.

ramic complexes seem to be concurrent with the decentralization of regional settlement patterns.

Other common Period II sherds are reminiscent of Monte Albán types, but could not be placed in a specific category. These sherds include brownware imitations of Period II creamwares, which were most likely of local manufacture; the few true creamwares were concentrated at site S39. Creamware is the most common ware category during Period II at Monte Albán (Caso, Bernal, and Acosta 1967), and the presence of true creamwares (i.e. with the Atzompa clay body) in other regions has been linked to Zapotec state administration (e.g. Redmond 1983; Feinman and Nicholas 1990a). Significantly, there is an especially high density of creamwares associated with the Period II public buildings at Site S39.

Sites and Their Characteristics

The growth at S39, a first-tier center, is coupled with a slight decline in average site size (3.23 ha) on the regional level, but Sola site sizes are still within the range of variation for Valley of Oaxaca subregions (Kowalewski et al. 1989:156). Sites have an average elevation of 1624 m, virtually unchanged from the prior phase. Five sites are terraced. Period II sites are most often located on irrigable piedmont land, immediately adjacent to the valley floor. There are more sites with mounds associated with Period II pottery (5 of 11) than in the prior phase, but this figure probably conflates surface pottery associations with actual construction phases. The comparative cases of S15 and S39 (described below) suggest that administrative functions were concentrated at the regional capital. Most Period II sites (8 of 11) are newly founded, though continuity in population and administrative control was maintained at S39.

S39 grew to 19.94 ha and had 53% of the estimated population in the region. Period II ceramics (particularly creamwares

Types G.12, C.7, and C.11 were the most common decorated ceramics in the Sola Valley. Other types were rare; only a single A.9 was recovered on survey. Type G.21 was found only once—at site S39. The limited number of C.20s surprises me because it was so common at Monte Albán (Caso, Bernal, and Acosta 1967:67-68), and because similar types often appear in Ic/II equivalent contexts in the Mixteca Alta (Spores 1972). Thus the subregional variation in ceramic complexes described for the Valley of Oaxaca (Kowalewski et al. 1989:164-82) can be extended to other regions. These growing distinctions in ce-

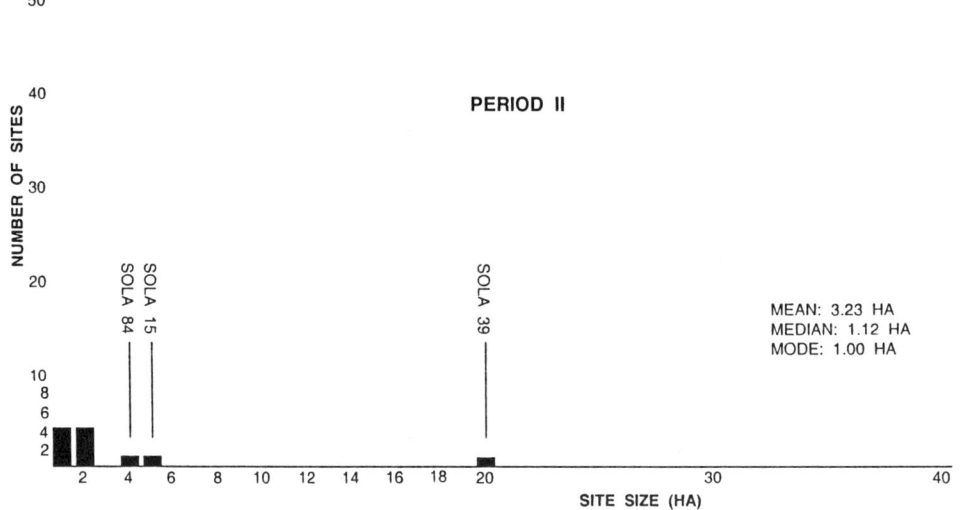

Figure 3.8. Histogram of Sola Valley site sizes during Period II.

TABLE 3.4. Population Centers in Sola, Ejutla, and the Southern Oaxaca Valley during Period II

Site	Region	Grid	Size (ha)	Population	Rank
OC-SMT-SMT-23	Valle Grande	N8E8	54.30	979	1
Ejutla	Ejutla			646	2
Texcoco (S39)	Sola	S2W2	19.94	440	2
Cuilapan	Valle Grande	N10E5	16.80	423	2
ZI-ZI-SN-3	Valle Grande	N6E6	19.60	343	3
Yogana	Ejutla			332	3
CE-SMC-SMC-19	Valle Grande	N10E8	17.60	308	3
ZA-ZA-ZA-8	Valle Grande	N9E6	15.80	277	3
Amatengo	Ejutla			267	3
OC-SJT-PG-4	Ocotlán	N3E9	5.30	250	3
SB Coyotepec	Valle Grande	N9E8	32.50	249	3
Ocotlán de M	Ocotlán	N5E8	13.20	231	3
SI Yatzeche	Ocotlán	N5E6	12.40	217	3
S Ana Zegache	Ocotlán	N6E7	11.00	193	3
ZI-VDF-LB-3	Valle Grande	N4E5	10.40	182	3
	Ejutla			164	3
ZI-SG-SG-2	Valle Grande	N4E5	3.50	161	3
Cerro Orcón (S84)	Sola	S1W1	2-6	150	3
ZA-ZA-ZA-12	Valle Grande	N9E5	1.80	132	3
	Ejutla			125	3

(Feinman and Nicholas 1997; Kowalewski et al. 1989: Table 7.4)

and their imitations) are more common and varied at S39 than other valley sites. The site's architectural configuration is difficult to infer, due to the overburden of later construction; still, an expanded building program likely began with the Plaza 3 structures that were associated with Period II ceramics (pending excavation to confirm the date of construction). The Plaza 3 structures are composed of two mounds of unequal length on either side of a small plaza that was partially enclosed by walls. S39 also had two I-shaped ball courts, both associated with Period II ceramics (though other phases are present as well). The north ball court was situated between Plaza 1 and 3 and could date to this period. The west ball court has the highest density of Formative ceramics (Period I and II) at the site; its initial construction could also date to the Ic or Early II phase.

The second-tier population centers were S15 and S84. S84 is difficult to interpret: Classic period construction obscured whatever Late Formative architecture was present, and surface visibility was poor, making site size and population estimates problematic. Sola 15 dates solely to Period II. Although the site was a population center, it had no formal architecture; however, on three successive levels the flattened slope was accentuated artificially. The remaining valley sites are considerably smaller, with no clear evidence for mounds. These comparisons suggest that S39 was the focus of regional administration.

Settlement and Land Use

Most of the Period II population continued to reside in the piedmont zone (Table 3.3). Settlement did shift, however, compared to the prior phase, to piedmont locations closer to valley-floor land. Sites are located near productive land—both irrigable piedmont and alluvium—but not necessarily the region's best quality land.

The Sola Valley's potential population (based on land quality) in occupied grid squares increased substantially, averaging 1837 persons per grid square compared to 917 from the prior phase. Two-thirds of all grid squares (6 of 9) with Type I land were occupied, accounting for 87% of all Type I land in the valley. But the specific distribution of population and center size in the valley is not related to land quality alone. The relationship between the potential and actual archaeological population is negative, with a correlation coefficient of -0.155 (Fig. 3.7). Even with a possible outlier site removed (S39), this relationship only improves to +0.244. Neither figure is significant at the 0.05 level; the scatterplot is dispersed, with no real relationship between the variables.

I would still argue against a strong relationship between land quality and settlement in this period. S39's grid square ranked only sixth out of seven occupied grid squares for potential popu-

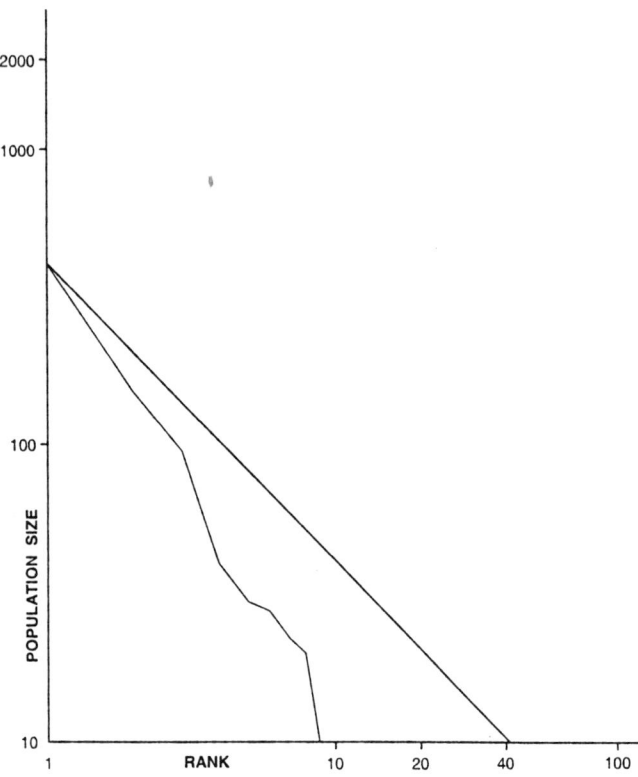

Figure 3.9. Rank-size graph for the Sola Valley during Period II.

lation. Overall, regional population was only 4.1% of its resource-based potential, down from 8.7% in the Ic phase. In the Valley of Oaxaca, there were also many highly productive zones left underexploited (Nicholas 1989). Population pressure cannot account for these patterns, although other factors suggest significant changes during Period II in the Sola Valley's productive output.

Sola's potential surplus production, however, increased substantially over the previous phase. All occupied grid squares were surplus producers in Period II. Available land and labor indicate that Sola farmers could potentially have produced corn for 2770 persons, or 335% of the estimated population of 833. These figures represent absolute as well as relative productive increases over the Ic phase.

Sola Valley farmers could have provided substantial tribute to the Zapotec state. Monte Albán's grid square accounts for 97% of the needed food imports into the Valley of Oaxaca (Nicholas 1989:496). Although the Sola Valley's surplus production probably did not support Monte Albán directly, it could have supported armies or Zapotec traders that passed through the region. Sola's potential surplus production could also have funded S39's expanded administrative apparatus (and made it a more densely occupied site).

Two major changes took place in Period II land use: (1) settlement shifted to sites on irrigable piedmont and valley-floor lands; and (2) potential productivity nearly doubled from the previous phase. Still, the regional population was well below its resource-based potential and declined by almost half. Sola's increased productivity—far in excess of local needs—took place in the central and western parts of the valley, near the regional center. Valley of Oaxaca survey data show a similar relationship between sites with administrative functions and irrigation potential (Kowalewski et al. 1989:156).

Regional and Macroregional Organization

Sola Valley population declined by 46% in Period II, a far steeper decline than the 19% regional decline believed to have taken place in the Valley of Oaxaca (Kowalewski et al. 1989:158-61). Sites in the southeast and elsewhere were abandoned as populations were concentrated near S39. Eighty-two percent of the valley population was located in the first- and second-tier centers (S15, S39, and S84). Seventy-one percent of the population resided in sites having more than 100 persons. Second-tier centers (S15 and S84) were within 8 km of the regional capital. These patterns were quite different from the dispersed Ic phase settlements, whose centers were spread to the limits of the valley.

Period II site-size histograms showed S39's emergence as the focal site in the region (Fig. 3.8). Once again there were three tiers in the settlement hierarchy, but with greater differentiation between levels than during the prior phase. S39 was the sole occupant of the first tier, with S15 and S84 on the second tier (these distinctions were especially pronounced in population estimates). S39 was the only Sola Valley site with probable administrative architecture. As noted above, there was evidence for new construction—including one, and possibly two, ball courts—beginning in Period II. Ejutla's Period II capital also grew in administrative complexity at this time (Feinman and Nicholas 1990a).

Rank-size was primate in distribution at this time; S39 was more than twice the size of the region's next largest site (Fig. 3.9). A primate distribution also was found in the southern Valley of Oaxaca, though not in the other valley subregions (Kowalewski et al. 1989:188). Sola's rank-size curve was relatively convex across the rank 2 spectrum, suggesting less integration between secondary centers (S15 and S84); valley interactions were most likely mediated by the regional capital. A steep descent below sites with fewer than 100 persons indicated that valley administration was limited to ranks 1 and 2.

S39 was probably articulated with a still larger settlement system. Oaxaca's emergent multiregional settlement hierarchy included adjacent subregions in the valleys of Sola, Ejutla, and Oaxaca (Table 3.4). San Martín Tilcajete resettled on a hilltop (SMT-23) above the Period I site, and remained the major center in the southern Valley of Oaxaca; Sola and Ejutla might have articulated with Monte Albán via SMT-23. These macroregional relationships continued into the next period.

Summary and Conclusions

Sola's Period II settlement system was more centralized than in Period I, with both population and administrative functions concentrated at a single regional capital. Site S39 emerged as the top-ranked center, and this change signaled a significant shift in macroregional relationships. Settlement was focused on S39 to the exclusion of highly productive lands elsewhere in the region. Sola's potential for productive surplus doubled over the previous phase; the population, however, was more strongly correlated with administrative than productive potentials. Other regional capitals were founded in Ejutla, Miahuatlán, and the Cuicatlán Cañada during Period II (Feinman and Nicholas 1990a; Markman 1981; Spencer and Redmond 1997). These developments cannot be understood without reference to Monte Albán and its extra-valley expansion.

Valley of Oaxaca settlement patterns were modified to better integrate Monte Albán's expanded political domain. Period II was characterized by valley-wide decentralization, as local centers arose to administer each subregion by growing in size and internal complexity (Kowalewski et al. 1989:198-200). As system scale increased, the degree of political centralization decreased via the delegation of authority to subregional centers. Valley of Oaxaca survey data showed a strong relationship between sites with administrative functions and productive potential (Kowalewski et al. 1989:156). These potential surpluses would have supplied Monte Albán with staple tribute, and supported the subregional centers' increased administrative expenditures. Sola and other nearby regions took part in the same process—their capitals growing in size and establishing key links in the Zapotec state's tributary network.

The Zapotec Expansion

Possible explanations for the Sola Valley's Ic phase colonization include the forced settlement of mobile mountain peoples, the arrival of colonists in search of new land because of population pressure, and the strategic resettlement of Valley Zapotec in the region. The various permutations on these themes depend on whether the Ic phase centers were semi-autonomous but linked to Monte Albán, or wholly independent and mutually antagonistic.

Sola's earliest settlers had no mobile precursors. Sola was virtually unoccupied before the Ic phase, and so could not have contributed to Monte Albán's founding population. Sola and other regions instead absorbed the population spillover on the southern margins of the valley. Sola, moreover, was a relatively unsettled frontier region during Period I, and would have provided less protection, and less access to potential markets, than existed for sites in the Valley of Oaxaca. Expansion of already settled Valley Zapotec into frontier regions during Period I is the simplest and best supported explanation for Sola's first settled villages.

Sola's ceramics, tombs, and settlement patterns link its earliest settlers to extant Valley Zapotec communities. Were these settlers driven by population pressure in search of new farmland? The answer is no, since population pressure has not been demonstrated for the Formative period Valley of Oaxaca. Population ranged from 7% to 20% of the regional potential during Period I and II, and the valley survey data shows no significant relationship between land and settlement at this time (Kowalewski 1982a; Nicholas 1989). If anything, many high quality lands in subregions such as the Valle Grande were underexploited during these periods.

Population pressure, nevertheless, could have been felt at levels below the regional carrying capacity, especially in regions not yet unified politically (Carneiro 1970; Santley 1992). Valley of Oaxaca land use analyses are predicated on the assumption that the entire valley was unified by the Ia phase. Monte Albán's potential sustaining area (Blanton et al. 1999: Fig. 3.2; Nicholas 1989: Fig. 14.10) would be reduced if the southern or eastern valley subregions remained autonomous in the Ia phase. Still, even local population stress (as yet unexamined) in the Valley of Oaxaca due to competing Period I polities (so that productive shortfalls could not be shifted from one subregion to the next) would not explain the specifics of the Sola land use patterns.

In the Sola Valley, the relationship between land and settlement is negative during Periods I and II. Some of the region's most productive grid squares were vacant or only sparsely settled, while less productive lands were heavily utilized. For example, one of the Ic phase centers (S61) was located on the valley's poorest agricultural land. By Period II, the regional capital (S39) was located in merely the sixth most productive out of seven occupied grid squares. Thus, early occupation cannot be tied to either population pressure in the Valley of Oaxaca or the search for optimal farmland in the Sola Valley.

The strategic resettlement model is tied to the issue of regional political organization. Was the Ic phase Sola Valley unified, semi-autonomous, or composed of mutually antagonistic sites? At first glance, the Ic phase settlement patterns (Fig. 3.2) might support a scenario of mutual antagonism among the regional centers. Yet, the overall settlement dynamics in the Valleys of Sola and Oaxaca were similar. Sola's population growth co-occurred with the expansion of settlement in the Valley of Oaxaca. The southern Valley of Oaxaca (the Ocotlán subregion), moreover, had a low-density occupation with limited hierarchy similar to the adjacent valleys of Sola and Ejutla (Table 3.2; Feinman and Nicholas 1990a: Fig. 7; Kowalewski et al. 1989: Map 3). If Sola and Ejutla were not integrated to some degree during the Ic phase, then neither was the southern Valley of Oaxaca. Hierarchical suppression was characteristic of regions near the limits of Monte Albán's political control (Redmond 1983:120).

The presence of a major subregional center at San Martín Tilcajete (grid square N7E8) makes the total autonomy of sites in the southern Valley of Oaxaca an unlikely proposition. On the other hand, it appears that the Tilcajete site may have remained autonomous until the end of Period I (Spencer, pers. comm.). Monte Albán could have bypassed the site, and begun constructing non-overlapping spheres of control (cf. Spencer 1982:256). Monte Albán–Tilcajete competition also could explain the underutilization of agricultural resources in the Valle Grande subregion.

I would argue that the Sola Valley was to some degree already integrated with an extraregional political authority by the Ic phase. Sola had the militarized character of a boundary region on the edge of a larger state's political territory. Hodge (1998:200), writing about the later Aztec state, distinguished *strategic* from *tributary* provinces: "The 38 tributary provinces in the *Codex Mendoza* (Berdan and Anawalt 1992) were located in the empire's interior and paid specified goods to Tenochtitlan. In contrast, strategic provinces were located on trade routes, militarily important points, and at trade entrepôts." Hodge (1998) further described strategic provinces as having "client-like" relationships with the Aztec capital that could be reciprocal, rather than one-sided. Sola's Ic phase relationship to Monte Albán could be understood as more strategic than tributary. Sola was colonized by the Valley Zapotec, but its relative autonomy from Monte Albán may have waxed and waned. By Period II, however, Sola and other regions from Cuicatlán in the north to Miahuatlán in the south, were more integrated into Monte Albán's tributary networks.

Sola's Ic phase centers (S39, S61, S82, and S84) were located on the periphery of the region in defensible locations. Boundary maintenance, therefore, was a consideration in the Ic phase settlement system (Kowalewski et al. 1983). At the same time, an inner sphere of settlement bisected the region, with sites located along the highland-coastal passage (S33, S47, and others). None of the innermost Sola Valley sites was on a par with the aforementioned centers, or even associated with one center in particular; it is unlikely that these small sites could have survived on their own without cooperation among valley centers. Establishment of a transport route to the coastal lowlands would have been in the interests of an emergent elite at Monte Albán. Ic phase Sola was most likely a militarized frontier region, a strategic province, rather than a tributary province of the Zapotec state.

What motivated the Zapotec expansion into the Sola Valley? Expansion into the region to exact tribute seems unlikely, given the absence of indigenous labor and desirable agricultural products like those available in the Cuicatlán Cañada (Spencer and Redmond 1997). Sola's Ic phase sites on the route of the modern highway (and the old *camino real* that pilgrims still walk from Oaxaca to Juquila) were significant in this regard. Control of a major transportation route to the coast seems the likeliest motive for expansion of the Zapotec frontier. The walled hilltop site of San Francisco Arriba first became prominent on the Oaxaca coast at this time, and that site had a ceramic complex similar to Monte Albán II (de Cicco and Brockington 1956). By Period II, there was a monument at Monte Albán that probably referred to this coastal region as tributary (Marcus 1992a; Marcus and Flannery 1996:195-98).

By Period II, the Sola Valley had become a tributary province of the Zapotec state. Settlement of the region was consolidated near a single regional capital (S39) that served as both population and administrative center. Potential food production increased more than threefold compared to the prior phase. Surplus production could have supported the regional capital's expanded administrative apparatus, a Zapotec garrison, or traders and military personnel that traveled through the region. Period II settlement in the Sola Valley was not as defensively situated as before, since the borders of the Zapotec state's political territory now lay beyond the Sola Valley (Marcus 1992a). If the Ic phase was the initial expansion of Valley Zapotec into the Sola Valley, then Period II was the formal consolidation of this frontier region into a tributary province of the Zapotec state.

Monte Albán was the center of Oaxaca's multiregional settlement hierarchy by Period II. As the Zapotec state incorporated Sola and other regions into its political sphere, regional capitals arose in Sola, Ejutla, Miahuatlán, and the Cuicatlán Cañada to administer the emergent empire's tributary domain. A similar series of regional and subregional reorganizations was underway even within the Valley of Oaxaca during Period II (Kowalewski et al. 1989:153-200). For the first time, there was an integrated rather than competitive network of first-, second-, and third-tier sites that interlocked each of the valley's three arms (e.g. Marcus and Flannery 1996:173-78). The new central place hierarchy extended uninterrupted throughout the valley, with Monte Albán at its apex. A seismic shift in Oaxaca's macroregional settlement hierarchy was underway by Period II. Sola Valley settlement patterns document the Monte Albán expansion, and the consolidation of state control in this study region.

Chapter 4

The Sola Valley in the Classic to Early Postclassic Period

The Classic period is often called Oaxaca's "Golden Age." Monte Albán was one of the great cities of ancient Mexico, but other cities existed in Oaxaca, and their growing autonomy characterized the period. Monte Albán's political territory gradually diminished, but population and complexity increased in the Valley of Oaxaca and nearby regions. This period of territorial contraction ended with Monte Albán's political decline and the emergence of multiple new polities and autonomous regions.

In the Valley of Oaxaca chronology (Caso, Bernal, and Acosta 1967), Monte Albán IIIa is the Early Classic. Monte Albán IIIb-IV is the Late Classic to Early Postclassic period that covers Monte Albán's collapse. Period IIIb-IV consists of difficult-to-separate ceramic subphases (Bernal 1965; Marcus and Flannery 1990), and is especially troublesome for surface survey (Kowalewski et al. 1989:251-54). Efforts to separate Period IIIb from Period IV continue (e.g. Martínez et al. 2000), but no published stratigraphic report so far enables surface survey to distinguish the two subphases. The problem is that changing sherd frequencies rather than presence/absence are necessary to separate the two subphases, and the subphase distinctions are further confounded by significant regional variation. I therefore refer to Period IIIb-IV as one long period in this volume, except in cases where excavated or epigraphic data allow for its division into IIIb and IV.

Sola entered the Classic period still integrated with Monte Albán, but this relationship ended with the later collapse of the Monte Albán state. Sola's emergence as a semi-autonomous region in the wake of Monte Albán's political decline was the counterpoint to the earlier Zapotec expansion. By the Late Classic, the Zapotec state had fractured into multiple competing centers, and the Sola Valley consisted of multiple small centers sometimes allied, sometimes independent.

Sola's new centers were small polities that probably competed with each other. The valley now showed a distinctive regional complex of carved stone monuments, pyramidal platforms grouped around small plazas, and a dispersed settlement pattern of several separate yet equal centers. Sola's Period IIIb-IV centers seem to have been precursors of the later *cacicazgos*, the small polities or *señoríos* of the Conquest era.

Oaxaca archaeologists will require multiple perspectives, both regional and site specific, to construct historical explanations of the Monte Albán collapse (Balkansky 1998b). Monte Albán's site specific history should no longer be conflated with the collapse of regional states. Monte Albán sustained its population and building projects even though some provinces were breaking away during the Classic period. The Sola Valley contributes to our understanding of this process, especially with regard to the resurgence of local political authority in newly autonomous regions.

Period IIIa (Early Classic)

In Period IIIa (ca. A.D. 200-500), continuous, high-density occupations linked the valleys of Sola, Ejutla, and Oaxaca (Fig. 4.1; Feinman and Nicholas 1990a: Fig. 10; Kowalewski et al. 1989: Map 5). Site S23 ("Los Chilillos"), the region's new major center, overlooked a mountain pass leading into the Sola Valley. S23 was twice the size of the region's next largest site, and could have functioned as the regional administrative node for the Zapotec state. Sola's population lived mostly on terraced hilltops, and these defensible positions formed part of Monte Albán's southern boundary (Feinman and Nicholas 1990a: Fig. 9). Sola's defensible sites overlooked the highland passage to the Oaxaca coast. Possibly Sola might have been defended because Monte Albán's outer provinces had begun to break away.

Period IIIa was a time of renewed immigration to the region. Regional population reached 7703 persons, a 925% in-

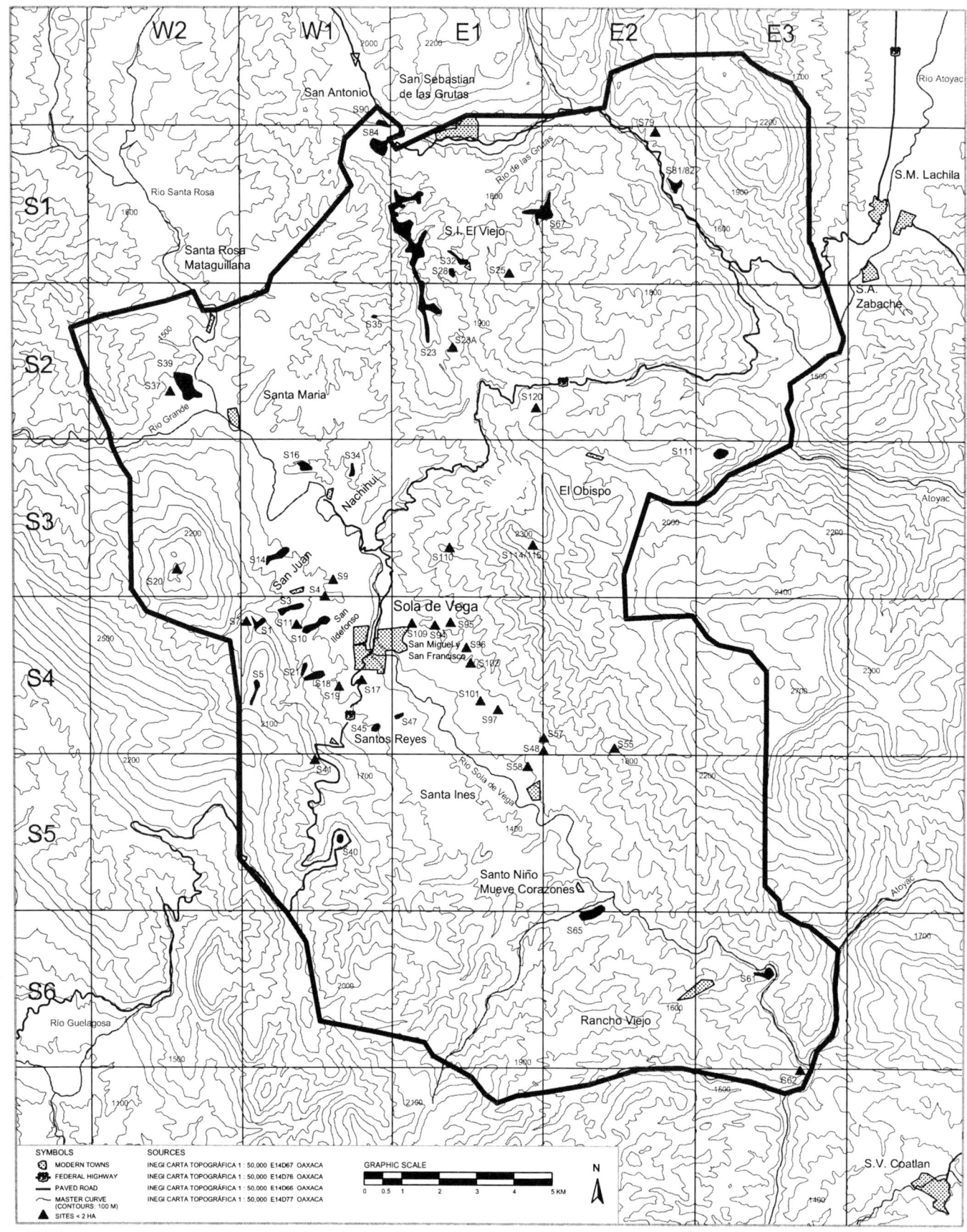

crease over the previous period. Sola's per annum growth rate of 0.74% exceeded the expected growth by natural increase (Cowgill 1975; Hassan 1981:125-42). Still, many large stretches in the region remained vacant, especially in the southern and northwestern sectors of the region. Sola was less densely occupied than the valleys of Ejutla and Oaxaca; only the Etla subregion had fewer persons per square kilometer (Table 2.6; Feinman and Nicholas 1990a: Table 1). Sola's population, even during this high growth phase, was not sufficient to fill the region and did not exceed carrying capacity.

Ceramics and Dating

Sola's Classic period ceramics are easily distinguished from the incised graywares and creamwares of the preceding period but are less decorated, and the complex includes fewer imports than most Valley of Oaxaca sites have. Sola nonetheless had access to decorated ceramics including type G.23 (and an oxidized yellow-orange equivalent), and the G.12, G.21, and C.7 types that sometimes continued into Period IIIa (Caso, Bernal, and Acosta 1967:79-84) (Plate 4.1). Sola's G.23s are outleaned-wall bowls or vases; none are of the hemispherical variety. No *floreros*, slab supports, or Thin Orange from Puebla were found on the surface of Sola Valley sites.

Sola's Period IIIa ceramic complex is dominated by G.35 bowls with outcurving walls and smoothed to roughened exterior surface finishes (Caso, Bernal, and Acosta 1967:80-82; Kowalewski et al. 1989:201; Kowalewski, Spencer, and Redmond 1978). G.35 analogues in the orange-brownware clay body, presumably made locally, are especially abundant. Brownware K.2 jars with raked necks are another common diagnostic.

Period IIIa utilitarian wares are bright orange, but become progressively paler, thicker, and less finished in later times. The preponderance of brownware and orange-brownware vessels in the Sola Valley is an indication of its marginality compared to subregions within the Valley of Oaxaca (Kowalewski et al. 1989:216). Sola's orange-brownwares likely represent a local ceramic tradition that developed into the region's Period V orange-creamware vessels.

One important point to clarify, however, is that the local settlement change, especially the shift of the Period II regional capital at S39 to the Period IIIa mountaintop urban center at S23, began during the II/IIIa transition (Caso, Bernal, and Acosta 1967). S39 and S23's population maximums, in other words, were not contemporary. This observation should be confirmed with excavations at S39 to show the hiatus in that site's occupational history.

Sites and Their Characteristics

Sola Valley sites are distributed widely but by no means fill the valley, since just 18 of 29 grid squares were occupied. The

Plate 4.1. Gray eagle-claw support and G.23.

52 Period IIIa sites occupy an area eight times greater than the previous period. Site size averages 5.71 ha compared to 3.7 ha in the Valley of Oaxaca (Kowalewski et al. 1989:205). Sola's median site size is 1.53 ha which indicates that Sola's propensity for larger sites was real, and not due to sampling bias against small sites (the mode was 0.50 ha). Sola site sizes are larger on average than in the Valley of Oaxaca, perhaps due to their more vulnerable location on the frontier. Valley of Oaxaca centers also would have provided more incentives—such as economic exchange and protection—to attract small communities to locate nearby.

Sola's Period IIIa terraced sites (27 of 52) include both major population centers (e.g. S23, S84) and smaller sites (e.g. S40, S55, S114) with lesser residential populations. Site locations average 1713 m in elevation, a significant upward movement over earlier periods. S23 was the only site with more than 50 residential terraces during Period IIIa; most terraced sites had small residential populations. Valley of Oaxaca sites often had hundreds of terraces, and populations estimated in the thousands (Kowalewski et al. 1989:202).

Most new building and platform construction took place at S23. But 13 of 52 (25%) Sola Valley sites have mounds associated with Period IIIa ceramics, and the percentage of sites with mounds is similar to the Valley of Oaxaca (Kowalewski et al. 1989:205). Sola's typical Period IIIa civic-ceremonial architecture consists of two mounds at either end of a plaza, constructed as single units in smaller centers (e.g. S40, S47, S61, S67), but found in long chains at the regional capital. S23 lacks the large central plaza that was typical of later phases; instead, the site has many small plazas with mounds or platforms along one axis

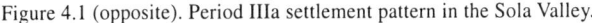
Figure 4.1 (opposite). Period IIIa settlement pattern in the Sola Valley.

TABLE 4.1. Sola Valley Settlement by Environmental Zone during Period IIIa

Environment	Sites	Total (ha)	Population	% Population
Low Alluvium	0	—	—	—
High Alluvium	4	1.78	47	—
Low Piedmont	29	132.22	3386	44%
High Piedmont	11	45.55	1284	17%
Mountain	8	117.92	2986	39%

and enclosed by low walls. This architectural arrangement is similar to Santa Cruz Mixtepec, Ayoquesco, and other nearby sites in the Valley of Oaxaca (Kowalewski et al. 1989). Other Period IIIa centers in the Sola Valley might have had this pattern, but their configurations were obscured by later construction.

S23 is a 71 ha mountaintop site that extends over 4 km on the El Obispo ridgeline north of the highway. S23 overlooks an important pass descending into the Sola Valley; it was a new center in Period IIIa, and not important politically before this time. The site has more than 20 mounds and a ball court that dated to the Classic period (Plate 4.2, 4.3). S23's mounds were aligned with the contour of the ridgeline, with residential terraces located on the east face of the hillside and adjacent to the mound groups. The occupants of these terraces faced the productive alluvial bottomlands near modern San Sebastián de las Grutas.

Sola's Period II center (S39) continued as one of the region's main secondary centers, although its Period IIIa architectural arrangement was obscured by the massive Period IIIb-IV buildup at the site. A third focus of settlement was located near San Juan Sola (S1, S3, and S10). The San Juan subregion, with its central location on the long axis of the valley and irrigable piedmont and valley floor land, was a favored location for the remainder of the prehispanic sequence. The San Juan sites and S39 grew at the expense of S23 during the Classic period. By Period IIIb-IV, S39 and other sites were relative equals in size and administrative complexity.

Other Period IIIa population centers (S61, S67, S82, S84, and S111) were located on the edge of the region; these centers combined central place functions (population and administration) with defensive advantages; each was a terraced hilltop site, and some had defensive walls. Several smaller sites were more specialized, and possibly functioned as defensive outposts or lookouts (S5, S20, S23A, S35, S40, S46, S55, and S114); these were terraced hilltop sites, often with fortifications located on inaccessible promontories but with low populations. Sola's defensive array was an extension of the Valley of Oaxaca and Ejutla pattern of defensive sites that controlled access to those regions (Feinman and Nicholas 1990a: Fig. 9). In the Sola Valley, most terraced sites (and regional population) were clustered on the main transportation route across the valley.

Settlement and Land Use

Period IIIa settlement shifted to higher elevations (Table 4.1). The low piedmont was still favored (44% of the regional population), but more than 56% of the population now lived in the high piedmont and mountain zones. S23, S67, S84, and S111 were high piedmont and mountain sites, and accounted for 40% of the regional population; immediate access to valley floor land was less important for the major centers than defensive and administrative functions. Occupied grid squares, however, account for 98.6% of Type I-II land in the region. These contrasting aspects of land use—the weak positive correlation with land quality but low surplus potential—are described below.

Sola Valley hamlets and small villages were often located in the low piedmont near productive valley floor land. The piedmont occupation recapitulated the Period Ic site locations, and is similar to the "piedmont strategy" in the Valley of Oaxaca (Kowalewski et al. 1989:212). Sola's smaller sites have limited public architecture (one or two low mounds, but sometimes none) and low population (probably less than 100 persons); these sites probably specialized in agricultural production to offset the productive deficits of the main centers.

S23 occupies only the third most productive grid square. Four sites—S23, S67, S82, and S84—encircle Type I land near San Sebastián de las Grutas, but at some distance from the region's most productive lands near the Río Sola. Settlement in the region is skewed similarly, with a weak positive correlation between population and land quality. The correlation coefficient is an anemic +0.258, and the removal of a possible outlier (S23) reduces the correlation to +0.107. Neither of these figures is significant at the 0.05 confidence level. The scatterplot (Fig. 4.2) is highly dispersed, and points straddle both sides of the regression line. There is no strong relationship between potential and actual population at this time.

Analysis of potential production (when considering available labor) shows that 12 of the 17 occupied grid squares are surplus producers, although S23's grid square is not. Still, the total surplus production could have fed 2310 more persons, or 130% of the regional population. Sola's bad-year productivity, however, would have been marginal, with outside inputs needed to offset productive shortfalls. Sola's limited surplus potential was a major change from the previous period, when surplus production could have supported more than three times the regional population.

Linda Nicholas (1989:497-99) argues that most Valley of Oaxaca sites of this period were not situated to maximize surplus production. Forty percent of the Valley of Oaxaca population by grid square was dependent on external food supplies, and this was a greater percentage than ever before. The south-

Plate 4.2. Everardo Olivera and Carmelo Aragón measure a structure at S23.

Plate 4.3. The ball court at S23, with a carved stone fallen in the center.

Regional and Macroregional Organization

Sola's Period IIIa settlement pattern is dispersed (similar to Period Ic), but more integrated than it was for previous periods. The site size histogram yields a four-tiered settlement hierarchy (Fig. 4.3); sites with public architecture are found on all four tiers. S23 had 25% of the region's population. By way of comparison, San Joaquín had 46% of Ejutla's regional population, and Jalieza had 25% of the southern Valley of Oaxaca's residents (Feinman and Nicholas 1997; Kowalewski et al. 1989). Jalieza was the largest of the three sites.

S23, S67, S82, and S84 formed Sola's demographic core with lower-order centers spread throughout the region. Sola's population was focused on San Sebastián de las Grutas and its small corner of the valley, and not the Sola Valley proper. Overall, 18 of 53 (34%) sites had populations greater than 100 persons; these sites accounted for 83% of the regional population. Thus, below the top rank site, nucleated populations were found in all corners of the valley, often at some distance from the regional capital. Since many lower-order sites became Period IIIb-IV centers, their later architectural buildup obscured information on the Period IIIa administrative hierarchy below the top level.

Sola's rank-size graph shows the coexistence of "separate" settlement systems with its primo-convex distribution; the regional capital, in other words, stands apart from a loosely integrated second tier of settlement (Fig. 4.3). The secondary centers would have been integrated directly with the regional capital, but not necessarily well integrated with each other. Sola's Period II-IIIa transition, marked by S23's emergence above the extant settlement system, contributes to the primo-convex rank-size graph (cf. Falconer and Savage 1995; McAndrews, Albarracin-Jordan, and Bermann 1997). But the region's primo-convexity could also reflect the growth of secondary centers (e.g. S1, S3, S10, and S39) at the expense of the regional capital during Classic times. By Period IIIb-IV, the Sola rank-size graph was entirely convex.

Sola's Period IIIa growth was part of a wider demographic shift to Ejutla and the southern Valley of Oaxaca. Jalieza ri-

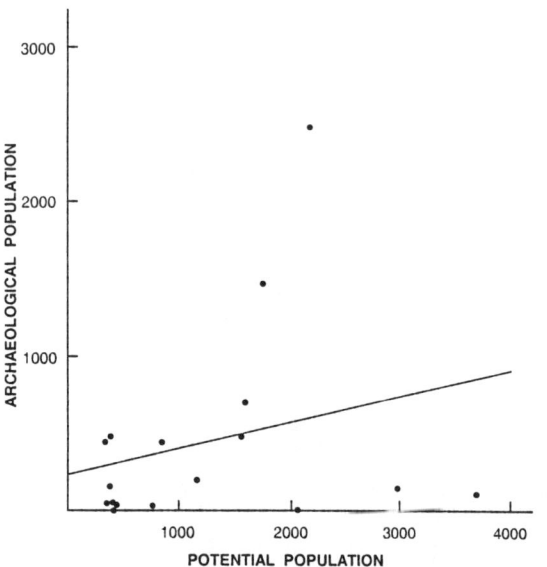

Figure 4.2. Period IIIa scatterplot of potential and actual population in the Sola Valley.

ern Valley of Oaxaca was one of the most dependent subregions. Valley of Oaxaca sites relied on an integrated regional exchange system to redistribute surplus. Sola Valley residents could have participated in the Valley of Oaxaca exchange sphere to mitigate bad-year risk.

In the Sola Valley during Period IIIa, land quality was a factor but not the sole determinant of settlement decisions. Sola's major population centers were not located near the region's best agricultural land, although overall agricultural production was adequate to make the region self-sufficient in most years. Sola's Period IIIa settlement pattern was similar to the Ic phase in that considerable interdependence was needed to offset local imbalances in agricultural productivity. Valley of Oaxaca sites also relied less on staple food surplus from other regions and more on efficient management of their own nearby lands (Nicholas 1989:497-99).

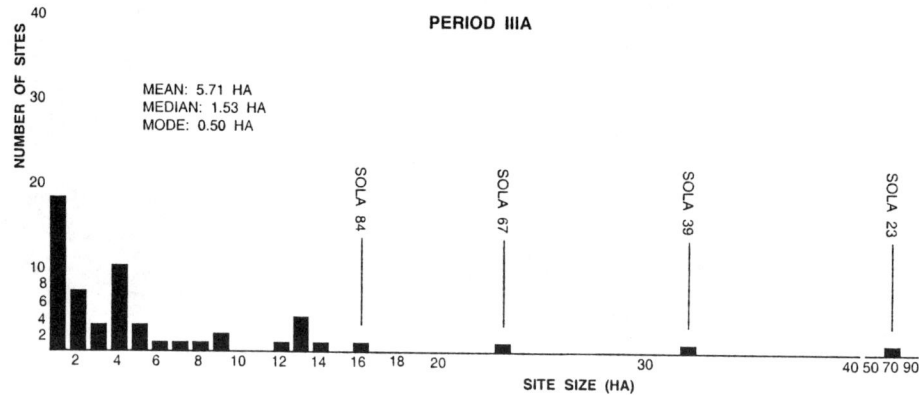

Figure 4.3. Histogram of Sola Valley site sizes during Period IIIa.

TABLE 4.2. Population Centers in Sola, Ejutla, and the Southern Oaxaca Valley during Period IIIa

Site	Region	Grid	Size (ha)	Population	Rank
Jalieza	Valle Grande	N7E9	408.10	12,835	1
San Joaquín	Ejutla			6,710	2
Sta C Mixtepec	Valle Grande	N6E3	49.40	3,219	3
SM Tilquiapan	Ocotlán	N4E10	109.40	2,746	3
Tejas de Morelos	Valle Grande	N4E6	99.30	1,937	3
Los Chilillos (S23)	Sola	S1E1	71.08	1,915	3
Ejutla	Ejutla			1,850	3
El Choco	Valle Grande	N2E3	9.10	1,320	4
T Zaachila	Valle Grande	N8E6	72.00	1,266	4
SJ Progreso	Ocotlán	N2E9	18.00	1,208	4
El Trapiche	Valle Grande	N4E3	11.00	1,178	4
SP Mártir	Ocotlán	N4E8	59.90	1,082	4
OC-SJT-PG-1	Ocotlán	N3E9	13.50	1,051	4
	Ejutla			1,016	4
P Guerrero	Ocotlán	N3E10	9.60	990	4
SA Tlapacoyan	Valle Grande	N3E4	51.50	902	4
ZI-SAT-SAT-5	Valle Grande	N3E4	13.70	825	4
La Soledad	Valle Grande	N8E7	46.50	814	4
Cuilapan	Valle Grande	N10E5	32.00	803	4
Texcoco (S39)	Sola	S2W2	31.06	713	4

(Feinman and Nicholas 1997; Kowalewski et al. 1989: Table 8.3)

valed Monte Albán as the largest site in the southern highlands; the central place network descended from Jalieza into Ejutla and Sola (Table 4.2). Sola's occupation was less dense, but its growth rate was comparable to these adjacent regions. A rank-size graph for Sola, Ejutla, and the southern Valley of Oaxaca is near log normal in distribution (Fig. 4.5). The Sola-Ejutla-southern Valley of Oaxaca macroregion was better integrated than the Valley of Oaxaca in general during this period (Kowalewski et al. 1989: Fig. 8.14).

Summary and Conclusions

The limits of Monte Albán's political domain during Period IIIa were the terraced and fortified sites in the southern Valley of Oaxaca, Sola, and Ejutla (Feinman and Nicholas 1990a: Fig. 9). Sola's rate of population growth matched that of the southern Valley of Oaxaca. Since few Sola sites were occupied continuously from Period II to IIIa, the regional population growth must be due partly to in-migration. The three valleys of Sola, Ejutla, and Oaxaca have continuous settlement patterns, including terraced sites through Sola on the highland passage to the coast. The continuous settlement suggests strong integration among these three regions.

Monte Albán's administrative network extended south to Jalieza, and then to San Joaquín (Ejutla), and S23 (Sola's "Los Chilillos"). S23's placement in the mountains close to the Valleys of Ejutla and Oaxaca indicates the heightened level of integration. The rank-size graph for these adjacent regions is near log normal. In addition to the continuity in settlement, these regions shared ceramics, terracing, and probably participated in the redistribution of surplus production. This zone was probably the southern boundary of the Zapotec state. S23 overlooked the exchange corridor, but secondary and tertiary centers in Sola were more dispersed. Sola's Period IIIa centers eventually became separate entities, for it was precisely along lines of initial colonization that the region would fracture with the political decline of Monte Albán in Period IIIb-IV.

Period IIIb-IV (Late Classic-Early Postclassic)

During Period IIIb-IV (ca. A.D. 500-1000) Sola was no longer as politically unified as it had been in the previous period (Fig. 4.6). S23 was diminished in importance, and valley settlement fractured into several competing zones of roughly equal size. The main center in each zone was 30-50 ha in size, yielding a top-heavy settlement hierarchy. Monte Albán's retreat from Sola is apparent—we see abandoned terraced sites and settlement discontinuities in the Sola-Ejutla-Valley of Oaxaca boundary zone (Fig. 4.6; Feinman and Nicholas 1990a: Fig. 11; Kowalewski et al. 1989: Maps 6, 7).

Sola's Period IIIb-IV centers are distinguished from prior phases by a characteristic architectural group: three to four mounds (with the east mound the largest) tightly knit around a small plaza, and a ball court adjacent to one of the lesser mounds. Six sites had ball courts either newly constructed or potentially in use during this period (S1, S10, S39, S65, S97, S104). Sola's ball courts date from the Classic period (if not before), but were

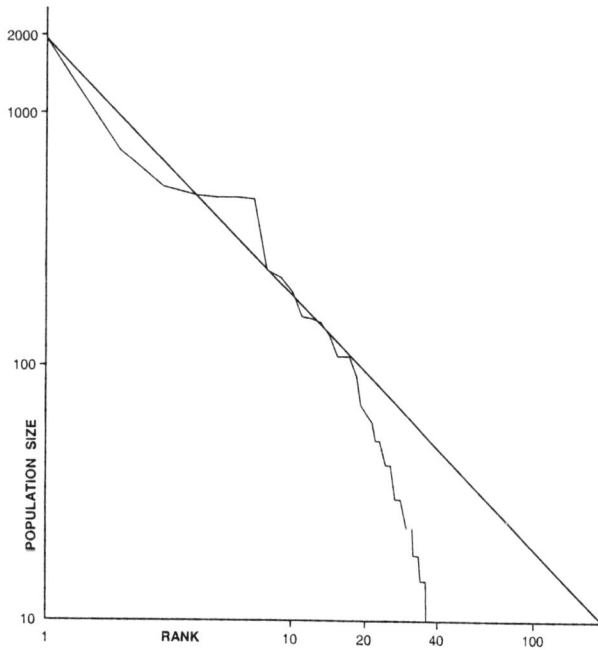

Figure 4.4. Rank-size graph for the Sola Valley during Period IIIa.

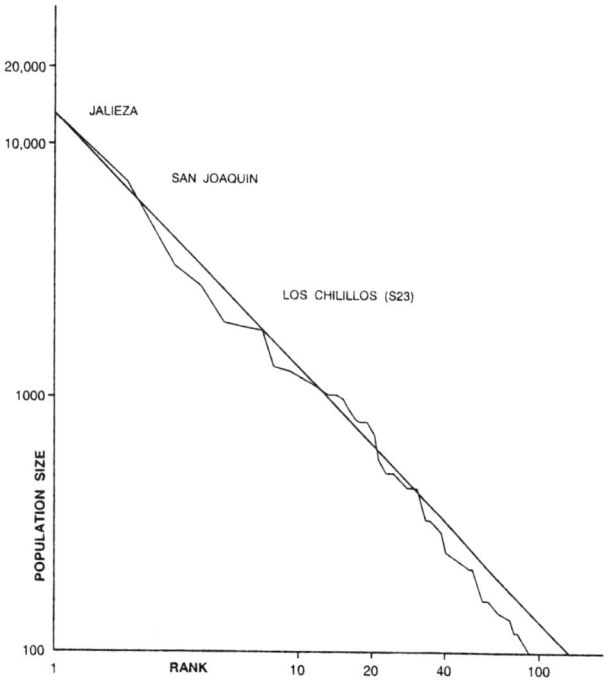

Figure 4.5. Rank-size graph for Sola, Ejutla, and the southern Oaxaca Valley during Period IIIa.

especially prevalent in Periods IIIb-IV and V. Period IIIb-IV centers often had secondary mound groups located away from the architectural core, but one principal mound group was always the regal-ritual focus of the site (cf. Kowalewski 1994).

Period IIIb-IV centers also have carved stones (S1, S3, S10, S23, S39, S97, and S111). Carved stone monuments were sel-

Plate 4.4. Brownware urn fragments typical of IIIb-IV sites in the Sola Valley.

Plate 4.5. Brownware brazier fragments from the top of the stone outcrop at S61, probably dating to late IIIb-IV.

dom encountered on the Valley of Oaxaca survey (Kowalewski et al. 1989), although many had been found prior to the 1960s. Sola's stone monuments were carved in Late Classic Zapotec style, and would not have been out of place in the valley proper (see Marcus, this volume). Berlin (1946, 1951) suggested that many Sola carved stones were linked to the ballgame; the Sola regional survey found this to be the case. Carved stones occur at sites with ball courts, and are often in direct association with the courts themselves. Berlin's (1946, 1951) finds, combined with the carved stones reported here, provide a total of more than 40 carved stones and 13 ball courts in the study region.

Figure 4.6 (opposite). Period IIIb-IV settlement pattern in the Sola Valley.

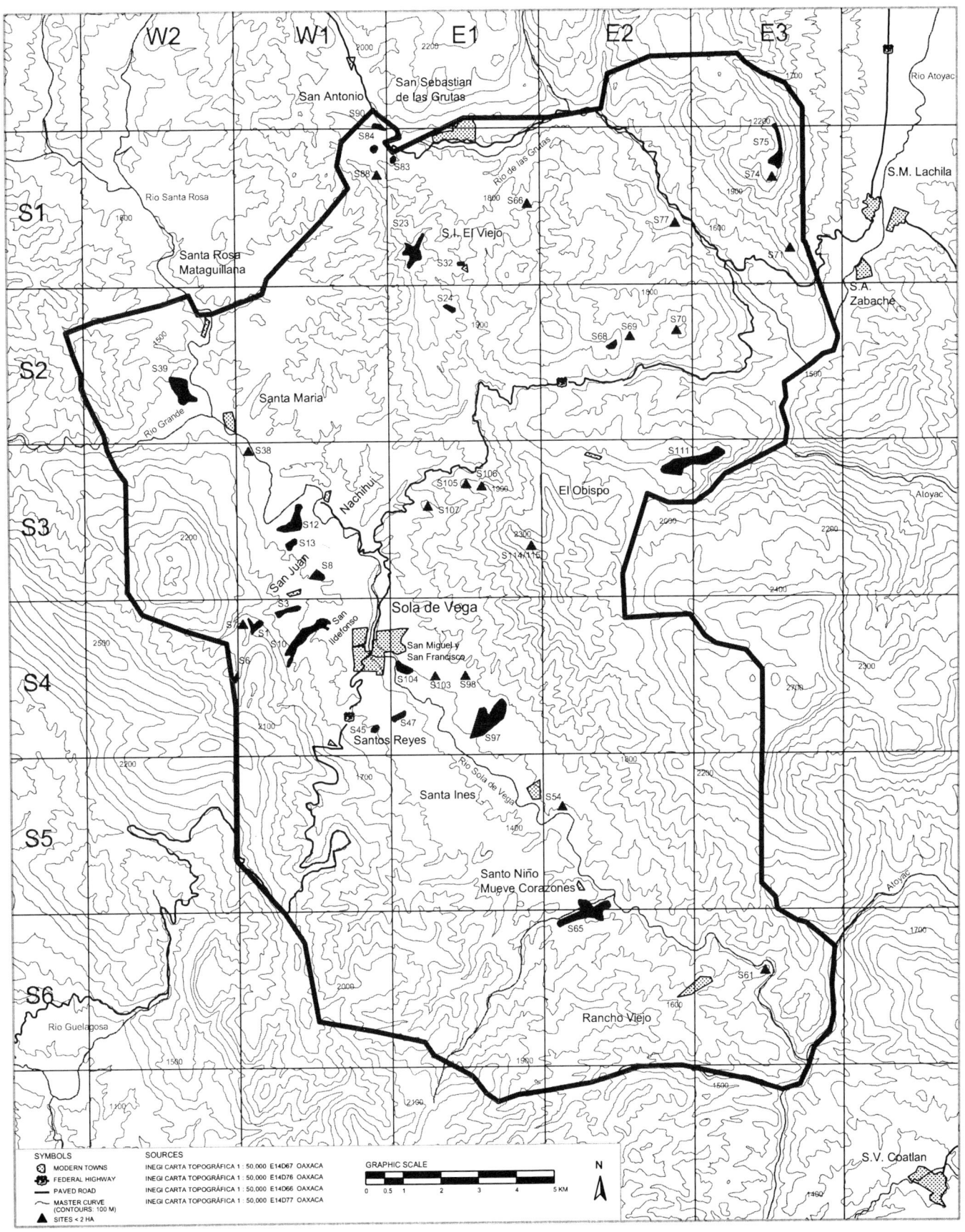

TABLE 4.3. Sola Valley Settlement by Environmental Zone during Period IIIb-IV

Environment	Sites	Total (ha)	Population	% Population
Low Alluvium	2	0.49	17	—
High Alluvium	6	84.65	1502	21%
Low Piedmont	9	128.90	2605	37%
High Piedmont	13	27.87	882	13%
Mountain	9	99.71	2060	29%

Ceramics and Dating

Sites were dated to Period IIIb-IV if they had ceramic wares that were the local variants of type G.35; these could be grayware, brownware, or orange-brownware G.35 analogues (Caso, Bernal, and Acosta 1967:84-86). The vessels are conical with straight, outleaned walls and rough exterior surfaces (Martínez et al. 2000). Hemispherical shapes also appear in the Sola collections. Another class of Sola ceramics resembles types K.14 and K.22, including brownwares with a gray slip. An apparent Sola variant is the brownware and orange-brownware bowl with a flattened rim.

Many of Sola's Period IIIb-IV ceramics are vessels with ritual associations. Brownware urn fragments, spiked braziers, and incensarios with wide-aperture tubular handles (Caso, Bernal, and Acosta 1967:434-36) were found in elite contexts at the major centers, and often recorded as isolated finds or at possible shrines (Plate 4.4, 4.5). Some isolated finds may fall near boundaries between Sola's competing centers.

Finally, subregional variation in clay composition is a feature of Sola's Period IIIb-IV ceramic complex, possibly due to a proliferation of local production centers, different exchange spheres, or temporal differences. Ceramic distinctions were most evident along the east/west gradient that divides the Sola study region, defined by the El Obispo ridgeline (Sites S23, S111, and their neighbors). Earlier and later periods were far more uniform in terms of ceramic clay composition than IIIB-IV.

Sites and Their Characteristics

The regional population numbered 7066 persons—an 8% decline from the previous period—but this decline is still within the margin of error for estimating prehispanic populations (see Chapter 2). Sola's total population was essentially unchanged from the previous period. Although the overall population was stable, the distribution of sites was not. Thirteen of twenty-nine grid squares were occupied. Site elevations average 1770 m— higher than in earlier periods—but the distribution is bimodal with peaks at 1825 m and 1425 m in elevation. Most major centers were located near valley floor lands except S111. There were 21 terraced sites out of 39 total sites in the region (54%). Sites with mounds that date reliably to Period IIIb-IV number 13 out of 39 (33%), yet the greatest construction effort was found in the main centers. Site size averages 8.76 ha, higher than any other period in Sola's prehispanic settlement history.

S39, S65, S97, and S111 were the major centers, spaced 6-10 km apart; these sites differed from all others in size, population, and public architecture (Plate 4.6). The second-tier sites at S1, S3, S10, S12, S23, S75, and S104 also were spaced widely in the region (Plate 4.7, 4.8). Seldom was the typical Period IIIb-IV center a site that had been of regional significance in earlier periods (S23 and S39 were exceptions). Each center was significant architecturally (and so were relatively small sites such as S104). Ball courts and carved stone monuments were common in the region; six (and possibly eight) Period IIIb-IV sites had ball courts in use during this period, and seven sites had carved stone monuments (Plate 4.9).

A third, but diverse, group of sites is smaller and often found on high promontories; these sites may have had defensive functions, but most did not resemble earlier defensible sites, since they lacked terraces or defensive walls. Isolated sites were found between major centers (often near modern community boundaries) and had ritual artifacts such as urns and braziers, often found on prominent landscape features or associated with small mounds. The isolated mounds were little more than low piles of stone rubble, and may have functioned as boundary markers. S6, S54, S61, S68, S69, S70, S74, S90, and S114 were examples of possible shrines or boundary marker sites (see Kowalewski et al. 1989:263-67). Period IIIb-IV sites anticipate Sola's Postclassic and modern settlement patterns better than those of any prior phase. Period IIIb-IV centers would become capitals of the region's Postclassic petty kingdoms; nine colonial and modern towns are located near these same centers.

Settlement and Land Use

More than any other period, Period IIIb-IV settlement patterns were closely tied to land quality. The Sola Valley's potential population in occupied grid squares averaged 1793 persons, compared to 600 persons in unoccupied grid squares. Several high production grid squares had major IIIb-IV centers. Correlation coefficients for potential and actual population (i.e. land quality) are +0.475, a stronger relationship than occurs in any other prehispanic period; for the corresponding scatterplot, see Figure 4.7. In contrast, regional population was only 22% of its resource-based potential (Fig. 2.5), and several grid squares provide prominent exceptions to the weak correlation (e.g. the underpopulated square S5E1 and the overpopulated S3E2). Sola's land/settlement correlation coefficient, moreover, is not significant at the 0.05 confidence level.

The low piedmont continued to be the favored site location in this period, with 9 sites and 37% of the regional population (Table 4.3). Period IIIb-IV sites also shifted to the high allu-

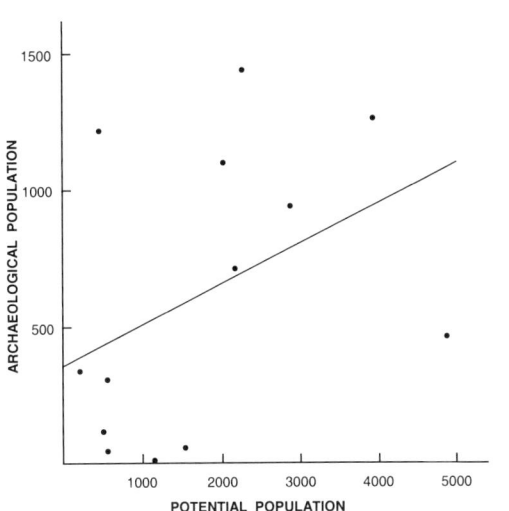

Figure 4.7. Period IIIb-IV scatterplot of potential and actual population in the Sola Valley.

vium, which was only sparsely settled in earlier periods but now accounted for 21% of the regional population. Valley floor locations were capable of exploiting the best quality Type I lands. High piedmont and mountain zones had the remaining 42% of the regional population. Sites strung along the Río Sola had most of the low piedmont and valley floor populations; the northeastern part of the region, nearest the Valley of Oaxaca and Ejutla, had the main high piedmont and mountain sites. It is possible that this spatial discontinuity in site location was due to temporal variation, but Sola's east/west split was already present in Period IIIa.

Sola's potential surplus production (based on resources and the distribution of labor) could have fed 8642 more persons, or 213% of the regional population. Potential surplus thus increased, but a destination for such surplus was not apparent.

Linda Nicholas (1989:499-501) notes that Period IIIb population in the Valley of Oaxaca was well distributed to support its major centers, but in Period IV much of the valley was at risk, and Jalieza would have been heavily dependent on exchange with sites in other grid squares. Yet settlement patterns for both IIIB and IV show vacant spaces where sites had once linked the Valleys of Sola and Oaxaca.

It may be that Sola's Period IIIb-IV food surpluses were destined for use in its own major centers, and funded expanded building programs. Sola's potential for surplus production was distributed across multiple grid squares, such that each center (except S111) could have subsisted independently of all others. Even the seeming exception of S111 may fit the pattern, since the nearby grid square S2E3 was relatively productive, and could have supported S111; our analysis, moreover, does not include productive lands in nearby Ejutla and the southern Valley of Oaxaca. S111 could have taken advantage of its gatekeeper position at the Sola region's edge, giving its leaders the leverage to obtain staple surplus from its neighbors.

Period IIIb-IV sites were closer to high quality land than sites in earlier periods (although the relationship is not statistically significant). The total population remained below what could have been supported, and surplus production could have increased with more optimally distributed population. Yet site placement was determined in part by land quality concerns, and Sola Valley settlements were apparently more autonomous with respect to potential production than those of earlier periods. It is possible that as the Monte Albán state broke down after Period IIIa, sites had to scramble for the best land until new institutions of exchange had replaced those of the regional state.

Regional and Macroregional Organization

Sola Valley population was virtually unchanged from the prior period, but the distribution of settlement was substantially altered. The former regional capital at S23 was much reduced, and multiple centers arose roughly equidistant from each other. Eighty-one percent of the Sola Valley population lived in the

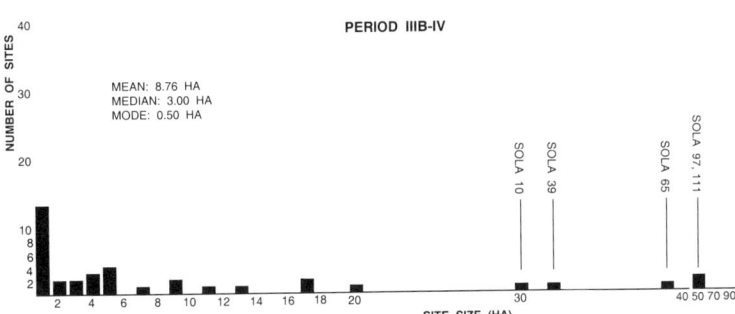

Figure 4.8. Histogram of Sola Valley site sizes during Period IIIb-IV.

Plate 4.6. Laura Stiver surveys near Structure 1 at S39, the most monumental IIIb-IV site in the Sola Valley.

Plate 4.7. The plaza and surrounding structures at S1, typical of the smaller IIIb-IV sites with architecture in the Sola Valley.

Plate 4.8. Structure 1, situated on the east side of the plaza at S1.

Plate 4.9. Surveyors walk through corn planted in the ball court at S1.

top two tiers of the settlement hierarchy. Ninety-two percent of the regional population was found at sites with more than 100 persons. These figures are not biased by the differential recovery of large sites; 15 of 39 sites (38%) have estimated populations of less than 25 persons, and 23 of 39 sites (59%) have estimates of less than 100 persons. Period IIIb-IV's modal population size is only 13 persons. Settlement nucleation in a few regional centers is thus a true reflection of the Sola Valley settlement pattern.

The site size histogram illustrates the top-heavy settlement hierarchy (Fig. 4.8). First-tier sites cover 30 to 55 ha; lower-order centers are not strongly differentiated, since sites from 2 to 20 ha have only three low modal peaks. A third class of sites measures less than 1 ha. A sort by population gives a clearer indication of the settlement hierarchy—ranks form at 1-12, 30-177, 250-519, and 713-1028 persons, giving us four tiers of settlement. A further subdivision might have split the third-tier sites (30-177 persons) into separate hierarchical levels, but I chose a more conservative approach in my analysis. I also lumped first-tier centers (713-1028 persons) into a single hierarchical level, since comparisons among site sizes and mounds, presence of carved stones, ball courts, and their location suggest that these sites were different from others.

The Sola Valley was divided into at least six core zones (S1-S3-S10, S23 and its neighbors, S39, S65, S97, and S111). As mentioned, each subregional center was able to sustain itself independently of other sites with the possible exception of S111. Site size and population were not good predictors for the presence of civic-ceremonial architecture, since even the smallest sites had pyramidal mounds, and relatively small centers (e.g., S1, S8, S12, S75, and S104) often had significant architecture. S104, for example, was only a 10 ha site but had nine structures, a ball court, and an architectural layout similar to the major centers. Public buildings—though found at widely dispersed sites—were nevertheless concentrated in the main centers.

Sola's rank-size graph illustrates the region's decentralization and top-heavy settlement hierarchy (Fig. 4.9). Extreme convexity was the rule in the region's topmost ranks, similar to the Valley of Oaxaca (Kowalewski et al. 1989: Fig. 9.18). Sola's rank-size curve descends sharply at sites with less than 300 persons, suggesting that administrative authority was especially concentrated in the top rank sites (the curves of earlier periods dropped off at sites less with than 100 persons). A partitioned settlement system alone cannot account for Sola's rank-size distribution, since survey maps for Sola, Ejutla, and the Valley of Oaxaca all illustrate the disintegration of the earlier macroregional hierarchy. Sola's rank-size convexity was due not just to the elimination of the former regional capital, but also to the continued growth of former secondary centers. Sola's rank-size convexity, wide distribution of major centers, and massive construction programs suggested that competing centers had a similar array of functions and redundant administrative institutions.

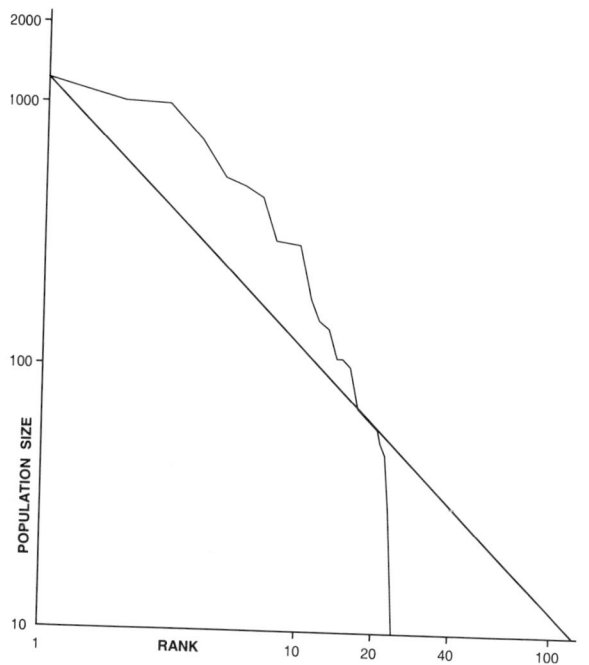

Figure 4.9. Rank-size graph for the Sola Valley during Period IIIb-IV.

Sola Valley settlement thus conformed to that of the combined Ejutla and southern Valley of Oaxaca regions (Feinman and Nicholas 1990a: Fig. 11; Kowalewski et al. 1989: Maps 6, 7). Sola Valley centers were much smaller than Valley of Oaxaca sites such as El Choco, Santa Cruz Mixtepec, or Jalieza, but fit comfortably within secondary and tertiary ranks on the macroscale (Table 4.4). Sola's regional population density best approximated that of the southern Valley of Oaxaca, and was far more robust than that of the Ejutla Valley (Table 2.6).

Summary and Conclusions

Many of Sola's characteristic regional traits coalesced during Period IIIb-IV: carved stone monuments, massive building programs, the proliferation of ball courts, and dispersed settlement patterns. Administrative authority was divided among multiple competing centers. Sola Valley leadership may have become more competitive with the contraction and retrenchment of the Zapotec state, with its emergent elite seeking monumental displays to help solidify power at each center.

Sola's decentralization was similar to the Valley of Oaxaca's, where separate site clusters occupied 25-50 km² and were each dominated by a different center (Blanton et al. 1993:91-99; Kowalewski et al. 1989:251-305). Valley of Oaxaca centers were larger, however, than their Sola Valley counterparts. Sola Valley population did not decline to the pronounced degree that occurred in neighboring Ejutla (Feinman and Nicholas 1990a). Survey data from the Miahuatlán Valley (Markman 1981) show

TABLE 4.4. Population Centers in Sola, Ejutla, and the Southern Oaxaca Valley during Period IIIb-IV

Site	Region	Grid	Size (ha)	Population	Rank
Jalieza	Valle Grande	N7E9	534.40	16,117	1
El Choco	Valle Grande	N2E3	53.40	4,047	2
Zaachila	Valle Grande	N9E7	232.00	2,135	3
SP Mártir	Ocotlán	N3E8	107.10	1,875	3
SC Mixtepec	Valle Grande	N5E3	11.90	1,501	3
Tejas de Morelos	Valle Grande	N4E6	64.50	1,215	3
A Trujano	Valle Grande	N11E8	52.90	1,121	3
Los Paderones (S111)	Sola	S2E2	53.00	1,028	3
Shilegua (S97)	Sola	S4E1	54.20	953	3
SM Tilquiapan	Ocotlán	N4E10	18.80	891	3
Cuilapan	Valle Grande	N11E5	30.70	839	3
Santos Niños (S65)	Sola	S5E2	38.61	797	3
Texcoco (S39)	Sola	S2W2	31.06	713	3
	Ejutla			529	4
OC-SJT-PG-1	Ocotlán	N3E9	19.60	522	4
San Ildefonso (S10)	Sola	S4W1	29.62	519	4
Los Chilillos (S23)	Sola	S1E1	19.22	475	4
San Joaquín	Ejutla			462	4
	Ejutla			371	4

(Feinman and Nicholas 1997; Kowalewski et al. 1989: Tables 9.2, 9.6)

similarities to Sola, with the region remaining strong even as other parts of highland Oaxaca were in sharp decline. We cannot tell if Ejutla was more reliant on San Joaquín's fortunes, or if its population was drawn into the Period IV urbanization at Jalieza.

The Territorial Limits of the Zapotec State

Monte Albán was a more powerful integrating force during Period IIIa than ever before, but not as a result of territorial expansion (Blanton et al. 1993:87-91; Kowalewski et al. 1989:249-50; Marcus 1992a). Monte Albán's Classic period domain was reduced compared to its prior expansionist phase (Marcus 1992a), even though the city itself was reaching its greatest size and monumentality (Acosta 1965; Blanton 1978). The Zapotec capital retreated from its most distant provinces, such as the Cuicatlán Cañada, and instead sought to concentrate population and administrative control closer to home. Monte Albán was now confronting potential rivals even within the Valley of Oaxaca at Jalieza and greater Dainzú (Balkansky 1998b; Kowalewski et al. 1989: Map 5), a change that began during the II/IIIa transition.

Monte Albán, Jalieza, and the greater Dainzú cluster formed a triangle enclosing the central part of the valley (Blanton et al. 1993:87-91), but this system was latent with potential conflict (Balkansky 1998b). Monte Albán maintained its edge in architectural monumentality, yet Jalieza and Dainzú also had the capacity to support and defend themselves by Early Classic times. The regional population hierarchy was composed of separate but equal centers; a second piedmont expansion focused on the southern and eastern subvalleys; and settlement was continuous between the latter two subregions (Kowalewski et al. 1989: Map 5). This transformation involved more than just change at the capital, since "not just localities but whole regions could take on a new character depending on their role in the new macroregional system" (Kowalewski et al. 1989:249). I would argue that the "new character" of these regions made their interrelationships more complicated than Monte Albán-centered explanations have allowed.

Valley of Oaxaca survey results indicate greater state involvement in economic activities, especially ceramic production and agriculture (Kowalewski et al. 1989:249-50). Efficient intraregional exchange was needed to balance agricultural risk (Nicholas 1989). Ceramic styles were more uniform from region to region; ceramic production was standardized, and associated with administrative centers near the regional core (Feinman 1982; Kowalewski et al. 1989:213-21). Carved stone monuments had a standardized art style and hieroglyphic system (Marcus 1983d). Valley of Oaxaca ceramics at this time showed little influence from other parts of Mesoamerica; Teotihuacan-style vessels were rare in Period IIIa, and generally restricted to elite precincts at the capital (Caso and Bernal 1965; Caso, Bernal, and Acosta 1967:311; Martínez 1994). Economic activity was redirected from the north to the southern Valley of Oaxaca, and extended into Ejutla, Sola, and Miahuatlán.

Sola-Ejutla parallels include the many terraced and defensible sites. Ejutla's Period IIIa capital moved closer to Monte Albán. Sola's Period IIIa capital (S23) was not in the valley proper, but in the mountains where Sola, Ejutla, and the southern Valley of Oaxaca converged. Ejutla could have provided some surplus agricultural production, but its principal role during Period IIIa seems to have been as a highland/coastal exchange route and boundary area (Feinman and Nicholas 1990a). Sola survey results imply similar functions within Monte Albán's territory.

Survey and excavation in Ejutla indicate that a primary role for that region was marine shell ornament production (Feinman and Nicholas 1992, 1993, 1995). Shell is difficult to date from surface collections, but was present at seven Sola Valley sites; based on surface associations the most probable date for the shell was the Classic period. Sola's marine shell was composed entirely of Pacific species; evidence for shell production was found at one and possibly three sites in the Sola Valley (Nicholas and Feinman, this volume). Further work will be required to elucidate the full range of shell work in Sola and compare it with the excavated results from Ejutla, but it is intriguing that both regions seem to have followed a parallel course in this craft specialty.

Monte Albán withdrew from the Cuicatlán Cañada by the Early Classic, perhaps due to expansionist pressures from Teotihuacan (Spencer and Redmond 1997:603-5). Cuicatlán's settlement pattern was reoriented for highest potential irrigation and staple food production. Sites were distributed with respect to the best agricultural land, and each subsector or alluvial fan was a separate focus of settlement with its own civic-ceremonial center. The Quiotepec sector that had housed the Zapotec military garrison was on the least productive land, and became the region's only subsector with a population decline. Cuicatlán's new centers underwent a construction boom that included multiple ball courts. The Cañada pattern of disengagement from Monte Albán was replicated somewhat later in time in the Sola Valley.

Period IIIb-IV was a time of "changing politics" (Flannery and Marcus [eds.] 1983) due to the growth of competing centers and a secondary elite who claimed political authority in temples, tombs, and hieroglyphic writing. Monte Albán was one of several large sites in the Valley of Oaxaca in Period IIIb-IV, along with Atzompa, Jalieza, Macuilxochitl, Lambityeco, and Mitla among others (Kowalewski et al. 1989: Maps 6, 7). Each arm of the Valley of Oaxaca was returning to its historical roots as an independent region.

The themes of carved stones at sites throughout Oaxaca reflected regional elite claims to political authority (Marcus 1983c). On the household level, there was a diversification of production in Late Classic times (see Balkansky, Feinman, and Nicholas 1997; Feinman and Nicholas 1993) that could reflect the growing economic autonomy of individual small polities. Atzompa was a major ceramic production site in early Period IIIb-IV (Blanton 1978). Craft debris is especially common on Period IIIb-IV residential terraces at Monte Albán (Blanton 1978; Blanton et al. 1993:93-96). Divergences among sites—their growing autonomy and specialization—are magnified on the macroregional scale.

Sola and Ejutla diverged by Period IIIb-IV, and the latter region went into sharp decline. Feinman and Nicholas (1990a:237) suspect that Ejutla's decline began earlier than at Monte Albán. Ejutla's Period IIIb-IV settlement pattern anticipated that of the petty kingdoms of Period V. Valley of Oaxaca survey data also suggest that the contiguous southern arm of the valley (as well as Tlacolula) went into decline prior to Monte Albán's Late Classic collapse (Kowalewski et al. 1989:251). Monte Albán's site-level dynamics and the Valley of Oaxaca's regional dynamics were not one and the same.

Sola's Period IIIb-IV setting was one of uncertain leadership and lack of political centralization or unity, indicated by the relatively flat hierarchy and the dead zones between major centers. Competition among elites of equal rank in the wake of Monte Albán's political decline best explains the proliferation of monument building and the fragmented settlement pattern.

Still, contacts with Monte Albán were not severed, as shown by stylistic affinities to the carved stone tradition of the Valley Zapotec (Berlin 1946, 1951), and the likelihood that political power in Sola was validated through ties to Valley of Oaxaca elites (Marcus, this volume). Sola elites looked to be allied or linked with Valley of Oaxaca elites on the same, rather than a subordinate, level. Other, comparable examples of factional competition among Classic period elites include the ritual ballgame in the coastal lowlands (J. F. Zeitlin 1993), monument building in the Maya area (Pohl and Pohl 1994), and the uses of political propaganda in Mesoamerican writing systems (Marcus 1992b:442-43). Sola's carved stones and architectural data may represent a political situation that was more negotiated and contingent than absolute, such that local rulers had to go to greater symbolic lengths to establish legitimacy.

Sola Valley texts recorded genealogical information on "nonpublic" stones such as the lintels, doorjambs, and wall panels of tomb antechambers (Marcus, this volume). When tombs were reopened for later interments, this genealogical information could be consulted by persons in attendance, and formed a kind of "horizontal propaganda" between elites of equivalent rank (Marcus 1992b:11-12, 281-85, 301-2). Such depictions appear in the Valley of Oaxaca with the political decline of Monte Albán, when each noble family began to arrange its own political alliances, and claim authority based on hereditary rules of descent. Tombs were an ideal setting to establish links to one's ancestors, with each claim documented in stone. The appearance of Sola's carved stones may signal new alliance building among Valley of Sola and Oaxaca centers.

Period IIIb-IV Sola Valley centers undertook major new construction programs that in most cases left earlier pyramid mounds buried under later buildings. The characteristic pattern was the three to four structure group (with a larger east structure) arranged around an enclosed plaza, with a ball court adjacent to one of the lesser mounds. Although ball courts in Oaxaca date from the Late or Terminal Formative (Kowalewski et al. 1991), most of Sola's ball courts were Period IIIb-IV and V constructions (based on surface ceramic associations and some single component sites). Ball courts in "Epiclassic" and Postclassic Oaxaca may have mediated conflict among competing centers (Kowalewski et al. 1991); similar arguments have been advanced for other parts of Mesoamerica and the Southwest (de Montmollin 1997; Whalen and Minnis 1996). Sola Valley ball courts occurred at the same widely spaced centers as the carved stone monuments, and possibly reflected elite competition in the new decentralized political climate.

Sola's Classic to Early Postclassic period growth occurred in counterpoint to the earlier Zapotec expansion. Period IIIa Sola was at the southern margin of Monte Albán's political domain, yet this episode of contraction once again brought population into the region. Sola's roles in the Zapotec state may have included boundary maintenance, and control of a key transport route linking the highlands to the Oaxaca coast. By Period IIIb-IV, Sola's ties to Monte Albán were diminishing in the wake of Monte Albán's own political decline. Sola then emerged as a core region of its own, semi-autonomous or autonomous from Valley of Oaxaca centers near Monte Albán, yet linked to other formerly lower-order Valley of Oaxaca centers. Political, ritual, and perhaps commercial ties were maintained between the two regions, as Sola Valley elites sought ties with other emergent centers. Sola's era of competing small polities continued into Period V and the contact period *cacicazgos*.

The roots of the Postclassic *cacicazgos* are visible in several Late Classic period societies, making the collapse a more continuous process than most scholars have imagined. We are predisposed to thinking that the "Epiclassic" everywhere means decline and collapse, but this is really a pre-settlement-survey view of ancient Mexico. Monte Albán's changing fortunes vis-à-vis other centers was relative and not representative of the entire valley—some sites, such as Jalieza and Lambityeco, had been prominent prior to the collapse and then grew in response to declines at the capital. Xochicalco and other Central Mexican centers had a similar dynamic with respect to Teotihuacan (Hirth 1989, 1995; Marcus 1992a). Other regional formations, such as the one in Sola Valley, flourished during the collapse era. If we are going to understand the collapse of regional states and the transition to the Postclassic, we must separate individual site histories (including that of Monte Albán) from our notions of regional and macroregional political structure.

Chapter 5

The Sola Valley in the Late Postclassic Period

In this chapter, I reconsider the origins of the petty kingdoms that the sixteenth-century Spanish conquerors called *cacicazgos*. By Period Monte Albán V, the era of territorial empires had passed, and dozens of small polities characterized by shifting alliances among relative equals inhabited Oaxaca (e.g. Hunt 1972; Marcus 1989; Marcus and Flannery 1983; Spores 1965, 1967, 1974; Whitecotton 1977). Even though the regional political structure was decentralized, social stratification was more pronounced than ever before. Nobles often moved from one kingdom to another through marital alliance and rules of inheritance and brought their dependents with them (including the class of landless peasants called *terrazgueros*), resettling wherever the latest shift in political fortunes allowed. For the noble class, ties owed less to regional or ethnic origin and more to lineage, marital ties, and skilled diplomacy. But not all interpolity links were political; some believe that Postclassic markets were an equally pervasive integrative mechanism, and persisted through changes in the fractious political scene (e.g. Blanton et al. 1993:99-103; Pohl, Monaghan, and Stiver 1997).

Ethnicity, especially the Postclassic Mixtec presence in the Valley of Oaxaca, underlies the political integration of *cacicazgos* and Postclassic origins. Mixtec kingdoms underwent a cultural florescence in Postclassic times (Spores 1969, 1983b). The presence of Mixtec speakers in Valley of Oaxaca towns during early Colonial times, plus "Mixtec-style" ceramics at Postclassic sites, once suggested a possible "Mixtec invasion" of the Valley of Oaxaca (e.g. Bernal 1966; Paddock 1966). Other migration and conquest scenarios mention Toltec influence or refugees from Teotihuacan's collapse to explain Postclassic origins (see Bernal 1965). But the effort to link material culture traits such as ceramics with ethnicity and presumed political control could be misleading. The locus of political action during the Postclassic period was the *cacicazgo*.

Current evidence best supports an *in situ* development of Postclassic societies in Oaxaca out of their Classic period forebears. The available stratigraphic record at Valley of Oaxaca sites such as Abasolo, Cuilapan, and Yagul shows Period IIIb-IV graywares changing into Period V G.3Ms, and these "Zapotec" graywares co-occurring with "Mixtec" red-on-cream and later polychrome vessels (Marcus and Flannery 1990). The same continuous transition is apparent from Saville's (1898) excavation of Period IIIb-IV tombs at Xoxocotlán (Balkansky 1998c). The Nochixtlán ceramic sequence likewise is uninterrupted (Spores 1972). Ceramics and ethnicity had no necessary relationship in Postclassic Oaxaca (Marcus and Flannery 1983). A more apt distinction would be elite (polychrome) versus non-elite (less fancy) wares.

Cacicazgos were the basic building blocks of all larger-scale social formations in late prehispanic times. It is characteristic of the Postclassic in Oaxaca that this organizational unit is recognizable from region to region. These polities replaced the regional states of earlier periods, and could be considered their breakdown products (e.g. Marcus 1989). Elite marriages cemented alliances among Postclassic kingdoms, but warfare, exchange, and ceremonialism also integrated polities on the macroregional scale (Spores 1974). I would suggest that the multiregional integration of *cacicazgos* and their origins are one and the same phenomenon. Mixtec-Zapotec ties are part of this process, but not in the sense of unidirectional influences. The multiregional convergence of settlement patterns and interpolity dynamics makes the Postclassic period less amenable to distinctions of ethnicity or regional politics, and seem more like a single macroregional settlement system.

Period V (Late Postclassic)

Period V (ca. A.D. 1000-1520) marked the end of the prehispanic sequence. After Monte Albán's collapse (ca. A.D. 800), the Sola region had fractured into several competing small

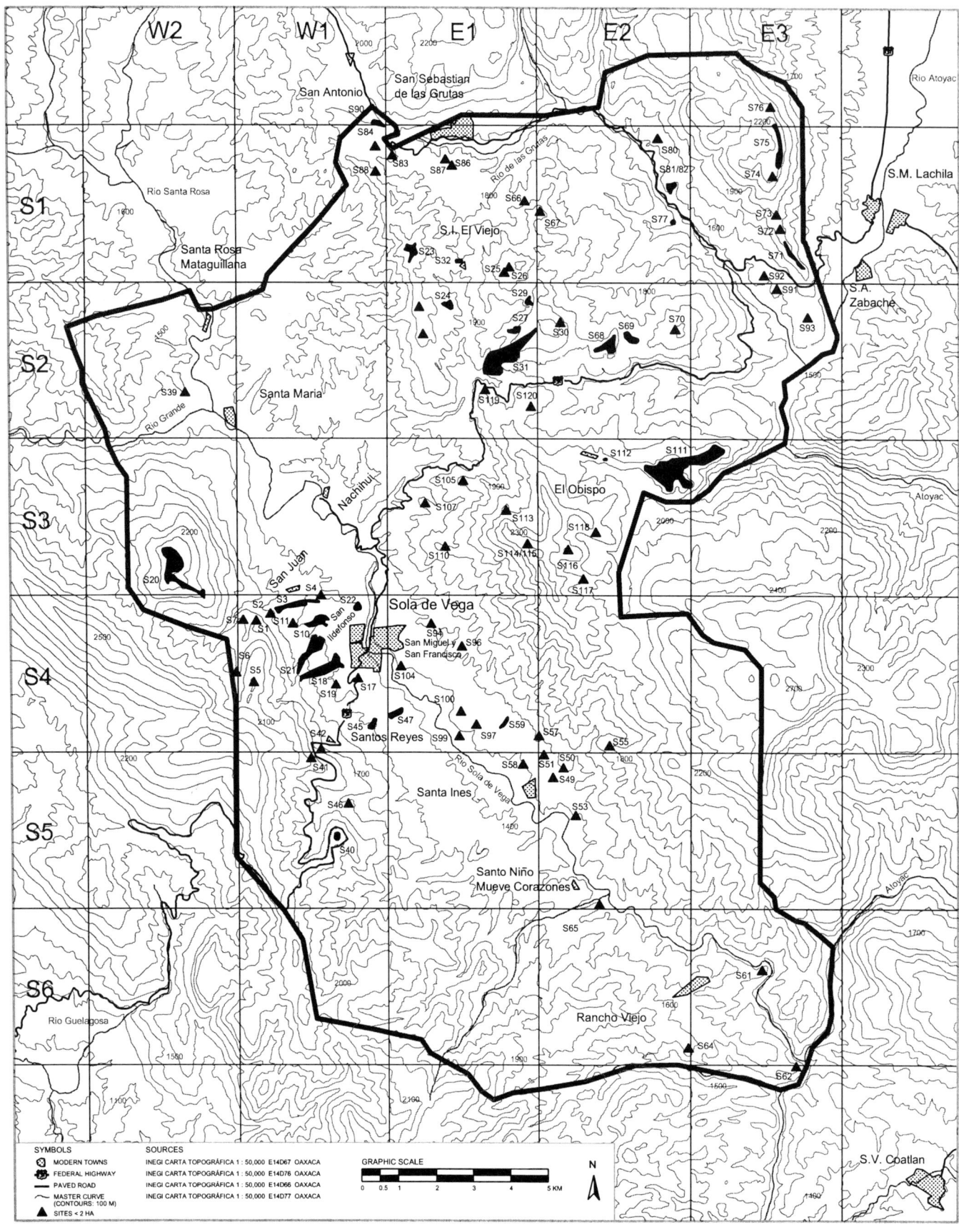

polities, similar to the historically known *cacicazgos*. By Period V only two of Sola's *cacicazgos* survived; they were located on opposite sides of the transport corridor through the valley (Fig. 5.1). Each polity differed in artifact complexes and architecture, and was delimited by the fall-off in settlement that separated these coexistent settlement systems. S23, S39, S65, and S97—sites that often had been major regional centers for centuries—were largely abandoned. S18/21 and S111 were new centers each on its side of the aforementioned transport corridor.

Sola still maintained aspects of a militarized frontier, with its site clustering, defensibility, several ball courts, and relatively low regional population density. But in other respects, the region was more like its highland neighbors than ever before.

Sola's regional settlement structure was identical to the valleys of Ejutla and Oaxaca, although its overall population was less than that of these regions (Table 2.6). This was a period during which Mixtec–Valley Zapotec ties were more pronounced than before, because the many separate but equal polities could form ties that ranged from economic to marital (e.g. Marcus and Flannery 1983). After the decline of Monte Albán, there was greater evenness in the size, distribution, and architectural complexity of sites in highland Oaxaca; no single center dominated an entire region, as sometimes occurred in earlier times.

Valley of Oaxaca survey results (Kowalewski et al. 1989:307-66) show a Period V regional settlement system shaped by market forces as never before. Craft production increased, with production sites no longer linked to administrative centers, but was situated to take advantage of multiple potential markets. The size and distribution of polities conformed to a cross-cultural "standard market area." Marketing was not wholly divorced from political structure, however; nobles used the market system to their advantage, especially in the exchange of exotic goods, and the sponsorship of long-distance traders and periodic festivals (e.g. Hunt 1972; Monaghan 1994; Spores 1984:82-84).

Some twenty *cacicazgos* occupied the Valley of Oaxaca (Kowalewski et al. 1989: Fig. 10.8), and averaged 8000 inhabitants, though there was considerable variation in polity size. The Monte Albán region featured one of the many Valley of Oaxaca *cacicazgos,* but the highest settlement densities had by then shifted to the Tlacolula subregion (e.g., Mitla, Yagul, Tlalixtac, and Macuilxochitl). The largest centers could exceed 10,000 persons, but the 2455 Valley of Oaxaca sites averaged just 66 persons per site (Kowalewski et al. 1989:310) and were more evenly distributed than ever before (Kowalewski et al. 1989: Map 8). In macroregional perspective, these small polities continued uninterrupted into the mountains and adjacent valleys (Finsten and Kowalewski 1999). Regional population densities reached their prehispanic maxima during Period V in most surveyed regions (Balkansky et al. 2000).

Ceramics and Dating

Period V ceramics are readily identifiable in surface collections, and similar to types known from across the southern highlands. Examples include the high fired, fine grayware type G.3M,

Plate 5.1. G.3Ms (some misfired) typical of Postclassic sites in the Sola Valley.

Plate 5.2. Sola Valley red-on creamwares, dating to the Postclassic period.

Figure 5.1 (facing page). Period V settlement pattern in the Sola Valley.

TABLE 5.1. Sola Valley Settlement by Environmental Zone during Period V

Environment	Sites	Total (ha)	Population	% Population
Low Alluvium	0	—	—	—
High Alluvium	7	5.20	119	1%
Low Piedmont	34	105.84	2609	29%
High Piedmont	17	32.11	856	10%
Mountain	25	234.86	5414	60%

so designated by Caso, Bernal, and Acosta (1967:445-71) because they mistakenly believed it was of Mixtec origin (hence the "M" suffix). Sola's G.3Ms include outleaned wall, composite silhouette, and semi-hemispherical bowls; none were differentially fired. Sola's G.3Ms were misfired frequently (i.e., not fully reduced) and can appear light brown to buff in surface color (Plate 5.1). Thin gray water jars or *ollas* also are common, as are thin brownware utilitarian vessels.

Sola's local ceramic tradition also continued into Period V. Most sites had fine orange-brownware vessels, often with a creamy white slip that resembles (and was perhaps a local imitation of) the fine creamwares of the Mixteca Alta (Spores 1972). Sola ceramic collections also include true Yanhuitlán Red-on-Cream, Graphite-on-Orange, and polychrome types thought to originate in the Mixteca Alta. Sola's version of Huitzo Red-on-Cream (which was the Valley of Oaxaca equivalent to the Yanhuitlán variety creamwares) was made on the local orange-brownware clay body (Plate 5.2). As will be discussed in greater depth below, there were differences in ceramic assemblage between Sola's eastern and western kingdoms, suggesting different spheres of interaction for each of the two polities.

Sites and Their Characteristics

Period V in the Sola Valley had the most sites (83), the greatest occupied area (378.01 ha), and the highest population (8998) of any period in the prehispanic era; only in the twentieth century did the region's population come to exceed that of Period V. Sola's Period V population grew by 2000 persons, a 27% increase over the previous period, but that rate of growth was modest compared to earlier growth phases in the Ic phase and Period IIIa. Period V lasted at least 500 years, making the region's per annum growth rate 0.05%. This figure suggests relative stability, with population growth only slightly above replacement. Sites occupy 18 of 29 grid squares, but are clustered in two distinct subsectors on opposite sides of the valley. Sola's two *cacicazgos* are delimited by the fall-off in settlement.

Period V site locations showed a shift to the mountains; the three largest sites (S20, S31, and S111), as well as 60% of the regional population, were located above 2000 m elevation. Some mountain sites were reoccupations of earlier settlements (S23, S75, and S111), but others became prominent for the first time (S20, S31, and S71). The average site elevation was 1802 m, higher than in any previous period. Of the 83 Period V sites, 38 (46%) had terraces associated with Period V ceramics (a slight decline from Period IIIb-IV). The incidence of terracing and fortifications suggest that defensive considerations were a significant factor in site location. Sola's defensible sites are clustered near the polity capitals, and at endpoints of the highland-coastal transport corridor (Plate 5.3).

Sola's population centers were more diverse than at any time since Period IIIa (see below). Sites averaged 4.55 ha, approximately half the average for the previous period. Valley of Oaxaca sites of this period averaged 3.2 ha, but the Sola Valley average is comparable to that of the Tlacolula and Ocotlán subregions (Kowalewski et al. 1989:310). Ejutla's site size average was 2.94 ha (Feinman and Nicholas 1988). Sola's frontier location could have discouraged individual householders from settling far from the major population centers and markets.

Sites with pyramidal mounds and platforms also contrast with the Valley of Oaxaca pattern. There are 36 Sola Valley sites (43%) that have mounds associated with Period V ceramics—the highest percentage in prehispanic times (although total mound volumes were less than those of Period IIIa and IIIb-IV). Only 13% of Valley of Oaxaca sites have Period V mounds (Kowalewski et al. 1989:310). Until excavation reveals the function of these mounds, we can only guess that Sola might have placed a higher premium on ritual activity. Ritual integration would have provided a means of keeping the peace and cementing political alliances among factions in the absence of an overarching political authority. Sola's location on the transport corridor, with its shifting boundaries, exchanges, and interactions, might have produced a less stable political climate than the Valley of Oaxaca, and hence a greater need for ritual integration.

Sola's Period V sites were diverse in architecture, site function, size, and location, and included administrative centers with several pyramidal mounds, isolated shrines or boundary markers, outposts, military installations, and caves. Site S1 near San Juan Sola, for example, overlies a substantial earlier occupation, but during Period V the site was much reduced in size and formed a gateway from the western kingdom's mountaintop redoubt and ritually significant cave (S20) to the major centers below (S3, S10, S18, and S21). One typical Postclassic architectural form was the sunken patio group (and an additional low mound at S1) placed near the entrance to the main plaza and its earlier Classic period structures. S1's sunken patio group consists of four low (1 m) structures placed around a small sunken plaza (12 × 10 m) with a narrow entrance. One green obsidian blade was found in the site's main plaza, an area that must be crossed before making the final ascent of the mountain. Other sunken patio groups in the Sola Valley (e.g. at Sites S23, S39, S75, and S111) are also associated with small Postclassic occupations or reuse of earlier centers, and are situated on routes leading between architectural foci. The ceremonial areas of Classic period centers seem often to have been reutilized for ritual purposes during the Postclassic period.

Other significant architectural forms in Postclassic Sola include ball courts, especially clustered in or near the two *cacicazgos*. S18/21 was the capital of the western kingdom. The ball court at S21 is 58 m long and was the site's only pyramidal structure; the long axis of the ball court forms a large plaza at the base of a series of massive elite terraces at the site. S22 nearby has remains of another possible ball court, but the site's extremely poor condition prevents a firm determination of its architectural layout. S22 is located at the valley's center, near modern Sola de Vega, and was a necessary crossing point to reach S21 and the passage out of the valley.

S111 was the capital of the eastern kingdom and has three ball courts, sunken patio groups, Classic period mounds reconfigured as Late Postclassic houses with interior courtyards, and two palace complexes (Plate 5.4, 5.5). S112 is on the outskirts of the capital center, and might be considered part of S111's boundaries. S112 has yet another large platform (20 m on a side) supporting a low mound, with two other structures defining a plaza. The dispersed nature of the S111/112 settlement, with its several ball courts, palaces, and other architectural foci, may signal the presence of elite factions within the site. S111/112 also was terraced and had defensive walls.

The relationship between population and architectural complexity varies. S18 and S71 have low platforms, supporting single mounds much smaller than their Classic period antecedents. S31 was a major population center, second only to S111, but has no monumental architecture; its location near S111 shows the way civic-ceremonial functions were especially concentrated at the polity capitals (but S31 may have dated later in time than S111, since it had a high density of polychrome ceramics while the latter center did not). Valley of Oaxaca survey results also indicate a concentration of mound and plaza groups, greater formality and elaboration of architecture, and the widest variety of temples, plazas, and palaces at its Period V first-tier centers (Kowalewski et al. 1989:330). It must be noted, however, that most Postclassic sites were isolated households or small farming communities located on the valley floor. S58 in Sola is a good example of this common site type.

Some low rubble mounds placed on hilltops near the edge of *cacicazgo* boundaries (e.g. S88, S90, S105, S110, and S116) may have marked boundaries or ritually significant locations. Other sites were defensive installations or lookouts (e.g. S5,

Plate 5.3. The fortress at S40, on the summit of this mountain near Santos Reyes and encircled by the highway, guarded the passage out of the valley and was reoccupied during the Postclassic period.

Plate 5.4. Structure 1 at S111, probably the ruler's palace.

Plate 5.5. The main ball court at S111.

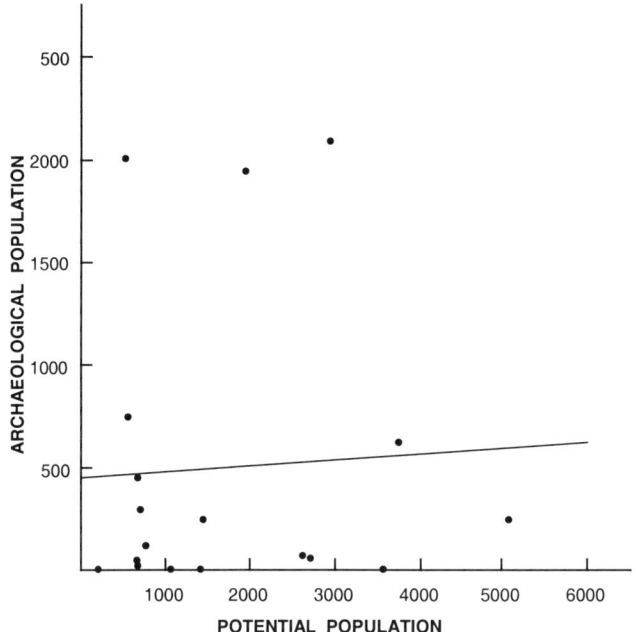

Figure 5.2. Period V scatterplot of potential and actual population in the Sola Valley.

Sola's caves, and determine the full range of activities conducted there.

Settlement and Land Use

Sola's Period V occupation was further removed from issues of land quality than the occupations of earlier periods. Sixty percent of the population lived in the mountains, with their shallow bedrock soils and limited irrigation potential (Table 5.1). Mountain and high piedmont sites together accounted for 70% of the regional population (though the low piedmont still had the most sites overall). A scatterplot of potential and actual population shows no relationship between these variables (Fig. 5.2); the correlation coefficient is insignificant at +0.045.

With the increased productivity of corn (Kirkby 1973), the potential population of Sola was reaching an exponential trajectory (Fig. 2.5), but the observed archaeological population was only 21% of the regional potential. If interpolity commerce was strong, then local production deficits could be redistributed through a market system (Blanton et al. 1993:99-103). Soltecos apparently had more exchange options and fewer environmental constraints during Period V than ever before. But contrary to the expectations of population determinists, Sola's Period V demographic trend was stable at an incremental 0.05% growth per annum. No advantage was taken of the potential productive surplus, and few sites were situated to maximize the best land.

The gap between potential population in occupied grid squares (1732 persons) compared to unoccupied grid squares (1108 persons) narrowed. Sola's most agriculturally productive grid square (S3W1) had no sites whatsoever. Thus, the region's major population centers were not found in the most productive grid squares; the main population centers (S3, S18, S20, S21, S31, and S111) were found in the fifth, sixth, eighth, and twenty-first most productive grid squares (S4W1, S3W2, S2E1, and S3E2, respectively). In fact, 56% of the regional popula-

S6, S68, S69, S70, S74, and S114). S113 is located on the prehispanic and Colonial transport route through the valley, which passed through S111 before crossing the El Obispo range at its highest point and descending into the valley. S113 has two low mounds that straddle the *camino real;* both Period V ceramics and Colonial era coins have been found at this site.

Finally, cave sites (S20, S26, S61, and S90) are another notable characteristic of the region. Sola's caves are associated with Period V ceramics, and some are still used today for ritual purposes. One informant from San Juan Sola stated that the cave near Site S20 was more important to the community than the modern church. It would be worthwhile to excavate some of

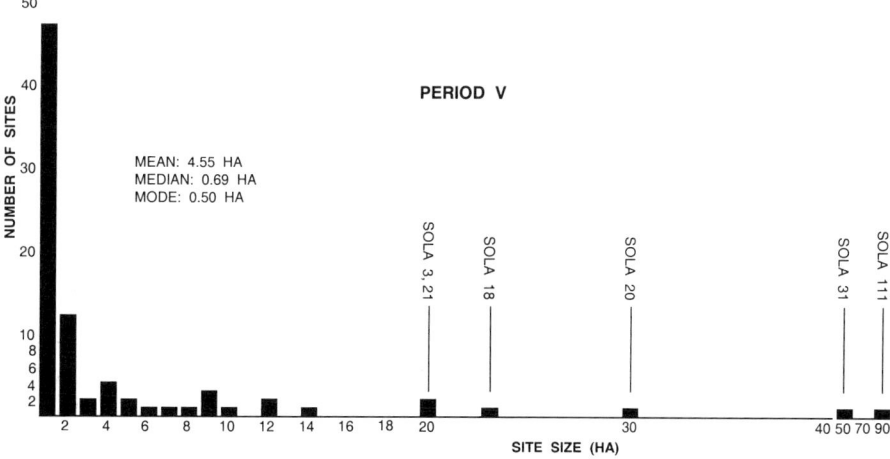

Figure 5.3. Histogram of Sola Valley site sizes during Period V.

tion was found in a deficit production grid square (no other period exceeded this level of risk). Given the distribution of labor, there was potential surplus production for 4943 additional persons, or 155% of the regional population. Still, Sola Valley farmers were producing much less than their labor-based potential would have allowed if population had been ideally distributed with respect to land (Table 2.7).

Some of the region's best quality valley-floor land was left abandoned, perhaps because it was located on the boundary between *cacicazgos*. Yet each polity apparently had sufficient surplus to subsist independently; the relatively marginal eastern kingdom also could have exacted additional surplus from productive lands in the Valley of Ejutla or southern Valley of Oaxaca.

Land use during Period V in the Valley of Sola more closely resembled the Valley of Oaxaca than in earlier periods (Nicholas 1989:501-5). Valley of Oaxaca population had reached its highest prehispanic level at this time, but still remained below its productive potential. Valley of Oaxaca sites were more dispersed than before, but not necessarily better situated with regard to natural resources. Many Valley of Oaxaca grid squares had greater populations than predicted by the productive potential, and major centers were not associated with better quality land (especially in the eastern Tlacolula subregion and the central part of the valley). Each subregion was nevertheless a potential surplus producer for the first time since pre-Monte Albán times. Valley of Oaxaca *cacicazgos* would have been self-sufficient in an average rainfall year, but in dry years an interpolity exchange system would have been needed to offset local shortfalls.

Sola's Period V land use exhibits two contradictory characteristics: it has the greatest potential production (and highest regional population densities), yet settlement was less well situated with regard to local resources than ever before. Settlement was focused on endpoints of the highland-coastal transport route through the region, with much of the valley's best land left abandoned. In fact, several key sites that had been of regional significance for centuries were largely abandoned, despite their location next to prime farmland. Sola's *cacicazgos* would have been self-sufficient in an average rainfall year, but in contrast to earlier times, there was no political organization beyond the region's individual two polities to redistribute productive shortfalls.

Regional and Macroregional Organization

Sola's Period V political divisions are apparent from the regional settlement pattern (Fig. 5.1). Sites were clustered near the polity capitals at S111 and S18/21 on either side of the topographic divide and interregional transport corridor through the valley, with a settlement fall-off in between. A contrast with earlier periods is that at least one of Sola's *cacicazgos* was tied to regions in the Mixteca Alta. The Sola Valley had always before shared exclusive ties with the Valley Zapotec.

Valley of Sola demographic structures are similar to those in the Postclassic Valley of Oaxaca. Twenty-five Valley of Oaxaca sites had over 1000 persons (more than any previous period). But a strong rural/urban dichotomy was present, with most sites being small, isolated hamlets; Valley of Oaxaca population estimates average just 66 persons per site. In the Sola Valley, two sites had over 1000 persons, and a third combined site (S18/21) approached this figure, but some two-thirds of all Sola Valley sites had fewer than 50 persons. Period V Sola had more sites and population, occupied more diverse environmental zones, and had sites more evenly distributed than any previous period—and each of these characteristics was shared by nearby regions (e.g. Balkansky et al. 2000; Feinman and Nicholas 1990a; Finsten and Kowalewski 1999; Redmond 1983). Valley of Sola and Oaxaca macroregional demographic trajectories were synchronous and any ceramic boundaries between them dissolved.

A histogram of Sola's Period V site sizes (Fig. 5.3) reveals several tiers of sites (see below), and the presence of the two aforementioned polities is revealed by settlement clustering. S31 and S111 are mountain sites that straddled the eastern pass leading into the Sola Valley. S3, S18, S20, and S21 are clustered at the western limits of the valley. If the adjacent Sites S18 and S21 are combined, then this polity capital is more comparable in size to the eastern valley. I consider each of these settlement clusters to form a distinct *cacicazgo*.

Sites below the upper two tiers of the settlement hierarchy may be divided with some difficulty into third- and fourth-tier

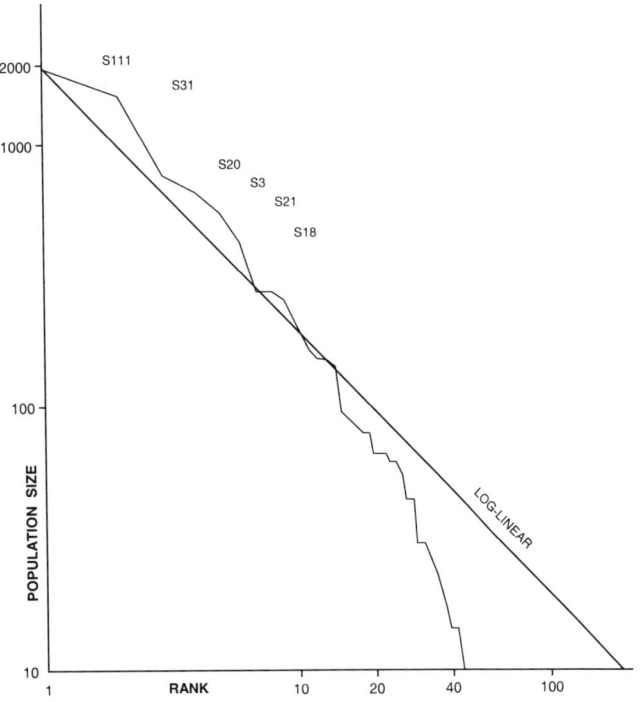

Figure 5.4. Rank-size graph for the Sola Valley during Period V.

TABLE 5.2. Population Centers in Sola, Ejutla, and the Southern Oaxaca Valley during Period V

Site	Region	Grid	Size (ha)	Population	Rank
Jalieza	Valle Grande	N7E9	149.10	6649	1
San P Mártir	Ocotlán	N3E8	156.60	3430	2
Taniche	Ejutla			2970	2
Sta L Ocotlán	Ocotlán	N3E8	90.0	2799	2
Coatecas Altas	Ejutla			2560	2
Ejutla	Ejutla			2358	2
OC-MO-MO-11	Ocotlán	N2E8	96.80	2353	2
Coyotepec	Valle Grande	N10E8	112.6	1968	2
Los Paderones (S111)	Sola	S3E2	89.20	1921	2
El Choco	Valle Grande	N2E3	18.60	1627	2
Sl El Viejo (S31)	Sola	S2E1	50.30	1561	2
La Cruz (S18/21)	Sola	S4W1	43.39	964	3
SM Tilquiapan	Ocotlán	N5E10	21.60	953	3
El Porvenir	Ocotlán	N3E9	35.60	867	3
Valdeflores	Valle Grande	N4E4	31.70	851	3
	Ejutla			826	3
ZIM-SCM-SCM-6	Valle Grande	N5E4	19.70	793	3
	Ejutla			730	3
	Ejutla			706	3
	Ejutla			665	3
La Cumbrita (S20)	Sola	S3W2	30.19	663	3

(Feinman and Nicholas 1997; Kowalewski et al. 1989: Fig. 10.2).

centers; the remaining majority of sites form a fifth tier at less than 2 ha in size. Each *cacicazgo* has its share of third-, fourth-, and fifth-tier settlements. Pyramidal structures can be present at even the smallest sites, but the vast majority of the region's monumental architecture is found at the polity capitals (especially S111, which had no architectural peer in the valley).

Sola's Period V rank-size graph (Fig. 5.4) is convex (suggesting poor integration among centers) and layered, due to the coexistence of separate settlement systems. S111 and S31 form the topmost layer, and S3, S20, S21, and S18 form an independent convex layer. Recall that these two layers are related to sites on opposite sides of the valley, forming the cores of separate *cacicazgos*. While both settlement systems are convex, combining S18/21 or S3/10/18/21 produces even greater convexity, much as was seen in the rank-size graph for Period IIIb-IV. Sola's western kingdom, with its several adjacent centers, is analogous to the multiple architectural complexes at S111, and possibly reflects a degree of intrapolity factionalism.

In the middle tiers of Sola's settlement hierarchy the rank-size graph is more linear, with secondary and tertiary centers tending to log-linearity. But these relationships among lower-order centers may be more apparent than real, the result of pooling independent kingdoms into a single rank-size analysis. Considered separately, the two kingdoms have rank-size graphs that are highly convex at the top, then plummet to lower-order centers, suggesting a concentration of administrative and economic functions at polity capitals. The western kingdom shows little development of its lower-order centers; the eastern kingdom has more strongly integrated centers among its lower ranks, tending to log-linear relationships.

What we see from these hierarchical considerations is a top-heavy system featuring two autonomous polities that are not closely integrated with each other. Whether viewed in regional perspective or as separate kingdoms, rank-size graphs are convex at all scales. The Sola Valley's two separate and distinct but comparably scaled small polities may reflect intrapolity factionalism which began in Period IIIb-IV. But intrapolity factionalism may be more relative than absolute, since each kingdom has its own distinct focal architectural complex (cf. Kowalewski 1994).

The *cacicazgos* of Sola, Ejutla, and the southern Valley of Oaxaca were evenly spaced with regard to each other. For example, the Ejutla "town site" and Coatecas Altas in the Ejutla Valley were 20-25 km from Sola's Site S111 ("Los Paderones"). The southern Valley of Oaxaca polities at Santa Cruz Mixtepec, Tlapacoyan-Valdeflores, and El Choco were all 15-30 km north of S111. No discernible boundary separated the three regions, as had been the case before. This spacing of *cacicazgos* resembled that of the Mixteca Alta (Balkansky et al. 2000; Spores 1972). The Sola Valley was less densely occupied than these other areas, however, and remained peripheral to demographic core regions in the central part of the Valley of Oaxaca, the Tlacolula subregion, and the Mixteca Alta.

Summary and Conclusions

Sola's Period V settlement was divided between two separate *cacicazgos*. S111 ("Los Paderones") measured nearly 1 km^2, had two palaces with standing walls, several house compounds with interior courtyards, three ball courts, and extensive terraces—similar to Late Postclassic Mitla and Yagul (Flannery 1983; Flannery and Marcus 1983c), albeit somewhat less elaborate. The full territory of the S111 polity likely extended into the adjacent valleys of Ejutla and Oaxaca (Plate 5.6).

In the western part of the valley, near modern Sola de Vega, a second cluster of sites was separated from S111 by the imposing ridgeline of Cerro El Obispo, and a fall-off in settlement. The main occupation of this western kingdom was at S18/S21. Several super-massive terraces descended to an open plaza and ball court that distinguished the capital of the *señorío* architecturally from nearby sites. The mountain site of S20 also had significant architecture, but based on ceramic styles, it was probably occupied earlier in the Postclassic than S18/S21.

Several independent lines of evidence suggest that the western kingdom had Mixtec contacts, or perhaps even Mixtec occupants. Characteristics of S18/S21 that are not shared by the S111 kingdom include a high incidence of Mixteca-Puebla polychrome pottery, Graphite-on-Orange, Red-on-Cream, and other fine creamwares characteristic of the Mixteca Alta (Spores 1972). To be sure, these imports are intermixed with the Period V G.3M grayware complex that was characteristic of both S111 and Valley of Oaxaca sites (Caso and Bernal 1965; Caso et al. 1967). However, there are additional differences in ceramic forms within the grayware: western Sola's G.3Ms are mostly outleaned-wall bowls, while G.3Ms from the east are predominantly composite silhouettes. Green obsidian is common on sites in the west, but nearly absent from eastern valley sites. These contrasts suggest that Sola's *cacicazgos* participated in different exchange spheres, and perhaps had different sets of alliances.

Sola's Historical Kingdoms

After the collapse of the Zapotec capital at Monte Albán (ca. A.D. 800), the Valley of Oaxaca and nearby regions broke up into small states until the Spanish Conquest. Such *cacicazgos* were variant forms of archaic states, and subjects of study for both the ethnohistorian and the archaeologist. Ethnicity, marriage, and economic alliances involving Mixtec and Zapotec royal dynasties underlie the political integration of *cacicazgos*. The inception of these inter-ethnic and interpolity ties on the macroregional scale was a catalyst for the Postclassic. Archaeologists and ethnohistorians have much to offer one another; long-term persistent patterns, meshed with unique events, yield better models. But the functions of historic era *cacicazgos* must not be confused with their prehistoric origins, for these are two separate research questions.

Crucial issues for archaeologists are the significance of Late Classic collapses at Monte Albán and Teotihuacan; the timing of incipient *cacicazgo* formation; the reasons for their eventual integration on the macroregional scale; and the role of historical actors such as 8 Deer of Tilantongo in Postclassic origins. Finally, there remains the thorny issue of how to best integrate the archaeological and ethnohistoric records. I argue that we need to reconceptualize these issues: first, in terms of how ethnohistoric sources are used to understand archaeological periods, and second, to better use continuities from Classic period and earlier societies to understand the Postclassic. I will suggest ways that the Sola Valley settlement data contribute to resolving the question of Postclassic origins.

The Classic to Postclassic transition is usually considered a time of chaos, whose temporal rift yielded a fundamentally different kind of society after Monte Albán's collapse (e.g. Blanton et al. 1993; Byland and Pohl 1994; Joyce and Winter 1996). This view is based at least in part on the received wisdom now several decades old, that Late Classic collapses were uniform across Mesoamerica. This view largely antedates full-coverage surveys in Mesoamerica. We now know that most Classic centers maintained significant (albeit reduced) populations into the Epiclassic and Postclassic, and that other sites flourished during this "collapse era" (e.g. Marcus 1992a). The cessation of monumental construction in Monte Albán's main plaza in early Period IIIb-IV (Acosta 1965) did not result in the site's total abandonment; significant populations continued in residence on the hilltop through Period V (Blanton 1978). Other major centers arose in the Valley of Oaxaca both before and during Monte Albán's decline (Kowalewski et al. 1989). I have argued elsewhere that Monte Albán probably lost political control over the Valley of Oaxaca sometime before the main plaza area was abandoned, and that its outlying provinces had long since broken away (Balkansky 1998b). There were also greater continuities among first-, second-, and third-generation states in Oaxaca than have often been acknowledged (cf. Spores 1972, 1983b).

Settlement pattern data from regions outside the Valley of Oaxaca have shown that *cacicazgos* predate Monte Albán's collapse (e.g. Balkansky et al. 2000; Redmond 1983; Spores 1983c). We may debate when the full range of institutions reported ethnohistorically first arose, but regional settlement structures that are otherwise identical to Postclassic *cacicazgos* first take form by Transition II-IIIa in the Mixteca Alta (Balkansky et al. 2000). By Period IIIb-IV, *cacicazgo* settlement patterns were the rule in the Valley of Oaxaca, and I suspect that all of that polity's diagnostic institutions are present by this time as well (cf. Flannery and Marcus 1983d). Semi-autonomous small polities existed in Classic times, and these embryonic kingdoms were preadapted for the Postclassic transition. The Epiclassic would be better understood if it were redefined as a continuum into the Postclassic.

The Sola Valley in the Late Postclassic Period 79

Plate 5.6. Architectural complexes from S111 are visible, as is Cabo de Hacha (the dark landscape feature center left of the frame) and the passage into the Valley of Oaxaca looking northeast.

Ethnohistorians (e.g. Jansen, Kröfges, and Oudijk 1998) are sometimes overly reliant on Whitecotton's (1977) summary of Oaxaca archaeology, which is now out of date, especially with respect to the regional survey results. Bernal (1965), Paddock (1966), and other leading scholars of their era likewise would not make the same arguments today, based on current archaeological data. We are more likely to see passenger pigeons or pterodactyls flying overhead than contemporary archaeologists waxing poetic over the influx of post-collapse Teotihuacan refugees in Oaxaca, or the machinations of Tula's "Quetzalcoatl" on Oaxaca politics. It is incumbent on archaeologists to communicate these new results to ethnohistorians, and on the ethnohistorians to assimilate it when they get it. Our interests overlap in the Postclassic.

This brings me to the Mixtec, the Zapotec, and the misuse of the 8 Deer "Tiger Claw" story from the Mixtec codices in understanding the origins of the Postclassic. 8 Deer lived in the eleventh century A.D. (summarized in Spores 1993). Let us first dispense with the notion that 8 Deer led a rebellion that overthrew Monte Albán's "Classic period centralized authority" in the Mixteca Alta (with varied permutations in Byland and Pohl 1994 and Jansen 1998) more than two centuries after the Zapotec capital had already collapsed (Balkansky 1998b, 1999). The related notion that Monte Albán maintained symbolic authority over the Mixtec (similar to the Aztec reverence for Toltec predecessors) cannot be supported archaeologically either.

Monte Albán did not control regions outside the Valley of Oaxaca in Late Classic times. Monte Albán's territorial expansion reached its greatest extent in Period II, and receded to the margins of the Valley of Oaxaca thereafter (Marcus 1992a). A distinct buffer zone separated Valley of Oaxaca sites in Etla and the central valley from Nochixtlán during Period IIIb-IV times (Kowalewski et al. 1989: Map 7). Moreover, Cerro Jazmín and Yucuñudahui, among other Classic period Mixtec cities, were in the same size class as Monte Albán proper, and cannot be considered secondary based on hierarchical measures (Balkansky et al. 2000). Claims for the Zapotec capital's continued interregional hegemony into Classic times ignore current archaeological reality, and return to decades-old cultural diffusion for explanation.

Oaxaca ceramics also converge on the macroregional scale by the Classic period (Balkansky et al. 2000). It is worth noting that the hundreds of graywares (G.35s) and orangewares from the Mixteca Alta that I have examined macroscopically are identical in composition and surface finish, meaning that most of these wares were produced locally. This observation must be tested through source studies of excavated collections, but I suggest that the old notion that "graywares = Zapotec" and "orangewares = Mixtec (or Teotihuacano)" during the Classic period is wrong. Spores (1972) demonstrated long-term continuities in Mixtec ceramics for the Nochixtlán Valley; the same is true for the Valley of Oaxaca sequence (Caso, Bernal, and

Acosta 1967). Classic and Postclassic graywares are widespread in highland Oaxaca, and do not reflect degrees of political control. I must also insist that Period V begins with the introduction of the red-on-cream horizon in Oaxaca; the extent to which this horizon overlaps with late Period IIIb-IV has implications for surface survey and Classic to Postclassic continuities, but this question will only be resolved stratigraphically.

To be sure, there are Mixtec-Zapotec connections, for the intensification of those ties correspond too closely in time with Postclassic beginnings to be coincidental. But I would argue against the older unidirectional models culminating with a Mixtec invasion, or at least hegemonic influence over Postclassic Oaxaca (e.g. Balkansky 1999). Mixtec-Zapotec interaction was more continuous and pervasive than this extreme view allows. The precursors to the historical kingdoms were already present in the Classic period, and reflected in the small polities that adhered to the margins of large regional states. The most recent settlement data indicate that this mosaic pattern of relative coequals was entrenched on the macroregional scale by Classic times (Balkansky et al. 2000). Warfare under these circumstances was among individual and allied towns, and not based on ethnic or geographic determinants. 8 Deer's epic conquests may have spurred the integration of already extant *cacicazgos* on the macroregional scale, but he did not create them.

The integration of Mixtec and Zapotec royal dynasties is where ethnohistorical models help resolve a decades-old archaeological conundrum—what were Mixtec doing in the Valley of Oaxaca during the Postclassic? Spores (1967, 1974) notes the multiregional integration of Mixtec *cacicazgos* via marital alliances, among other factors. Flannery and Marcus (1983d) extend this reasoning on a still larger scale, and argue that the Mixtec presence in the Valley of Oaxaca in Postclassic times reflects Mixtec-Zapotec royal marriages. 8 Deer, for his part, was at best a catalyst of this process. Oaxaca's multiregional integration of coequal polities was underway by Late Classic times, and these polities were identical in settlement structure and location to the *cacicazgos* of the Postclassic period.

Ethnohistorians, however, have sometimes confused the functional integration of *cacicazgos* with the question of origins. In a recent review of the marital alliance data, Oudijk (1998) shows that Mixtec-Zapotec intermarriage was a normal occurrence; when conflicts arose, it was over land claims and title, not inter-ethnic warfare. Oudijk (1998) dates the first recorded marital alliances to the late thirteenth and fourteenth centuries—and then concludes that the influx of Mixtecs into the Valley of Oaxaca also began during these years. What was happening during the 500 years after Monte Albán's collapse? Oudijk's (1998) inferred dates could represent the limits of historical memory in this instance. Historical sources illustrate the process, but not the origins of the alliance system. Archaeology is needed to address the question of origins.

Now let us turn to Sola's historical kingdoms and compare this region to the rest of Postclassic Oaxaca. Valley of Oaxaca *cacicazgo* capitals numbered about twenty and were spaced 20- 25 km apart from one another (Kowalewski et al. 1989:325). Valley of Oaxaca occupation was densest in the central part of the valley and the Tlacolula subregion, at Monte Albán-Cuilapan, Macuilxochitl, Tlalixtac, Yagul, and Mitla. The spacing and settlement density of *cacicazgos* in the Mixteca Alta was comparable to the Valley of Oaxaca (Balkansky et al. 2000). The major *cacicazgos* often had smaller, satellite polities in their orbits, separated from other polities by fall-off in settlement. This mosaic pattern of settlement continued uninterrupted into the mountainous Peñoles area (Finsten and Kowalewski 1999), the Sierra Norte (Drennan 1989), and Sola, creating a continuous intervalley settlement system (Table 5.2). The description of larger sites, such as Mitla, amounting to a "nearly continuous belt of discontinuous settlement" fits the Oaxaca macroregion as a whole (Kowalewski et al. 1989:317).

Sola was structured similarly, but occupied less densely than its neighbors (Sola had 0.21 sites per km^2, Ejutla 0.86, and Oaxaca 1.14). Sola's *señoríos* resembled third-tier sites (or less) compared to Valley of Oaxaca centers (Kowalewski et al. 1989: Fig. 10.3); they were more like those in Etla and Ocotlán, regions farthest from the Valley of Oaxaca demographic core in the central and Tlacolula subregions (Table 2.6). Still, in most respects, the Sola Valley was more akin to its neighbors than ever before. Sola's individual polities—like those in the macroregion as a whole—forged their own alliances independent of their neighbors. Sola Valley settlement remained focused on the highland-coastal corridor through the valley; it was no coincidence that Sola's two *cacicazgos* settled directly on the valley's access points. Sola remained a throughway from the highlands to the coast, and could potentially link polities from the Valley of Oaxaca, the Mixteca Alta, and the Mixteca de la Costa.

Cacicazgo ties during the Postclassic remain difficult to discern without recourse to the historical record. But as Kowalewski et al. (1989:348) note, the archaeologically observed settlement patterns may reveal the more enduring relationships. It is significant that core/periphery structures are still evident: the demographic centers of gravity in the central Valley of Oaxaca, Tlacolula, and parts of the Mixteca Alta stand out relative to those of Sola and other regions. But on the macroregional scale, the Valley of Oaxaca and surveyed areas of the Mixteca Alta had equivalent Postclassic occupational densities, a situation that contrasts with the demographic imbalances of the preceding Classic period (Balkansky et al. 2000). Postclassic Oaxaca was thus composed of multiple demographic cores, buffered by multiple secondary occupations.

Sola's western kingdom provides an important archaeological contribution to studies of the Postclassic Mixtec presence in the Valley of Oaxaca (e.g. Flannery and Marcus 1983d; Kowalewski 1983). The rulers of the Sola Valley's western kingdom probably intermarried with Mixtec nobles, and might even have been incorporated into an expansionist polity like the one 8 Deer ruled from Tututepec (summarized in Spores 1993). However, the Mixteca-Puebla polychrome pottery and painted fine creamwares found in sites of Sola's western kingdom are more typical of the Mixteca Alta. Green obsidian was also common at these sites, but like the polychrome and other ceramics, nearly absent in the eastern part of the valley.

Sola's western kingdom sites also produced at least one copper ax of the type common in Mixtec tribute payments (Berlin 1951). Other characteristics of western valley sites that suggest Mixtec connections were *lama-bordo* terraces, a specialized agricultural system whose origin lay in the Mixteca Alta (Spores 1969). No *lama-bordo* terraces were found in the east. One woman near Santos Reyes still makes palm-leaf *petates,* or woven mats, another common Mixtec specialization (Warner 1976). The Mixtec ballgame is still played at Santos Niños and Rancho Viejo in the Sola Valley. We also heard consistent statements from knowledgeable Soltecos that generations ago both Zapotec and Mixtec speakers inhabited the Sola Valley. And Sola de Vega's indigenous toponym refers to a Zapotec-Mixtec royal marriage (Bradomín 1992).

The ultimate origins of the *cacicazgo* are a more difficult question. Sola, Cuicatlán, and, possibly some subregions within the Valley of Oaxaca broke away from Monte Albán before its collapse, and began to form settlement structures recognizable as *cacicazgos. Cacicazgos* were extant in the Mixteca Alta by this period as well (Balkansky et al. 2000; Spores 1972, 1983c). This period of incipient *cacicazgo* formation took place by IIIb-IV times; these polities' direct precursors had occupied the margins of Classic period regional states. These small Classic period polities were preadapted for the Postclassic transition, making the latter transition more continuous than most scholars allow (Balkansky 1998b). The *cacicazgo* was an enduring political formation, and its origins predate the Postclassic; the ethnohistorical sources can tell us how *cacicazgos* worked, but cannot describe their origins.

Sola's historical kingdoms were no longer tied to a single political center, as they had been during the millennium of Monte Albán's regional preeminence. Still, the region remained articulated (at least in part) to the Valley of Oaxaca, which by now was not the realm of a single large center, but a demographic center of gravity consisting of multiple small polities at least nominally autonomous. Postclassic Oaxaca was thus a mosaic of major and minor *cacicazgos* on the macroregional scale, and the small Sola Valley polities fit within the interstices of core regions in the Valley of Oaxaca, Mixteca Alta, and coastal Oaxaca. Despite the partly legendary histories of its Conquest-era polities, we would know little about late prehispanic Sola without recourse to archaeology.

Chapter 6

Summary and Conclusions

I have been back to Oaxaca more than once since the Sola Valley project ended in 1996. My colleagues and I have even managed to collect another 1500 or so square kilometers of regional settlement data elsewhere in Oaxaca (Balkansky et al. 2000). So where do we stand now with respect to macroregional concerns? The macroregional database has grown, but what kinds of observations are we generating from it? How do we explain the settlement patterns both within Oaxaca's own continuum, and with regard to general evolutionary principles operating in Mexico and beyond?

The moment of truth had arrived, and Kowalewski asked, "Where are all the macro models?" It was an apt question. We had just had a two-hour session earlier that day on macroregional models, and how the latest Oaxaca survey data could be fit to them. But there was an eerie silence in a roomful of macro thinkers.

There were about 10,000 square kilometers of cumulative survey experience—and several books worth of primary empirical contributions—sitting around a long seminar-room table in Athens, Georgia. It was April, 2000, and we were meeting to discuss the latest survey results. The Oaxaca surveyors' macrotheoretical guru Rich Blanton was there. So was Steve Kowalewski, who plans to continue surveying until he hits Guerrero someday. Laura Finsten, who the old surveyors know is the best of us all in the field, sat in silent readiness. So did Chuck Spencer, who along with Elsa Redmond surveyed the most theoretically compelling 52.1 km^2 anywhere in Oaxaca outside Monte Albán. Ron Spores, the Mixtec tiger now roaming Coixtlahuaca and setting the stage for the next round of surveys, was there too. Another dozen or so students, from places stretching from Madison to Mexico City, also sat in attendance. Some of them already had mud on their boots. And there was silence. Dead silence.

My thought was that those maps of surveyed regions tacked to the wall had finally busted through our old set of half-truths about Oaxaca prehistory. But what new set of better truths would fill the void? How would we account for the spatial patterning? It was no solution for me to turn Sola into a mini Valley of Oaxaca or even Ejutla. It was not working now to turn our latest Mixteca Alta results into *Monte Albán's Hinterland, Part III*. The Mixtec tiger had made that point just a few minutes before. Blanton studiously avoided using the words "core," "periphery," or "world system" in any context the entire weekend. He stated matter of factly that the new survey data had superseded all extant macroregional concepts. The Sola Valley was another piece of the puzzle still circulating in my head.

I will suggest ways out of this quandary in the coming pages. Go back to the field—that is my first answer. I never learned anything worthwhile in seminar rooms like this one. Take some questions posed from the survey data and start digging—that is my second answer. Surveyors do not like to admit it, but we simply do not have enough chronological control to answer many of the biggest questions even on the regional level. And those darned sherds simply do not burrow upward to the surface in direct proportion to their conditions down below. We have to dig to get the site-level details to fill the macroregional picture frame. The surveys must continue as well—that is my third and final answer. The stunned silence in the room was argument enough to continue the survey program.

I have a few theoretical bones to pick as well. The macrolesson for today is that the old models no longer suffice—not the culture histories that surveyors helped to bury with discovered regional variation in the 1960s; not the regional cultural ecology dead since surveyors went macroregional in the 1970s and 1980s. Even the attempt to apply "world system" models has fallen in the face of actual data about peripheries in the 1990s and beyond. There is also the matter of the historical character of many of the key transitions in Oaxaca prehistory. The surveyors have shown the profound degree of synchronicity for major transitions across regions, even though each regional trajectory differs in significant ways. The catalysts of major macroregional changes are often local in origin and short-term in duration. We will be hard-pressed to generate a new master framework anytime soon, but the known variation within dynamic interacting regions is going to play a big part.

I decided that we were not going to figure this thing out in seminars like this one. It was time to start packing the truck again. The truth is out there.

What Sola Tells Us about Monte Albán—What Monte Albán Tells Us about Sola

It is time to reconsider the Zapotec expansion into the Sola Valley, its relationship to state formation at Monte Albán, and the emergence of complex societies elsewhere in Late/Terminal Formative Oaxaca. The new macroregional problem also concerns the Classic to Postclassic transition. Monte Albán and the Zapotec state disintegrated into petty kingdoms, but not all at once. The challenge is to join these separate regional trajectories into a unified body of theory.

The Sola Valley case study is relevant to macroregional issues in several respects: the effects of the Zapotec expansion outside the Valley of Oaxaca, and the changing configuration of the later Zapotec state. Most significant is Sola's place in defining the full range of variation in Oaxaca's prehispanic settlement patterns. As we have seen, the specific regional trajectories were not all alike—but their differences allow us to build better macroregional models.

A phase-by-phase review of the Sola Valley's settlement history follows. I then answer frequently asked questions about the Sola Valley; compare the Sola Valley's long-term trajectory to other surveyed regions; and consider what these comparisons tell us about Monte Albán. The final section of this chapter considers broader theoretical implications. Monte Albán cannot be studied in isolation, or as a matter internal to the Valley of Oaxaca, but must be modeled at the central Oaxacan scale and perhaps beyond. Sola and other regions had varied articulations with Monte Albán and with each other. This macroregional variation is critical to understanding Monte Albán's evolutionary dynamics.

Sola Valley Settlement Patterns, 500 B.C.-A.D. 1521

I designed the Sola Valley Settlement Pattern Project to examine Monte Albán's territorial expansion and contraction, and the local response to the Zapotec state's changing boundaries. The "Solteca" had been visited intermittently before my project, so I knew that the region's prehispanic occupation was tied to the Valley Zapotec, including its tradition of carved stone monuments (Berlin 1946, 1951; Bernal 1965). San Juan Sola was also the site of an Inquisition, proceeding during the seventeenth century, to investigate the persistence of preconquest religious practices (Balsalobre 1988 [1656]; Berlin 1957; Carmagnani 1988). The answers to specific questions about the prehispanic Sola Valley required systematic survey data to put these earlier studies in context, and provide the basis for further research.

Data on Monte Albán's Period II political territory suggested that the Sola Valley was incorporated into the Late/Terminal Formative Zapotec state (e.g. Marcus 1992a). The precise means of incorporation—whether conquest, colonization, or some other mechanism—and its archaeological signature were unknown. Sola's position on a possible transport corridor to the coast made it an ideal candidate to evaluate the Zapotec expansion. Extant regional surveys in Cuicatlán (Redmond 1983) and Ejutla (Feinman and Nicholas 1990a) already showed significant variation within the more general Zapotec expansion.

Sola's later settlement history was also unknown. The Classic and Postclassic settlement patterns should reflect the dissolution of the Zapotec state. The key data would concern Sola's degree of autonomy from Monte Albán, and the manner in which Postclassic settlement patterns arose. These later developments also required a broad spatial perspective to compare variation in regional trajectories.

The Ia phase (ca. 500-300 B.C.). Sola's first settled village was Texcoco (Site S39), on valley-floor land near the Río Sola (Fig. 3.1). Sola was occupied much later than the valleys of Ejutla and Oaxaca, which were settled by the Early Formative period (Feinman and Nicholas 1990a; Kowalewski et al. 1989:55-83). Sola's Ia phase ceramics were in the Valley Zapotec tradition. Monte Albán's foundation seems to have had limited impact on the Sola Valley. The full colonization of the region did not begin until the next phase.

The Ic phase (ca. 300-200 B.C.). The Zapotec colonization of the Sola Valley centered on four terraced sites (S39, S61, S82, and S84) at strategic entrances to the valley (Fig. 3.2). These sites ranged up to 12-15 ha in size and had public architecture. Several smaller sites crossed the interior of the Sola Valley on the highland-coastal transport route. This transportation route continued to be a focus of settlement for the rest of the prehispanic sequence. Ceramics continued in the Valley Zapotec tradition, and included decorated graywares (types G.12/G.17). The land use study suggested that colonization was a strategic resettlement, rather than a random search for new farmlands. Monte Albán's expansion into the Sola Valley seems intended to control this boundary region for its access to the coast.

Period II (ca. 200 B.C.-A.D. 200). S39 became the region's single major population and administrative center (Fig. 3.7). The potential for surplus production was three times greater than during the prior phase (even though the correlation of good land and settlement was still negative). Sola's Period II sites were less defensible than in the prior phase, suggesting that Monte Albán's political boundary now lay beyond this region. Artifacts, architecture, and settlement patterns continued in Valley Zapotec traditions. Monte Albán consolidated its hold over Cuicatlán Cañada, Ejutla, and Miahuatlán by Period II (Feinman and Nicholas 1990a; Markman 1981; Spencer and Redmond 1997). Valley of Oaxaca administration also decentralized with the growth of subregional capitals (Kowalewski et al. 1989).

Period IIIa (ca. A.D. 200-500). Sola was another region of Classic period Oaxaca characterized by new urbanization at terraced sites (Fig. 4.1). S23 (Los Chilillos) became the regional capital during the transition into Period IIIa. S23 was 71 ha in size—more than twice the size of the next largest site in the Sola Valley. S23's architectural complexity far surpassed other Sola Valley centers and was similar to site plans in the southern Valley of Oaxaca. The site overlooked the pass into the Sola Valley. The regional population grew nearly tenfold, but was concentrated on terraced sites near S23. Sola's population growth might have been due to returning colonists from Monte Albán's outer provinces. Sola was on the southern boundary of the Classic period Zapotec state.

Valley of Oaxaca settlement hierarchy changed drastically beginning with Transición II/IIIa (Kowalewski et al. 1989:226-36). Monte Albán reorganized its immediate hinterland after losing its outer provinces, but remained preeminent politically in the Valley of Oaxaca (e.g. Blanton et al. 1993:87-91). Monte Albán might have declined briefly before reasserting itself within the valley. Valley of Oaxaca centers at Jalieza and DMTG (Dainzú-Macuilxochitl-Tlacochahuaya-Guadalupe) suggest that Monte Albán's degree of control was not static or uniform during the Classic period. Sola might have been semi-autonomous from Monte Albán during IIIa times; it might also have articulated directly with the capital, independent of Jalieza in the southern Valley of Oaxaca. These possibilities are not mutually exclusive.

Period IIIb-IV (ca. A.D. 500-1000). Sola's Late Classic/Early Postclassic occupation split into several 20-50 ha sites dispersed throughout the valley (Fig. 4.7). Monte Albán no longer administered the Sola Valley. Earlier hilltop terrace sites were abandoned; unoccupied buffer zones separated the valleys of Sola, Ejutla, and Oaxaca (Feinman and Nicholas 1990a: Fig. 11; Kowalewski et al. 1989: Maps 6, 7). Sola's position on the highland-coastal exchange and transport route could explain the region's continued high population level. Río Viejo was a major coastal center at this time (Joyce 1993a), and Sola could have mediated highland-coastal exchange. Ejutla suffered a major population decline at this time (Feinman and Nicholas 1990a).

Sola's Period IIIb-IV public architecture was more massive, complex, and evenly distributed than ever before. Sola's carved stone tradition was concentrated at major Period IIIb-IV centers. These carved stones were made in Valley Zapotec style, and could signal new alliances among emergent Sola and Valley of Oaxaca centers after Monte Albán's political decline (see Marcus, this volume). The construction of ball courts also accelerated. More than 40 carved stones and 13 ball courts were recorded on the survey project. With the contraction and retrenchment of the Zapotec state, leadership in the Sola Valley may have become more symmetrical, as competitive local elites sought to effect monumental displays to help solidify their power. This was the period of *cacicazgo* origins in the Sola Valley.

Period V (ca. A.D. 1000-1521). Sola coalesced into two separate petty kingdoms by the Late Postclassic, allied to different Mixtec and Zapotec regions (Fig. 5.1). Sola Valley population was now at its highest prehispanic level. Sola's *cacicazgos* were located on opposite ends of the passage across the valley. Postclassic occupation now extended uninterrupted from the Valley of Oaxaca to Ejutla, Sola, the surrounding mountains, and the Mixteca Alta. *Señoríos* were located every 20-25 km across the Oaxaca macroregion. Multiple demographic cores occupied this zone. Sola remained linked to larger-scale networks of interaction, but via alliances, ritual, and exchange rather than political subordination.

Answering Questions about the Sola Valley

1. What persistent macroregional factors linked the valleys of Sola and Oaxaca through successive political fluctuations?

Ethnicity was one factor, meaning shared Zapotec culture, starting with the initial colonization of the Sola Valley. Highland-coastal exchange was another persistent theme of Sola Valley occupation. Sola also played the potential role of demographic safety valve, and was a defensive buffer, for the Valley of Oaxaca during certain periods.

2. How did Sola Valley settlement patterns shift over time, compared to other regions in Oaxaca?

Variation in settlement patterns is the key lesson from ongoing Oaxaca surveys. Sola was not the Valley of Oaxaca in miniature, nor even identical to the nearby Ejutla Valley. Sola was not colonized until the Ic phase, but its Period II configuration was remarkably similar to that of nearby regions incorporated into the Zapotec state. Sola's transition into Period IIIa was similar to that of the valleys of Ejutla and Oaxaca, but different from Cuicatlán's trajectory. By Period IIIb-IV, however, the Sola Valley's small kingdom or *cacicazgo* settlement pattern provided a significant contrast to adjacent portions of Ejutla and the Valley of Oaxaca. The key to building better models is recognizing how regional differences were related to episodic transitions (e.g. the changing trajectories of Ic/II, II/IIIa, or IIIb-IV times).

3. What was the precise timing of the Sola Valley's initial occupation?

Colonization occurred during the Ic phase. A series of outposts on terraced hilltops guarded passages into the valley. High quality farmland was often ignored in favor of controlling the exchange corridor to the coast. This single result (the Ic phase timing) is crucial to understanding the Zapotec expansion in this region. Other highland regions had very different initial occupation dates.

4. How did population/resource balances affect Sola Valley settlement patterns over time?

Sola's earliest settlers were not seeking the best agricultural land, regardless of the population situation in the Valley of Oaxaca. Monte Albán might have had local resource stress until it took control over the entire Valley of Oaxaca. This stress could have figured in the expansion equation. Sola, however, was significant for its access to the coast rather than as a breadbasket. The earliest colonization in the Ic phase had a strong political dimension because of its defensive nature and control over an important exchange route. Even in later periods with higher regional population, the Sola Valley never approached its theoretical carrying capacity. Sanders, Parsons, and Santley's (1979:360) expectation that 80% of regional settlement patterns are explained by land use is probably closer to 20% in the areas so far surveyed in Oaxaca.

5. How significant was Monte Albán's foundation (the urban dimension) for understanding other social innovations (such as state formation)?

These are separate questions. Monte Albán's founding at the onset of the Ia phase occurred a century or two before archaeological manifestations of an early Zapotec state (integrated multi-tiered regional hierarchies and excavated building plans of state institutions) start to consolidate in the Ic phase. It is not before the onset of Period II that the full package of state indicators comes together. The political organization of Sola's Ia phase is ambiguous at best. The occupation looks like the unsystematic budding-off of one small group of colonists from a nearby Middle Formative village. It was not until the Ic phase that a massive population influx of Valley Zapotec occurred, and this influx was clearly part of a targeted effort to control the region for political purposes. Monte Albán's rulers possibly sought access to the Oaxaca coast, where Zapotec ceramic styles show up. Zapotec state formation thus occurred in the context of territorial expansion (e.g. Spencer 1998).

6. If Monte Albán controlled a multiregional political territory, then how did processes of incorporation manifest themselves in regions outside the Valley of Oaxaca?

Highland regions such as Cuicatlán had an influx of grayware and creamware imports and imitations of Valley of Oaxaca ceramics. The Zapotec expansion is associated with the Oaxaca grayware expansion, but the ceramics could signify differing kinds of interaction. The question becomes how to differentiate simple exchange, whatever its equivalence, from alliance, colonization, and conquest among other possible interactions. Each subject or affected region also grew in administrative complexity. Regional centers in Cuicatlán, Miahuatlán, Ejutla, and Sola were remarkably similar in their architectural layouts, at least in terms of scale and complexity relative to the Valley of Oaxaca. The Ic phase to Period II transition had pervasive, multiregional shifts, from colonization/conquest to formal incorporation into the Zapotec state administrative network; yet each region was not necessarily affected in the same way. Monte Albán conquered Cuicatlán, colonized Sola, raided Mixtec centers, and co-opted (with alliance and the potential threat of force) Ejutla and Miahuatlán. These differing regional trajectories were related historically. Sola was colonized to act as a buffer zone against rival powers and to gain access to distant provinces.

7. Why did complex societies emerge in regions outside Monte Albán's political control?

Political evolution on the central Oaxacan scale was a two-way street. State institutions did not arise at Monte Albán and spread outward, but were dispersed among several participating societies beginning in Ic times and coalescing in Period II. Monte Negro's temples (Acosta and Romero 1992); Tilcajete's multiroom palace and temple (Spencer and Redmond 2001); and the earliest ball courts (Kowalewski et al. 1991) were part of a shared elite political culture beyond single sites and regions. Monte Albán's expansion catalyzed Oaxaca's urban revolution, but cannot account for all its constituent parts. The co-occurrence of early state formation in the Mixteca Alta and at Monte Albán was more reciprocal than unidirectional in origin.

8. How was Monte Albán–coastal interaction connected to the Sola Valley, and does the timing of sequential expansion fit?

Sola's Ic phase colonization coincided with Oaxaca graywares appearing on the Pacific coast (e.g. Joyce, Winter, and Mueller 1998:20-36). Graywares came to dominate lower Río Verde Valley ceramic assemblages, including imports and local imitations of Valley of Oaxaca ceramics (Joyce 1993b). It is unlikely that these imported ceramics simply washed down from the highlands on their own. Not coincidentally, G.17 "fish plates" replaced earlier terrestrial species on effigy vessels at Monte Albán and other highland regions in Ic times (Caso, Bernal, and Acosta 1967:32-35; Spencer and Redmond 1997:161-62). Coastal population growth and changing social complexity also began during the Ic phase, just as Monte Albán began its extraregional expansion (e.g. Joyce 1993a; Joyce, Winter, and Mueller 1998). Settlement shifted (apparently) to the hills, and some sites such as Río Viejo were urbanized.

There are other data suggesting significant highland–coastal interaction. San Francisco Arriba was a walled hilltop site that became prominent on the Oaxaca coast at this time, and had a ceramic complex similar to Monte Albán I and II (de Cicco and Brockington 1956). The site overlooks modern Tututepec, shown on the Building J conquest monuments as one of the provinces claimed by Monte Albán during Period II (Marcus and Flannery 1996:196-98). Access to coastal products and more distant sources of exchange fueled the Valley Zapotec political economy. Such activities are evident in the conquest of the tropical Cuicatlán Cañada, the movement of marine shell into the highlands, and the appearance of Valley of Oaxaca ceramic styles on the coast. San Francisco Arriba is a candidate for a Zapotec outpost or at least interacting local center. Monte Albán's expansion and concurrent changes on the Pacific coast were not coincidental.

9. How did macroregional dynamics shift after Monte Albán's decline?

Sola's break from Monte Albán gives one timeline on the collapse of the Zapotec state. The Period IIIa situation was more ambiguous and probably less static than is often supposed. Sola's II/IIIa transition into the Classic period was part of broader macroregional shifts, and could indicate an earlier cycle of decline at Monte Albán. Subsequent ties to the Zapotec state—even a renewed capital—would have been structured differently from Formative times. By Period IIIb-IV, the Sola Valley was fully autonomous, being inhabited by multiple small polities similar in size and regional structure to later *cacicazgos*. Sola's Period IIIb-IV centers were forming new alliances with Valley of Oaxaca centers, probably independently of one another. These new alliances are suggested by the regional settlement structure, and especially by the proliferation of hieroglyphic texts in the Sola Valley. Sola's carved stones signify elite claims to political authority, and are similar to the Valley of Oaxaca tradition (see Marcus, this volume).

10. Have we surveyed enough by now?

In a recent NSF proposal review, I was told that Oaxaca's continuing regional surveys would soon be *counterproductive* for understanding macroregional issues; that more analysis was required of extant regional data sets (something always true for all data sets); and that intensive surveys and excavations were needed to clarify chronological and other issues (another truism). In thinking about these remarks today (after having just finished another 1500 km² of survey), I still do not understand them. We cannot talk about macroregional issues in the absence of data about regions that remain unknown archaeologically. The issue is not really to choose survey over excavation or the reverse but to do both. The number one lesson of the Oaxaca surveys is the continuing surprises that come with expanding the survey coverage (e.g. Finsten and Kowalewski 1999). We still do not realize the full range of variation in regional settlement patterns—and until we do, there are questions that cannot be resolved. I have more to say about this point in "Study Implications" below.

How the Regional Trajectories Compare

The five highland valleys covered in this section are among Oaxaca's most important comparative cases on the regional level. There are several ethnic groups, and multiple microenvironments, in the valleys of Nochixtlán, Oaxaca, Cuicatlán, Ejutla, and Sola. Most important, however, is that their regional trajectories vary, often drastically. It is my contention that the separate trajectories were related historically during times of transition—and that this variation is one basis for better models of state formation and collapse. The field methods and publication standards employed in the five survey areas are comparable. These regions interacted with one another in times past.

They also revolved geographically on Monte Albán's axis—though their specific characters often owed as much to local factors as to Monte Albán's influence. I will describe the research background, the main results for issues of state formation and collapse, and how the macroregional perspective replaces Monte Albán–centered views with more comprehensive explanations.

Nochixtlán Valley (1966-1999)

Modern survey work in the Nochixtlán Valley began with Ronald Spores in 1966, and his efforts to find the prehistoric origins of Mixtec social stratification and the *cacicazgo* (Spores 1972). Subsequent regional research in Nochixtlán has considered urbanism at Yucuita (Plunket 1983) and *cacicazgo* origins at Tilantongo and Jaltepec (Byland and Pohl 1994). The most recent regional survey was in 1999, and covered western Nochixtlán as part of a multi-valley survey (Balkansky et al. 2000). Nochixtlán's several crossings and recrossings continue to yield new insights.

The origins of Mixtec cities and states are often sought in conquest by Monte Albán, or other ill-defined influences emanating from the Valley of Oaxaca (Balkansky 1999). The direction of influence is usually reversed for the Postclassic, including a purported "Mixtec conquest" of the Valley of Oaxaca. Classic period Mixtec cities have been generally overlooked, but their interrelationships underlie the Postclassic transition. Alliance-building among coequals now seems the best explanation for the Postclassic Mixtec presence in the Valley of Oaxaca (Flannery and Marcus 1983d). Mixteca Alta regions interacted with Monte Albán and other Valley of Oaxaca polities from Late Formative times onward, but the extreme conquest and control models are overdrawn, as are considerations of exclusive regional-level autonomy.

Regional studies of the Mixtec urbanization are based on Huamelulpan, Monte Negro, Yucuita (reviewed in Balkansky 1998b; 1999), and now Cerro Jazmín (Balkansky et al. 2000). The Mixtec urban pattern consisted of dense occupations on terraced hilltops (Spores 1983a). Multiple *lama-bordo* (agricultural) terraces descended from hilltops even within urban settings. Monte Albán never conquered large portions of the Mixteca Alta, but militarism was a factor in Mixtec urbanization.

Scholars who favor Monte Albán conquest base their interpretations on the presence of Valley of Oaxaca graywares at Mixtec sites (e.g. Plunket 1983:355-72), or the assumption that since conquest occurred elsewhere, it must also explain the Mixteca Alta (Byland and Pohl 1994:55). Yet the local ceramic continuity is ignored. The relevant settlement patterns, especially their underlying continuities across the urban threshold, are likewise discounted (see Spores 1983a). The consistent cross-valley patterning of the Mixtec urbanization makes the notion of widespread conquest by Monte Albán even less tenable (Balkansky et al. 2000).

Monte Negro was the quintessential early Mixtec urban center (e.g. Acosta and Romero 1992). As regional surveys have progressed (e.g. Byland and Pohl 1994), the site has come to be seen as one of several early urban variants (Balkansky et al. 2000). Monte Negro's mountaintop site plan consists of a linear array of sunken courtyards, flanking buildings (including excavated temples), and columns surrounded by residential terraces. The buildings were numerous (extending for 200 m along the hilltop) but not massive (no structure was higher than 3 m). Monte Negro was built and abandoned within the Monte Albán Ic phase. The site measured 78 ha, and had an estimated 2500-5000 persons in residence. Monte Negro's foundation coincided with the abandonment of its local precursor site at La Providencia and its satellites. As in other parts of the Mixteca Alta, there was convincing evidence (timing and population size) for a shift from the earlier extended communities to the successor urban center.

Huamelulpan was located west of the Nochixtlán Valley; its urbanization also began during Monte Albán's Ic phase expansion, but continued into Period II (Balkansky 1998a; Gaxiola 1984). Huamelulpan's founding was coincident with the abandonment of its local precursor site at Tayata. Graywares appeared at Huamelulpan, but in such limited numbers that they never replaced the local tradition. Huamelulpan continued as a major center into Period II, by which time the site was 205 ha in size with a minimal population estimate of 5000-10,000 persons. Huamelulpan had over twenty mounds in varied arrangements, five formal plazas, two monumental multi-tiered platforms, carved stones with Zapotec-style glyphs, and a ball court. Huamelulpan was surrounded by multi-tiered site and architectural hierarchies. Yucuita followed a similar trajectory in the Nochixtlán Valley (Plunket 1983; Spores 1972, 1983a).

Mixtec cities consolidated for defense, but were limited territorially by Monte Albán and each other. Cerro Jazmín and Monte Negro were founded and abandoned within the Ic phase. Huamelulpan and Yucuita were in the same size class as Monte Albán, and located on terraced, defensible hilltops. These latter two Mixtec centers survived into Period II as the capitals of autonomous states. Other kinds of interaction, short of outright conquest, account for these coevolving early states and the extensive local continuities in the Mixtec sequence.

Archaeological research in the Mixteca Alta has focused on the origins of urbanism and the *cacicazgo,* but at the expense of the Classic period. Yucuñudahui was the archetype of the Classic period Mixtec site, similar to Monte Albán in the Valley of Oaxaca (Caso 1938). This analogy, however, has never been tested over a broad area. The transition from the Classic period regional state to the Postclassic *cacicazgo* is another matter. Bernal (1965) found discontinuous Classic and Postclassic ceramic horizons in his Mixteca Alta excavations. Spores (1972, 1983c), however, recognized regional settlement continuities, and further suggested that Yucuñudahui was one of several Classic period Nochixtlán Valley polities. I would suggest that the integration of Classic period Mixtec polities is related to the issue of Classic to Postclassic continuity.

The Classic to Postclassic transition in the Mixteca Alta must be understood in the absence of a centralizing power such as the Monte Albán state. Classic Mixtec states belonged to the second wave of urbanization, and each center occupied its own small valley (or sector of the larger Nochixtlán Valley). Earlier hill-forts were reoccupied, but many new terraced sites were constructed. The reoccupation of rural areas began during Transición II/IIIa, concurrent with population losses at Huamelulpan and Yucuita. The major new Nochixtlán centers included Cerro Jazmín, Etlatongo, Jaltepec, the Tilantongo cluster, and Yucuñudahui. These sites occupied the same hilltops—and controlled similarly sized territories—as the Postclassic *cacicazgos.* By the time of the local Period IIIb-IV equivalent, some Mixteca Alta regions had been abandoned, but occupation was continuous in the Nochixtlán Valley.

Cerro Jazmín is representative of the Mixteca Alta urban pattern in Classic times. The Jazmín site was reoccupied and expanded with new mound, plaza, and residential terrace construction. Classic Cerro Jazmín measured 228 ha, placing it among the first tier of Early Classic centers in Oaxaca. Other centers in this size class were Yucuñudahui in Nochixtlán, and Monte Albán and Jalieza in the Valley of Oaxaca.

There were nonetheless significant site-level differences among the regions, whether or not one considers Monte Albán. Valley of Oaxaca civic-ceremonial centers were more monumental and varied than their counterparts in the Mixteca Alta. Mixteca Alta public building was more dispersed, but with significant architectural mass relative to site size. Monte Albán was set apart from competing centers by its architectural monumentality. The Early Classic Mixteca Alta and most of its regional polities were relatively decentralized.

The Late Classic population losses affected some regions but not others. Cerro Jazmín and Tilantongo continued as leading centers; so did Yucuñudahui and other Nochixtlán Valley sites. Yet no region west of the Sierra de Nochixtlán maintained its population at Early Classic levels. As many as six polities occupied the Nochixtlán Valley in Late Classic times, and these centers continued into the Postclassic. The Monte Albán state had disintegrated into competing polities by this period (Kowalewski et al. 1989; Marcus 1989).

In macroregional perspective, results from Nochixtlán and other Mixteca Alta valleys restrict earlier models, especially those favoring mass migrations or outside conquest to explain the origins of Mixtec civilization. This observation holds true for both the origins of cities and the later *cacicazgos.* Monte Albán's Ic/II expansion sparked a chain reaction in the Mixteca Alta. Earlier valley-floor sites were abandoned, and new Mixtec cities were built on terraced hilltops. The transition was local and continuous. The explosive growth of Cerro Jazmín, Huamelulpan, Monte Negro, and Yucuita began during the Ic phase; by Period II, the regional settlement hierarchies suggest that small states existed at Huamelulpan and Yucuita.

Classic Mixtec cities expanded into unoccupied lands surrounding the earlier centers. This expansion began as the original Mixtec states declined during Transición II/IIIa. On the macroregional scale, this redistribution of population made each small valley a relative equal. Classic Mixtec Alta cities were too large, too well defended, and shared too many continuities with earlier periods to sustain arguments for external control. Epiclassic settlement was continuous at several sites, including Tilantongo and Cerro Jazmín in Nochixtlán, making it possible to model the Classic to Postclassic transition without external migrations or conquest.

Archaeological models for the Mixteca Alta often alternate from unique culture histories to unidirectional influences emanating from outside the Mixteca Alta. Yet the cumulative survey results show significant variation, such that Mixtec civilization cannot be reduced to one evolutionary trajectory. Mixtec–Valley Zapotec interaction figures in processes of change, but not in simplistic conquest-migration scenarios.

Valley of Oaxaca (1971-1980)

Systematic survey of the Valley of Oaxaca began in the 1970s with Blanton's (1978) urban survey of Monte Albán, and subsequent coverage of the valley extended over successive stages (Blanton et al. 1982; Kowalewski 1976; Kowalewski et al. 1989). Monte Albán was missing its regional context, and comparisons with the primary civilizations of other world areas (e.g. Adams 1981; Sanders, Parsons, and Santley 1979) required a large-scale context. Monte Albán was another case of emergent civilization in a large river valley, and answers about its environmental underpinnings and territorial management were dispersed among thousands of valley sites.

Blanton and colleagues moved away from ecologically functional explanations early in their research, and preferred a systems framework to balance social variables with population and environment. Today's debates (e.g. Blanton et al. 1999; Marcus and Flannery 1996) still revolve on the Monte Albán/valley survey empirical axis, mute praise for the monumental scope of this research. My own perspective (Balkansky 1998b) involves reassessing the valley survey results in the still larger macroregional context now available. We are still asking the same basic questions—where did Monte Albán come from, and what happened at the end of the Classic period?

Monte Albán was founded on a hilltop in the center of the Valley of Oaxaca in 500 B.C. Blanton (1978; Blanton et al. 1993, 1999) and his colleagues argue that Monte Albán's function as a decision-making center explains its location at the central hub of the valley and that the site represents a confederation of chiefdoms. But Monte Albán's rulers may have had different goals; competition among emergent leaders and constant raiding among competing chiefly centers could explain Monte Albán's origins on a defensible hilltop (Marcus and Flannery 1996). And what was the final cause of this transition to urban and state society—systemic needs, or ambitious rulers, militarism and its ideology, and random elements of success or failure?

Evidence for conflict among Oaxaca's pre-urban chiefdoms includes the high frequency of burnt daub found on the surface of Rosario phase sites (Kowalewski et al. 1989:70), the likely result of select structures being targeted and burned in raids. The wattle-and-daub temple that sat atop Structure 28 at San José Mogote was destroyed by deliberately-set fire (Marcus and Flannery 1996:128-29). One Rosario phase village had a defensive wall (Elam 1989). The three arms of the valley and their communities were separated by a buffer zone (Kowalewski et al. 1989:75; Marcus and Flannery 1996:124-25, Fig. 128). Monument 3 from San José Mogote depicts a slain captive that prefigures the more than 300 similar Period I monuments at Monte Albán (Marcus and Flannery 1996:129-30). San José Mogote's rulers might have responded to this social environment by moving into the unoccupied buffer zone separating the valley chiefdoms (though Blanton and others would dispute this point).

Monte Albán's founding population can be traced from the Etla chiefdom at San José Mogote and its satellites (Marcus and Flannery 1996). In contrast, the competing Rosario/Ia phase centers in the Zaachila and Tlacolula subvalleys grew in size, suggesting that these sites did not participate in Monte Albán's foundation (Kowalewski et al. 1989: Tables 4.2, 5.9; Spencer and Redmond 2001). Arguments for state formation based on settlement hierarchies cannot be sustained without these sites in Monte Albán's confederacy. Urban origins preceded state origins, if only slightly in time.

Monte Albán's population grew threefold during the Ic phase, and the density of nearby sites multiplied as a result of the "piedmont strategy" of concentrated rural settlement near the capital. These sites were necessary for protection and food production until the entire valley was unified (Marcus and Flannery 1996:164-65). Monte Albán's defensive wall was completed by the end of Period I (Blanton 1978). Monte Albán's Period I gallery of slain enemies (the so-called *danzantes*) also suggests the intensification of conflict with competing valley chiefdoms. Monte Albán still had significant competition from all sides, making the final consolidation of its home valley uncertain before the end of Period I. However, some regions outside the valley were being conquered and colonized at this time (e.g., Cuicatlán and Sola).

By Period II, Monte Albán's consolidation of valley secondary centers, and more distant provincial capitals, included the dispersal of state architectural canons including the standardized two-room temple, I-shaped ball court, palaces, and "grand plaza" design from Monte Albán into the valley and beyond (Marcus and Flannery 1996:178-91). The unification of the valley is related to the decentralization of administrative control. Significantly, Period II marked the end of the "piedmont strategy" of dense rural settlement near the capital, suggesting that Monte Albán could now expect support from the entire valley.

Monte Albán's conquests were commemorated on Building J monuments. The deciphered conquest monuments refer to places outside the Valley of Oaxaca, especially in locations near the coastal lowlands, or "hot country" locales such as the Cuicatlán Cañada. The highland-coastal connection is evident in the pattern of conquered territories, and the further exchange route into Central Mexico. Each new province was located outside Monte Albán's immediate sustaining area for staple foods, and may demarcate its territorial boundaries much as sixteenth-century Zapotec rulers had done (Marcus and Flannery 1996:195-98). The full array of Zapotec state institutions arises together with the unification of the valley and imperial expansion by the onset of Period II.

Monte Albán's Classic period territory receded from its earlier expansionist phase (Marcus 1992a), but the city itself was growing in size and monumentality (Acosta 1965; Blanton 1978). Monte Albán's growth was part of a second urban climax in Oaxaca prehistory, beginning in Period IIIa with the rise of competing centers within the valley, most notably at Jalieza and the DMTG cluster (Kowalewski et al. 1989). By Period IIIb-IV, Monte Albán had lost control over the valley, and settlement patterns broke into balkanized kingdoms (e.g. Flannery and Marcus [eds.] 1983; Kowalewski et al. 1989). The proliferation of carved stone monuments at these same Period IIIb-IV centers signifies regional elite claims to political authority (Marcus 1983c, 1992b). Monte Albán's urban population history, however, is not necessarily the same thing as the rise or fall of its regional state. I argue that Monte Albán's final collapse was prefigured during Transición II/IIIa, as the capital was losing its distant provinces, competing centers were arising within the valley, and new macroregional ties, especially with Teotihuacan, were instituted. Monte Albán's cyclical rises and falls make it more like other ancient states, and less the monolithic and unchanging entity that most models of the Classic period still convey.

The second urban climax of Period IIIa saw another episode of piedmont settlement, but this time in sectors of the valley more distant from Monte Albán. This new top-heavy regional system promoted circumstances under which the state might collapse. Jalieza, the DMTG cluster, and their neighbors were terraced sites, located on defensible hilltops and situated to maximize local agricultural production. Monte Albán, Jalieza, and DMTG occupied separate arms of the valley, and were in the same population size class (although Monte Albán still had the most monumental architecture). Jalieza and DMTG, moreover, were connected to the densest agglomeration of sites in the valley, a linkage that by-passed Monte Albán (Kowalewski et al. 1989: Map 5). This situation could have promoted latent instability within the valley, and the potential for within-valley conflict (see Blanton et al. 1993:87-91 for an alternative view).

Monte Albán's initial crisis or collapse may have occurred during the transition into Period IIIa. This was the time that the original Mixtec states went into decline (Balkansky et al. 2000). It was also the time that significant reorganization began within the Valley of Oaxaca (Kowalewski et al. 1989:249-50). The Period II subregional centers declined, and were replaced by new hilltop capitals, some with populations equal to Monte Albán. Monte Albán withdrew from its northernmost province in the Cuicatlán Cañada (Spencer and Redmond 1997). Shortly thereafter, Teotihuacan visitors appear on carved stones at Monte Albán (Marcus 1983d). Monte Albán also established a colony at Teotihuacan (Paddock 1983). This Basin of Mexico contact could reflect Monte Albán's efforts to build alliances, or simply gain prestige to support its weakened position at home. The significance of reconsidering the II/IIIa crisis is that it puts Monte Albán in its proper context with the simultaneous decline of states in the Mixteca Alta, and the recurrent cycles of expansion and contraction in other ancient states. Study of the II/IIIa transition also affords insight into what actually occurred at the end of the Classic period.

Period IIIb-IV was a time of "changing politics" (Flannery and Marcus [eds.] 1983), during which a secondary elite founded new centers and constructed monuments independently of Monte Albán. This new construction included pyramid building, carved stone monuments with genealogical registers, and elaborate burials (see Balkansky 1998b). Regional settlement patterns cannot support the continued belief in a monolithic Zapotec state ruled from the center of the valley during this period (Kowalewski et al. 1989: Maps 6, 7). Monte Albán was one of several large IIIb-IV centers in the valley, including Jalieza and a series of sites in the Tlacolula subregion. Monte Albán's own local area was broken into equal-size centers; even the nearby site of Atzompa is best considered separate from Monte Albán at this time. The removal of a center of Atzompa's size and monumentality from Monte Albán proper further diminishes claims for the latter site's continued regional control. Monte Albán's loss of control over the valley brings us into the Postclassic period, but its Period IV decline had been presaged more than once in the past, and the final decline of the city took place sometime after its regional state already disintegrated.

The processes of state formation and collapse are worth reconsidering in macroregional perspective. Zapotec state formation likely came in fits and starts, but occurred over decades rather than centuries. The Ia phase lacks convincing evidence for recognizable Zapotec state institutions or the consolidation of Monte Albán's control over the Valley of Oaxaca. The Ic phase and subsequent Period II have the best current evidence for state formation, concurrent with the Zapotec expansion into outlying regions. This macroregional aspect to the process of state formation could only be guessed at in the past, but today there is an empirical basis for modeling Zapotec expansion. The directional trends in key factors such as population, warfare, exchange, and agricultural intensification alone have not revealed the timing or manner of Zapotec state formation. Ancient Oaxaca's transformation into state society was as much a matter of ambitious leaders expanding Monte Albán's political territory, as it was an ecological necessity or outcome of proper system function.

Monte Albán's particular site-level history and decline is another question, separate from regional and macroregional political structure. Classic period Oaxaca underwent successive convulsions, beginning in Transición II/IIIa when Monte Albán lost, if only temporarily, its control of some valley neighbors. The capital seems to have reasserted itself through warfare and alliance building, and remained strong for the next several centuries, but its control over the valley probably oscillated more than is now recognized. Other sites rose to prominence in Oaxaca at this time, also at the expense of the local first generation states. Some of these places were former Zapotec-controlled provinces, others came from autonomous regions, but both established local polities similar in their regional structure to the later *cacicazgos*. In other words, Monte Albán's rulers had lost control over the valley even before the cessation of monumental construction and population decline in the city. The origins of the Postclassic kingdoms must be sought in this Classic period context of competing centers, not in mass migration of new peoples or "systemic regional adjustments" at the instant of final collapse.

Cuicatlán Cañada (1977-1978)

An integrated program of regional survey and excavation followed the identification of the Cuicatlán region on one of the Monte Albán conquest monuments (Redmond 1983; Spencer 1982). The Cuicatlán Cañada is a narrow pocket of *tierra caliente,* or hot country, among more temperate surrounding highland valleys. This unique environment supports fruit and nut trees normally found in the tropical lowlands; the region was also a passageway into Central Mexico. These factors could have motivated the Period Ic/II Zapotec conquest. By Early Classic times, the Cañada was once again autonomous—long before Monte Albán's Late Classic collapse.

During the Zapotec conquest, Spencer and Redmond (1997) report the elimination of formerly independent chiefdoms coincident with a settlement shift to higher ground. A Zapotec fortress at Quiotepec controlled access into the region from the north. Agricultural production changed, emphasizing tropical products often sought in tribute at the expense of staple foodstuffs. A skull rack was constructed at La Coyotera as an instrument of imperial control. Other evidence of conquest includes burned and abandoned structures, unburied dead, and the imposition of a Valley Zapotec community pattern at Cañada sites. Monte Albán's takeover began in the Ic phase and continued into Period II.

Cuicatlán was, however, among the first regions to break away from Monte Albán. Expansionist pressure from Teotihuacan, troubles within the Valley of Oaxaca, or both could have led to the Zapotec withdrawal. This process was underway by Transición II/IIIa (beginning ca. A.D. 200). Teotihuacan-style ceramics show up on Cerro de Quiotepec, the only site on that part of the Cañada with significant occupation continuing into the Classic period. The remainder of the Quiotepec area's imperial facilities were abandoned, and settlement patterns shifted toward a better fit between population and environment. Excavated botanical remains show that staple foods began to replace the earlier emphasis on tribute items. The public sectors of sites were moved, and a local construction boom took place, including many new plazas, mounds, and ball courts. The area of the skull rack at La Coyotera was abandoned. Redmond (1983:145), writing about the changed settlement landscape, concludes that "the specialized and artificial character of Zapotec military control" waned, along with a change to dispersed occupations similar to *cacicazgos.*

The Late Formative Cuicatlán conquest now appears to be one of several variants on the theme of Monte Albán expansion. Cuicatlán was located along an exchange corridor with Central Mexico, and its unique *tierra caliente* environment provided an opportunity for ambitious Zapotec rulers to obtain exotic foodstuffs and material. Cuicatlán and the Valley of Oaxaca had had a prior trading relationship that could have presaged the later conquest. Cuicatlán also is believed to have had an ethnically distinct local population of non-Zapotec speakers, organized into minimal chiefdoms. Monte Albán needed to conquer the Cuicatlán Cañada in order to incorporate this region into the Zapotec state.

Cuicatlán's post-Zapotec conquest settlement history provides significant data on Monte Albán's changing northern boundary. It was during Transición II/IIIa that the Zapotec withdrew from the region, perhaps due to expansionist threats emanating from Central Mexico (Spencer and Redmond 1997:604). Each subsector of the region then organized itself into an independent small polity, similar to a Postclassic *cacicazgo*. Earlier Zapotec-imposed ceremonial areas were abandoned, and new public sectors were constructed, including many ball courts. This pattern of local readjustment in the absence of pervasive state power was replicated in region after region as Monte Albán's political territory shrank during the Classic period.

Ejutla Valley (1984-1985)

The Ejutla Valley survey was a southern extension of the Valley of Oaxaca surveys (Feinman and Nicholas 1990a). This study provides another perspective on Monte Albán's changing territorial boundaries and its relations with an increasingly distant hinterland. Ejutla connects to the larger Miahuatlán Valley, which eventually leads out of the highlands toward the Pacific. The survey results suggest significant changes in the Ejutla Valley during the Late/Terminal Formative. Excavation in a Classic period site attested to the significance of highland-coastal exchange (Feinman and Nicholas 1993). Monte Albán most likely controlled the region by Period II, but any takeover probably "involved episodes of rebellion and co-option" over a long period (Feinman and Nicholas 1990a:234).

Ejutla's Monte Albán Ia occupation was low density, with little or no settlement hierarchy or nonresidential architecture at sites. Surface ceramics were less diverse at Ejutla Valley sites than in the bordering Valley of Oaxaca. By the Ic phase, Ejutla had grown substantially in population, and regional settlement hierarchies began to form. These changes included the presence of public sectors and nonresidential building at some sites.

The top-level sites also had access to a greater variety of ceramics. By Period II, the Ejutla town site had become the regional capital, and featured substantial new public buildings. This single site was far larger and more monumental than any other site in the region; it also had greater access to valued creamware ceramics, the principal ceramic ware at Monte Albán during this period. The Ejutla Valley was relatively undefended at this time, suggesting that Monte Albán control extended beyond this region.

By Period IIIa, the site of San Joaquín had replaced the Ejutla town site as the major center in the valley. This new center was 5 km closer to the Valley of Oaxaca, and its location could suggest new forms of integration with Jalieza and Monte Albán. The Ejutla Valley also had hilltop terrace sites monitoring transport corridors into the valley. Excavation of a Classic period household at the Ejutla town site shows a diversity of craft production, especially shell work, that suggests part of the Ejutla Valley–Valley of Oaxaca connection. Pacific marine shell arrived whole and uncut, and was then worked into various mosaics, disks, beads, bracelets, and other fine jewelry, presumably for elite consumers at Monte Albán, among other locations.

Ejutla's regional trajectory provides more clues about Monte Albán's expansion and contraction. Ejutla was located along another exchange route to the coastal lowlands, but was a region where colonization and co-option (with possible tribute payments) would be effective, since it was already occupied by Zapotec peoples. Ejutla's new provincial administrative center arose during Period II. Miahuatlán (Brockington 1973; Markman 1981) was the next valley to the south, providing even greater access to the coast; it had a similar trajectory of change, including the rise of a Period II provincial capital (Marcus and Flannery 1996:200-201).

Ejutla's Period IIIa changes could reflect Monte Albán's consolidation of its shrinking territory, and the concentration of population close to its home valley. As in the case of Sola, the many terraced sites in the Ejutla region could reflect defensive concerns on the southern margin of the Zapotec state.

The Ejutla Valley population crashed during Period IIIb-IV, possibly because many residents were drawn into Jalieza's growing urban sphere to the north. This pattern is the opposite of what occurred in the Sola Valley. This could suggest that Ejutla's Classic period ties to the Valley of Oaxaca were of a different order than those in the Sola Valley. Monte Albán's varied mechanisms of interaction and degrees of political control over other Classic period centers in highland Oaxaca should become an area for future research.

Sola Valley (1995-1996)

Sola was yet another regional trajectory altered by contact with the Valley Zapotec. The full coverage survey reported here was another comparative case of Monte Albán's expansion and contraction. The extent to which regions varied—from the strong conquest pattern in Cuicatlán, the similarities between Sola and nearby Ejutla, and Monte Albán's impact on coastal polities—were among the guiding research objectives. Specific questions included placing its famous carved stones in their regional context and determining the time of initial colonization.

Sola Valley settlement began much later than Ejutla's or the Valley of Oaxaca's. Sola's Ic phase colonization came in the form of hilltop terrace sites guarding access points into the valley. Several smaller sites crossed the mid-valley transport route to the coast. The grayware ceramics fit the Monte Albán sequence. Yet these earliest sites were not especially well situated for food production, whether for farmers wanting the best land or for tribute payment. Monte Albán's desire for control over transport routes to the coastal lowlands might better explain Sola's initial colonization.

Sola's Period II occupation could reflect its transition into a tributary province of the Zapotec state. The regional population was consolidated at a single provincial capital; Monte Albán-style ceramics (especially decorated creamwares) were concentrated there. Sites were better located to increase potential food production, perhaps to support the regional capital's new administrative apparatus, or for Zapotec traders and military personnel that could have traveled through the region. Sola's Period II sites were not as defensible as in Ic, suggesting that the region lay well within Monte Albán's political territory.

Sola's Classic period settlements show mechanisms whereby local elites sought to establish their autonomy during Monte Albán's decline. By Transición II/IIIa, the earlier regional capital was losing population to new mountaintop settlements that overlooked the pass into the valley. Sola during Period IIIa looked similar to Ejutla, with a new regional capital situated closer to the Valley of Oaxaca, and the establishment of many fortified sites on the boundary of the Zapotec state. We see a second wave of colonization, possibly coming in the reverse direction, as Zapotec outposts or colonies nearer the Pacific coast were abandoned. By Period IIIb-IV, Sola Valley centers were scattered throughout the region, each with its own monumental precinct, ball court, and carved stones. The carved stones conveyed themes of genealogical descent and legitimacy, and signify the region's relative autonomy. Ejutla's population crashed at this time, but Sola's optimal placement on the coastal exchange route was one factor allowing it continued Late Classic vitality. Successful alliance-building with new Valley of Oaxaca polities was another factor.

Sola thus demonstrates yet another regional trajectory within the general parameters of the Zapotec expansion. Some parts of the expansion model find support from the fact that Sola was colonized in the Ic phase, when an already complex settlement system existed in the Valley of Oaxaca. Sola's occupation was likely designed to gain control of an exchange corridor to the Oaxaca coast, which would have provided Valley Zapotec rulers with coveted exotics, including fish and marine shell, tropical foodstuffs, and access to even more distant exchange spheres. By Period II, the growth of Sola's single regional capital matched events in other nearby regions.

Monte Albán's territorial contraction is evident by Period IIIa in the Sola Valley, when colonists returning from the south could account for the steep population growth and the defensible settlements. Sola's Period IIIb-IV occupation likely reflects Monte Albán's final collapse with its ensuing local scramble for prestige and authority. Sola's emergent local leaders used monumental displays carved in stone, massive building programs (perhaps including ball courts to mediate interpolity conflict), and efforts to create new alliances and thereby solidify their power.

How the Macroregion Changes Views about Monte Albán

Since the 1960s, contributions from the regional survey program have changed our views about Monte Albán, putting the Zapotec capital into its proper spatial context. Monte Albán's population history was once equated with the political history of the Valley of Oaxaca. Monte Albán and the Zapotec state were often assumed to be dual aspects of the same phenomenon, and to have arisen and collapsed in the same time and manner. However, this conflated two separate phenomena: the events surrounding the rise and fall of a great city, and the larger-scale processes of state formation and collapse. The macroregional comparisons just discussed suggest that these events must be decoupled before better models can be constructed. The key evolutionary transitions were convergent processes, with interaction on the macroregional scale linking each local trajectory historically. In other words, we need a more dynamic model of social evolution to encompass the growing range of regional variation.

Monte Albán's urban population history must be viewed separately from our models of political structure in the Valley of Oaxaca. This single observation is perhaps the most significant contribution of the Oaxaca survey program, even though many of my fellow surveyors themselves refuse to see it. A second important observation is that evolutionary trends alone cannot account for the range of variation that is now apparent in macroregional perspective. That is why I suggest social action theory (Marcus and Flannery 1996:29-31) to model the expansionist early states and their impact on other regions, and the later emergent elite factions vying for political authority as regional states broke apart (Balkansky 1998b). Evolutionary-ecological structures still remain important, but selection operates on the variation introduced by human agency (e.g. Spencer 1990, 1993). An exclusive focus on evolutionary trends forces scholars to link Monte Albán's origin with state formation, and its collapse with the fall of the Zapotec state. Current results suggest that the two are not linked in that way.

Monte Albán's Ia phase foundation on an isolated hilltop, away from the valley's best agricultural land in Etla, exemplifies the role of human agency in the city's origins. Hilltops were sacred, and could bolster a ruler's argument for resettling thousands of Zapotec from centuries-old valley-floor villages; hilltops also served defensive and offensive aims, and could provide a redoubt from which to overwhelm rival valley chiefdoms.

Monte Albán began expanding into regions outside the Valley of Oaxaca by the Ic phase. This Zapotec expansion was a context for change throughout ancient Oaxaca, though its effects varied from region to region. Monte Albán conquered Cuicatlán, colonized Sola, and possibly raided Mixteca Alta centers by Ic times, yet may not have controlled the entire Valley of Oaxaca prior to the onset of Period II. Ejutla and Miahuatlán were annexed or co-opted diplomatically by Period II.

Monte Albán's Period II territory extended from Cuicatlán to the Pacific piedmont (e.g. Marcus and Flannery 1996:195-207). The architectural manifestations of Zapotec statecraft (two-room temples, palaces, and ball courts) form a unitary complex by this time—present at the capital, at Valley of Oaxaca secondary centers, and at provincial capitals outside the valley proper. Monte Albán's expanding territorial size put constraints on management, and required qualitatively different forms of administration than its precursor societies (e.g. Spencer 1998). State formation was crucially linked to the process of Zapotec expansion, but there was yet another dimension to this transition. Monte Albán's expansion also set off a chain reaction that catalyzed the emergence of complex societies in the Mixteca Alta and possibly on the Oaxaca coast. Mixtec polities nucleated to resist Zapotec expansion and formed their own states. This is one more example of the synergies binding early complex societies, a reminder that the directionality of change did not radiate exclusively from Monte Albán outward, but had reciprocal evolutionary effects (Balkansky 1998b, 1999).

Monte Albán and its contemporaries illustrate the role of agency in the urban transition—the walled cities were located on defensible hilltops far from the best local farmland, a rapid transition without parallel in Oaxaca prehistory. Each center also had a slightly different configuration, suggesting a range of experimentation at the early capitals. What long-term evolutionary causes underlay this transition? There is no doubt that a minimum demographic density is a necessary but not sufficient causal factor. The shift toward terraced hilltops also created the potential for local population stress. Warfare, however, was endemic among Oaxaca's pre-urban chiefdoms, and this was perhaps a key contextual factor. Marcus and Flannery (1996:241) write that it is "in such historic settings, when the power-building goals of leaders are rationalized by an external threat to their followers . . . that great evolutionary transitions are possible." This fundamental shift in settlement patterns and lifeways was not caused by the blind material forces of population pressure or too little farmland, but in the purposeful resettlement of rural populations into Mesoamerica's first cities.

As the early centers grew in size and power, they soon threatened their neighbors; from their hilltop redoubts, paramount chiefs could more effectively project themselves against their rivals. Generations of Zapotec rulers embarked on campaigns of extra-valley conquest, diplomatic subterfuge, co-option, hegemonic advantage, and population replacement to defend imperial boundaries, and gain access to coveted lowland goods.

Their successes (and claims) were inscribed on conquest monuments set in the arrowhead-shaped Building J on the main plaza at Monte Albán. Zapotec rulers sought not only staple items in tribute, but also access to distant exchange networks and exotic goods to fuel the elite political economy within their territories. On the Zapotec frontier, other societies either adopted changed strategies of territorial control, or would cease to exist. State formation was a political strategy in this context, the outcome of countless trials, and not forced upon societies by myriad systemic pressures alone.

Monte Albán abandoned its outer provinces during the beginning of the Classic period, and new centers emerged in those areas (Marcus 1992a). This transition into Period IIIa was a significant crisis for Monte Albán, although its rulers re-established their relative hegemony, if not outright control, over other valley centers. New alliances or contacts with Teotihuacan also played a role at this time (e.g. Marcus and Flannery 1996:216-21). This was another short-lived transition, similar in duration to the Ic phase.

Valley of Oaxaca political structure was latent with the possibility for within-valley conflict by Period IIIa. The Tlacolula and Valle Grande/Ocotlán subregions began to disengage from Monte Albán. The populations of Dainzú-Macuilxochitl-Tlacochahuaya-Guadalupe and Jalieza populations were now equal to Monte Albán, and the densest valley occupation was not near Monte Albán (Kowalewski et al. 1989: Map 5). Sites in the eastern and southern valleys were situated for subsistence and defense, being part of a second "piedmont strategy" of dense hilltop settlement (Kowalewski et al. 1989:213). Site clustering also suggests that at several scales, Monte Albán, DMTG, and Jalieza operated independently (Kowalewski et al. 1989:210, Fig. 8.1). Valley of Oaxaca subregions were becoming independent polities again.

The Classic to Postclassic transition was another instance of self-interested actors reshaping the limits of the possible during a time of crisis. Period IIIb-IV settlement patterns (Kowalewski et al. 1989: Maps 6, 7) show Monte Albán encircled by lesser sites in Etla and the central valley; to the south, giant Jalieza stood alone on a defensible mountain ridge; to the east, large sites were spaced equidistant to the valley's edge. Period IIIb-IV Jalieza would rival Monte Albán as the largest site ever in the Valley of Oaxaca; semi-independent centers arose in other parts of the Valley of Oaxaca. On the household level, craft producers diversified to offset risk, to bolster the economic autonomy of local polities, and to exploit emerging markets after the decline of regional states. Carved stones contained noble claims to legitimacy at Period IIIb-IV centers. More than ever, writing was a tool for ruling class nobles "in their endless competition for positions of leadership, prestige, territory, tribute, and politically advantageous marriages" (Marcus and Flannery 1996:242).

Monte Albán's royal palaces, painted tombs, and carved stone lintels and doors could suggest a competitive political climate even within the capital. Noble genealogies were carved in stone and expressed through elaborate burial ritual (Marcus 1992b). Monte Albán had fourteen temples on its main plaza that may correspond to the fourteen subdivisions of the city (Blanton 1978:69), suggesting the potential for factional conflict at the capital. Monte Albán's early Period IIIb-IV monumentality may have been as much the product of within-site competition among noble lineages as the reflection of power vis-à-vis other Valley of Oaxaca centers.

Monte Albán finally lost control over the Valley of Oaxaca, and that moment marked the beginning of the Postclassic kingdoms. The small kingdom or *cacicazgo* settlement pattern was already in place by Period IIIa in some parts of the state of Oaxaca, as polities became less territorial and royal houses allied on a macroregional scale. Classic period Mixtec cities rarely held significant territory beyond their home valleys, except in situation-specific contexts where one small polity briefly controlled another (Balkansky 1999; Spores 1983c). Mixtec *cacicazgos* arose somewhat earlier than those of the Zapotec, though nascent Valley of Oaxaca petty kingdoms were visible by Early Classic times. Mixtec and Zapotec societies were arriving at a similar end, albeit from separate evolutionary trajectories. By Period IIIb-IV Mixtec-Zapotec political ties had intensified, triggering a rapid transition to the pattern seen in ethnohistoric documents.

Evolutionary transitions of short duration present opportunities for human agents to generate variation, which then becomes subject to selection. When we use social action theory to augment evolutionary models, specific persons and social groups are articulated with their broader socioenvironmental systems. The broad evolutionary structures condition social change, but do not determine its ultimate course. That is why, within the limits of our archaeological chronologies, I emphasize episodic transitions within which the effects of social actors might be postulated. Actor-based social and evolutionist perspectives are complementary processes in this framework.

Our traditional theoretical frameworks are inadequate to describe historically unique social transformations, where prevailing models emphasize evolutionary trends to greater social complexity without attention to the historically contingent (unpredictable and nonlinear) features of culture change. Some older models project evolutionary trends through time, but fail to predict accurately the timing and sequence of change in the absence of a more comprehensive framework. As we chart ancient Oaxaca's successive social transformations into regional states and civilizations, and their collapse and reconfiguration into petty kingdoms, we must allow for the role of human agency in reshaping the system.

Implications of This Study

Empirical results of this study include data on the relationship of the state to territorial control. Methodological results include determining the relevant scale of analysis for the study of early states. Theoretical results provide explanations for the relationships among divergent regional trajectories. The Sola Valley now has settlement pattern data comparable to other surveyed regions. These data have something to say about the Zapotec expansion; the possible codevelopment of clusters of states; the collapse of earlier states and the transition into the Postclassic; and the utility of ecological, evolutionary, and other interaction models. I conclude my analysis with suggestions for future work in the Sola Valley. We cannot understand Sola without reference to a scale of analysis at least the size of highland central Oaxaca, including Monte Albán and other interacting regions. We may now measure local change in the Sola Valley against macroregional scale factors of social evolution. The general theoretical implications of this research follow.

Monte Albán and the Zapotec Expansion

Monte Albán's expansion beyond the Valley of Oaxaca began as the Zapotec state was forming during the Ic phase and early Period II. Our understanding of this process requires perspectives from Monte Albán and the Valley of Oaxaca, but also its outer provinces and other interacting regions (e.g. Marcus 1992a). The specific regional trajectories varied from case to case, but this variation is crucial to understanding the overall process of state formation. Monte Albán's impact on distant regions was contingent on their pre-existing conditions—demographic density, societal scale and complexity; their distance and accessibility to Monte Albán; and specific Zapotec designs and territorial ambitions. Some of the altered regional trajectories may have been nonadaptive in an ecologically functional sense, a fact that underscores their intentionality.

Sola was one variant on a more general pattern of colonization and conquest (Marcus and Flannery 1996:195-207). The Sola Valley was not occupied before Period I. The Zapotec colonization of Sola began during the Ic phase, and its full political incorporation by Period II clarifies aspects of the expansion. But what motivated the Zapotec expansion into the Sola Valley? Zapotec domination to exact tribute was unlikely, since Sola had no indigenous labor or unique agricultural products, as had been the case with the Cuicatlán Cañada. Zapotec communities, moreover, had already moved into nearby Ejutla centuries before, part of a gradual expansion into unoccupied land (Feinman and Nicholas 1990a). Sola's rapid colonization reflects political motives, rather than the gradual movement into a new ecological zone.

Zapotec colonization and conquest occurred in rapid bursts elsewhere. A Zapotec fortress was built in the least productive subsector of Cuicatlán and its land use reorganized (Spencer and Redmond 1997). Cuicatlán's new productive regime far outstripped local needs, and shifted toward tropical exotics rather than staple foodstuffs. Sola, in contrast, was colonized by Zapotec settlers who seem to have ignored the best available farmland; its sites guarded the passage between the highlands and coast. Monte Albán's territorial expansion seems to have been designed not for staple food production, but to control exchange routes between Central Mexico, the Southern Highlands, and the Pacific Coast. Exotic marine shell is found on sites in the Sola Valley and at sites located along other coastal passages through Miahuatlán (Markman 1981) and Guirún (Feinman and Nicholas 1996). Valley of Oaxaca graywares appeared suddenly on the coast during Ic times (Joyce, Winter, and Mueller 1998).

Monte Albán had claimed the province of Tututepec by Period II (Marcus and Flannery 1996:196-98), and Sola fits squarely between Monte Albán and coastal-piedmont Tututepec. Hilltop terrace sites controlled access points into the Sola Valley, while other sites ranged across the highland-coastal transport route. The possible Zapotec outpost at San Francisco Arriba in the coastal piedmont may have funneled coveted exotics, including marine shell and tropical foodstuffs, into the highlands. By Period II, the consolidation of Zapotec control is a plausible explanation for the rise of S39 as the Sola Valley's administrative center, and for the less defensive posture of sites in the region. Sola's settlement history is thus consistent with expectations of the Zapotec expansion model.

The Monte Albán state formed in the context of this expansion (e.g. Spencer 1990, 1998). As the Zapotec incorporated external regions into their political sphere, regional capitals arose in Sola, Ejutla, Miahuatlán, and the Cuicatlán Cañada to administer Monte Albán's tributary domain. A similar series of regional and subregional reorganizations was underway even within the Valley of Oaxaca during Period II (Kowalewski et al. 1989).

Emergent Complexity on the Zapotec Frontier

Monte Albán's growing complexity had reciprocal evolutionary effects on other societies with which it interacted; in other words, "influences" were not simply moving from the center of the system outward, but reverberating back toward the Zapotec capital, spurring further changes. The effects of Zapotec expansion varied, but were contributing factors in each region's changing social complexity. Some societies were protected by distance and rugged terrain from the Zapotec capital, and had the capacity to resist political domination; indeed in some regions, local leaders probably used the militaristic threat to promote themselves. Early Mixtec urbanization was one possible example of this kind of promotion. The interaction among competing centers was such that states formed in clusters in ancient Oaxaca.

Monte Albán's distance and the intervening rugged terrain contributed to interactions between Monte Albán and the Mixteca Alta being more indirect (e.g. Balkansky et al. 2000). Mixteca Alta population densities and levels of organizational complexity also gave cities like Huamelulpan and Yucuita the capacity to resist Zapotec domination. Nevertheless, Monte Albán's expansion was a catalyst in the appearance of cities and states in the Mixteca Alta during Late Formative times. Huamelulpan and Yucuita defended themselves with greater centralization and sociopolitical complexity, and the expansion of their own political domains co-occurred with the Zapotec expansion. Monte Albán's militaristic aggression sparked a chain reaction in the highlands, forcing societies on the Zapotec frontier to take a more militaristic posture or lose their autonomy.

Río Viejo on the Oaxaca coast also grew in complexity during the Zapotec expansion (Joyce, Winter, and Mueller 1998:81-94). The site urbanized rapidly beginning in the phase equivalent to Monte Albán Ic on the coast. Grayware ceramics on the coast indicate influence from the highlands, although whether via trade, emulation, or takeover remains controversial (Zeitlin and Joyce 1999). Hilltop terrace sites in the coastal piedmont, such as San Francisco Arriba, also became prominent at this time (de Cicco and Brockington 1956). Coastal sites such as Cerro de la Cruz appear to have evidence for a massacre, suggesting that the militarism of the highlands had found its way to the Pacific (Balkansky 2001; and see Matadamas 1999 for a possible massacre at a site near Huatulco). The earliest coastal hieroglyphic writing shows ties to the highlands (Urcid 1993). A glyph for Tututepec on Monte Albán's Building J suggests the Zapotec claimed that coastal piedmont region (Marcus and Flannery 1996:196-98). In this context, the rise of Río Viejo bears too many similarities to the aforementioned Mixtec cases to ignore. Río Viejo's rulers could have used the Zapotec military threat (or demand for coastal products) to promote themselves beyond the limits of chiefly political authority.

Monte Albán's interaction with frontier regions beyond its direct control created a synergistic effect. Mixtec states were not secondary developments in the traditional sense, but part of a broader, co-evolving system. Monte Albán's Ia phase movement to a terraced hilltop was matched by similar shifts at Yucuita and La Providencia (Monte Negro's precursor site) in the Mixteca Alta. Mixtec urbanization was underway by the Ic phase, a time during which Monte Albán's own population grew threefold, and it began incorporating rivals. Competition between these emergent polities may have selected for greater hierarchical development, and the trigger for these changes may have been Monte Albán's militaristic expansion, but Mixtec states were too large and show too much continuity from predecessors to be explained solely by outside conquest.

Monte Albán's Classic Period Dynamics

Monte Albán's Classic period political territory shrank, even though the city itself was more populous and monumental than ever before. Marcus's (1992a) model of a Classic period retrenchment of the Zapotec state's territory is confirmed by the Sola Valley survey results. Monte Albán's Period II territorial limits extended beyond the Sola Valley, but by Period IIIa the region was once again at the edge of the Zapotec state. Still uncertain, however, are the varying degrees of political control within this shrinking territory during the Classic period. The means of integration chosen within the Valley of Oaxaca and nearby regions during Period IIIa probably has much to do with the timing and nature of Monte Albán's Period IIIb-IV decline.

Monte Albán's hold over the Sola Valley during Classic times was less absolute than might be supposed. Beginning with the transition into Period IIIa, Sola's infrastructural buildup in administrative architecture, fortified and defensible sites, and population growth (possibly from returning colonists) reflects local administrative changes, the potential for greater autonomy, and the region's location on a boundary. The valleys of Ejutla and Oaxaca had even more extensive buildups—a second wave of urbanization—such that Monte Albán's control over new population centers should no longer be assumed.

Monte Albán's decline during Period IIIb-IV left a power vacuum in the highlands. The Sola Valley broke up into small polities, similar to the historical *cacicazgos*. The precise timing of this occurrence vis à vis Monte Albán's population history is a subject for future research. Sola/Valley Zapotec cultural ties nonetheless continued, especially in ceramic styles and carved stone monuments. Marcus (this volume) considers Sola and Valley of Oaxaca polities to be coparticipants in a writing tradition; Sola's carved stones would not be out of place in the Valley of Oaxaca, suggesting that emergent centers in both regions were forging new ties during and after Monte Albán's decline.

Sola's participation in the "ballgame cult" associated with the coastal lowlands in Epiclassic times (J. F. Zeitlin 1993) suggests yet another level of macroregional integration. The Epiclassic florescence of coastal Oaxaca (Joyce 1993a) suggests that highland-coastal exchange routes still included the Sola Valley at this time. Pacific marine shell on Sola Valley sites further attests to likely highland-coastal exchange ties (Nicholas and Feinman, this volume).

Scale of Analysis

Some Mesoamerican scholars believe that enough survey has been done, and that we should now focus exclusively on site-intensive research and excavation. I would agree, but only to a point. The two methodologies—regional survey and excavation—should both continue, and be integrated to the fullest extent possible. Some questions require further expansion of highland survey to answer; other questions need refined data from excavation. The point is that the full range of variation in settlement patterns is not yet established, and this variation is one key to understanding the overall system and its sources of change.

The results from the Sola Valley illustrate the interpretive power of placing even small study regions next to larger survey blocks. The combined Sola, Ejutla, and Valley of Oaxaca study area now exceeds 3000 km² in size; this is part of an even larger area of 7000 km² in highland Oaxaca. Variation in regional trajectories and interactions among regions at this spatial scale becomes the basis for building better macroregional models. Sola's trajectory was not identical to that of other regions, yet knowledge of the whole helps us to understand the Sola Valley.

As one example, Sola's settlement shifts over time could not have been anticipated solely from knowledge about its larger macroregion. It turns out that Monte Albán's role in shaping the region's settlement history was greatest from Sola's Ic phase colonization to the beginning of Period IIIa, and attenuated thereafter until the region was fully autonomous by Period IIIb-IV. Each region on the Zapotec frontier must thus be evaluated independently in order to understand its relationship to Monte Albán.

Ecological Functionalism

Models of Oaxaca settlement patterns have ranged from narrow ecological functionalism (Sanders and Nichols 1988) to broader sociopolitical concerns (Marcus [ed.] 1990). I have already mentioned Sanders, Parsons, and Santley's (1979:360) estimate that the environment (and indirectly the population densities) explains 80% of regional settlement patterns. My response is that in highland Oaxaca only 20% of the settlement pattern is explained by the environment, with the rest explicable via less strictly materialist concerns. Another way to make the distinction is to separate necessary pre-existing demographic densities from sufficient explanations of culture change. Oaxaca's macroregional database (with its differing regional trajectories, irrespective of environmental similarities and differences) offers one of the most damaging critiques yet for ecologically functional models of culture change.

Zapotec colonization accounted for Sola's specific regional trajectory during Ic/II times. Ecological functionalists might well predict that Sola's initial settlement history was a local matter, best explained by Valley of Oaxaca population pressure, and the settlement of new lands to boost agricultural productivity. In fact, Valley of Oaxaca population pressure is so far undemonstrated (Nicholas 1989), although I would suggest that locally acute food shortages following the shift to hilltop terrace sites could be one factor exacerbating interpolity conflict. Ecologically functional expectations force us to ignore the broader context of changes throughout Oaxaca, including the possible Zapotec rationale for tapping coastal resources. Correlation of land quality to settlement, for example, was negative during Sola's Ic/II colonization. Sola, moreover, was probably too far from Monte Albán to make tribute in staple foods energetically rational (e.g. Drennan 1984).

Ecological functionalists would also expect that Sola's initial colonization should occur on the most productive alluvial lands, and that sites with the best land would have the greatest population growth, with population pressure (defined with reference to carrying capacity) causing culture change. The correlation between land quality and the distribution of population should also increase over time as the population grows. Yet in the Sola Valley, our data show that population never correlated with agricultural potential, and the region was never near its maximum potential population. Archaeological population estimates range from 21% to 31% of the valley's resource-based potential during Period IIIa, IIIb-IV, and V (Sola's most populous periods). Sola's inhabitants at that time usually lived near *good* land, but not necessarily the region's *best* agricultural land. In fact, Sola's Period IIIa regional capital—and the most demographically dense subsector of the survey area—was not even in the Sola Valley proper, but located on the mountain pass leading into the valley. At no point were Sola's largest site and most populous grid square by phase ever located on the best agricultural land. There is a political dimension to settlement patterns that goes far beyond issues of population and the environment.

Instead of fulfilling the predictions of ecological functionalists, Sola underwent a series of varied transitions, different from but synchronous with those of neighboring regions. Sola's occupation was often associated with the transport corridor through the region that linked the highlands to the coast, and this conveys a sense of the larger-scale linkages in Sola's settlement history. The recurring themes in Sola Valley settlement were extra-regional trade, political alliance-building, and defense. Sola's land use was only one of many factors in settlement decisions, and population pressure cannot be invoked to explain the regional settlement pattern in any phase. It is this downsizing of the causal priority given to land use and ultimately population pressure that separates ecological functionalism from more inclusive models.

Why "World System" Models Just Won't Work

Was the Sola Valley part of a Monte Albán "world system?" I asked this question in my original grant proposal for the Sola Valley survey. What I found, from the Sola perspective, was that a strict Wallersteinian (1974) synthesis did not apply—this supposed periphery was more active in structuring its exchange relations, and its economic organization was more variable, than the world system model allows. I then considered using one of the many currently popular looser definitions, in which multiregional interaction constitutes a "world system" (e.g. Ekholm and Friedman 1985; Peregrine 1996; Santley and Alexander 1992). But by that definition, what kind of interaction would *not* constitute a world system? World system defined simply as large-scale interaction becomes a catchall model that covers gaps in data, masks local processes, and diverts attention from more fundamental causal relationships.

Sola in Period Ic/II times was colonized and incorporated into the Zapotec state; the peripheral issue in this case was Monte Albán's effect on coastal Oaxaca beyond the Sola Valley. The Oaxaca coast reached new levels of complexity in part because of its interaction with expansionist highland societies, although the local processes promoting that complexity were probably equally significant (Balkansky 1998b). Río Viejo's urbanization (e.g. Joyce 1993a) and the possibility that an autonomous coastal state formed in Period II times—an assumption based on present data—is not a good case for Wallersteinian systematic exploitation and local underdevelopment (e.g. Frank 1967; Wallerstein 1974).

Sola in Period IIIa/IIIb-IV times grew in population, and by the Late Classic flourished even though nearby regions, including parts of the Valley of Oaxaca, lost population precipitously (e.g. Feinman and Nicholas 1990a; Kowalewski et al. 1989: Maps 6, 7). This comparison suggests that Sola's varied relationship with Monte Albán differed from its relationship with other regions, including Ejutla. Sola polities were on the margins of the Zapotec state during Classic times, yet were arguably autonomous by Period IIIb-IV. Monte Albán declined while Sola grew in complexity (architecture, stone carving, and inferred alliances) during Period IIIb-IV, making the "peripheral" issue moot (cf. Kohl 1987). The operation of world systems implies an exchange differential, an extraction of resources or labor that benefits core states. This exchange differential must be demonstrated rather than assumed.

The best case to be made for world system effects can be found during Period IIIa, a time worth examining in detail. Ejutla is our best-studied Classic period example (e.g. Feinman and Nicholas 1990a, 1992, 1993). Ejutla was not underdeveloped, but growing, during Period IIIa; finished goods, such as shell ornaments, were shipped to the Monte Albán core, the reverse of Wallersteinian expectations. Excavations reveal diversity of production, rather than overspecialization and consequent dependency (e.g. Feinman, Nicholas, and Middleton 1993). Economic differentiation by region did not occur as it should under world system expectations. Ejutla might seem superficially underdeveloped because it had fewer true graywares (similar to the Sola situation), but San Joaquín in Ejutla was among the most populous sites in highland Oaxaca. The Ejutla Valley probably served important gateway functions, accounting for the unusual size of its capital center.

Sola's trajectory during Period IIIa was similar to Ejutla's. Sola's ceramics suggest its relative marginality compared to Valley of Oaxaca sites. Type G.23s (Monte Albán's main decorated serving bowl in Period IIIa) were seldom found in the Sola Valley; G.23 imitations in a yellow-orange clay body were present, but not numerous. The bulk of Sola's ceramics were undecorated orange-brownware serving bowls and brownware jars, not the true grayware complex typical in the Valley of Oaxaca. Sola's orange-brownware G.35 analogues, along with a few true G.23s, could mean that Sola was not closely integrated with the Valley of Oaxaca during this period.

Was the Sola Valley exploited, or even underdeveloped, at this time? It is possible, but the alternative is equally likely—that the region was at least semi-autonomous politically, and so did not receive an abundance of preferentially exchanged decorated ceramics from Monte Albán and nearby Valley of Oaxaca sites; this condition would not preclude Sola's participation in other kinds of exchange with Valley of Oaxaca sites. Sola's demographic core of terraced sites near S23 could have operated semi-autonomously at this time also. The greater autonomy of the Sola Valley during Period IIIa could explain its successful continuity into the IIIb-IV era, when the nearby Ejutla Valley crashed.

Sola appears to have received little obsidian during the Classic period. Marine shell, however, was relatively abundant on the surface, and there is evidence of local production (though not on the scale of the Ejutla Valley). If much of the Sola Valley shell dates to the Classic period (a reasonable inference, based on surface associations), then it becomes possible that the Sola region was systematically exploited for its labor, some performed craft specialization, and strengthened control of a boundary zone, but received little from Monte Albán in return. This possible underdevelopment is reminiscent of the world system argument made for the Ejutla Valley (Feinman and Nicholas 1992, 1993); the problem is that Sola's shell work could be *Late* Classic in date, making systematic exploitation from Monte Albán unlikely since that city was in decline. Sola's carved stone tradition was not yet important in IIIa times, suggesting that while Early Classic Sola was economically incorporated into the Zapotec state, Sola elites were not equal participants in the Valley Zapotec writing tradition. Thus, evidence from ceramics, shell, obsidian, and carved stones could point to the Sola Valley being marginal economically within the Zapotec state during Period IIIa.

But what sort of "world system" would account for the Sola Valley data? *Most* places would have been economically marginal compared to Monte Albán; this observation alone says little. It would also be a mistake to smooth over Sola's differences with Ejutla, especially its different fate during Period IIIb-IV. The means of integration among regions during Classic times remains so poorly understood that world system models do more to cover gaps in data than to illuminate actual processes of interaction.

In short, there is too much variation on the Zapotec periphery to reduce it all to "world systems." The growing variation in peripheral development now apparent from similar worldwide case studies (e.g. Stein 1998; Stern 1988) suggests that local processes are being downplayed to make the scheme fit, a situation not so different from decades-old diffusionist thinking. The uncritical application of Wallerstein's (1974) concept, or modified formulations thereof (e.g. Peregrine 1996), also risks something greater—masking and diverting attention from more fundamental evolutionary relationships. Besides, even Wallerstein would probably say that because the penetration of world capitalism into native economies was not involved, his model would not be appropriate to the prehispanic New World.

Evolution and Agency

Social action theories originated from dissatisfaction with evolutionists' efforts to explain culture change (Marcus and Flannery 1996:29-31). Criticisms of evolutionism are based on its occasional determinism, especially single-factor and system-stress models of culture change that ignore unique historical factors and human agency, and on reliance on typological constructs insufficiently dynamic to model variable transitions in the archaeological record. Archaeologists are working to resolve these problems by incorporating social action, or agency, into evolutionary models of culture change (e.g. Spencer 1990, 1993).

Agency and evolution are complementary, not opposing explanatory approaches. Evolutionary structures describe the periods of relative stasis over centuries or millennia between episodes of rapid social evolution. Evolutionism alone, however, cannot explain the proximate causes of culture change, no matter how many long-term trends are tallied; it can only explain their outcomes. Agency allows a look inside actual processes of change. One implication of this approach is that episodes of transition that are historical in character are of equal significance for both understanding culture change and the relative stasis of evolutionary stages. It is during the shorter duration of episodic social transformations that social actors become proximate causal agents. How do we define the nested structures within which social actors operate? How do we recognize agency in the archaeological record?

The error that some proponents make is to ignore evolutionary structures altogether in favor of agency. Joyce and Winter (1996) commit this error for Oaxaca, making their model just as functional and static as the neoevolutionary typologies they seek to replace. Their approach is to create a laundry list of "things ideological" whose detailed enumeration is supposed to generate culture change. But Oaxaca archaeologists have always known that pyramids, palaces, tombs with carved stones, funerary urns, and prestige goods from far-off lands convey ideological messages. Endless litanies of such items offer little insight into processes of change.

Agency (in this case transposed into ideology) thus becomes the latest prime mover argument, no different from population pressure, trade, warfare and the rest: the single ideological factor is followed over time until it passes an undefined critical threshold and transforms culture. Ancient Oaxaca's cities and states were therefore the result of a homogeneous elite population transforming ideology and becoming "ritual specialists." The later collapse of cities and states was due to an apparent overabundance of ideology: nobles made ever-increasing demands on commoners until crossing an undefined critical threshold, after which societies questioned the dominant ideology. Agency in the form of individuals and social groups—to say nothing of broader social institutions and evolutionary structures—is never part of the discussion. It is simply the changing sets of ideas—each new idea being an elite manipulation—about rulership and the cosmos that cause social evolution.

This approach results in agency without actors, power without social structure, and ideology as a commonplace evolutionary trend. Such verbal legerdemain cannot replace actual data on social action, or knowledge of the structural limitations of societies, their prior histories, internal contradictions, and potential for change. The social actors we are looking for exist in Oaxaca ethnohistory; their potential roles in culture change are discernible in material constraints and the institutional structures of their time. Without a dynamic model of social evolution, it is impossible to explain culture change.

The Sola Valley case study can provide a first step toward incorporating agency into more general evolutionary explanations of the Oaxaca survey data. I suggested in the first chapter that two criteria for recognizing the effects of social actors on settlement patterns were (1) settlement characteristics not attributable to ecological necessity; and (2) the variation in regional trajectories due to disjunctive historical events. Social actors operate within nested socioenvironmental structures from household to site level, and from region to macroregion. The survey data obviously apply best to the region and macroregion. More intensive work on the site and household levels will be required to extend these arguments further.

Sola's terraced sites of the Monte Albán Ic phase made little sense in terms of ecological necessity, but fit the general pattern of Zapotec expansionism, in this case toward the Oaxaca coast. Monte Albán colonized Sola, conquered Cuicatlán, and forged alliances with Ejutla and probably Miahuatlán. This small sample does not exhaust the full range of possibilities, but the point is that the regional variation was all related historically to the Zapotec expansion and reflects variable decisions made by specific actors.

The II/IIIa transition saw the origins of urbanism in the Sola Valley. The former Period II capital was abandoned for a densely nucleated cluster of terraced sites in the mountains. This pattern was replicated in parts of the Valley of Oaxaca, and could represent local efforts toward greater autonomy. Monte Albán soon abandoned more distant provinces like Cuicatlán altogether, and changed its relationship with Teotihuacan in ways still not well understood.

This restructuring presaged events during Period IIIb-IV. The Sola Valley was fully autonomous by that time, and its population broke up into a pattern not unlike today's dispersed rural settlement. The architectural elaboration and carved stones at IIIb-IV centers in the Sola Valley could signal local elite claims to political authority and the growth of the kind of alliance system, both within and between valleys, that characterized the Postclassic period. The interplay between these large-scale structures and the short-term disjunctive events that produced them must inform any future discussions of agency in the Sola Valley.

Agency, properly balanced with evolutionary processes, maintains the comparative backdrop of material constraints and social structures within which change occurs. Evolutionary constructs provide essential reference points on the antecedent conditions of society, the key trends, and their ultimate outcomes. But to understand unique occurrences such as pristine state formation we require more historically informed perspectives. Zapotec state formation and collapse are processes both unique to Oaxaca prehistory and the product of common evolutionary structures seen worldwide.

Some Suggestions for Future Research in the Sola Valley

The principal results of this study raise issues about integration within bounded territories, and relationships among autonomous political units over time. Questions raised by the survey data are answerable, but will require new and independent data sets. I conclude this volume with suggestions for future work in the Sola Valley that address these challenges.

First and foremost, we need to expand the survey coverage around the Sola Valley (yes, we still need more survey). There are about 100-150 km² of high mountains separating the Valley of Sola from Ejutla that should be covered. In the 1995-1996 survey project, we pushed as far as possible eastward toward Ejutla, but in the end we lacked the financial and logistical capacity to finish the job. Our first priority was to survey the Sola Valley proper, and anything beyond that was desirable but not essential.

We now need to close the Sola-Ejutla coverage gap, and not just for the sake of completeness. Determining the boundaries of Postclassic *cacicazgos* and Sola's connection to Ejutla during the Classic period are significant issues. We managed to cover the pass that connects Sola, Ejutla, and the Valley of Oaxaca, but not the long mountainous axis that separates Sola from Ejutla. I expect that those high mountains were unoccupied in Formative times, given the focus on Sola's transport corridor and its overall low-density occupation compared to Classic and Postclassic times. But this is informed guesswork; we need to find out. This mountain survey could be completed as a prelude to excavating a Classic-Postclassic boundary site such as S111.

The other desirable future survey in Sola's immediate vicinity would be the small valley surrounding Santa María and San Vicente Lachixio. This region to the north of the Sola Valley would be an ideal dissertation project, and would lead logically to follow-up excavations at one of the surveyed sites. A good survey in Lachixio would cover 200-400 km², depending on logistical difficulties and the density of occupation. There is some minimal Colonial documentation on the area (e.g. Garzón 1994 [1777]; Gerhard 1972), so we know that it had a late prehispanic occupation of some kind. I would like to know whether a Postclassic Mixtec presence could be documented in the region, and understood eventually from excavated data. I would like to compare the regional organization of Sola, Ejutla, and Lachixio during the Classic period, to see if yet another specific local pattern emerges. I would also like to know the Late/Terminal Formative settlement history of the Lachixio Valley. This region lacks Sola's direct coastal access, so I wonder if its settlement history also differs. Some of the principal conclusions of the Sola Valley survey could be tested in an adjacent valley such as this one.

The Lachixio surveyors could also cover more of the high mountains west of the Valley of Oaxaca, and with a sufficient stride reach the Peñoles area. Oaxaca's high mountains contain sites that are in pristine condition. The architectural preservation is amazing, though it can be difficult to date these sites from the surface remains. That is why it is important that we start excavating these sites. You need only trowel away 500-1000 years of leafy detritus to find sites that look as if they were abandoned yesterday. Some of the best pristine mountain sites are in the Peñoles and Guirún areas (Feinman and Nicholas 1996; Finsten and Kowalewski 1991), but more would arise from a Lachixio survey. This type of work would require camping, and an affinity for the wilderness experience.

I might now mention that there are sites worth excavating in the Sola Valley, and good reasons for doing so. There are detailed site descriptions for each of the 120 sites recorded for the Sola Valley in Appendix A. Some of the most promising candidates are Sites S1, S10, S20, S23, S39, S75, S82, S84, and S111. I like these sites because they are among the best preserved and accessible (some would require camping to excavate), and were significant centers during episodes of transition. Excavations at any of these sites would complement the existing regional data and clarify major issues raised from the survey. I will focus here on S39 (near the towns of Santa María Sola and Texcoco), whose major occupation spans the Late Formative to Late Classic periods.

The site's architectural core and latest main occupation was Late Classic (IIIb-IV). S39 has the largest number of carved stones in the Sola Valley, now found in the walls of the church at Santa María Sola. The terraced hilltop would be a good place to start work, by taking apart some of the terraces, houses on those terraces, and probable tombs near or underneath house floors. This work could focus on the reestablishment of local political authority and elite identity during Monte Albán's decline. The extent of the underlying Period IIIa occupation could be measured. (I suspect the site was mostly abandoned, or at least underwent a significant hiatus in construction, during the II/IIIa transition.) Elite ties to the Valley of Oaxaca and its new political centers could be better understood. We also need to measure changes in local economic activities against the large-scale backdrop of changing political structures.

Earlier periods of transition were also significant, and Site S39 was a crucial player during Sola's Ic phase colonization and Period II integration into the Zapotec state. S39 was Sola's regional capital during Period II, and had a significant architectural complex by this time. It would not be feasible to remove much of the Classic period overburden, but the two ball courts are accessible, and Structures 25-26 are of manageable size. I suspect that one or both of the ball courts, and the entirety of Structures 25-26, had their beginnings in Ic/II times. It is important to know when ball courts were first constructed in Oaxaca, since they evolved into later Zapotec state institutions. There are also several terraces near Structures 27-31 with Ic/II houses accessible near the surface. A good sample of excavated ceramics would suggest the timing and means of the site's integration with the Zapotec state. Were the Ic graywares and Period II creamwares at S39 manufactured locally, or were some imported from the Valley of Oaxaca? Which households had access to the real thing? What kinds of local productive activities took place within these households? What might we learn about highland-coastal interaction during these times?

Many of the same questions would apply to other Sola Valley sites, and it would be a mistake to overlook the Early and Late Postclassic periods. Site S75 has some dozen houses, sunken patio groups, and larger mounds waiting in nearly pristine condition on Cabo de Hacha. S111 has Postclassic architecture and a massively terraced hillside reminiscent of the Mitla Fortress. S20 was another Postclassic mountain site with impressive architecture and a ritually significant cave nearby. Studies at these sites could tell us about integration within and between territories during late prehispanic times. I like to think that work in the Sola Valley has just begun.

Conclusions

Zapotec state formation was not the result of ecological necessity or systemic stress, but the contingent territorial ambitions of Zapotec rulers. Their aim was to pave an unbroken pathway between the highlands and the coast, gaining access to exotic preciosities in a network stretching from Central Mexico to the Pacific Coast. The state in this context was a new strategy to maintain control over their recently acquired tributary domain. Other state societies outside the bounds of Monte Albán's political control arose in response to Zapotec expansion. The evolutionary context including demography, political structure, and warfare was necessary but not sufficient to explain the rise of the state. The origin of the Zapotec state was not predicated on directional evolutionary trends alone, but also on the historical events of frontier expansion.

The origin of the *cacicazgo* was another episodic transition, shaped by human intention as much as it was shaped by long-term trends in socioenvironmental structures. The crisis of the II/IIIa transition left political structures more equivalent than hierarchical on regional and macroregional scales. As the Classic period Zapotec state receded from its former territorial extent, more distant regions became autonomous, while places closer to the Valley of Oaxaca were still enmeshed in the Zapotec state's core polity. Monte Albán's relationships, however, were not defined simply by concentric circles of territory, but by a series of policies ranging from outright control to alliances and more indirect interactions. In this setting, ambitious local rulers could succeed in forging their own alliances independent of the Zapotec capital. Monte Albán's final decline left a vacuum filled by multiple competing centers, but with many continuities from Classic to Postclassic society.

The things we still do not know could fill a book. The large-scale political structure of Ic/II times is clear in its rough outlines, but not in the specific means of integration among regions. We do not fully understand how specific goods and people flowed, and via what channels within Monte Albán's territorial boundaries. We do not know the extent to which early states arose responsively in clusters, rather than as the result of Monte Albán's "influence" flowing outward from the center. I argue against using "world system" and other center-based models that simply cover missing data; this is just diffusionism by another name. Studies to fill gaps in data must be taken down to the household level.

The specific means of integration among sites and regions is even murkier for the Classic period. Even within the Valley of Oaxaca, subregions and individual sites were not necessarily articulated with Monte Albán in the same ways. I have tried to draw attention to Transición II/IIIa as an overlooked starting point to understand the collapse of regional states during Period IIIb-IV. The Classic to Postclassic transition, moreover, had stronger cultural continuity than most "Chaos of the Epiclassic" approaches allow (this last phrase is another rhetorical cover for missing data). The value of recognizing settlement continuities is that it enables us to use ethnohistorical sources, with their named individuals and institutions, to model earlier periods. We can raise all these issues from the standpoint of regional survey, but not yet answer them. Still, raising the right questions is what full-coverage survey is all about.

Chapter 7

Carved Stones from the Sola Valley

Joyce Marcus, University of Michigan

Zapotec writing first appeared at two sites within the Valley of Oaxaca—at San José Mogote (ca. 600 B.C.) and Monte Albán (ca. 500 B.C.). Hundreds of years later, Zapotec-influenced writing began to appear on stone monuments *outside* the Valley of Oaxaca, first at sites like Huamelulpan in the Mixtec highlands (Figs. 7.1-7.3) and later at sites in the Valley of Sola de Vega.

After describing and illustrating the carved stones of the Sola Valley in the first section of this chapter, I will try to put them into macroregional context by addressing six questions: (1) Why did Zapotec writing appear outside the Valley of Oaxaca? (2) Why did such writing appear when it did? (3) What was the content of those texts and carved monuments? (4) What do the Sola de Vega stones tell us about Sola's relationship to the Valley of Oaxaca? (5) Why has the decipherment of Zapotec writing lagged behind that of Maya writing? and (6) How does the discovery of carved stones in the Sola Valley further the task of decipherment?

The Sola Valley and the Pioneering Work of Heinrich Berlin

Approximately forty carved stones have been reported for the Sola region, the vast majority of them removed from their original context by accident or by looting. As is the case with the overall corpus of Zapotec monuments, we cannot be precise about the number of carved stones in the Sola region because it is constantly in flux. During each decade, new monuments come to light and some of those previously reported are lost or destroyed.

The first systematic effort to record the carved stones of Sola de Vega was that of Heinrich Berlin in the 1940s (Berlin 1946, 1951). Berlin set himself two principal tasks—linking the stones he found to specific archaeological sites and to specific contexts within those sites—both of which proved to be difficult. The monuments he recorded in the 1940s were no longer *in situ* in the walls of public buildings, palaces, or tombs. Most had been removed from their archaeological sites and reused in the construction of churches or municipal buildings (Heinrich Berlin, pers. comm.).

During his full-coverage survey in the 1990s, Andrew Balkansky photographed all the carved stones he came across in the Sola Valley. In the process, he ended up finding new carved stones, some still located at archaeological sites (Balkansky 1997). He also tried to relocate all the monuments found earlier by Berlin, but some had been moved or lost.

Berlin's survey of the Sola region involved three separate trips: 1946, 1947, and 1948. Berlin had been drawn to the area in part by Gonzalo de Balsalobre's seventeenth-century manuscript, which relates the "idolatrous acts" conducted by speakers of Soltec (a variant of the Zapotec language) living in the Sola region (Balsalobre [1656] 1892; Berlin 1957). Balsalobre had described thirteen "heathen gods" worshiped by the natives of Sola, and Berlin hoped to find stone monuments depicting some of these prehispanic "deities." Each time he came upon a carved stone, Berlin tried to link the figure depicted on it to one of Balsalobre's "gods." By his own admission, this endeavor was unsuccessful.

With the wisdom of hindsight, we can say that Berlin's initial effort was frustrated by several incorrect assumptions. The first was Balsalobre's assumption that all the names he had collected were those of deities. The names on Balsalobre's list included words like *Nozana*, "ancestor" or "progenitor," and *Coqueetaa* (*sic*), "great lord" or *coquitào*, making it likely tha.

Figure 7.1. Carved surface on the south face of a lintel located in the southeast corner of Building C at San Martín Huamelulpan. In addition to the lizard (carved in high relief), there are two Zapotec calendar signs: 9 J (on the left) and 13 O (Monkey) (on the right). Whether these two signs commemorated important dates or were the names of an important marital couple is not known. See Caso and Gamio 1961, Gaxiola 1976, Moser 1977, Marcus 1983d. [Photo by author]

Figure 7.2. Carved surface on the east face of a lintel located in the southeast corner of Building C at San Martín Huamelulpan. Four calendar signs were recorded on this side: 2?; 9 Tiger; 5 Monkey; 6? Water. Whether these two signs commemorated important dates or the names of two marital pairs is not known (see Caso and Gamio 1961, Gaxiola 1976, Moser 1977). [Photo by author]

Figure 7.3. Carved surface on the east face of a lintel located in the southeast corner of Building C at San Martín Huamelulpan, which may record the name 13 Bat? See also Caso and Gamio 1961, Gaxiola 1976, Moser 1977. [Photo by author]

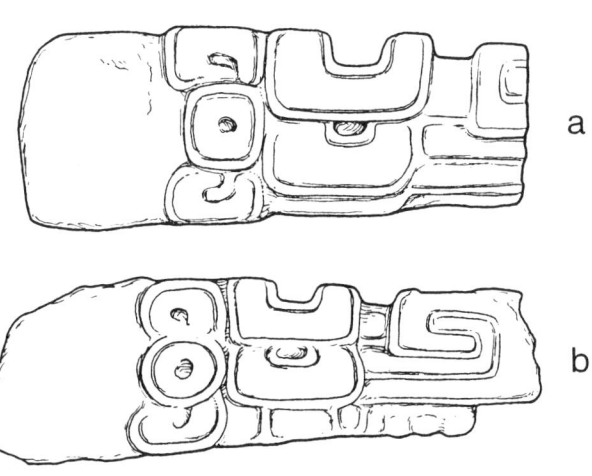

Figure 7.4. Two carved stones embedded in the wall of the church at San Francisco Sola, possibly from Balkansky's Site 111. Both stones depict a long-nosed supernatural (*Cociyo* or Lightning) and were evidently tenoned into a wall. Each has a superorbital element that is U-shaped and similar ear ornaments. [Redrawn from photos in Berlin 1951: Figs. 4 and 3, and photos taken by Andrew Balkansky]

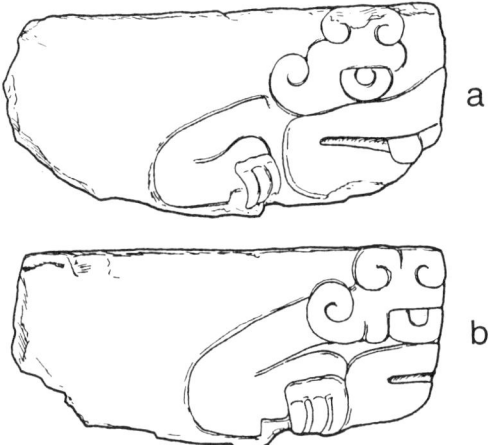

Figure 7.5. Two carved stones embedded in the wall of the church at San Francisco Sola, possibly from Balkansky's Site 111. Both stones were evidently tenoned into a wall. Although not drawn here, the upper surfaces of these stones have very similar tripartite elements. [Redrawn from photos in Berlin 1951: Figs. 5, 6 and photos taken by Andrew Balkansky]

Figure 7.6. Two carved stones, evidently intended to be tenoned into a wall. Both stones depict a long-nosed supernatural (*Cociyo* or Lightning), but the face associated with the earplug is anthropomorphized in both cases. *a*. This stone was found standing in the plaza at San Juan Sola. *b*. This stone was found in the local school at San Francisco Sola. [Redrawn from photos in Berlin 1951: Figs. 9 and 2]

Figure 7.7. Carved stone found at Reyes Etla. Maximum length is 1.9 m.

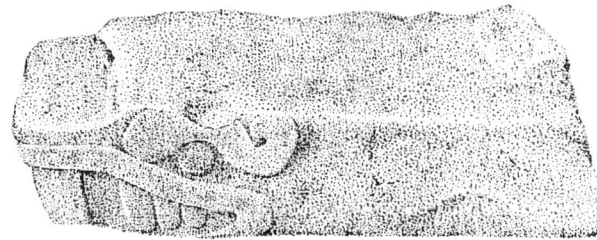

Figure 7.8. Carved stone found in the ball court at Reyes Etla. Maximum length is 1.9 m. [Drawing by Mark Orsen]

his informants were referring not to gods but to deceased and revered native lords. Another of the names on Balsalobre's list was *Lociyo*, the Soltec version of *Cociyo* or "Lightning," a powerful supernatural force.

Berlin, like other Mesoamerican epigraphers in the 1940s, did not know that the figures carved on Maya and Zapotec stone monuments were likely to be royal humans rather than gods; this situation was to change with Caso's later work on the Mixtec codices (Caso 1949) and with Berlin's (1958, 1959) and Proskouriakoff's (1960, 1962, 1963) work on Maya monuments. A further impediment to Berlin's initial effort was the fact that most of the Sola monuments he found seemed to date to the period from A.D. 600 to 900. In other words, those carved stones preceded the conquest by so many centuries that it was unlikely that many "deities" found on them would still be prominent in a seventeenth-century manuscript.

Despite his initial frustration, Berlin made a pioneering contribution to the study of Sola's monuments. He found the region "especially rich in stone sculptures" (Berlin 1951:4), most of them removed from their original contexts and incorporated into buildings in the towns of Santa María Sola, San Juan Sola, and San Francisco Sola. Fortunately Balkansky (1997, and in this volume) has found other carved stones still associated with prehispanic structures such as ball courts, altars, tombs, or platforms. These associations provide us with likely contexts for some of the stones found earlier by Berlin.

Berlin did find one kind of monument that he considered a deity, but which he believed had no seventeenth-century counterpart. Of this situation Berlin (1951:4) says, "I have not succeeded in identifying beyond doubt this god with any of Balsalobre's list and would therefore prefer to call him the Sola God throughout this paper." We will discuss Berlin's "Sola God" at greater length below. Similar depictions of the same figure are known from the Valley of Oaxaca itself, making it clear that the "*Sola* God" was not restricted to the Sola Valley as its label might suggest.

Classifying the Sola Monuments

One convenient way to classify the carved stones from the Sola de Vega region is to divide them into two groups: those with hieroglyphic texts and those without.

Carved Stones without Hieroglyphs

Prominent among the stones without hieroglyphs are those that appear to have been tenoned into walls (Berlin 1951: Figs. 2-6). One end of each stone was left uncarved, since it would be hidden when tenoned into a prehispanic structure (see Figs. 7.4-7.6 in this chapter). It is on the carved portions of these stones that Berlin first identified his "Sola God," a long-nosed supernatural being (e.g. Berlin 1946: Figs. 1b, 1c). These depictions look like "Lightning," the powerful force that the Valley of Oaxaca Zapotec called *Cociyo* and the Soltec called *Lociyo* or *Loziyo* (Balsalobre [1656] 1892). Another version of "Lightning"—apparently an anthropomorphic *Cociyo*—was still standing in the plaza in San Juan Sola in the 1940s (Berlin 1951: Fig. 9; see Fig. 7.6a in this chapter).

Berlin noted that when tenoned stones depicting his "Sola God" were found in archaeological sites, they were associated with ball courts. At least five such cases are known from the Sola region, and other cases are known from the Valley of Oaxaca (Marcus 1975). In 1974 I photographed the carved stone

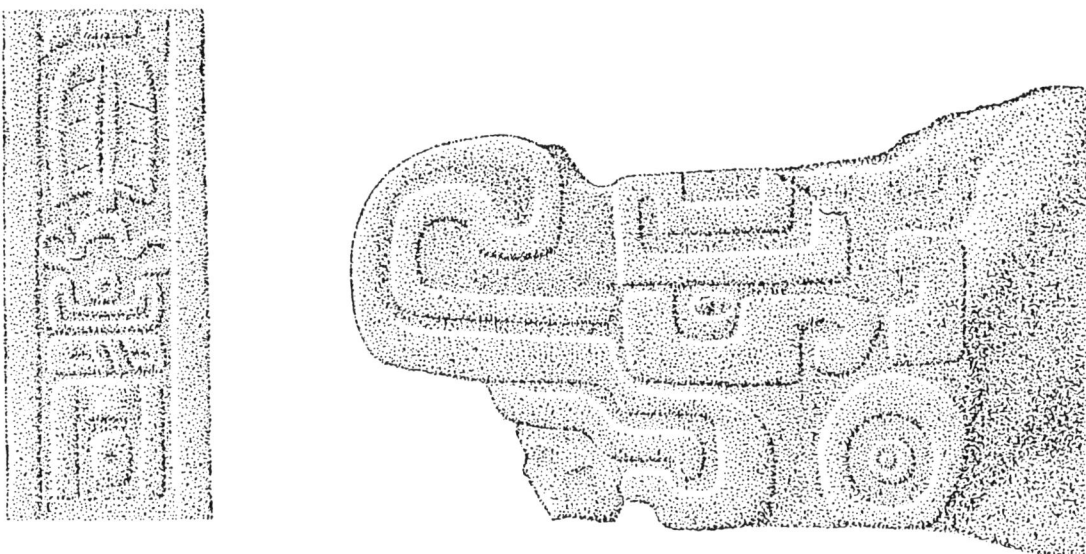

Figure 7.9. Carved stone found at Zaachila. At left is the short hieroglyphic text carved on the upturned nose of this supernatural being. At right is the profile view of the long-nosed supernatural. Although carved to be tenoned into a wall, this stone is now out of context; it stands in the plaza at Zaachila. [Drawing by Mark Orsen]

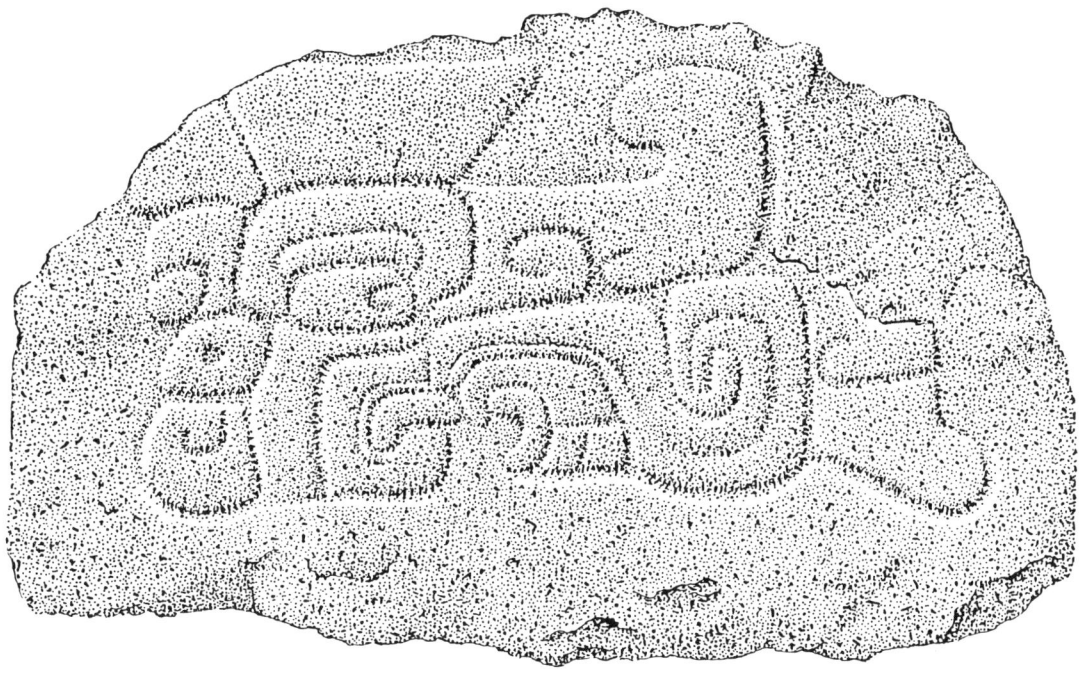

Figure 7.10. Carved stone at Tlacochahuaya. [Drawing by Mark Orsen]

(see Fig. 7.7) at Reyes Etla, a large site just north of San José Mogote in the Etla arm of the Valley of Oaxaca (Marcus 1976b). The Reyes Etla stone is 1.90 m long and 0.50 m high. Of its 1.90 m length only 0.79 m was carved (Fig. 7.8). The uncarved portion would probably have been tenoned into one of the walls of the ball court. The carving shows a fairly realistic serpent, perhaps a reference to "Lightning" as a sky-serpent or fire-serpent (Marcus 1989a; Marcus and Flannery 1996:95). The ball court at Reyes Etla has not been excavated, but the site seems to have reached its peak size during period Monte Albán IIIb-

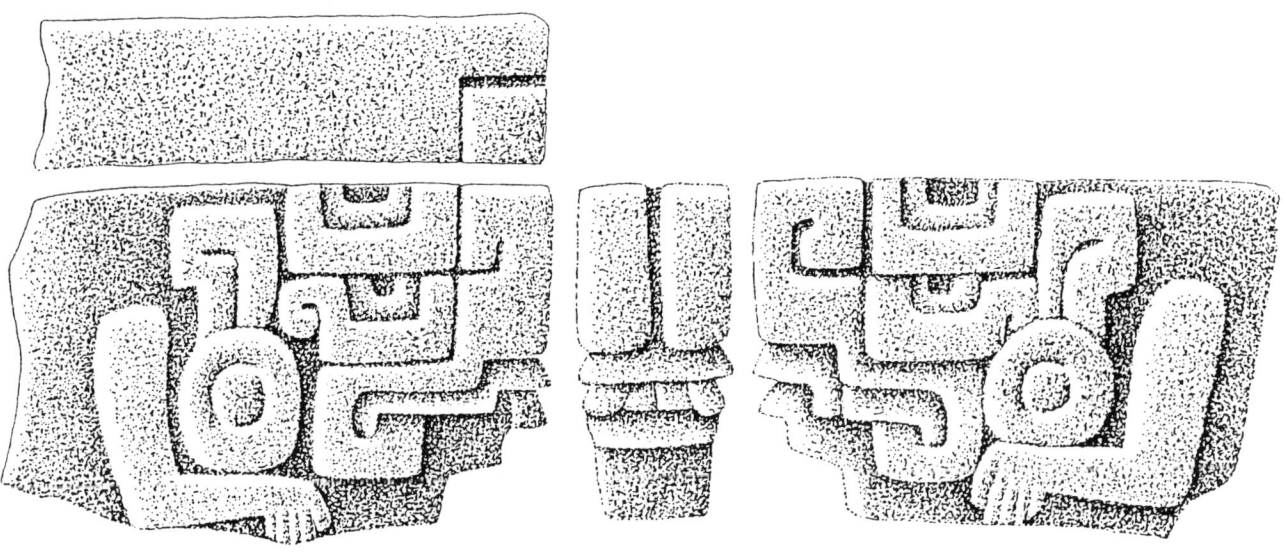

Figure 7.11. This carved stone was found in 1954 during excavations in the Yagul ball court. It was set in a wall of the ball court, but evidently not *in situ*, since only one of its three carved surfaces was visible. The long-nosed supernatural includes many elements seen on other stones (see Figs. 7.4-7.6), but this Yagul example includes a human arm. This stone is on display in the regional archaeological museum (Santo Domingo) in Oaxaca de Juárez.

IV, based on population estimates derived from surface survey data (Kowalewski et al. 1989).

Other depictions of *Cociyo* are known from Zaachila (Fig. 7.9), Tlacochahuaya (Fig. 7.10), Yagul (Fig. 7.11), Mitla (Fig. 7.12), and Monte Albán (e.g., in the ball court at El Plumaje and in the South Platform) in the Valley of Oaxaca. The Zaachila stone (Fig. 7.9), removed from its original context many years ago, appears to have been designed for insertion into the wall of a building. The Tlacochahuaya slab (Fig. 7.10) is carved on only one surface (rather than being a three-dimensional tenoned stone like those from the Sola region), but it also seems to depict a version of *Cociyo* (Marcus 1976b).

The stone from Yagul (0.80 m high, 1.25 m long, and 0.38 m wide) was designed to have been tenoned (see Fig. 7.11). It was found in 1954 by Oriol Pi-Sunyer and Charles Wicke during excavation of the Yagul ball court (Wicke 1957: Fig. 30). Wicke (1957:68) describes it as follows:

> This was a large block of stone carved in the shape of a serpent head which had been re-used to make up part of the wall. The head is very stylized and exhibits arms and hands. The hands show five fingers with nails. The arm develops an earplug from which a feather extends upward. The rectangular eye is pitted by a deep pupil and a superior and inferior plate surrounds it. The nose, which turns upon itself, is continuous with and balanced by the mouth, which also turns in a similar manner. The prominent front teeth are set in equally prominent gums that jut out slightly.

Although this tenoned *Cociyo* was found in the Yagul ball court—in the southwest corner of the eastern end zone—it was no longer *in situ* (see Fig. 7.13). It appears to have been moved and re-set into the end zone wall in such a way that only one of the three carved sides could be seen. In its original location the stone should logically have been set so that both sides, as well as the front carved surface of its nose, could be seen.

Unlike some Oaxaca ball courts whose long axis runs north-south (e.g. those at Reyes Etla, Monte Albán, and San José Mogote), the Yagul ball court is oriented east-west. Despite its different orientation and lack of corner niches, the Yagul ball court resembles the one on the Main Plaza at Monte Albán in that both lack stone rings and have benches with extensions (see Fig. 7.14).

A carved stone bearing a theme similar to that of the stone from Yagul's ball court (Fig. 7.11) was reused in Tomb 7 at Mitla (Fig. 7.12):

> At the back of the tomb was found a carved stone, which was utilized as part of the construction material and covered with stucco. It undoubtedly represents the god Cocijo's eye and ear adorned with an earplug. [Oliver 1955:64-66, citing Caso and Rubín de la Borbolla 1936]

While he did not make the connection between his "Sola God" and the Zapotec *Cociyo*, Berlin clearly noted the association of tenoned stones with ball courts in the Sola Valley. He stated that

Figure 7.12. Carved stone found in Tomb 7 at Mitla. [Redrawn by John Klausmeyer from Oliver 1955: Fig. 39]

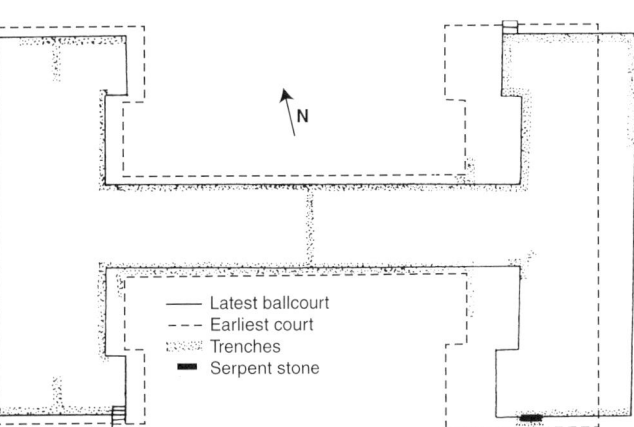

Figure 7.13. Ball court at Yagul. Note the location of the carved *Cociyo* or "serpent" stone. [Redrawn by John Klausmeyer from Wicke 1957: Fig. 30]

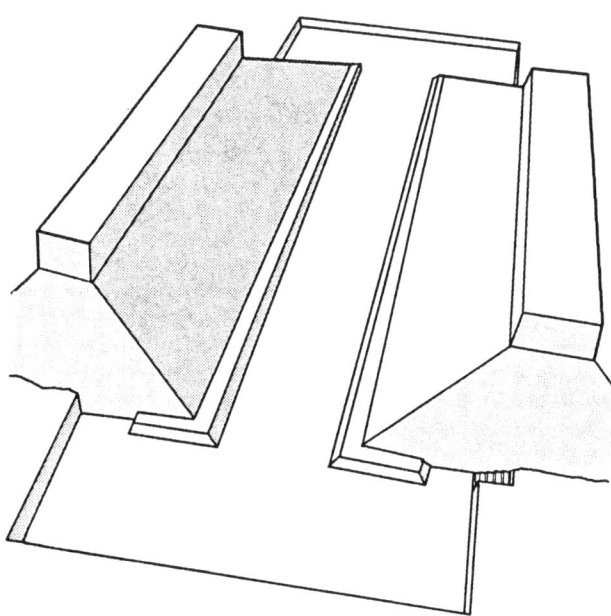

Figure 7.14. General view of a Oaxaca ball court. [Redrawn by John Klausmeyer from Wicke 1957: Fig. 28]

the function of these Sola God stones must have had an intimate connection with the ball game (substitutes for the "rings," used in Aztec and more recent Maya ball courts?) and that the double T shown on top of the God's face is with him no arbitrary ornament but a symbol related with his function. On the inner walls of the large parallels forming the ball court stucco rests were still found. [Berlin 1951:15]

Obviously, confirmation of the ideas presented by Caso, Rubín de la Borbolla, and Berlin will come when future investigators find tenoned *Cociyo* stones *in situ* in ball courts. If such serpent sculptures were set in ball courts, we need to determine why and how Lightning was linked to the ballgame, and why certain ball courts had such stones and others did not. As Berlin suggests, tenoned heads may have been the Zapotec counterpart to the stone rings used in the Maya region; if so, a pair of tenoned stones may have been inserted into the side walls of the long central court.

Now that Balkansky has thoroughly surveyed the Sola region, we can say something about the spatial distribution of both ball courts and carved stones. According to Balkansky's survey, the Monte Albán IIIa capital of the Sola Valley was his Sola 23, a site with a ball court in which a carved stone was found.

During Monte Albán IIIb-IV, the six main administrative centers were Balkansky's Sola 1, 39, 65, 84, 97, and 111. Each of these important centers covered 40-60 ha, and were spaced roughly equidistant from each other. Sites 1, 39, 97, and 111 had both ball courts and stone monuments. Balkansky located a carved stone in the center of the ball court at Sola 39 (Fig. 7.15). Although incomplete and damaged, this carved stone (Figs. 7.16-7.18) appears to be another example of a *Cociyo* stone carved especially for a ball court. During Monte Albán V, the El Obispo site (Site 111) became the Sola Valley's largest center, but since its carved stones are fragmentary we can say little about them.

At Site 10 in the Sola Valley, Balkansky found a fairly crude carved stone (Fig. 7.19). This monument was in the northwest corner of Mound 7, and today serves as a boundary marker (Balkansky, pers. comm.). The exposed portion of the stone measures 1.0 m in height. This simple carving is atypical of the Sola Valley corpus; it has punched-in eyes and mouth, a two-part element above the face, and in its chest we see a tri-lobed element similar to the one in the chest of the sacrificial victim

Figure 7.15. Sola 39 ball court. Note the carved stone at the center of the playing field, between Structures 10 and 11, the structures flanking the court. The carved stone is shown in Figures 7.16-7.18. [Photo by Andrew Balkansky]

Figure 7.16. Carved stone found in the center of the ball court at Sola 39. This carved surface of the stone is the south face. [Photo by Andrew Balkansky]

depicted on Monument 3 at San José Mogote in the Valley of Oaxaca (Marcus 1976c: Fig. 2; Marcus and Flannery 1996:129). The date of the Site 10 monument is not known.

Carved Stones with Hieroglyphic Writing

Most of Sola's monuments with hieroglyphic writing appear to belong to Monte Albán IIIb-IV on stylistic grounds, and they usually feature the nobles and their relatives. Such a focus on genealogy, as well as the style and arrangement of the hieroglyphic writing, link the Sola de Vega stones to contemporaneous monuments in the Valley of Oaxaca. In the latter region, genealogical information was often recorded on slabs whose scenes and hieroglyphs were relatively small in size; they were clearly intended to be read from up close (Marcus 1980, 1983a:191, 1992a:238). Not surprisingly, when found *in situ* such IIIb-IV stones seem to have been designed as integral parts of tombs—as lintels, jambs, doors, or wall panels set into the antechambers or interior chambers (Caso 1928, 1965a, 1965b; Miller 1991, 1995).

The most splendid of the Sola carved stones is set above the entrance to the church in Santa María Sola. The version shown in Figure 7.20 is based on various photographs taken by Andrew Balkansky, one of which is shown in Figure 7.21. The monument was probably removed from Balkansky's Site 39, a Monte Albán IIIb-IV administrative center. From its shape and overall dimensions—1.7 m long and 0.27 m high—we can infer that the stone was probably a tomb lintel. From its content, we can suggest that its genealogical information was intended to honor one or more of the nobles buried in the tomb. And, although we lack information on the number of individuals in

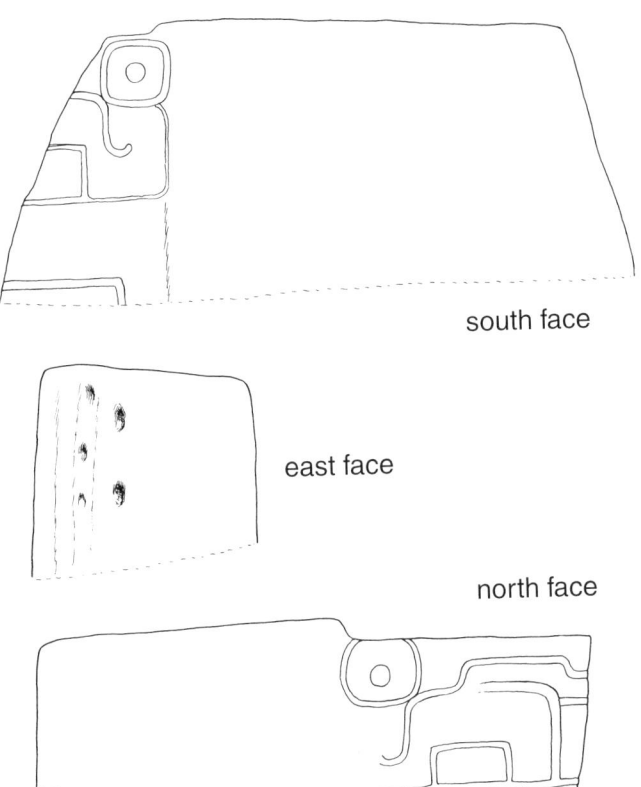

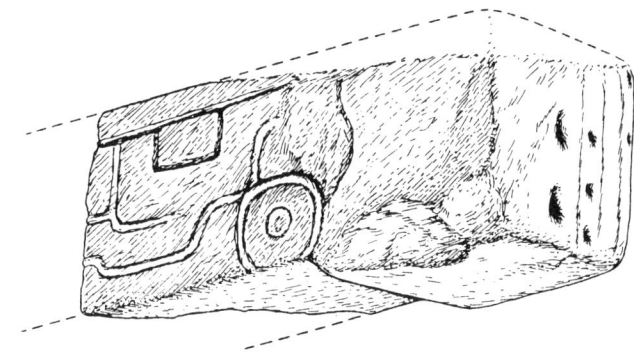

Figure 7.18. Carved stone found in the center of the ball court at Sola 39. This carved stone lies upside-down in the ball court; in this drawing, we see its probable original position. When complete, it was probably tenoned into a wall of the ball court. [Drawing by John Klausmeyer]

Figure 7.17. Carved stone found in the center of the ball court at Sola 39. Three surfaces were carved. [Drawn by John Klausmeyer from Laura Stiver's field drawings]

Figure 7.19. This carved stone from Sola 10 shows a human figure and a tri-lobed motif. Today this stone serves as the boundary marker dividing the lands of San Juan Sola, San Ildefonso, and San Miguel Sola de Vega. The exposed portion of the stone measures 1.00 m in height. [Drawing by John Klausmeyer]

that tomb, we might infer that the tomb itself was a "family mausoleum," similar to contemporaneous Valley of Oaxaca tombs found below the patios of palaces.

At the top of the Santa María Sola carving we see the so-called *Fauces del Cielo* or "Jaws of the Sky," a motif used to establish noble descent (Caso 1928; Marcus 1983a:191, 1992a:238). The "Jaws of the Sky" motif usually frames the central scene. Such scenes include royal weddings, claims of royal descent from revered ancestors, or tableaux of nobles conducting rituals of drinking, sacrifice, or copal-burning. The "Jaws of the Sky" can include a variety of elements such as open jaws (*chita rua*), a front-facing human head, a man in profile holding a rope, necklace, bird, leaves, shells, feathers, or precious beads (see Fig. 7.22 for several examples). In the case of the Santa María Sola lintel, the Jaws of the Sky motif is a simple version, featuring just a few jade beads suspended from the bottom of the jaw motif.

Typically on such monuments we see one marital pair just below the Jaws of the Sky; on the Santa María Sola lintel, however, we see two couples. The men and women alternate, from left to right, as follows: man/woman/man/woman. The man at the far left has a large earplug, large bead necklace, and loincloth. The woman sitting next to him wears a *huipil* and skirt, jade earplug, and bead necklace. She, in turn, faces a second man with a beard, jade necklace, and loincloth. Finally we see a second woman with bead necklace, earplug, *huipil*, and a skirt. While it is likely that these two couples are marital pairs, their relationship to each other is not

Figure 7.20. Lintel set into the church of Santa María Sola. [Drawing by Kay Clahassey and John Klausmeyer from photos taken by Andrew Balkansky]

Figure 7.21. Lintel set into the church of Santa María Sola. [Photo by Andrew Balkansky.]

clear; we do not know whether they are contemporaries or belong to different generations (e.g., one member of the pair on the left might be the offspring of the couple on the right).

On the far left of the scene we find the number 13 carved in the style typical of Monte Albán IIIb-IV. The number is below the day sign and consists of two bars (5 + 5) tied with bands or ribbons, then three dots below them. This number 13 is done the same way as numbers on Lápida 1 from Zaachila (Caso 1928: Fig. 81; Marcus 1992a: Fig. 8.15), a genealogical register from Noriega (Marcus 1992a: Fig. 9.13), a genealogical register from Suchilquitongo (Méndez Martínez 1988; Miller 1991, 1995), and other Valley of Oaxaca monuments assigned to Monte Albán IIIb-IV.

The day sign above the number 13 resembles Caso's Glyph M (Caso 1928:40-41), and I will tentatively refer to it as such, even though I am not convinced that it closely fits any of Caso's categories. Elsewhere (Marcus 1975) I developed a new classification that incorporates Caso's A-Z glyphs as well as others that do not fit into any of his categories. Directly in front of the name 13 M, we see a seated man with a bare chest, his left hand resting on his right upper arm. He is associated with a deco-

rated speech scroll, presumably indicating "song" or "flowery speech" (*tichatij*). Above the speech scroll is a glyph that resembles the Zapotec "hill sign," associated either with this man or with the woman seated in front of him. Normally one would expect to find an additional element above or within the hill sign, specifying the name of the place; in this case, however, we see only a few transverse bands (a generic characteristic of many hill signs at Monte Albán). Evidently it was not important for the carver to specify the man's (or woman's) place of origin.

The seated woman to the right of this man is presumably his wife. Her hair seems to be braided and coiled into what was once a widespread Zapotec woman's hairstyle, one that survives even today in towns like Yalalag (Caso and Bernal 1952). In front of the woman's face is a speech scroll, and below that is a group of small hieroglyphs that should contain her name. It is not clear whether this name is 5 V or 6 V in Caso's system, just above a possible 1 M. Moving to the right on the lintel, we see a hand plus two footprints that seem to ascend to the Jaws of the Sky. The hand—with its thumb and index finger raised—may convey the ordinal number *tini*, which the Zapotec used to indicate

Figure 7.22. Examples of the "Jaws of the Sky" (*Fauces del Cielo*) motif. [Drawing by John Klausmeyer]

"second-born son" (see Córdova 1578b:213; Marcus 1983c:93). To the right of the footprints are two more day-names—1 Owl(?) above and 1 Monkey below. The name 1 Owl(?) may be associated with the footprints leading to the Jaws of the Sky. One possible interpretation is that a second-born noble son named 1 Owl(?) had ascended to heaven as an ancestor.

Moving further to the right we come to a bearded man who (perhaps significantly) lacks a speech scroll. Judging by the glyph near his lower torso, his name may be 1 Monkey. Behind him is the name 1 M(?). Above that day-name we see one footprint ascending; then comes a speech scroll associated with the old woman sitting behind him, presumably his wife. Behind her are two large calendar signs, 3 P(?) and 4 Monkey(?). It is not clear whether these last glyphs are dates or day-names. If they are dates, they might correspond to the birth and death dates of the individual buried in the tomb from which the lintel came. Whatever the case, it is significant that the man and woman on the right of the scene are depicted as being wrinkled and older than the couple on the left; they might therefore belong to an earlier generation.

From A.D. 300 to 600, such genealogical data were often given in murals, especially in the tombs at Monte Albán (Caso 1938, 1965b; Marcus 1983b:139-43; Miller 1995). From A.D. 600 to 900 genealogical data were more likely to be given on stone slabs set in tombs, and such tombs were often opened and re-used by relatives and descendants (Marcus 1992a:281; Middleton et al. 1998). The scene carved on the Santa María Sola lintel is one more example of the importance of genealogy, marital pairs, and perhaps even the apotheosis of noble ancestors among the Zapotec during the period A.D. 600-900 (Marcus 1992a: Chapter 9; Marcus and Flannery 1994:71; Miller 1995; Winter et al. 1994:23).

The period Monte Albán IIIb-IV saw an explosion of genealogical information on carved stone monuments in the Zapotec area, both inside and outside the Valley of Oaxaca (Caso 1928, 1938, 1965b; Marcus 1976a, 1983a, 1989b, 1992a; Urcid 1993).

Figure 7.24 (above). Stone found in the church wall at Santa María Sola. [Redrawn by John Klausmeyer from photo in Berlin 1951: Fig. 10 and photos taken by Andrew Balkansky]

Figure 7.23 (left). Photo of carved stone embedded in the church wall at Santa María Sola. [Photo by Andrew Balkansky]

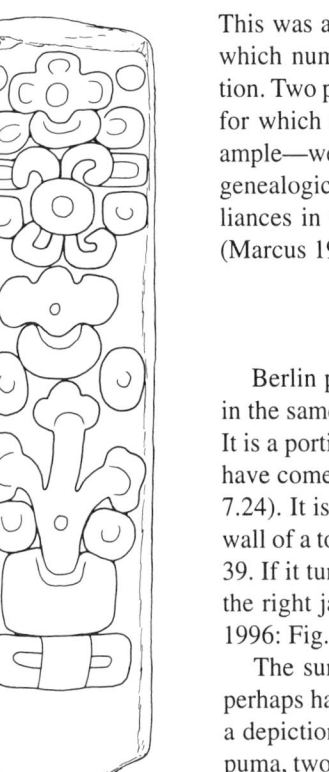

Figure 7.25. This carved stone bears four calendar dates that may have been the names of important Zapotec individuals. [Drawing by John Klausmeyer from photo in Berlin 1946: Fig 1a]

This was a period of increasing political balkanization during which numerous competing small polities jockeyed for position. Two popular themes on stone monuments of that period—for which the Santa María Sola lintel provides one more example—were (1) the establishment of one's right to rule through genealogical claims, and (2) politically important marriage alliances in which both noble husband and wife were depicted (Marcus 1980, 1983a).

A Second Stone from Santa María Sola

Berlin published a second monument with hieroglyphs, set in the same church at Santa María Sola (Berlin 1951: Fig. 10). It is a portion of a stone 1.28 m high and 0.60 m wide that may have come from a tomb; however, it is not a lintel (Figs. 7.23-7.24). It is more likely to have been a jamb or panel set in the wall of a tomb antechamber, probably at the nearby site of Sola 39. If it turns out to have been a jamb, it could be compared to the right jamb of a tomb at Reyes Etla (Marcus and Flannery 1996: Fig. 256).

The surviving portion of the stone shows a human figure, perhaps half of a marital pair. In this figure's headdress we see a depiction of Lightning (*Cociyo*) and the head of a jaguar or puma, two elements associated with Zapotec nobles. Above the figure's head are three dots that probably formed part of the

Figure 7.26. Ejutla carved stone showing a Zapotec noblewoman possibly named 13 Dog. [Drawing by John Klausmeyer from slide and photos supplied by the American Museum of Natural History]

Figure 7.27. Ejutla carved stone showing human figure with crossed arms; such "crossed arms" usually signify that a person is deceased. The top of this stone probably depicted the person's head. [Photo by Gary Feinman and Linda Nicholas]

Figure 7.28. Ejutla carved stone showing human figure with crossed arms; such "crossed arms" usually signify that a person is deceased. [Drawing by John Klausmeyer]

individual's calendar name. Although the name is not clear, Berlin (1951:12) tentatively identified it as "Mr. 1 Tiger." Because the monument is not complete, this identification must remain only one possibility. Stylistically, this stone (now set in the east wall of the Santa María Sola church) resembles monuments from the site of Tlacochahuaya and elsewhere in the Valley of Oaxaca.

A Stone from San Juan Sola

Another monument originally described by Berlin comes from San Juan Sola. This was Berlin's "Stone 3, stela with glyphs" (Berlin 1946: Fig. 1a). This carved stela or tomb jamb measures 1.35 m in height, 0.33 m in width, and 0.30 m in thickness (Fig. 7.25). It displays four day-signs from the Zapotec calendar. Berlin (1946:35) read them from bottom to top as 7 J, 2 D, 7 L, and 2 D, using Caso's (1928) glyph designations. Berlin's glyph designations are probably right, but I think it is possible the sequence was read from top to bottom.

Since no individuals are pictured with these hieroglyphs, we do not know whether this stela (or tomb jamb) refers to dates, or to the names of two noble marital pairs, or even to four noble ancestors. Like other Sola monuments with hieroglyphs, the style of this stone appears to be Monte Albán IIIb-IV.

Discussion

Now we can return to the six questions posed at the start of this chapter.

Figure 7.29. Ejutla carved stone of a crouching jaguar, shown consuming a stylized human heart, perhaps a metaphor for "sacrifice" or "conquest." Similar depictions are known from murals at Teotihuacan where jaguars are associated with hearts that have blood dripping from them (see Figs. 7.31-7.32). [Photo by Gary Feinman and Linda Nicholas]

Figure 7.30. Ejutla carved stone of a crouching jaguar, shown consuming a stylized human heart, perhaps a metaphor for "sacrifice" or "conquest." [Drawing by John Klausmeyer]

1. Why did Zapotec writing appear outside the Valley of Oaxaca?

Within the Zapotec region, Monte Albán nearly had a monopoly on writing for the first 600 years of its occupation. Only after A.D. 100 did carved stones and writing begin to appear at subordinate sites within the Valley of Oaxaca, as well as at sites outside the valley.

It seems clear that the initial appearance of Zapotec writing *outside* the Valley of Oaxaca coincided with the expansion of the Zapotec state. Such expansion seems to have been achieved in a variety of ways—blatant conquest, the threat of conquest, peaceful political incorporation, or colonization of a sparsely occupied region. The Zapotec noble administrators who were shipped to outlying regions provided the glue that held the empire together.

After several generations had passed, some of these Zapotec nobles commissioned the carving of stone monuments at their bases of power outside the Valley of Oaxaca. Their marriage ties to other noble families, whether recent or in the past, were commemorated in stone. Such a strategy aided the nobles residing in outlying valleys by helping them to secure certain privileges and laying the foundation for such privileges to be passed down to their offspring. If we had more detailed data, we might find that some even referred to marriage partners from the Valley of Oaxaca, perhaps even from Monte Albán itself.

2. Why did such writing appear outside the Valley of Oaxaca when it did?

As suggested above, writing first appeared outside the Valley of Oaxaca when the Zapotec state was expanding into neighboring regions, some of which featured a range of goods not produced in the Valley of Oaxaca. Some outlying regions were occupied by Zapotec speakers, and some were occupied by Mixtec, Chatino, and other groups. The hieroglyphic texts of Huamelulpan in the Mixteca are Zapotec in style, suggesting that some neighboring groups may have borrowed the script (Marcus 1983d:125-26). By Monte Albán IIIb-IV, however, there were so many Zapotec nobles living outside the Valley of Oaxaca that their tomb lintels and jambs strongly resembled valley prototypes.

3. What was the content of those texts and carved monuments?

During Monte Albán IIIb-IV, one of the important contexts for the display of Zapotec writing was the noble tomb. We would thus expect that elite genealogy, with the naming of ancestors and descendants, would be important themes; and indeed, we find that Sola Valley nobles were recording their names and life histories in such contexts. Just as in the Valley of Oaxaca (Marcus 1992a), the nobles of Sola were using tombs as the

Figure 7.31. Painted mural at Teotihuacan, showing a jaguar consuming human hearts with blood dripping from them. [Redrawn from Séjourné 1966: Fig. 15]

Figure 7.32. A stylized human heart with blood dripping from it. [Redrawn from Séjourné 1966: Lámina XLIX]

venue for recording their ties by blood or marriage to other elite families, possibly including families in the Valley of Oaxaca.

A second context for the display of carved stones in the Sola Valley was the ball court. The monuments associated with the ball court, however, have different themes; they display *Cociyo* or *Lightning*, and were carved to be tenoned. These tenoned *Cociyos* also have prototypes in the Valley of Oaxaca, most notably in the Valle Grande (or Zaachila region) which lies along the route from Monte Albán to Sola.

4. What do the Sola de Vega stones tell us about Sola's relationship to the Valley of Oaxaca?

An emerging state can use any number of techniques for expansion; the Zapotec state centered at Monte Albán used several. In the case of the Cuicatlán Cañada, it seems to have employed military conquest. In the case of the valleys of Ejutla and Miahuatlán, the Zapotecs seem to have used diplomacy and alliance building to incorporate and reorganize their neighbors. In the case of the Sola region, Monte Albán seems to have simply colonized an extremely underpopulated region.

According to Balkansky, the oldest settlements in the Sola region are few in number and date to Monte Albán Ia. His survey reveals four main sites by Monte Albán Ic or early Monte Albán II. Three sites are on terraced hilltops and the fourth (Sola 39) is at the base of a defensible hilltop similar to the setting of Dainzú in the Valley of Oaxaca. Even though we are uncertain as to the precise political ties among the Sola sites or their relations (if any) during Monte Albán Ic, we can say that the regional settlement pattern in Sola is continuous with that of the Valley of Oaxaca. During Monte Albán Ic it appears that the site of San Martín Tilcajete was overrun and its palace burned, and that the Sola Valley itself was colonized in greater numbers by the Valley of Oaxaca Zapotec. This Period Ic colonization of the Sola Valley, as well as colonization and incorporation of other parts of the periphery, is tied to the process of Zapotec state expansion. Unfortunately, no hieroglyphic monuments from the Sola Valley are known to date to this crucial period. This lack of writing in the Sola Valley is not surprising, since Monte Albán seems to have virtually monopolized writing during this time period (Caso 1947; Marcus 1976a, 1976c, 1983c).

By late Monte Albán II, Balkansky believes that all settlements in the Sola Valley had been incorporated into Monte Albán's political sphere. This relatively late incorporation may reflect the fact that the two areas produced similar goods (whereas Cuicatlán, for example, offered tropical fruits, nuts, and other items; see Redmond 1983; Redmond and Spencer 1994; Spencer and Redmond 1997). It may also reflect the fact that areas like Cuicatlán lay on more strategic routes, leading to the Tehuacán Valley and the north. The northern route appears to have been part of the Zapotec state's initial thrust; when Sola was finally taken over, it may have been because it lay along the route to the Pacific piedmont where truly different products were available (Balkansky 1997:15; Marcus 1992a:396, 1998; Spencer 1982; Spencer and Redmond 1997).

Zapotec control of the Sola region was centralized, with site Sola 39 becoming larger at the expense of its satellite communities (Balkansky 1997). This situation is similar to the pattern in the Ejutla Valley to the east of Sola, where Feinman and Nicholas (1990, 1993) discovered that Monte Albán II inhabitants had been pulled away from smaller sites and concentrated at one large center near the present town of Ejutla.

By Monte Albán IIIa, continuous strings of fortified or defensible hilltop centers extended from the Valley of Oaxaca to Sola and to Ejutla (Feinman and Nicholas 1990). These hilltop centers overlooked the "corridor to the tropics" that led from the Valley of Oaxaca to Juquila and Tututepec on the Pacific

Coast, leaving little doubt what the Zapotecs' intentions were (Marcus 1992b:401, 1998:69). In the Sola Valley, the site called Sola 23 covered 71 ha and emerged as the local capital for the region. Nevertheless, there are no hieroglyphic monuments from Sola that can be securely dated to Monte Albán IIIa.

During Monte Albán III, Monte Albán's grip on some of its most distant colonies began to weaken (Marcus 1989b, 1998). By Monte Albán IIIb, the Zapotec state had retreated from areas like the Cuicatlán Cañada and Tututepec.

During Monte Albán IIIb-IV the string of hilltop sites linking the Valley of Oaxaca to Sola was abandoned, and site Sola 23 was greatly diminished in size. It appears that between A.D. 600 and 900 the Sola Valley fragmented into several polities, each seeking its own base of political power.

Monte Albán IIIb-IV is the period to which I would assign most of the currently known Sola monuments with hieroglyphs. Furthermore, the themes of those carved stones are similar to period IIIb-IV monuments in the Valley of Oaxaca proper. As Monte Albán's political and military power waned, competing Valley of Oaxaca political centers like Zaachila/Noriega, Cuilapan, Suchilquitongo, Lambityeco, and Matatlán rose to prominence (Marcus 1983a, 1989b). By then, Monte Albán's virtual monopoly on hieroglyphic texts in tombs had been broken, and competing centers on the valley floor were carving monuments that established their rulers' credentials. Particularly common were (1) genealogical registers that gave each local ruler's version of his noble ancestry, and (2) scenes of marital pairs conducting sacred rites that had implications for political alliance and consolidation of power (Marcus 1992a).

Most of the currently known Sola monuments with hieroglyphs represent an extension of this Monte Albán IIIb-IV pattern. The writing system is Zapotec; the concern with nobles, marriage, and elite rituals is similar; and there is the same preoccupation with genealogy, although the Sola Valley so far lacks genealogical monuments divided into two or three registers.

Both Sola and Valley of Oaxaca nobles considered tombs to be appropriate places to display such genealogical monuments. Sola's elite during period IIIb-IV seem to have considered themselves the equals of elite families in the Valley of Oaxaca. This period is the first time in Sola's history that we can suggest that this is the case, and I doubt that the Sola elite would have been allowed to do so while Monte Albán was at its apogee.

A fascinating but unanswered question is, "might some Sola marriage alliances have been hypogamous?" In other words, might noble women from the Valley of Oaxaca have been sent to Sola to marry local lords? The lintel from Santa María Sola features at least two noble women, and the so-called "Lord 1 Tiger" stone from the same church may feature a third noble woman. There appears to be yet another noble woman on a carved stone from the Ejutla Valley, located to the east of Sola (see Fig. 7.26). If some of these women were from the Valley of Oaxaca, it would indicate that patterns of noble hypogamy—amply demonstrated for the Postclassic—had considerable time depth. Hypogamy is likely to have played a role in the Zapotec strategy of incorporating surrounding valleys, but cannot be confirmed in this case without extensive excavation at such sites as Sola 39.

Another clear tie between Sola and the Valley of Oaxaca can be found in the tenoned monuments associated with ball courts. These stones, often carved with depictions of the powerful Zapotec supernatural *Cociyo*, have been found at Monte Albán, Reyes Etla, Zaachila, and Yagul in the Valley of Oaxaca. In the Sola region, they have been found with ball courts (or in the case of some out-of-context examples, in small civic-ceremonial plaza complexes near ball courts) (Berlin 1946, 1951; Balkansky 1997).

During Monte Albán V, the final prehispanic period, Balkansky considers Sola to have been divided into two *cacicazgos*, each affiliated with a different neighboring region. So far no carved stone monuments can be assigned to this period in the Sola Valley. This fact is not surprising, since very few carved monuments in the Valley of Oaxaca proper date to Monte Albán V. The Late Postclassic was an era in which perishable codices or "books" on deer hide had become the preferred medium for genealogical and political information. This medium allowed rulers to produce palimpsests, or "rewrite history," in a way that had not been possible with the stone monuments of earlier times.

As the corpus of monuments from Sola de Vega grows, our understanding of Zapotec writing will also increase. We may eventually be able to document some of the nonmilitary strategies the Zapotec used as their empire expanded and incorporated surrounding regions.

5. Why has the decipherment of Zapotec writing lagged behind that of Maya writing?

While the decipherment of Maya writing has accelerated rapidly in recent years, the pace of Zapotec decipherment has remained rather slow. There are several reasons for this contrast.

a) Several thousand Maya texts are known. In contrast, Zapotec monuments with hieroglyphic texts number only in the hundreds. Thus the Maya sample is much larger.
b) Maya texts are often long, and reveal the same sequences of glyphs over and over. Zapotec texts tend to be short, and have few long clauses that show repetitive sequences of signs. This lack of repetitive clauses impedes decipherment.
c) Many Maya glyphs occur scores of times in the corpus of texts; many Zapotec glyphs occur less than five times, and some only occur once.
d) Maya writing is far more syllabic than Zapotec; Zapotec writing appears to be more logographic.
e) Bishop Diego de Landa provided a syllabary for sixteenth-century Yucatec Maya, and that syllabary has been used as a "Rosetta Stone" for the phonetic decipherment of Maya hieroglyphs (see Tozzer 1941:170 for Landa's syllabary). No comparable Zapotec syllabary exists.
f) Luckily for Mayanists, Landa was able to get his six-

teenth-century Yucatec informant to draw, in order, the glyphs for the twenty days of the Maya calendar. Later a label was written next to each day sign in the European alphabet, identifying each day by name and easing the way for decipherment (see Tozzer 1941:134). We lack sixteenth-century drawings of the twenty Zapotec day glyphs, placed in order, each labeled with its name. Such drawings would allow us to link sixteenth-century Zapotec day names (Córdova 1578b) to the hieroglyphs for those days.

6. How does the discovery of carved stones in the Sola Valley further the task of decipherment?

All the early efforts at reconstructing Zapotec history were focused on monuments from Monte Albán (Acosta 1958-1959; Batres 1902; Caso 1928, 1947, 1965a, 1965b). To make more progress, we must expand outward from the Zapotec capital to include many new monuments from Monte Albán's dependencies, located both within and outside the Valley of Oaxaca.

Monuments found outside the Valley of Oaxaca include those from Sola de Vega and from the Ejutla Valley (see Figs. 7.26-7.30). One monument from Ejutla shows a human figure with crossed arms, an arm position often associated with revered ancestors (Figs. 7.27-7.28). The top of the stone appears to have been broken off, which is probably why this individual lacks a head; however, if the individual's head was not part of the original sculpture, we might conclude that the figure was a decapitated sacrificial victim like those at Cerro Sechín (Marcus 1992a: Fig. 11.32). Another monument from Ejutla (Figs. 7.29-7.30) shows a jaguar eating what may be a stylized human heart, a motif known from Teotihuacan (Figs. 7.31-7.32).

These new monuments expand our knowledge of the themes used on stone sculptures outside the Valley of Oaxaca. With more survey and excavation in the Sola de Vega and Ejutla region, we would expect our corpus of monuments to increase, thereby expanding our understanding of the timing and nature of Zapotec imperial expansion.

Our knowledge of Zapotec writing will also be aided by the discovery of new texts. A larger corpus of texts will increase our sample of specific hieroglyphs and clauses, thereby expediting Zapotec decipherment as well as contributing to the reconstruction of Zapotec dynastic history. The fact that Balkansky's work provides provenience and context for many of the new monuments increases their importance.

Bibliography

Acosta, Jorge R.
1958-59 Exploraciones arqueológicas en Monte Albán, XVIII temporada. Revista Mexicana de Estudios Antropológicos 15:7-50.

Balkansky, Andrew K.
1997 Archaeological Settlement Patterns of the Sola Valley, Oaxaca, Mexico. Ph.D. dissertation, University of Wisconsin, Madison.

Balsalobre, Gonzalo de
1892 Relación auténtica de las idolatrías, supersticiones, vanas observaciones de los indios del Obispado de Oaxaca. Anales del Museo Nacional de México, Primera Epoca, Tomo VI: 225-60. Mexico.

Batres, Leopoldo
1902 Exploraciones de Monte Albán. Mexico: Casa Editorial Gante.

Berlin, Heinrich
1946 Three Zapotec stones. Carnegie Institution of Washington, Division of Historical Research, Notes on Middle American Archaeology and Ethnology, pp. 34-36. Washington, D.C.
1951 A survey of the Sola region in Oaxaca (Mexico). Ethnos 16(1-2):1-17.
1957 Las antiguas creencias en San Miguel Sola, Oaxaca, México. Beiträge zur mittelamerikanischen Völkerkunde, Herausgegeben von Hamburgishen Museum für Völkerkunde und Vorgeschichte, no. 4.
1958 El glifo "emblema" en las inscripciones mayas. Journal de la Société des Américanistes 47:111-19.
1959 Glifos nominales en el sarcófago de Palenque. Humanidades 2 (10):1-8. Universidad de San Carlos, Guatemala.

Blanton, Richard E.
1978 Monte Albán: Settlement Patterns at the Ancient Zapotec Capital. New York: Academic Press.

Caso, Alfonso
1928 Las estelas zapotecas. Talleres Gráficos de la Nación, México, D.F.
1938 Exploraciones en Oaxaca, quinta y sexta temporadas, 1936-1937. Instituto Panamericano de Geografía e Historia, Publicación 34. Mexico.
1947 Calendario y escritura de las antiguas culturas de Monte Albán. In Obras Completas de Miguel Othón de Mendizábal: un homenaje, Vol. 1, pp. 5-102. Mexico: Talleres de la Nación.
1949 El mapa de Teozacoalco. Cuadernos Americanos 8 (5):145-81. Mexico.
1965a Zapotec writing and calendar. In: Handbook of Middle American Indians, edited by Robert Wauchope and Gordon R. Willey, Vol. 3, part 2, pp. 931-47. Austin: University of Texas Press.
1965b Sculpture and mural painting of Oaxaca. In: Handbook of Middle American Indians, edited by Robert Wauchope (general editor) and Gordon R. Willey (volume editor), Vol. 3, part 2, pp. 849-70. Austin: University of Texas Press.

Caso, Alfonso, and Ignacio Bernal
1952 Urnas de Oaxaca. Memorias del Instituto Nacional de Antropología e Historia 13. Mexico.

Caso, Alfonso, and Daniel Rubín de la Borbolla
1936 Exploraciones en Mitla, 1934-1935. Instituto Panamericano de Geografía e Historia, Publicación 21. Mexico.

Caso, Alfonso, and Lorenzo Gamio
1961   Informe de exploraciones en Huamelulpan. Manuscript in the archivo del Instituto Nacional de Antropología e Historia, Mexico.

Córdova, fray Juan de
1578a Vocabulario en Lengua Zapoteca. Mexico: Pedro Charte y Antonio Ricardo.
1578b Arte en Lengua Zapoteca. Mexico: Pedro Balli.
1942   Vocabulario en Lengua Zapoteca, edited by Wigberto Jiménez Moreno. Mexico: Instituto Nacional de Antropología e Historia.

Feinman, Gary, and Linda Nicholas
1990   At the margins of the Monte Albán state: settlement patterns in the Ejutla Valley, Oaxaca, Mexico. Latin American Antiquity 1:216-46.
1993   Shell-ornament production in Ejutla: implications for highland-coastal interaction in ancient Oaxaca. Ancient Mesoamerica 4:103-19.

Gaxiola, Margarita
1976   Excavaciones en San Martín Huamelulpan, 1974. Tesis profesional, Escuela Nacional de Antropología, México, D.F.

Kowalewski, Stephen, Gary M. Feinman, Laura Finsten, Richard Blanton, and Linda M. Nicholas
1989   Monte Albán's Hinterland, Part II: Prehispanic Settlement Patterns in Tlacolula, Etla, and Ocotlán, the Valley of Oaxaca, Mexico. Memoirs of the University of Michigan Museum of Anthropology, No. 23. Ann Arbor.

Marcus, Joyce
1975   The Zapotec Calendar. Report submitted to the National Endowment for the Humanities, Washington, D.C.
1976a The iconography of militarism at Monte Albán and neighboring sites in the Valley of Oaxaca. In: The Origins of Religious Art and Iconography in Preclassic Mesoamerica, edited by Henry B. Nicholson, pp. 123-39. Los Angeles: Latin American Center at UCLA.
1976b An Analysis of the Ancient Zapotec Writing System. Report submitted to National Endowment for the Humanities, Washington, D.C.
1976c The origins of Mesoamerican writing. Annual Review of Anthropology 5:35-67.
1980   Zapotec writing. Scientific American 242: 50-64.
1983a Changing patterns of stone monuments after the fall of Monte Albán, A.D. 600-900. In: The Cloud People: Divergent Evolution of the Zapotec and Mixtec Civilizations, edited by K.V. Flannery and J. Marcus, pp. 191-97. New York: Academic Press.
1983b Stone monuments and tomb murals of Monte Albán IIIa. In: The Cloud People: Divergent Evolution of the Zapotec and Mixtec Civilizations, edited by K.V. Flannery and J. Marcus, pp. 137-43. New York: Academic Press.
1983c The first appearance of Zapotec writing and calendrics. In: The Cloud People: Divergent Evolution of the Zapotec and Mixtec Civilizations, edited by K.V. Flannery and J. Marcus, pp. 91-96. New York: Academic Press.
1983d The style of the Huamelulpan stone monuments. In: The Cloud People: Divergent Evolution of the Zapotec and Mixtec Civilizations, edited by K.V. Flannery and J. Marcus, pp. 125-26. New York: Academic Press.
1989a Zapotec chiefdoms and the nature of Formative religions. In: Regional Perspectives on the Olmec, edited by Robert J. Sharer and David C. Grove, pp. 148-97. Santa Fe, NM: School of American Research and Cambridge University Press.
1989b From centralized systems to city-states: possible models for the Epiclassic. In: Mesoamerica after the Decline of Teotihuacan A.D. 700-900, edited by Richard A. Diehl and Janet C. Berlo, pp. 201-8. Washington, D.C.: Dumbarton Oaks.
1992a Mesoamerican Writing Systems: Propaganda, Myth, and History in Four Ancient Civilizations. Princeton: Princeton University Press.
1992b Dynamic cycles of Mesoamerican states. National Geographic Research & Exploration 8:392-411.
1997   The Carved Stones from Sola. Manuscript in possession of the author.
1998   The peaks and valleys of ancient states: an extension of the dynamic model. In: Archaic States, edited by Gary M. Feinman and Joyce Marcus, pp. 59-94. Santa Fe, NM: SAR Press.

Marcus, Joyce, and Kent V. Flannery
1994   Ancient Zapotec ritual and religion: an application of the direct historical approach. In: The Ancient Mind, edited by Colin Renfrew and Ezra B.W. Zubrow, pp. 55-74. Cambridge: Cambridge University Press.
1996   Zapotec Civilization: How Urban Society Evolved in Mexico's Oaxaca Valley. New York: Thames and Hudson.

Méndez Martínez, Enrique
1988   Tumba 5 de Huijazoo. Arqueología 2:7-16. Dirección de Monumentos Prehispánicos, Instituto Nacional de Antropología e Historia, México.

Middleton, William D., Gary Feinman, and Guillermo Molina V.
1998   Tomb use and reuse in Oaxaca, Mexico. Ancient Mesoamerica 9(2):297-307.

Miller, Arthur G.
1991   The carved stela in Tomb 5, Suchilquitongo, Oaxaca, Mexico. Ancient Mesoamerica 2:215-24.
1995   The Painted Tombs of Oaxaca, Mexico: Living with the Dead. New York: Cambridge University Press.

Moser, Christopher L.
1977   Ñuiñe Writing and Iconography of the Mixteca Baja. Vanderbilt University Publications in Anthropology 19, Nashville, Tennessee.

Oliver, James P.
1955   Architectural similarities of Mitla and Yagul. Mesoamerican Notes 4:49-68. Department of Anthropology, Mexico City College, Mexico.

Proskouriakoff, Tatiana
1960   Historical implications of a pattern of dates at Piedras Negras, Guatemala. American Antiquity 25:454-75.
1962   Historical data in the inscriptions of Yaxchilan, part 1. Estudios de Cultura Maya 3:149-166.
1963   Historical data in the inscriptions of Yaxchilan, part 2. Estudios de Cultura Maya 4:177-201.

Rabin, Emily
1970 The Lambityeco friezes: notes on their content. Boletín de Estudios Oaxaqueños 33. Mitla, Mexico.

Redmond, Elsa M.
1983 A Fuego y Sangre: Early Zapotec Imperialism in the Cuicatlán Cañada, Oaxaca. Studies in Latin American Ethnohistory & Archaeology, Vol. I. Memoirs of the University of Michigan Museum of Anthropology 16. Ann Arbor.

Redmond, Elsa M., and Charles S. Spencer
1994 The cacicazgo: an indigenous design. In: Caciques and Their People: A Volume in Honor of Ronald Spores, edited by J. Marcus and Judith F. Zeitlin, pp. 189-225. Anthropological Papers of the University of Michigan Museum of Anthropology 89. Ann Arbor.

Séjourné, Laurette
1966 Arquitectura y pintura en Teotihuacan. Mexico: Siglo XXI Editores.

Smith, Mary Elizabeth
1973 Picture Writing from Ancient Southern Mexico: Mixtec Place Signs and Maps. Norman: University of Oklahoma Press.

Spencer, Charles S.
1982 The Cuicatlán Cañada and Monte Albán: A Study of Primary State Formation. New York: Academic Press.

Spencer, Charles S., and Elsa M. Redmond
1997 Archaeology of the Cuicatlán Cañada, Oaxaca. American Museum of Natural History Anthropological Paper No. 80. New York.

Tozzer, Alfred M.
1941 Landa's Relación de las Cosas de Yucatán, edited by Alfred M. Tozzer. Peabody Museum of Ethnology and Archaeology, Harvard University, Vol. 18. Cambridge.

Urcid, Javier
1993 The Pacific Coast of Oaxaca and Guerrero: westernmost extent of the Zapotec script. Ancient Mesoamerica 4:141-65.

Urcid, Javier, and John Paddock
1989 Cuando los kilómetros no miden la distancia. In: Etcetera, suplemento semanal, segunda época, número 32.

Wicke, Charles
1957 The ball court at Yagul, Oaxaca: a comparative study. Mesoamerican Notes 5:37-76. Department of Anthropology, Mexico City College, Mexico.

Winter, Marcus, Javier Urcid, Raúl Matadamas, Damon E. Peeler, and Benjamín Maldonado
1994 Escritura zapoteca prehispánica: nuevas aportaciones. Contribución No. 4 del Proyecto Especial Monte Albán 1992-1994. Oaxaca, Mexico.

Chapter 8

Shell from Sola de Vega

Linda M. Nicholas and Gary M. Feinman
The Field Museum

In June 1996, we examined 16 pieces of shell that were collected by Andrew Balkansky as part of the archaeological settlement survey of the Sola Valley. Shell was found at seven localities in Sola, compared to 21 settlements in the Ejutla Valley and 20 settlements in the much larger Valley of Oaxaca. If we consider the number of sites found in each of these survey regions, shell was found at roughly 5% of the total number of localities in Sola and Ejutla but less than 1% of the settlements in Oaxaca (Feinman and Nicholas 1992). Although such comparisons are preliminary at best, we would advance the hypothesis that access to shell was greater in these two smaller peripheral valleys than it was in the Valley of Oaxaca.

The Sola shell sample was composed entirely of Pacific marine varieties (Table 8.1). Six different genera were noted. Of 12 Sola shell pieces that could be identified to genus, five were identified as the nacreous pelecypod, *Pinctada* (*mazatlanica*). *Pinctada mazatlanica* also was the most abundant species in a shell ornament manufacturing context that we excavated at the Ejutla site (Feinman and Nicholas 1993). Three other taxa (*Oliva, Patella,* and *Spondylus*) found in the Sola surface collections also were well represented in the Ejutla excavations, and are marine varieties that long have been recognized as having been used for ornamentation in prehispanic Mesoamerica (Kolb 1987; Suárez 1981). The fifth taxa that was identified

TABLE 8.1. Marine Shell from the Sola Valley

Site	Item	Class	Genus	Species
Sola 3	unfinished triangular placa 2.3 × 1.8 × 0.4 cm	pelecypod	*Pinctada*	*mazatlanica*
Sola 3	unidentified fragment			
Sola 3	fragment	gastropod	*Patella*	*mexicana*
Sola 3	burnt hinge	pelecypod	*Pinctada?*	*mazatlanica?*
Sola 3	fragment	gastropod	*Patella?*	
Sola 3	finished rectangular placa 2.4 × 1.5 × 0.3 cm	pelecypod	*Spondylus*	
Sola 10	hinge fragment	pelecypod	*Pinctada*	*mazatlanica*
Sola 10	placa abraded rim	pelecypod	*Pinctada*	*mazatlanica*
Sola 23	fragment	pelecypod	*Pinctada*	*mazatlanica*
Sola 39	unmodified whole shell	pelecypod	*Tellina*	
Sola 39	unfinished disk	gastropod		
Sola 41	finished broken pendant	gastropod	*Oliva*	*porphyria*
Sola 41	fragment	gastropod	*Oliva*	*porphyria?*
Sola 42	finished whole pendant 2.0 × 2.0 cm with rough hole punched near beak	pelecypod	*Noetia*	*reversa*
Sola 61	fragment	pelecypod		
Sola 61	whole conch (looter's collection photographed)	gastropod		

(*Tellina*) also was recorded at the Ejutla site, although the last Sola shell variety (*Noetia reversa*) was not.

Given the small sample of Sola shell found at eight different sites, it is difficult to discern much about the use of this good across the region. At present, we can say that there are no indications of shell-working at Sola 23, 41, 42, and 61, where, respectively, one, two, one, and one pieces of shell were found (a complete conch shell came from a cave offering at Sola 61 found by looters). In contrast, we do see the possibility for ancient shell-working activities at both Sola 10 and 39. At each of these sites, two pieces of shell were collected. Yet, more importantly, one of the pieces at each of these sites was an unidentified worked ornament. At Sola 10, this piece was a *Pinctada mazatlanica* plaque with an abraded rim, while at Sola 39, the unfinished piece was a disk from an unidentifiable gastropod columella. Such unfinished, but still clearly worked, shell pieces were abundant in the shell-working contexts at the Ejutla site. The strongest current evidence for shell-working was observed at Sola 3, where a total of six shell artifacts, representing at least three different species (*Patella, Pinctada, Spondylus*) were identified. One of these pieces was an unfinished triangular plaque of *Pinctada mazatlanica*, while a second piece of *Pinctada* (a hinge) was burnt. A finished *Spondylus* rectangular plaque also was found at Sola 3. None of the Sola sites provides the wealth of evidence for shell-working that we found on the surface of the Ejutla site, but further work clearly will be needed to compare the intensity of production at the two sites.

In sum, we suggest that shell ornaments likely were fashioned at minimally one prehispanic site in the Sola region and possibly more. Only three of the sixteen pieces of Sola shell were finished ornaments, thus it seems highly unlikely that marine shell only arrived from the coast in Sola as a finished product. Some shell likely entered the Sola region as whole shells or large finished pieces from which ornaments were then crafted. This was the case at the Ejutla site, where the volume and nature of shell debris indicates that finished shell ornaments likely then were exported to other sites and regions (Feinman and Nicholas 1993, 1995). At present, it is unclear whether the shell that arrived in Sola eventually made its way outside the Sola Valley to Monte Albán and other sites in the Valley of Oaxaca, but that hypothesis certainly cannot be eliminated at this time.

Chapter 9

Resumen en Español

Traducción de Verónica Pérez Rodríguez

Los estudios de patrones de asentamiento realizados en el valle de Oaxaca y sus alrededores formularon preguntas acerca de los orígenes y dinámicas que contribuyeron, a largo plazo, a la formación del primer estado zapoteco. Un asunto central de esta investigación es la relación que hubo entre la capital zapoteca (Monte Albán), con otras regiones más allá del valle de Oaxaca. Monte Albán tuvo contacto con regiones adyacentes a su territorio inmediato, ya sea por medio de relaciones de comercio, diplomacia, migración o guerra. Sin embargo, los mecanismos que unieron a Monte Albán con regiones más alejadas no siempre fueron los mismos. Este estudio del valle de Sola examinará modelos de la expansión sociopolítica de Monte Albán y de los efectos que ésta expansión tuvo en el desarrollo de la complejidad socio-política de las demás regiones de Oaxaca. La información proveniente del valle de Sola es además relevante al estudio de la declinación de Monte Albán y contribuirá al conocimiento de los mecanismos que fueron implementados durante la época Posclásica, para establecer una autoridad política a nivel local.

En 1995-1996 se realizó el proyecto de recorrido arqueológico del valle de Sola, Oaxaca. El propósito de éste estudio fue el de evaluar las interacciones dinámicas que hubo entre el valle de Sola, Monte Albán, y los valles aledaños. El valle de Sola se encuentra en un punto estratégico, en el trayecto de transporte que conectaba las tierras altas y los valles centrales con la costa. En los años cuarenta (1940s), en el valle de Sola, Heinrich Berlin reportó haber visto extensos sitios con estructuras piramidales, juegos de pelota, y piedras grabadas con iconografía semejante a la de Monte Albán. Este proyecto tenía como objetivos el de situar las observaciones de Berlin en un plano empírico, y el de comparar los patrones de asentamiento registrados a través de las regiones de tierras altas del estado de Oaxaca. Se utilizaron métodos de recorrido arqueológico de cobertura total y se registraron 120 sitios prehipánicos en un área de 370 km². Como resultado, los datos reflejan la variación total encontrada en los patrones de asentamiento del valle de Sola.

La expansión de Monte Albán durante el Formativo

En el valle de Sola no se registraron sitios anteriores al periodo Monte Albán I. El primer sitio fue establecido durante la primera fase (Ia). Después hubo una rápida colonización del valle, seguida por importantes transformaciones en los patrones de asentamiento durante la fase Ic. Los sitios de la fase Ic se concentran alrededor de los primeros asentamientos establecidos en las cimas de los cerros. Esta localización daba acceso a cualquier punto de los valles. Para el periodo Monte Albán II se había establecido una capital a nivel regional (el Sitio S39 se encuentra cerca de Santa María Sola), la cual contaba con arquitectura monumental y cerámica decorada de pasta crema fina. La mayoría de la población se concentraba alrededor de este centro regional. Los patrones de asentamiento del periodo II no tenían un carácter defensivo como lo habían tenido los asentamientos de épocas anteriores. Esto sugiere que el territorio político de Monte Albán se extendía más allá de ésta región. El valle de Sola fue colonizado durante la fase Ic, luego fue incorporado al estado zapoteco en el periodo II, probablemente debido a su localización estratégica como punto de coneccíon entre las tierras altas y la costa de Oaxaca.

La formación de los primeros estados mesoamericanos y la expansión de Monte Albán tuvo lugar durante los periodos Formativo Tardío y Terminal. Estos estados primarios aparecieron casi al mismo tiempo en distintas regiones que evidentemente tenían contacto entre si. Monte Albán buscaba controlar las rutas de intercambio desde el valle de Oaxaca al valle de México y hacia la costa del Pacífico. El valle de Sola, al igual que otras regiones, era esencial para el control y defensa del territorio zapoteco. La trayectoria de desarrollo sociopolítico de las distintas regiones variaba de tal forma que actualmente es necesario estudiar cada región y su desarrollo de manera individual. Monte Albán colonizó el valle de Sola, atacó la Mixteca y varias poblaciones de la costa, conquistó la Cañada de Cuicatlán e incorporó por medio de una hábil diplomacia o por la fuerza los territorios de Ejutla y Miahuatlán. Nuestros modelos teóricos de urbanización y de desarrollo de los estados primarios deben explicar estas variadas trayectorias regionales.

El colapso de Monte Albán durante la época Clásica tardía

Los datos de patrones de asentamiento provenientes del valle de Sola, durante las épocas Clásica y Posclásica tienen relevancia al estudio de la declinación de Monte Albán y del orígen de los cacicazgos Posclásicos. Durante el periodo IIIa Sola tuvo un importante crecimiento poblacional y urbanístico alrededor de una nueva capital regional (S23), incrementó al mismo tiempo la llegada de grupos de colonos al valle de Sola, provenientes de provincias lejanas. Los patrones de asentamiento del periodo IIIb-IV sugieren que Sola era una región autónoma a las demás regiones. Sin embargo, la región parece haber estado dividida internamente en varios centros políticos. Fue durante éste periodo que los centros subregionales invirtieron labor en grandes proyectos arquitectónicos en los sectores públicos; esto se ve reflejado en la proliferación de juegos de pelota y de monumentos de piedra grabada, éstos especialmente se encuentran asociados a las tumbas de las élites. La declinación política de Monte Albán se ve asociada en el valle de Sola al surgimiento de un mayor grado de competencia a nivel local. Además de esta competencia, surgió la formación de alianzas entre los distintos centros políticos autónomos.

El territorio de Monte Albán se redujo considerablemente entre los periodos IIIa al IIIb-IV. Sin embargo, ésto sucedío mientras que la población de las regiones aledañas a Monte Albán y la monumentalidad del sitio aumentaban. Las regiones que anteriormente fueron provincias de Monte Albán se separaron durante este periodo, formando nuevas configuraciones de asentamientos que se asemejaban a los cacicazgos de la época Posclásica. Monte Albán abandonó sus colonias en la Cañada de Cuicatlán durante la época de transición II/IIIa. Sola, Ejutla y algunas otras provincias cercanas permanecieron integradas al estado zapoteco durante ésta época. También en este momento Jalieza y otros asentamientos en el valle de Oaxaca se urbanizaron rápidamente. Estos cambios reflejan la inestabilidad y competencia que habia dentro del mismo valle de Oaxaca. Durante el periodo IIIb-IV, antes de su colapso parcial, Monte Albán no era más que uno de varios sitios que competían por supremacía política a nivel regional. La trayectoria regional de Sola nos da otra perspectiva más de la declinación de Monte Albán durante la época Clásica tardía.

Monte Albán y una perspectiva multi-regional

La expansión política y demográfica de Monte Albán hacia regiones distantes ha sido, y sigue siendo, un proceso muy controversial. Sin embargo, los modelos con los que contamos para estudiar estos procesos de expansión tienen indicios que pueden ser reconocidos y examinados a nivel regional. Si Monte Albán controló un territorio político multiregional, ¿Cómo se manifestaron estos procesos de incorporación en áreas fuera del valle de Oaxaca? ¿Cómo afectaron estos procesos a las distintas regiones? Otro asunto de interés es la eventual disolución de los primeros estados en Oaxaca. En el momento en que el estado zapoteco perdió control sobre las regiones vecinas, ¿cómo se llevó a cabo esa transición del Clásico al Posclásico? ¿Cómo cambia una región de una provincia de Monte Albán a una región autónoma? ¿Cómo pueden los datos del valle de Sola mejorar los modelos que tenemos de la declinación de Monte Albán y la consecuente transición al periodo Posclásico? El estudio de los patrones de asentamiento a nivel macroregional es indispensable para entender estos temas.

Las interacciones entre Monte Albán y el valle de Sola influyeron los patrones de asentamientos locales durante la época prehispánica. Sin embargo, en el valle de Sola ésto sucedió de manera distinta a otras regiones. Los primeros asentamientos en el valle de Sola indican que la región fue parte de una provincia externa de Monte Albán. Luego, a través de la secuencia prehispánica, la región se volvió cada vez más autónoma, y en el momento de la Conquista, la región estaba dividida en varios reinos independientes. La expansión territorial de Monte Albán estaba vinculada a la formación de los primeros estados en el valle de Sola, aunque en esta región la secuencia fue distinta a la de otras regiones que fueron conquistadas o colonizadas. Esto sugiere que los primeros estados Mesoamericanos usaron múltiples estrategias para incorporar nuevas regiones a sus territorios.

La declinación de Monte Albán se ve reflejada en las construcciones monumentales que formaron parte de estrategias originadas por las élites, con el fin de legitimizar su autoridad política en una región lejana a Monte Albán. Los resultados demuestran la importante contribución que aportan las perspectivas macroregionales en el estudio de desarrollo y cambio cultural pre-hispánico.

Appendix A

Site Descriptions

SITE 1
Municipio: San Juan
UTM: E612000/N1827400
Environment: High piedmont/1800 m
Site Size: 8.50 ha
Periodization: IIIa, IIIb-IV, V
Condition: Excellent

Description: Sola 1 was located in the high piedmont 1 km southwest of modern San Juan Sola. The site was cleared of pine and oak cover, and had heavy secondary growth in places. Water was available from *barrancas* on all sides of the site. The site had a commanding view of the valley. Cabo de Hacha—a prominent landscape feature in the southern Valley of Oaxaca—was visible from the uppermost portion of the site.

The survey mapped multiple structures and 37 terraces. Most of the terraces were not plowed, and were overgrown with grass, low shrubs, and cactus. Still, there was a wide range of artifacts, including ceramic, lithic (chert flakes, green and gray obsidian), and a carved stone. The carved stone was associated with the adoratorio in the center of the main plaza. Other features recorded were a looted tomb, defensive wall and ditch, two plazas, an altar, ball court, and many ruined terraces (not mapped) below the defensive wall. Very low artifact density below the defensive wall could suggest that these were primarily agricultural terraces, but the erosion was too severe to be certain. Houses near Mound 5 and its platform had plaster floors. Mound 1 and 2 also had exposed plaster floors.

An extremely steep drop-off from the north and west sides made the site inaccessible and highly defensible. The only possible approach was covered by the defensive wall and ditch. Natural bedrock outcrops immediately below this wall could have been utilized for defensive purposes as well. A chert point was found in the area of ruined terraces below the defensive wall.

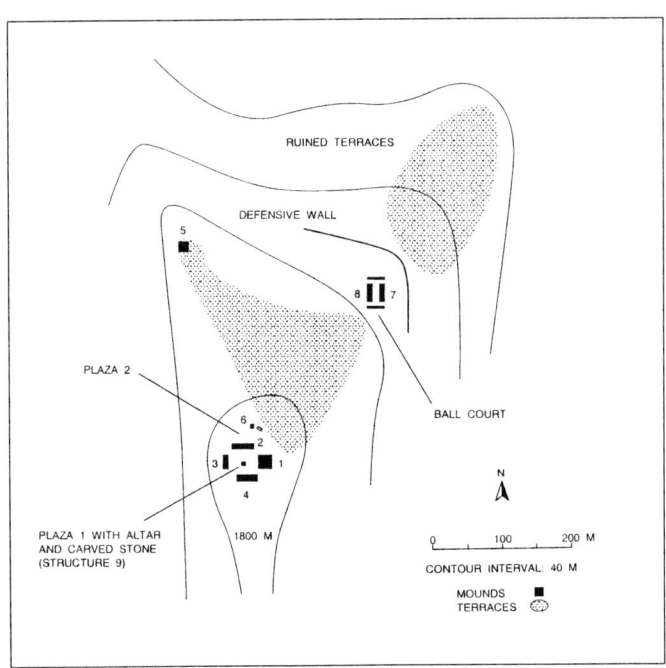

Figure A.1. San Juan Sola (S1).

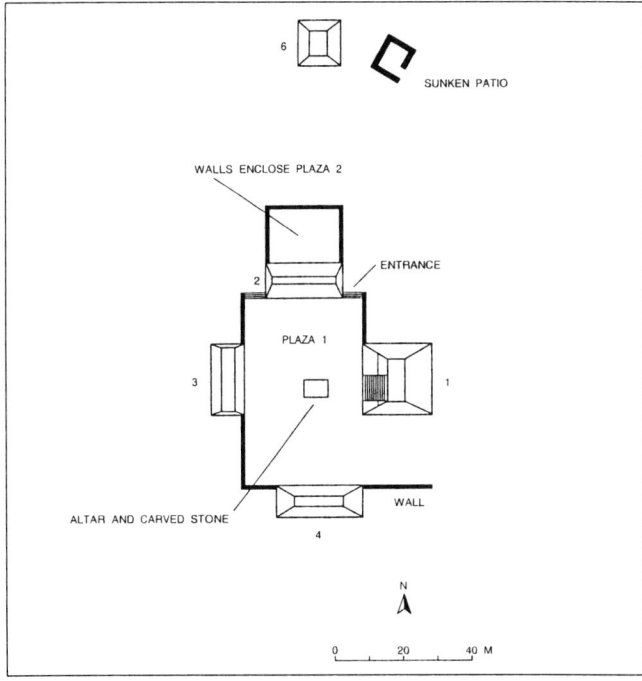

Figure A.2. Detail of the civic-ceremonial core at San Juan Sola.

Sola 1 was a key IIIa site in the western Sola Valley. Ceramic distributions suggest this was its phase of initial occupation, although the site continued to be important into IIIb-IV. Modern use includes periodic farming and grazing. There was an isolated residence within the site limits. Irrigation canals and check-dams were used at lower elevations, near the modern town. Residents of San Juan consider the site to be their Pueblo Viejo. The presence of a small Period V component offers some support for this view (but see Sola 20).

Phase-by-Phase Site Size and Population Estimates:

Phase	Area (ha)	Low	High	Mean
IIIa	8.50	200	408	304
IIIb-IV	8.50	200	408	304
V	1.20	12	30	21

SITE 2
Municipio: San Juan
UTM: E612800/N1827400
Environment: Low piedmont/1620 m
Site Size: 0.02 ha
Periodization: V
Condition: Fair (plowed)

Description: The site was located on the same piedmont slope below Sola 1. *Barrancas* on either side of the site provided ready water sources 100 m distant. The site was cleared for maize and peanut cultivation. The prehispanic remains consisted of an isolated Late Postclassic house. The collection included Red-on-Cream and polychrome pottery. No other artifacts were recorded.

Phase-by-Phase Site Size and Population Estimates:

Phase	Area (ha)	Low	High	Mean
V	0.02	5	10	8

SITE 3
Municipio: San Juan
UTM: E613500/N1827800
Environment: Low piedmont/1580 m
Site Size: 20.47 ha
Periodization: II, IIIa, IIIb-IV, V
Condition: Fair (eroded)

Description: Sola 3 was located at a lower elevation on the same piedmont ridge as Sola 1, 250 m south of modern San Juan Sola. The site extension along the long, low, nearly flat piedmont slope was over 1200 m. Most of the site area was highly eroded. This part of the piedmont near San Juan was cleared of vegetation, although many fruit trees were grown on the adjacent valley floor. *Barrancas* on either side of the *loma* provided water sources from 100-150 m distant. The site terminated just above the alluvium.

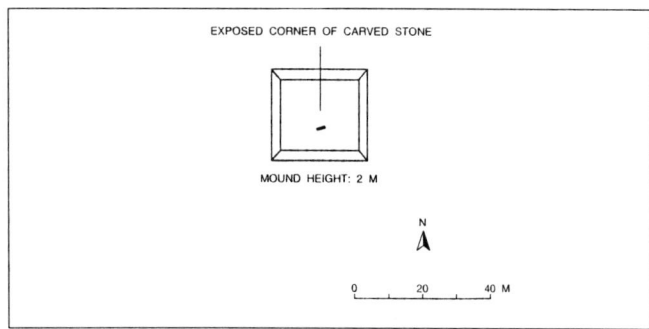

Figure A.3. Detail of Mound 2 at Sola 3.

Sola 3 was distinguished by three dispersed mounds strung along the *loma*, each built over a natural rise. A badly eroded carved stone was found jutting out from the top of Mound 2. This same mound serves as a *punto trino* marking the boundaries of San Miguel, San Juan, and San Ildefonso. These mounds overlooked highly productive alluvium on either side of the *loma*. Artifacts included ceramics, chert tools and flakes, and heavy densities of green and gray obsidian.

More obsidian was collected here than at all other sites combined. Heavy densities of shell were associated with the obsidian, including evidence for shell production. In this same portion of site, there was possible evidence for ceramic production with a large number of incompletely fired orange-brownware vessels (jars and a *sahumador*) and a waster with mat impressions. This shell/obsidian zone had multiple occupations dating from Periods II-V, but had the greatest density of Period V material on the surface. This included a probable elite residence with red-painted plaster floor. Period V pottery included polychrome, Graphite-on-Orange, Huitzo Red-on-Cream, and G.3M. Unfortunately, this portion of the site was completely destroyed by agriculture and badly eroded; future excavations would be unlikely to find undisturbed deposits. Earlier ceramics included a G.23, and imitation plumbate. Finally, a *mano* fragment was associated with an area of ruined houses between Mounds 1 and 2. Other features included a looted tomb, and retention walls to control erosion. Population estimates used a higher density figure for the terraced area.

There was modern use over nearly the entire site, with several dispersed residences, while the *loma* was used for agricultural purposes; nearly all the available land was either in cultivation or left fallow but recently plowed. Fruit trees were grown near streams on both sides of *loma*.

Phase-by-Phase Site Size and Population Estimates:

Phase	Area (ha)	Low	High	Mean
II	1.12	28	56	42
IIIa	12.00	300	600	450
IIIb-IV	12.00	100	400	250
V	20.47	355	812	584

SITE 4
Municipio: San Juan
UTM: E714300/N1828000
Environment: Low piedmont/1520 m
Site Size: 1.66 ha
Periodization: IIIa, V
Condition: Good

Description: Sola 4 was located on the path between San Juan and San Ildefonso Sola. The site was not utilized when surveyed, but appears to have been cultivated in the recent past. A *barranca* provided water 150 m to the south. Well-watered alluvial bottomlands were located nearby.

The site had outstanding views of the valley in all directions. Since the Period IIIa and V sites were far smaller than other contemporaneous sites, they might have functioned as observation points. Ceramics were Classic utilitarian wares and G.3Ms. The Period V occupation was restricted to a small portion of the site, and was likely an isolated residence.

Phase-by-Phase Site Size and Population Estimates:

Phase	Area (ha)	Low	High	Mean
IIIa	1.66	17	42	30
V	0.02	5	10	8

SITE 5

Municipio: San Juan
UTM: E612100/N1826000
Environment: Mountain/2100 m
Site Size: 3.17 ha
Periodization: IIIa, V
Condition: Fair (plowed/eroded)

Description: Sola 5 was located on the hilltop known as "El Mogote de Piedra"—perhaps owing to the many rock outcrops that make for a difficult ascent. The hill was extremely steep, but the summit was broad and flat. Pine forest prevailed at this elevation. The site was located near the origin of several mountain streams, but these were not readily accessible given the steep slope. Modern use included rainfall farming of the hilltop (maize), grazing, and exploitation of forest resources. The site was plowed at the time of the survey.

A small mound was located on the east side of the hilltop, overlooking the valley. Terraces were built on the hillside near the summit—facing the only possible ascent—and near the mound (approximately 8 terraces in total). The terraces were too damaged from plowing and erosion to map. The site was one of a string of IIIa hilltop terraced sites that defined the western ridgeline of the valley. Even though the Sola 5 hilltop was plowed and the surface visibility was excellent, there was a very low ceramic density, suggesting that residential functions were limited. No house foundations or ground stone was recorded; there were only trace density of chert and quartz flakes. The Period IIIa site may have served as an outpost, observation point, or fort. The site was similar in these respects to Sola 40 and 55. The nature of the Period V component was unclear; there was no indication of a residence.

Phase-by-Phase Site Size and Population Estimates:

Phase	Area (ha)	Low	High	Mean
IIIa	3.17	68	150	109
V	0.01	5	10	8

SITE 6

Municipio: San Juan
UTM: E611500/N1826300
Environment: Mountain/2040 m
Site Size: 3.84 ha
Periodization: IIIb-IV, V
Condition: Fair (plowed/proded)

Description: The site was located at the confluence of two mountain streams that eventually pass Sola 1 and continue to the valley floor. There were many ruined terraces that could not be formally mapped (approximately 15 terraces total). A lone mound was located on a higher level of ridgeline, above the terraced area. It was a highly defensible site location.

The mound was located along a narrow *montura* that links the lower portion of the ridgeline to the high sierra that defines the valley's watershed. The terraced area likely included many houses, seen in occasional foundation stones still in place, and the utilitarian nature of the artifact assemblage. Artifacts included utilitarian orange brownwares (analogs to the G.35), an urn fragment or possible waster, lithics, including a chert point, other chert and quartz flakes, obsidian, and a basalt ax fragment.

The Period IIIb-IV site would have been a small satellite of Sola 1. The Period V component was most likely an isolated residence. Population estimates used a higher density figure for the terraced area. Modern use included farming, grazing, and exploitation of forest resources.

Phase-by-Phase Site Size and Population Estimates:

Phase	Area (ha)	Low	High	Mean
IIIb-IV	3.84	61	134	98
V	0.01	5	10	8

SITE 7

Municipio: San Juan
UTM: E612100/N1827300
Environment: High piedmont/1820 m
Site Size: 0.69 ha
Periodization: IIIa, IIIb-IV, V
Condition: Fair (plowed)

Description: Sola 7 was located only 150 m from Sola 1, but a deep *barranca* separated the two sites. Water was 100-150 m distant. The site was cleared of vegetation and plowed. Ceramics, a chert scraper, chert flakes and debitage, and a gray obsidian blade were recovered. The pottery was a mix of utilitarian orange brownwares and graywares. Modern use included agriculture, grazing, and an isolated residence.

Phase-by-Phase Site Size and Population Estimates:

Phase	Area (ha)	Low	High	Mean
IIIa	0.20	5	10	8
IIIb-IV	0.20	5	10	8
V	0.69	7	17	12

SITE 8

Municipio: San Juan
UTM: E714200/N1828600
Environment: Low piedmont/1520 m
Site Size: 6.37 ha
Periodization: II, IIIb-IV
Condition: Fair (plowed)

Description: Sola 8 was located near three *barrancas*, two of which originated within the site limits, and overlooked highly production alluvial terrain. The Río Grande was 250 m distant. There was an excellent view of the valley floor. San Juan Sola was 800 m west.

The site had two mounds and an enclosed plaza. A possible third structure was placed south of the plaza, but was too destroyed to clearly define. The construction style was similar to Sola 1, albeit built to a smaller scale. Stucco floors were exposed on top of both mounds, and in the plaza. Mound 2 was too narrow for habitation. A gray obsidian blade was found atop Mound 1. Chert flakes were found in an area of ruined houses away from the mound group. Ceramics included a G.21, A.9, G.35s, and several thick orange brownwares.

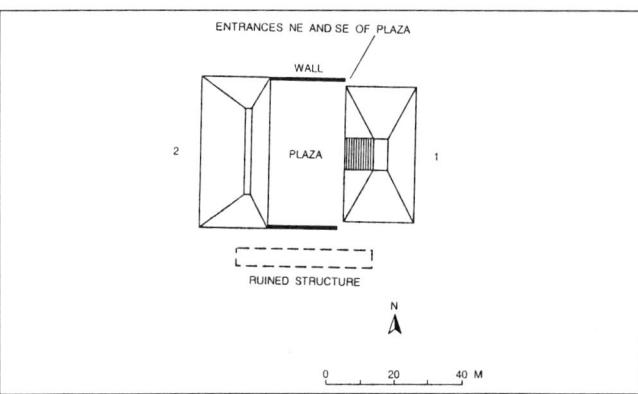

Figure A.4. Detail of the civic-ceremonial core at Sola 8.

Modern use included several dispersed households. Much of the site was planted with maize, *garbanzo, frijol*, and *calabaza*. Fruit trees were grown on the valley floor adjacent to the site.

Phase-by-Phase Site Size and Population Estimates:

Phase	Area (ha)	Low	High	Mean
II	0.20	5	10	8
IIIb-IV	6.37	64	159	112

SITE 9
Municipio: San Juan
UTM: E714600/N1828200
Environment: Low piedmont/1500 m
Site Size: 0.15 ha
Periodization: IIIa
Condition: Good

Description: Sola 9 was located at the foot of the piedmont, overlooking the well-watered alluvium 1 km from the Río Sola. *Barrancas* were located on either side of the *loma*, 100 m from the site. The alluvium below was irrigated, although the site itself was not under cultivation. Ceramics consisted of orange brownware jars; chert flakes also were present. The site was defined as an isolated Period IIIa residence.

Phase-by-Phase Site Size and Population Estimates:

Phase	Area (ha)	Low	High	Mean
IIIa	0.15	5	10	8

SITE 10
Municipio: San Juan/Ild
UTM: E714000/N1827000
Environment: Low piedmont/1540 m
Site Size: 29.62 ha
Periodization: II, IIIa, IIIb-IV, V
Condition: Excellent

Description: Sola 10 was located at the confluence of two *barranca* streams, overlooking highly productive alluvium near modern San Ildefonso Sola. Water is available year-round. The Río Sola was 1 km east. Modern irrigated agriculture takes place at the site; corn, beans, and squash are planted with fruit trees grown near *barranca* streams on the valley floor. Local tree species included *lentisco, moral, algarrobo, enebro, guaje*, and *copal*. There was an isolated residence. A carved stone serves as a *punto trino* today, defining the boundaries between San Ildefonso, San Juan, and San Miguel.

Separate mound groups defined the occupied area, each located on higher ground separated by an alluvial terrace. Three residential terraces were constructed near the principal mound group, each having high-density ceramic assemblages. The principal mound group had a ball court, adoratorio in the plaza, and a small structure atop Mound 1. Mound 1 measured 3 m in height from the plaza, and 15 m in height from its south side. Walls defined the main plaza; the plaza originally had a stucco floor, now destroyed by plowing. A low, narrow stone-wall runs down the long axis of the ball court.

The secondary mound group was oriented toward the main plaza group, and had a carved stone monolith on the basal NW corner of Mound 7. An erosion control wall supported Mounds 7 and 8. On the east side of the secondary mound group, near the *barranca*, multiple looted tombs were exposed. Artifacts at the site included shell; chert and quartz flakes and debitage; a chert borer and scraper; gray obsidian blades; and heavy ceramic densities. Ceramics included orange brownware utilitarian wares, a misfired gray eagle claw support, G.35s, a brownware urn fragment, Huitzo Red-on-Cream, and Graphite-on-Orange. Basalt *mano* fragments were found in the *bajío* below the principal mound group, near Mound 7, and on Terrace 2. Shell was found on Terraces 1 and 2, and associated with the looted tombs near the secondary mound group.

Sola 10 was remarkable for having been one of the few sites in the region to have had significant occupation from the Late Formative until the Late Postclassic. Periods IIIa, IIIb-IV, and V were particularly robust, with high occupational densities, and many decorated ceramics associated with these occupations. Despite its intensive series of occupations, Sola 10 remains well preserved, and would be an excellent candidate for excavation.

Phase-by-Phase Site Size and Population Estimates:

Phase	Area (ha)	Low	High	Mean
II	1.24	12	31	22
IIIa	12.80	128	320	224
IIIb-IV	29.62	296	741	519
V	11.71	117	293	205

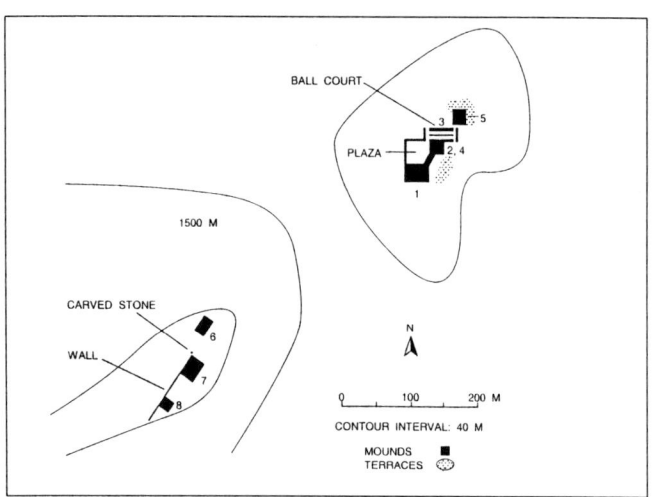

Figure A.5. San Ildefonso Sola (S10).

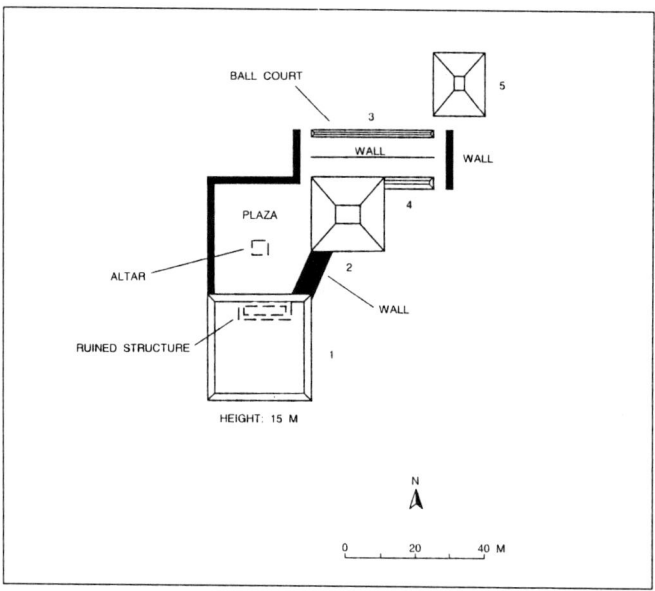

Figure A.6. Detail of the civic-ceremonial core at San Ildefonso.

Appendix A: Site Descriptions

SITE 11
Municipio: San Juan
UTM: E714000/N1827300
Environment: High alluvium/1520 m
Site Size: 1.27 ha
Periodization: IIIa, V
Condition: Fair (plowed)

Description: The site was located on an alluvial terrace, with slightly sloping terrain. A *barranca* was 50 m from the site. Irrigated bottomlands were immediately east. The site was cleared for agriculture; maize, beans, and squash were planted. An isolated residence was nearby.

The site was located halfway between Sola 3 and 10. A chert burin and ceramics were recovered. Ceramics included utilitarian orange brownwares and graywares, Graphite-on-Orange, and Huitzo Red-on-Cream. No other surface features were visible, due to intensive plowing and the degree of alluviation.

Phase-by-Phase Site Size and Population Estimates:

Phase	Area (ha)	Low	High	Mean
IIIa	1.27	13	32	23
V	0.96	10	24	17

SITE 12
Municipio: San Juan
UTM: E613600/N1830000
Environment: High alluvium/1460 m
Site Size: 16.21 ha
Periodization: IIIb-IV
Condition: Fair (plowed/eroded)

Description: Sola 12 was located in center of a small "valley" between piedmont ridges that separate the upper basin of the Río Sola from the central part of the Sola Valley at San Miguel. The Río Sola crossed along the north edge of the site. Sola 12 had been cleared for agriculture in the past, but fallow when surveyed and overgrown with *copal*, *enebro*, *huizache* (a spiny bush), and *algarrobo*. Irrigated alluvium was nearby.

There were two dispersed mounds at the site, both heavily damaged by the plow, looter's pits, and erosion, overgrown with secondary vegetation. Mound 1 was oriented 300 degrees west. Mound 2 had a large stone slab (1.80 × 0.30 m) exposed in a looter's pit; but the stone was not inscribed on its visible surfaces, and was too heavy to turn over. Surface visibility was poor due to the secondary growth, but bare patches and looter's pits revealed a light density of utilitarian orange-brownware and grayware sherds, a single chert flake, and a *mano* fragment. No other artifacts were observed.

Phase-by-Phase Site Size and Population Estimates:

Phase	Area (ha)	Low	High	Mean
IIIb-IV	16.21	162	405	284

SITE 13
Municipio: San Juan
UTM: E613500/N1829700
Environment: High alluvium/1440 m
Site Size: 4.11 ha
Periodization: IIIb-IV
Condition: Fair (eroded)

Description: Sola 13 rested on an alluvial terrace, completely cleared of vegetation; soils were thin, sandy, and poor. In the nearby *bajío*, however, the land was extremely productive and well watered. A *barranca* was 200 m south; the Río Sola was 600 m northeast. There was a solitary mound at the site. Utilitarian orange-brownwares were on the surface; no other artifacts were observed.

Phase-by-Phase Site Size and Population Estimates:

Phase	Area (ha)	Low	High	Mean
IIIb-IV	4.11	41	103	72

SITE 14
Municipio: San Juan
UTM: E613000/N1829200
Environment: Low piedmont/1560 m
Site Size: 6.20 ha
Periodization: IIIa
Condition: Poor (eroded)

Description: Sola 14 was badly eroded, nearly entirely exposed bedrock, and without vegetation. *Barrancas* provided water 75 m from the site. The site likely had terraces, but the extreme erosion has erased the surface. House foundations were observed on a small, flat portion of the site. Ceramics were utilitarian brownwares; no other artifacts were observed.

Phase-by-Phase Site Size and Population Estimates:

Phase	Area (ha)	Low	High	Mean
IIIa	6.20	62	155	109

SITE 15
Municipio: San Juan
UTM: E613000/N1829100
Environment: Low piedmont/1520 m
Site Size: 5.44 ha
Periodization: II
Condition: Poor (eroded)

Description: Sola 15 was spread across a long, narrow piedmont slope with three successive flat areas giving the appearance of "steps" leading down to the valley floor. Water was between 50-100 m distant in *barranca* streams on either side of the *loma*. The predominant tree species were *enebro* and *guaje*. Modern farming has plowed much of the site in recent years, although the land was fallow at the time of the survey. Contemporary artifacts included colonial and modern pottery, and a *mano*. An off-site mineral sample was collected near Sola 15.

On three successive levels, the *loma* was flatter, and this condition may have been artificially accentuated—remnant stonewalls supported portions of each flattened area. The site was terraced on the east side of the *loma*, facing the central part of the valley; but these may have been colonial or modern agricultural terraces—the site was too badly eroded to be certain. Population estimates may be somewhat low, since the nature of the terraced area was ambiguous, and I did not count the ruined terraced area as prehispanic. Looter's pits in the flat portions of the site revealed a large capstone, possibly from a tomb. The prehispanic artifacts were Period II ceramics with red paint, two chert burins, and a *mano*.

Sola 15 reflected the Period II reorganization of the valley, as sites were abandoned in many areas and the regional population focused on nearby Sola 39, in the northwestern portion of the valley.

Phase-by-Phase Site Size and Population Estimates:

Phase	Area (ha)	Low	High	Mean
II	5.44	54	136	95

SITE 16
Municipio: Santa María
UTM: E613500/N1831600
Environment: Low piedmont/1520 m
Site Size: 5.07 ha
Periodization: IIIa
Condition: Fair (plowed/looted)

Description: Sola 16 had once been plowed, but heavy secondary growth, *copal*, *tepeguaje*, and thorn bushes covered much of the site. Rainfall farming was practiced on a small portion of the site, with maize, beans, and squash grown. Water was available from a *barranca* stream, 200 m distant.

A four-mound group surrounded a sunken plaza. Entrances to the plaza were located on the NW and NE sides. Mounds 1 and 3 were badly sacked; a tomb was exposed in Mound 1. Orange-brownware and grayware ceramics, and a chert point, burin, flakes and debitage were recovered. There was considerable building stone strewn about site; the stone was likely from house foundations and perhaps a few terraces destroyed by plowing.

Sola 16 was ideally located for visual communication between the northern and central portions of the valley, otherwise obscured by the long piedmont ridges that extend across this portion of the valley.

Phase-by-Phase Site Size and Population Estimates:

Phase	Area (ha)	Low	High	Mean
IIIa	5.07	51	127	89

SITE 17
Municipio: San Miguel
UTM: E715100/N1826000
Environment: Low piedmont/1480 m
Site Size: 0.75 ha
Periodization: Ic, IIIa, V
Condition: Poor (eroded)

Description: Sola 17 rested on a flat piedmont spur that was a prominent observation point overlooking modern San Miguel. The highway wrapped around this small rise as traffic headed out of the Sola Valley toward the coast. Heavy erosion, due to road construction and overgrazing, has left the site in a shambles. There was no vegetative cover. Water in a *barranca* stream was 150 m distant. Ceramics included a Period Ic brownware with red paint (K.3), Period IIIa orange-brownwares, and Period V graywares (G.3M) one of which was misfired. A fence surrounds the site, defining the dance ground where the local *Lunes del Cerro* celebration is held each year.

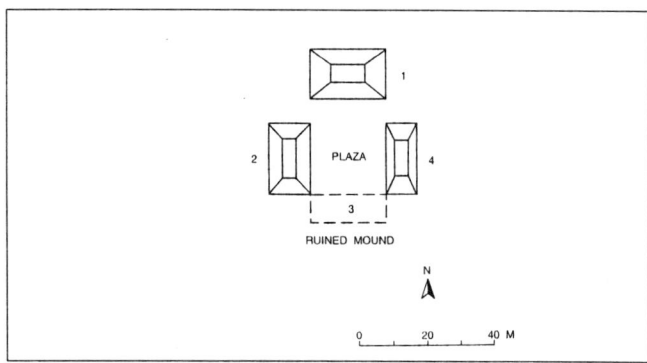

Figure A.7. Detail of the civic-ceremonial core at Sola 16.

Phase-by-Phase Site Size and Population Estimates:

Phase	Area (ha)	Low	High	Mean
Ic	0.01	5	10	8
IIIa	0.75	8	19	14
V	0.75	8	19	14

SITE 18
Municipio: San Miguel
UTM: E714000/N1826000
Environment: Low piedmont/1700 m
Site Size: 23.19 ha
Periodization: IIIa, V
Condition: Poor (plowed/eroded)

Description: Sola 18 extended for over 1200 m from high in the piedmont zone to the edge of the valley floor overlooking modern San Miguel. The site was steeply sloping at its highest elevations, and eventually flattened out near the base of the *loma*. Water was available from *barranca* streams immediately adjacent to each side of the *loma*. This piedmont zone was irrigated. Vegetation included *ocote*, *enebro*, *anona*, and *hijo blanco*, with pine forest limited to the highest elevations. Portions of the site were plowed, with several dispersed residences located within the site limits. Maize, beans, and squash were cultivated; the area was heavily grazed and eroding. Only a narrow, steep *barranca* separates sites 18 and 21.

A single mound had been located on the flat ground at the foot of the *loma*; it was completely plowed away with the recent construction of a water tank. Highly burnished G.3M (Period V) grayware bowls were found where the mound had been located. The uppermost portion of the site had been terraced (approximately 10 terraces) but was in ruins and not mapped. Ceramic densities were high in plowed portions of the site. A small chert collection was taken, including a burin, flakes, and debitage. An ax fragment was found on the uppermost portion of the *loma*. Ceramics included orange-brownwares, a G.23, Huitzo Red-on-Cream, Graphite-on-Orange, and G.3Ms.

Population estimates used a higher density figure for the terraced area. These upper terraces were first occupied in IIIa, and apparently served as a small elite precinct in V (considering the distribution of decorated Postclassic ceramics). An indeterminate number of other terraces may have been located further down slope, but plowing has erased them. The site was naturally defensible with the edge of the *loma* having a sheer drop to the valley floor. Sola 18 was one of the main period V sites in the western part of the valley.

A large blue cross made the site visible throughout the central part of the valley. Known as "La Cruz del Carmen," this was the original location of the local *Lunes del Cerro* celebration, later moved to Sola 17 after the new highway was constructed.

Phase-by-Phase Site Size and Population Estimates:

Phase	Area (ha)	Low	High	Mean
IIIa	7.80	93	220	157
V	23.19	247	605	426

SITE 19
Municipio: San Miguel
UTM: E714700/N1725800
Environment: Low piedmont/1500 m
Site Size: 1.38 ha
Periodization: IIIa, V
Condition: Fair (plowed)

Description: Sola 19 was nearly cleared of vegetation, although a few pine trees remained. A *barranca* provided water 150 m to the north. The site was planted with maize, beans, and squash. Ceramics consisted of orange-brownwares (IIIa), Huitzo Red-on-Cream (V), and thin, gray *olla* bodies (V). Chert and quartz flakes and debitage were on the surface.

Phase-by-Phase Site Size and Population Estimates:

Phase	Area (ha)	Low	High	Mean
IIIa	1.38	14	35	25
V	0.25	5	10	8

SITE 20
Municipio: San Juan
UTM: E610200/N1829000
Environment: Mountain/2400 m
Site Size: 40.19 ha
Periodization: IIIa, V
Condition: Fair (plowed/overgrown)

Description: Sola 20 was located on the hilltop known locally as "La Cumbrita". Modern San Juan Sola was 3.25 km east and 800 m down slope from the site. Multiple *barrancas* originated within the site limits. Rainfall farming has been practiced on the hilltop in times past, but the site was not under cultivation when surveyed. Heavy secondary vegetation covered most of the site. Local tree species included *encino*, *ocote*, and *enebro*.

Within the site limits a cave (40 × 45 m) was associated with prehispanic ceramics and still used for ritual purposes by the residents of San Juan Sola. The area in front of the cave was artificially flattened, forming a small patio (17 × 15 m). A series of five dispersed terraces began immediately above the cave, all with house foundations. At the summit, there were two separate mound groups, with seven low structures. Most of these structures were badly damaged by plowing. House foundations were found atop Mound 1. Mound 4 supported a small structure 1.5 m high, similar to Mound 1 at Sola 10.

Period V ceramics encompassed the full area of the site, including the cave. Period IIIa ceramics were restricted to bare patches on the summit. Given the degree of vegetative cover, however, future studies should reevaluate the occupational sequence and site size assessments. Ceramics were the only artifacts observed.

Phase-by-Phase Site Size and Population Estimates:

Phase	Area (ha)	Low	High	Mean
IIIa	1-5	30	75	53
V	40.19	350	975	663

SITE 21
Municipio: San Miguel
UTM: E714000/N1826500
Environment: Low piedmont/1680 m
Site Size: 20.20 ha
Periodization: IIIa, V
Condition: Poor (plowed/eroded/looted)

Description: Sola 21 was located in the foothills directly west of modern San Miguel Sola de Vega, 1100 m from the Río Sola. The site was plowed over its entire area; there was considerable erosion, with the bedrock exposed in places. *Barrancas* provided ready access to water immediately adjacent to the site limits on all sides; this zone is irrigated today. The uppermost portion of the site was on a *montura* that linked the high mountains that define the west side of the valley. Pine forest prevailed at the upper elevations of the site, while mixed pine and oak were found at its lower reaches. There was an isolated modern residence. Maize, beans, and squash were planted over most of the site; fallow areas were heavily grazed.

Sola 21 nearly connected with Sola 18 at its highest elevation; further down slope the sites were separated by a deep *barranca* that downcuts to the valley floor. The steep slope at the highest elevation of the site had approximately 10 terraces, ruined by plowing, overgrazing, and subsequent erosion. House foundations were found among these terraces. Further down slope multiple ruined residential terraces and heavy ceramic densities were seen. These terraces could not be systematically mapped due to their poor condition, but I estimate that 40-50 terraces had once stood on this portion of the site (Sola farmers systematically destroy prehispanic terrace walls to obtain greater surface area for planting). A poorly preserved ball court was mapped at the base of a succession of large terraces. The ball court was in an exclusively Period V context; unfortunately only two of its component structures survive, and they have been further distorted by farming, looting, and reuse of building stone. The ball court was oriented N/S; its approximate inside length was 56 m.

The west wall of the ball court formed a "plaza" 46 × 40 m that joined the base of a flight of large terraces. On what appears to have been the largest terrace at the site (approximately 45 × 56 m), looting had revealed a red-painted stucco floor and three tombs with many decorated Yanhuitlán Red-on-Cream and polychrome ceramics in the looters' backdirt. On this same terrace were foundation stones of a multi-room structure, with approximate dimensions of 30 × 40 m. The large terrace with the looted tombs was situated 4 m above the next terrace level, connected to the rest of the site by a narrow walk. Access was limited.

High densities of Huitzo Red-on-Cream were found across the entire site; true Yanhuitlán Red-on-Cream, however, was restricted to the aforementioned large terraces and tomb. *Mano* and *metate* fragments were recovered in the zone of ruined terraces, and at least 5 polished ax fragments were seen. Chert flakes and debitage, along with green and gray obsidian were recovered. Terracing extended into the *barrancas* on either side of the site. These terraces did not support houses and had low artifacts densities; it is possible that they were exclusively agricultural.

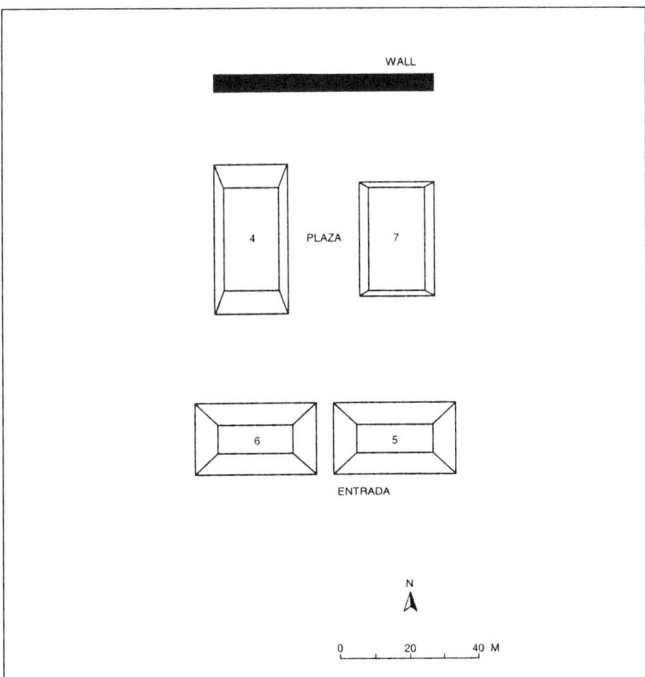

Figure A.8. Detail of the civic-ceremonial core at La Cumbrita (S20).

Population figures used the estimated number of terraces in the calculation. The size of the site, ball court, large elite terraces, multi-room structure, and density of decorated ceramics suggest that Sola 21 was the seat of a Postclassic kingdom in the western valley (see discussion in text). As noted above, the proximity of Sola 18 and 21 suggests these two sites were functionally similar, and might be considered the same settlement.

Phase-by-Phase Site Size and Population Estimates:

Phase	Area (ha)	Low	High	Mean
IIIa	3.06	70	150	110
V	20.20	350	725	538

SITE 22
Municipio: San Ildefonso
UTM: E715300/N1827900
Environment: Low piedmont/1460 m
Site Size: 4.64 ha
Periodization: V
Condition: Poor (plowed)

Description: Sola 22 lies next to the community cemetery on the *loma* above modern San Ildefonso Sola. The site directly overlooked the Río Sola, 125 m east; several *barrancas* originate from the Sola 22 *loma*. In addition to the cemetery, the site was located adjacent to several contemporary households and their *milpas*. Maize, beans, and squash were grown; this zone was irrigated. Apart from farming, there was little vegetation on the site; local tree species included *guaje* and *algarrobo*.

Sola 22 had a single mound, cardinally oriented, with the unusual dimensions of 22 × 6 × 2 m. There were few artifacts visible, despite recent plowing that has clearly exposed much of the site. It is possible that other mounds (perhaps forming a ball court) had been associated with this structure, but were erased by the intensive contemporary occupation. Artifacts included ceramics, two *mano* fragments, and a gray obsidian blade. An example of Huitzo Red-on-Cream was found among the utilitarian brownware ceramics.

Phase-by-Phase Site Size and Population Estimates:

Phase	Area (ha)	Low	High	Mean
V	4.64	46	116	81

SITE 23
Municipio: Sta. María/Ild
UTM: E717000/N1834600
Environment: Mountain/2300 m
Site Size: 71.08 ha
Periodization: II, IIIa, IIIb-IV, V
Condition: Fair (terraces plowed away but architecture intact)

Description: Sola 23 was found north of Highway 131, on the high ridgeline that extends from Cerro El Obispo north to San Sebastián de las Grutas. Several *barrancas* originated within the site's terraced slopes. Pine forest prevailed, but was cleared by plowing in places. Surface visibility was poor over much of the site, particularly in that portion of the site associated with the principal mound group. Other parts of the site, however, especially the main residential area, had been plowed in recent years providing good surface visibility. The long axis of the ridgeline marks the territorial division between Santa María and San Ildefonso Sola.

Sola 23 was a long, narrow site that extended for over 4000 m on an imposing ridgeline, overlooking the natural pass leading into the Sola Valley. More than 20 mounds—including platforms, a ball court, sunken patio group, and successive plazas—were distributed along the long axis of the site. The mound groups were oriented with the natural contour of the ridgeline. A carved stone was found in the center of the ball court, just as at Sola 39. The terraced area between Mounds 1 and 2 had several looted tombs. This area was the location of the shell debris recovered. Other opened tombs were discovered in association with Mounds 5 and 25. Ceramics, chert, and obsidian artifacts were recovered. Most of the larger structures at this site were well preserved.

A *montura* separated Sola 23 at roughly its midpoint; for convenience, the site was divided into two segments that correspond to both the natural division and the organization of the site. These two sections were the Cueva Negra group—associated with the site's principal architecture—and the Portillo group with its several dispersed mound groups and the majority of the residential terraces. Unfortunately, the majority of the terraces were obliterated with the recent plowing of the hillside; only a small percentage of the original terraces could be mapped. Every effort was made, however, to obtain accurate data on the distribution and approximate number of original terraces, and their phase or phases of occupation. The total of the mapped plus estimated terraces numbered 162, although this figure is probably an undercount. Although relatively modest compared to Valley of Oaxaca centers, Sola 23 was by far the largest and most populated Sola Valley site during the Early Classic period (IIIa). Population figures for Period IIIa utilize the terrace estimate.

Postclassic site size and population estimates lump three dispersed settlements (see Period V settlement pattern map). The main Postclassic occupation was associated with the Portillo group. This area included a sunken patio group (believed to date to IV/V). In comparison, the dispersed Period V occupations associated with the Cueva Negra group were found in both residential and ceremonial contexts. Late Postclassic

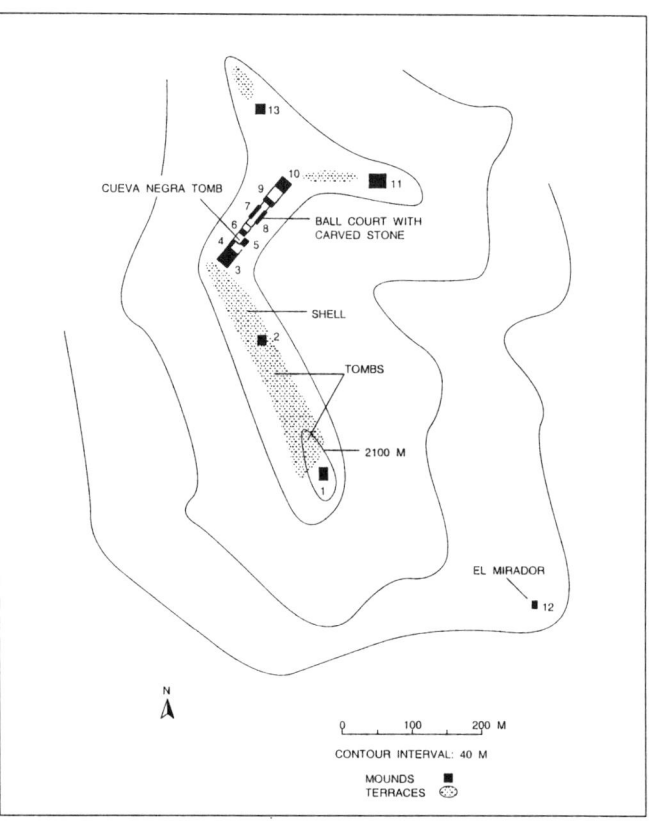

Figure A.9. Los Chilillos, Cueva Negra Group (S23).

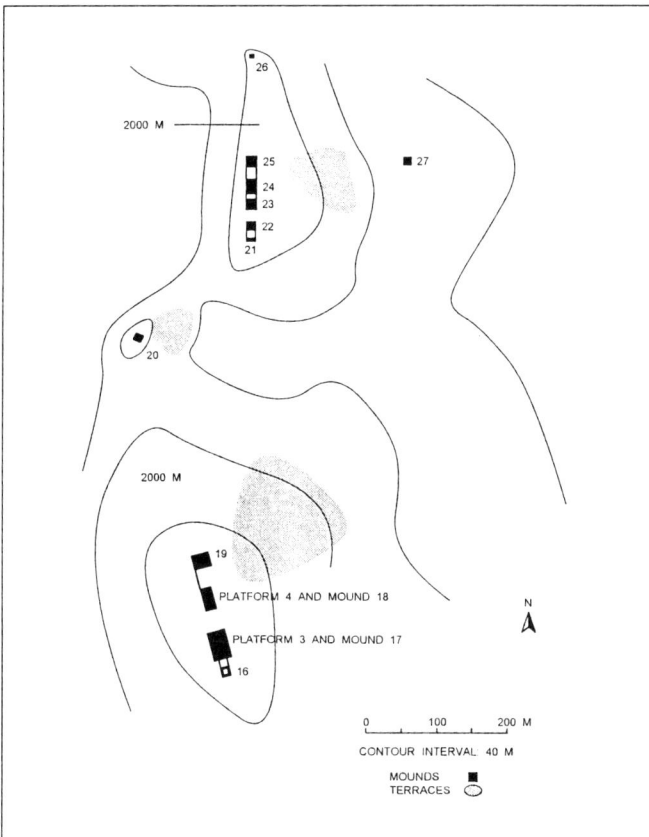

Figure A.10. Los Chilillos, Portillo Group (S23).

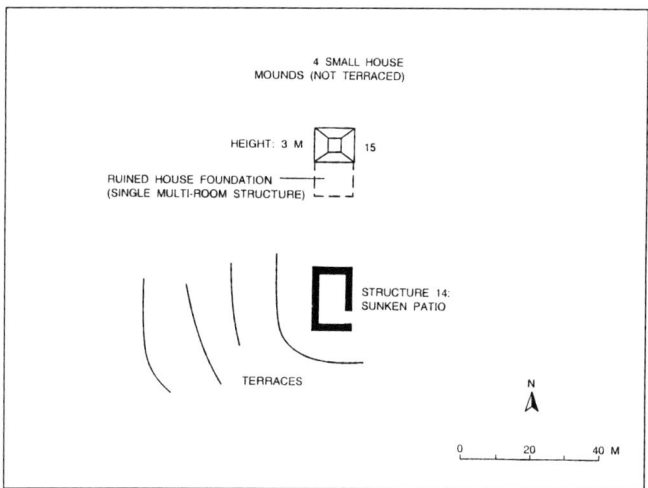

Figure A.12. Detail of Structures 14-15 at Los Chilillos.

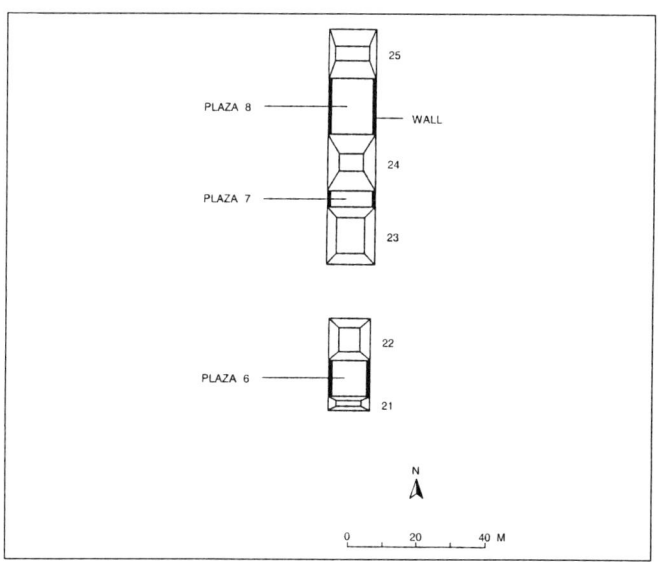

Figure A.13. Detail of Structures 21-25 at Los Chilillos.

pottery—that was not directly associated with particular mounds or plazas—had many misfired G.3M graywares suggesting a possible locus of ceramic production. As noted above, however, surface visibility was obscured by dense foliage in the Cueva Negra group; Period IIIb-IV and V site size estimates may therefore need revision. See Berlin's (1951) description of this site that he called "Los Chilillos."

Phase-by-Phase Site Size and Population Estimates:

Phase	Area (ha)	Low	High	Mean
II	1.65	17	41	29
IIIa	71.08	1210	2620	1915
IIIb-IV	19.22	300	650	475
V	13.41	159	385	272

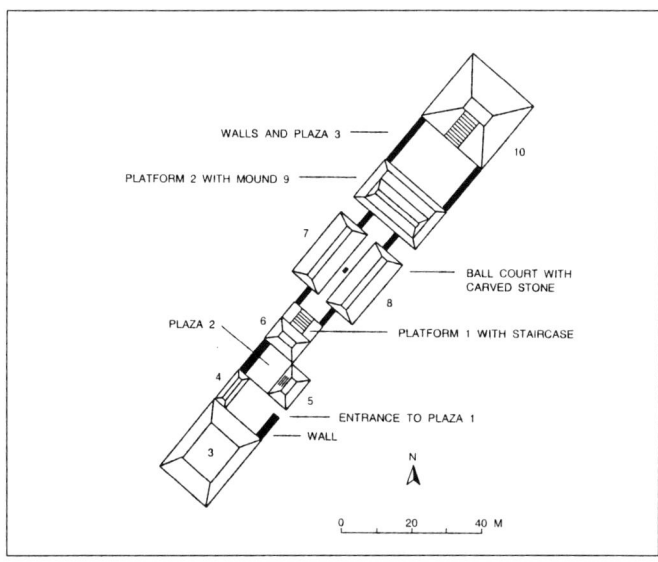

Figure A.11. Detail of the civic-ceremonial core at Los Chilillos.

SITE 24
Municipio: San Ildefonso
UTM: E717900/N1835400
Environment: High piedmont/1980 m
Site Size: 5.09 ha
Periodization: IIIb-IV, V
Condition: Poor (plowed/eroded/looted)

Description: Sola 24 was located 500 m east of the Sola 23 ridgeline, near the Agencia of Palo Blanco. The site was completely cleared of vegetation; erosion was heavy, with bedrock exposed in places. A *barranca* stream was 200 m distant. The site had a low mound, heavily damaged from plowing, and three looted tombs. A house foundation was recorded. There was considerable chert and quartz chipping debris. Ceramics included a G.35, Huitzo and Yanhuitlán Red-on-Cream, and G.3M. Modern use was limited to grazing.

Phase-by-Phase Site Size and Population Estimates:

Phase	Area (ha)	Low	High	Mean
IIIb-IV	3.50	35	88	62
V	5.09	51	127	89

SITE 25
Municipio: San Ildefonso
UTM: E719500/N1836000
Environment: Mountain/2200 m
Site Size: 1.88 ha
Periodization: IIIa, V
Condition: Excellent

Description: Sola 25 was a hilltop site situated north of Highway 131 near San Ildefonso El Viejo. Pine forest covered the site. Despite some looting, the site was in excellent condition; it was not plowed. Although there were no nearby streams, the site was well watered with many underground channels accessible at the surface.

Eleven Late Postclassic house foundations were recorded. These houses often employed natural bedrock outcrops as part of the foundation. The inhabitants of Sola 25 likely used the nearby cave (Sola 26) for ritual purposes. The site was inaccessible and highly defensible due to bedrock outcrops and a steep ascent. Period V population estimates use the house count. The Period V G.3M grayware complex was present.

Phase-by-Phase Site Size and Population Estimates:

Phase	Area (ha)	Low	High	Mean
IIIa	0.40	5	10	8
V	1.88	55	110	83

SITE 26
Municipio: San Ildefonso
UTM: E719500/N1836200
Environment: Mountain/2180 m
Site Size: 0.01 ha
Periodization: V
Condition: Good

Description: Sola 26 was a cave site located on the *montura* 150 m northeast of Sola 25. The area was covered in pine forest, not farmed, and had no modern settlement. Utilitarian brownwares, a deer incisor, and a green obsidian blade were found inside. A few brownware sherds were scattered within a 10 m radius of the cave entrance, but no clear indication of a permanent occupation was found. Period V ceramics and cave use were probably associated with nearby Sola 25. The cave could have been used during other time periods as well, but there has been considerable infilling and the recovered ceramic assemblage may not represent all periods of use.

Phase-by-Phase Site Size and Population Estimates:

Phase	Area (ha)	Low	High	Mean
V	0.01	5	10	8

SITE 27
Municipio: San Ildefonso
UTM: E719400/N1834700
Environment: Mountain/2100 m
Site Size: 4.66 ha
Periodization: V
Condition: Poor (eroded)

Description: Sola 27 was badly eroded due to plowing, overgrazing, and lack of vegetation; bedrock was exposed. Tree species in the vicinity of the site included *enebro* and *encino*. A *barranca* was adjacent to the site. Irrigated farming takes place today; an isolated modern household was located nearby.

The site was terraced, but these were built in the style of colonial and modern terraces; the extent of prehispanic terracing could not be determined. Consequently, population estimates refer only to site area, and not the greater density figure associated with terracing. Artifacts included Huitzo Red-on Cream, a light density of chert flakes, and a gray obsidian blade fragment.

Phase-by-Phase Site Size and Population Estimates:

Phase	Area (ha)	Low	High	Mean
V	4.66	47	117	82

SITE 28
Municipio: San Ildefonso
UTM: E717500/N1836200
Environment: High piedmont/1940 m
Site Size: 3.72 ha
Periodization: IIIa
Condition: Poor (plowed)

Description: The site was located near the valley floor 1 km east of the Sola 23 ridgeline. There was no vegetative cover. Water was immediately available from adjacent *barrancas*. Modern use consisted of a small *milpa* and household. There was a small two-mound group with plaza, all badly damaged by plowing. Ceramics were the only artifacts observed. There was no indication of terracing. Another possible mound was located further down the *loma*, but it was too destroyed to be certain.

Phase-by-Phase Site Size and Population Estimates:

Phase	Area (ha)	Low	High	Mean
IIIa	3.72	37	93	65

SITE 29
Municipio: San Ildefonso
UTM: E720000/N1835900
Environment: Mountain/2120 m
Site Size: 6.37 ha
Periodization: V
Condition: Excellent

Description: Sola 29 was a hilltop site 2.5 km north of highway 131, near San Ildefonso El Viejo. The site was not plowed; surface visibility was poor. Water was available from *barrancas* on either side of the site, 75 and 125 m distant. Tree species included *ocote*, *encino*, and *medrón*. This zone is exploited for forest products, especially firewood. Excellent lines of sight extended into the Sola Valley. There were 10 intact terraces, but no mounds. It is possible that other time periods were present, but these were not possible to identify based on the limited surface visibility. Only Period V brownwares were recovered. No other artifacts were seen. Sola 29 was similar in location and layout to its much larger neighboring site, Sola 31.

Phase-by-Phase Site Size and Population Estimates:

Phase	Area (ha)	Low	High	Mean
V	6.37	100	225	163

SITE 30
Municipio: San Ildefonso
UTM: E720500/N1835000
Environment: Mountain/2160 m
Site Size: 0.01 ha
Periodization: Ic, V
Condition: Good

Description: Sola 30 was a cave site. No water source was in the vicinity. Pine forest covered the area. Sola 30 was located near the summit of the hilltop with sites Sola 27, 29, and 31—all of which were Period V sites. The cave was used during the Late Formative and Late Postclassic. Ic ceramics were decorated types C.20 and G.12. There was no evidence of residential activity. Postclassic ceramics were limited to a few undecorated brownware sherds. No other artifacts were seen. The cave is used today as a shelter during inclement weather.

Phase-by-Phase Site Size and Population Estimates:

Phase	Area (ha)	Low	High	Mean
Ic	0.01	5	10	8
V	0.01	5	10	8

SITE 31
Municipio: San Ildefonso
UTM: E719000/N1834000
Environment: Mountain/2220 m
Site Size: 50.30 ha
Periodization: V
Condition: Poor (plowed)

Description: Sola 31 was located on the north side of Highway 131, near the Agencia of El Nogal. Water was available from the confluence of several mountain streams both along the hillside and at the base of the site. Nearly the entire site was plowed; fields were irrigated on the lower slopes and planted with corn. Many modern households were located on the site and in the vicinity.

The site was in extremely poor condition. Few intact prehispanic terraces remained. House foundations were observed among the ruined terraces. Ceramics included polychrome. Population estimates use a higher density figure for the terraced area. This site's main occupation dates later in the Postclassic than its neighbor at Sola III, and could be its successor. Sola 31 was likely the Pueblo Viejo of San Ildefonso Sola.

Phase-by-Phase Site Size and Population Estimates:

Phase	Area (ha)	Low	High	Mean
V	50.30	986	2081	1534

SITE 32
Municipio: San Ildefonso
UTM: E718100/N1836500
Environment: High piedmont/1920 m
Site Size: 8.44 ha
Periodization: II, IIIa, IIIb-IV, V
Condition: Poor (plowed/eroded)

Description: Sola 32 was located at the confluence of three mountain streams, between Sola 23 and modern San Ildefonso El Viejo. Fields were irrigated; several modern households were in the vicinity. The site was cleared of vegetation, with heavy erosion and exposed bedrock in places.

The site had a mound and small plaza defined by a low wall. A second small mound was located 150 m from the mound/plaza; this latter mound was in very poor condition from plowing and erosion. A few terraces remained intact; modern plowing has ruined most of the original terraced area. A stucco floor was seen among the terraces. The Period II component included creamwares with red paint.

Phase-by-Phase Site Size and Population Estimates:

Phase	Area (ha)	Low	High	Mean
II	0.62	6	16	11
IIIa	8.44	84	211	148
IIIb-IV	2.78	28	70	49
V	2.49	25	62	44

SITE 33
Municipio: San Miguel
UTM: E718400/N1831800
Environment: High piedmont/1820 m
Site Size: 4.33 ha
Periodization: Ic
Condition: Fair (looted)

Description: Sola 33 was located at the top of a steep hill, immediately adjacent to the modern highway as it crossed the mountain pass and descended into the Sola Valley. Deep, incised *barrancas* provided water 120 m below. Rainfall farming was practiced at the site, although it was not plowed at the time of the survey. Tree species included *enebro*, *encino*, and *copal*.

One structure and five terraces were mapped. There was an erosion control wall, and a looted tomb with human bones strewn about. Lithics included a chert scraper, three gray obsidian blades, and an ax. Pottery included two G.12s (combed bottom), and types C.2/C.4. The site was highly defensible. The location of the site suggests that it controlled traffic into the Sola Valley during the Late Formative.

Phase-by-Phase Site Size and Population Estimates:

Phase	Area (ha)	Low	High	Mean
Ic	4.33	65	150	108

SITE 34
Municipio: San Juan
UTM: E715000/N1831100
Environment: Low piedmont/1520 m
Site Size: 2.28 ha
Periodization: II, IIIa
Condition: Poor (eroded)

Description: Sola 34 overlooked highly productive alluvium near the modern town of Nachihui. *Barrancas* provided water 200 m distant. The area was irrigated; the site, however, was not plowed at the time of the survey and was overgrown with heavy secondary vegetation and cactus. Soils were thin and eroded. Maguey was cultivated.

There was a light density of ceramics including a C.7 (most likely Period II), and utilitarian orange-brownwares (Period IIIa). No other artifacts were seen. Sola 34 was located further east than any II/IIIa site in the San Juan sector of the valley, nearest the new regional capital at Sola 23.

Phase-by-Phase Site Size and Population Estimates:

Phase	Area (ha)	Low	High	Mean
II	0.01	5	10	8
IIIa	2.28	23	57	40

SITE 35
Municipio: Santa María
UTM: E716000/N1835100
Environment: High piedmont/1920 m
Site Size: 2.39 ha
Periodization: IIIa
Condition: Good

Description: Sola 35 was located 1 km west of the Sola 23 ridgeline. The site was overgrown, but had been cultivated in the past. Mountain streams flowed down the ridgeline, 200 m from the site. Low piedmont zones below the site are irrigated today. Tree species included *encino*, *algarrobo*, and *tepeguaje*.

There was a small mound and low platform at the site. Sola 35 rested on the same ridgeline as Sola 23, and was its satellite (or could be considered part of the same site). Sola 35 had a commanding view of the western Sola Valley. It was probably an observation point for the west side of the valley; a similar function was provided by the El Mirador extension of Sola 23 to the east. Only brownware ceramics were seen on the unplowed surface. The site was not terraced, but had a highly defensible location, and could have communicated easily with Sola 23.

Phase-by-Phase Site Size and Population Estimates:

Phase	Area (ha)	Low	High	Mean
IIIa	2.39	24	60	42

SITE 36
Municipio: Santa María
UTM: E611300/N1833600
Environment: High alluvium/1480 m
Site Size: 0.08 ha
Periodization: Not defined
Condition: Good

Description: Sola 36 was located adjacent to the Río Santa Rosa, directly east of Sola 39. These were highly productive alluvial lands where the Río Santa Rosa and Río Grande join to form the Río Sola. Permanent water was 150 m distant. The area is irrigated today. Heavy secondary growth covered the site; vegetation was composed of grasses, *huizache*, and *pájaro bobo*. Sola 36 had two mounds and a small plaza defined by low walls. These structures were cardinally oriented N/S. The site was completely overgrown; no ceramics were visible on the surface. Architecture suggests a Classic period occupation. No other artifacts or terracing were seen. Future work must re-evaluate site size and chronology.

Phase-by-Phase Site Size and Population Estimates:

Phase	Area (ha)	Low	High	Mean
Not Defined	0.08	—	—	—

SITE 37
Municipio: Santa María
UTM: E610100/N1833200
Environment: High alluvium/1480 m
Site Size: 0.02 ha
Periodization: IIIa
Condition: Good

Description: The site was located 500 m west of Sola 39, on an alluvial terrace adjacent to highly productive bottomlands. The area is cultivated today with *guirasol*, an orange flower common in the valley used during Day of the Dead ceremonies. Nearby fields were irrigated; maize, beans, and squash were cultivated. A *barranca* was adjacent to the site; the Río Grande was 600 m distant. Period IIIa orange-brownwares were recovered; there were no other artifacts or architecture on the surface.

Phase-by-Phase Site Size and Population Estimates:

Phase	Area (ha)	Low	High	Mean
IIIa	0.02	5	10	8

SITE 38
Municipio: Santa María
UTM: E612200/N1832000
Environment: Low alluvium/1420 m
Site Size: 0.48 ha
Periodization: IIIb-IV
Condition: Fair (plowed)

Description: Sola 38 was located alongside the Río Sola. The surface was plowed but not planted during the survey. Large river cobbles showed that periodic flooding has buried the site—obscuring the true size and nature of settlement. Utilitarian brownwares and graywares were present, but no other artifacts were found.

Phase-by-Phase Site Size and Population Estimates:

Phase	Area (ha)	Low	High	Mean
IIIb-IV	0.48	5	12	9

SITE 39
Municipio: Santa María
UTM: E610600/N1833300
Environment: Low piedmont/1520 m
Site Size: 31.06 ha
Periodization: Ia, Ic, II, IIIa, IIIb-IV, V
Condition: Excellent

Description: Sola 39 was located at the origin of the Río Sola, near the Agencia of Texcoco, adjacent to the region's richest farmland. This zone is irrigated today; maize, beans, squash, and a variety of fruit trees are grown. Two isolated residences were within the site boundaries, but the disturbance from modern farming was minimal. Any future visitor to the site, however, should be aware of the conflict over control of the site and its surrounding land between Texcoco and nearby Santa María Sola.

The site's ceremonial precinct was located on relatively flat, low-lying terrain, but the main residential area was a terraced hilltop. Sola 39 had the widest variety of ceramic types of any site in the valley, and the greatest total volume of mounded architecture. Artifact collections included heavy densities of ceramics across the site, and some evidence for ceramic production; chert tools and obsidian; ax fragments and ground stone; shell; and many out of context carved stones set into the church at Santa María Sola. The carved stones were all reported to have originated at Sola 39; interviews with local residents helped to identify the original provenience for many of these monuments.

Appendix A: Site Descriptions

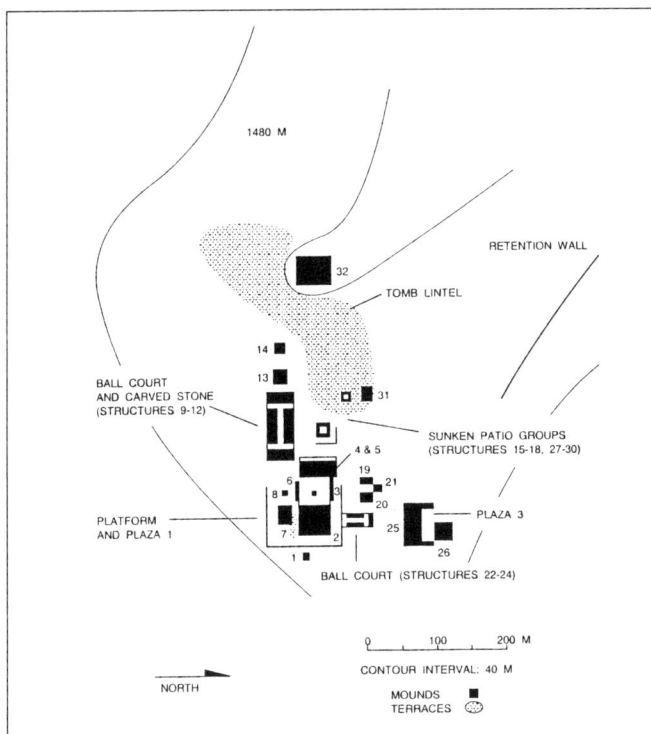

Figure A.14. Texcoco (S39).

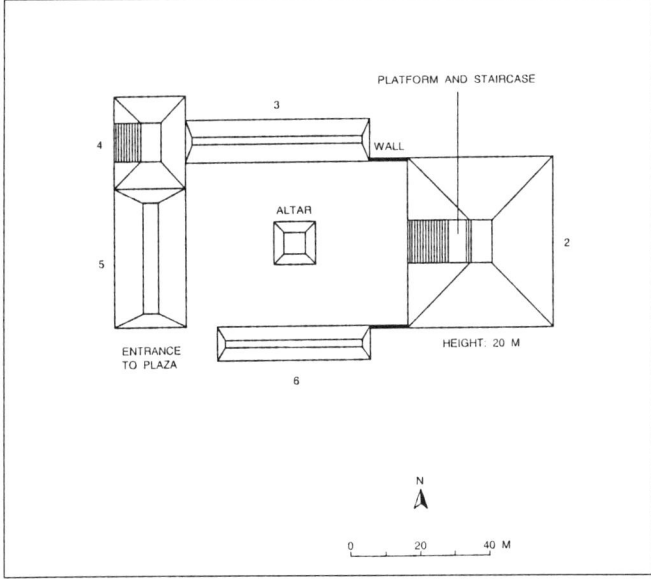

Figure A.15. Detail of the civic-ceremonial core at Texcoco.

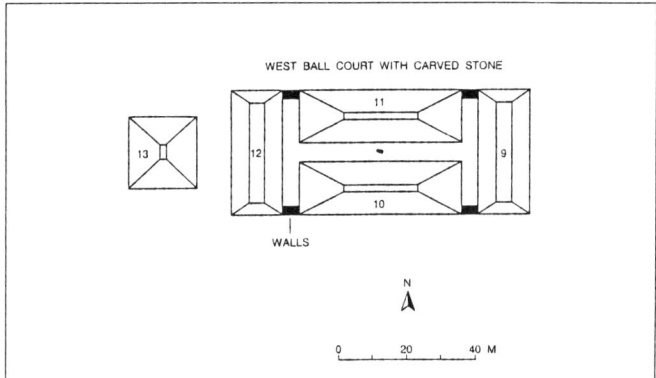

Figure A.16. Detail of the West Ball Court at Texcoco.

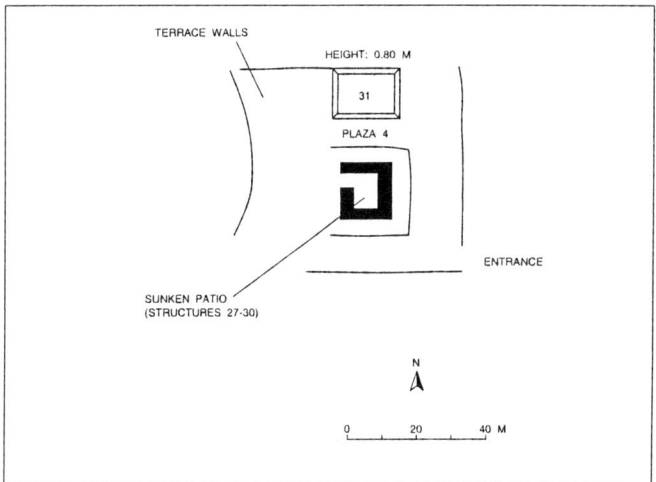

Figure A.17. Detail of Structures 27-31 at Texcoco.

Sola 39 had the earliest occupation in the valley, dating from the Ia phase. The occupational sequence continued uninterrupted through Colonial and modern times. More than 30 structures and 54 terraces were mapped. Structures included two ball courts, multiple plazas, an altar, and several enormous buildings—the largest of which was 20 m high. Monumental construction began as early as the Ic phase, based on observations of profiles and mound fill from recently dug irrigation canals.

In the Ic phase, Sola 39 had been one of several sites in the region of roughly equivalent size and monumentality. By Period II, many centers were abandoned and Sola 39 became the focus of regional settlement. Sola 39's main phase of occupation was Period IIIb-IV. During the transition into Period IIIa, Sola 39 and most sites in the western part of the valley experienced population declines or were abandoned as regional settlement shifted to Sola 23 and its satellites. The IIIb-IV site was again one of the principal settlements in the region. This was the time when the region's carved stone tradition was at its apex. Site size and population estimates for Period IIIa and IIIb-IV were assumed to be identical since the terraced hilltop was not plowed preventing finer distinctions for these phases. Period V occupation was limited, although a small elite precinct continued to be inhabited. Postclassic occupation was limited to 6 residential terraces adjacent to the sunken plaza groups. There appears to have been Late Postclassic ceremonial activities (based on the presence of decorated serving vessels) on the summits of Mound 1 and 2.

Sola 39 was the only site in the project area to have been occupied continuously from the Ia phase until the end of the prehispanic sequence, with the possible exception of a brief hiatus after the II-IIIa transition. The site is well preserved and its occupation sufficiently discrete such that each of these periods could be studied intensively.

Phase-by-Phase Site Size and Population Estimates:

Phase	Area (ha)	Low	High	Mean
Ia	0.33	7	17	12
Ic	14.81	220	500	360
II	19.44	277	602	440
IIIa	31.06	450	975	713
IIIb-IV	31.06	450	975	713
V	1.58	40	85	63

SITE 40
Municipio: Santos Reyes
UTM: E714700/N1721800
Environment: Mountain/2180 m
Site Size: 4.12 ha
Periodization: IIIa, V
Condition: Good

Description: Sola 40 was a terraced hilltop site 2.5 km southwest of Santos Reyes. Highway 131 circumnavigates this hilltop as it passes out of the Sola Valley. The terrain had an extremely steep slope; the hilltop was a 2.5-hour climb from the valley floor. The nearest water source was over 100 m down slope. Pine forest covered the site (*pino* and *encino*). The site—known locally as "Mogote Riliquis"—is used today for collecting firewood and charcoal production.

A small platform and low mound were on the hilltop, and encircled by 18 residential terraces. Surface visibility was poor. Utilitarian orange-brownware and grayware ceramics were collected; no other artifacts were recorded. The ceramic collection was not especially diagnostic, so future work must better define the site's occupation. The Period IIIa occupation could have been contemporary with Sola 55, making these two sites hill-fort outposts for Sola 23. The Period V occupation at this site was probably contemporary with that of Sola 20, based on similar looking ceramics, and so would date early in the Postclassic period.

Sola 40 has a commanding view of the valley; the distinctively shaped hilltop is visible from all parts of the Sola Valley. The site overlooks the modern highway and Colonial period *camino real* to the coast. It was a highly defensible location, terraced, with a steep slope. Defensive walls were below the residential terraces located along only the possible approach to the site.

Phase-by-Phase Site Size and Population Estimates:

Phase	Area (ha)	Low	High	Mean
IIIa	4.12	105	218	162
V	4.12	105	218	162

SITE 41/42
Municipio: Santos Reyes
UTM: E715100/N1723900
Environment: Low piedmont/1640 m
Site Size: 1.50 ha
Periodization: Ic, II, IIIa, V
Condition: Poor (modern use)

Description: Sites 41 and 42 have been combined. Sola 41/42 was located immediately west of Santos Reyes Sola, bisected by Highway 131. A *barranca* runs along the southern edge of the site; lands nearby were irrigated. What had originally been described as Sola 42 (east of the highway and nearest to Santos Reyes) is currently under cultivation. The Sola 41 component (west of the highway) sat atop an open-air rock shelter; no artifacts were found in association with this feature. The area was not plowed.

Modern highway construction has heavily damaged the surface remains. Several ruined terraces were found west of the highway, but were too damaged to map. Both parts of the site had Ic phase and Period V; only the Sola 41 occupation had Period IIIa, found among the ruined terraces. The Period II designation was not definitive, being based on several ambiguous sherds that could be grouped with the Ic phase or even II-IIIa material. Ceramics included C.2/C.4, burnished red storage jars, orange brownwares, Huitzo Red-on-Cream, and thin gray jars (some slightly misfired). In addition to ceramics, shell artifacts were recovered. No other artifacts were recorded. Sola 41/42 may have been larger, but the modern disturbance has obscured its original configuration.

Phase-by-Phase Site Size and Population Estimates:

Phase	Area (ha)	Low	High	Mean
Ic	1.50	15	38	27
II	1.50	15	38	27
IIIa	0.20	5	10	8
V	1.50	15	38	27

SITE 43
Municipio: Santos Reyes
UTM: E613000/N1724100
Environment: Mountain/2200 m
Site Size: 0.01 ha
Periodization: Not defined
Condition: Poor (isolated find)

Description: Sola 43 was located on a steep mountain slope west of Santos Reyes. The origins of two mountain streams were nearby, some 300 m distant in each case. These streams irrigate lands of Santos Reyes below. Pine forest prevails at this elevation. This mountain zone is used today for the collection of firewood and charcoal production. Artifacts consisted of a single gray obsidian blade fragment and a quartz flake. No pottery was found. The area was overgrown, however, and surface visibility was poor. The next nearest site, Sola 41/42, was more than 2 km distant. The most likely (but conjectural) date for these artifacts would be Postclassic.

Phase-by-Phase Site Size and Population Estimates:

Phase	Area (ha)	Low	High	Mean
Not Defined	0.01	—	—	—

SITE 44
Municipio: Santos Reyes
UTM: E715000/N1724900
Environment: Low piedmont/1540 m
Site Size: 0.01 ha
Periodization: Ic
Condition: Poor (modern use/looted)

Description: Sola 44 was a looted tomb. No other surface indications of a settlement were found beyond this disturbed area. Water was available from *barrancas* less than 100 m on the north and south sides of the site. Sola 44 was not under cultivation. Ceramics, chert flakes, and an ax fragment were recovered. Human bones were associated with the tomb. The ceramics included a G.12 (combed bottom) and K.3 with an everted rim. It is possible that highway construction has removed other indications of settlement.

Phase-by-Phase Site Size and Population Estimates:

Phase	Area (ha)	Low	High	Mean
Ic	0.01	5	10	8

SITE 45
Municipio: Santos Reyes
UTM: E715000/N1724800
Environment: Low piedmont/1500 m
Site Size: 3.76 ha
Periodization: IIIa, IIIb-IV, V
Condition: Poor (plowed)

Description: Sola 45 was located along the old *camino real* that leads up from the valley floor and passes Santos Reyes before exiting the Sola Valley. Water from a *barranca* was 150 m distant. There was an isolated modern residence within the site limits; the site area was cultivated. Many fruit trees were grown near the site, including lemon, orange, banana, and avocado. Alfalfa and *guaje* were grown as well. There appears to have been a low platform at the site, but it was too badly damaged by agriculture to measure. Only ceramics were recovered. The Classic period ceramic materials were not definitive, and could date to either Period IIIa or IIIb-IV exclusively. The Period V collection included Huitzo Red-on-Cream.

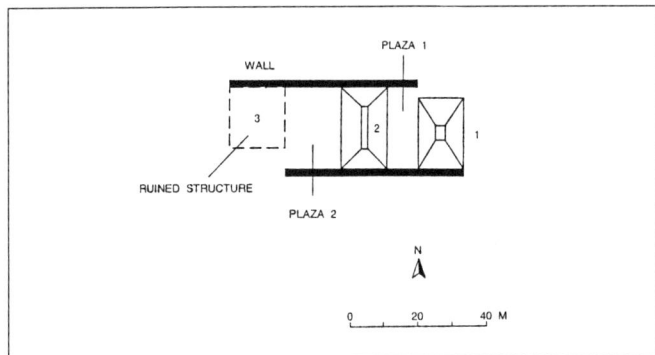

Figure A.18. Detail of the civic-ceremonial core at Sola 47.

Phase-by-Phase Site Size and Population Estimates:

Phase	Area (ha)	Low	High	Mean
IIIa	3.00	30	75	53
IIIb-IV	3.00	30	75	53
V	3.76	38	94	66

SITE 46
Municipio: Santos Reyes
UTM: E715000/N1722800
Environment: Low piedmont/1720 m
Site Size: 0.03 ha
Periodization: V
Condition: Poor (eroded)

Description: Sola 46 was located at the summit of a 30 m high rock outcrop; the site was inaccessible and highly defensible. The mountaintop fortress at Sola 40 was less than 1 km to the southwest. A *barranca* was less than 100 m distant. Only ceramics were recovered, and these sherds looked similar to those from Sola 20 and 40. This site was one of several fortifications on the western side of the valley that probably date early in the Postclassic. There was no modern occupation or utilization of the site. A relict (*lama-bordo*) terraced field was located nearby, but not necessarily associated with the site.

Phase-by-Phase Site Size and Population Estimates:

Phase	Area (ha)	Low	High	Mean
V	0.03	5	10	8

SITE 47
Municipio: Santos Reyes
UTM: E716300/N1725000
Environment: Low piedmont/1460 m
Site Size: 8.05 ha
Periodization: Ic, II, IIIa, IIIb-IV, V
Condition: Fair (plowed/looted)

Description: Sola 47 rested on a piedmont spur surrounded by high alluvial terraces less than 1 km from the Río Sola. *Barrancas* on the north and south sides of site were less than 100 m distant; modern fields were irrigated. *Enebro* and *copal* trees grew within the site limits. The site had been farmed in recent years, but was not cultivated at the time of the survey. Sola 47 was located on the natural route leading out of the Sola Valley, and had outstanding views in all directions.

The site consisted of three mounds (uncertain date of construction) with two intervening plazas and three dispersed terraces. There was a looted tomb, with partially exposed lintels, located down slope on Terrace 1 to the north of the mound group. Surface visibility was poor, though ceramics were collected from several looter's pits near the mound group and tomb. Ceramics included a Formative figurine, G.12, burnished creamwares, gray *sahumador* with wide tube, orange brownwares, G.35, and G.3M. The Ic phase and Period V components were the best-defined occupations ceramically, but there was also a Classic period presence at the site making inferences about construction phases problematic.

Phase-by-Phase Site Size and Population Estimates:

Phase	Area (ha)	Low	High	Mean
Ic	4.65	47	116	82
II	1.10	11	28	20
IIIa	4.00	40	100	70
IIIb-IV	8.05	81	201	141
V	8.05	81	201	141

SITE 48
Municipio: Santa Inés
UTM: E720000/N1724200
Environment: Low piedmont/1460 m
Site Size: 0.01 ha
Periodization: IIIa
Condition: Poor (eroded)

Description: Sola 48 was located on steeply sloping land just above the alluvium of the Río Sola. The area was overgrown with grasses and low shrubs. An irrigation canal diverted water to nearby fields from *barrancas* on either side of the *loma*. Ceramics were found eroding from a vacant posthole. It is probable that Sola 48 was formed by slopewash from Sola 57, located on the *loma* above. For the present analysis, however, these sites will be kept analytically separate.

Phase-by-Phase Site Size and Population Estimates:

Phase	Area (ha)	Low	High	Mean
IIIa	0.01	5	10	8

SITE 49
Municipio: Santa Inés
UTM: E720200/N1723300
Environment: Low piedmont/1500 m
Site Size: 1.35 ha
Periodization: V
Condition: Poor (eroded)

Description: Sola 49 was located on a piedmont spur overlooking modern Santa Inés. This piedmont zone has been farmed in recent years, but was not under cultivation at the time of the survey. Water was available from a *barranca* 250 m distant. The lower reaches of the Santa Inés piedmont zone were irrigated. Highly productive alluvial lands were 500 m distant.

Ceramics included utilitarian brownwares, a grayware jar body, and modern San Marcos *comales*. No lithics or other artifacts were observed. The site was in a defensible location, though no evidence of terracing or other fortification was seen. Sola 49 is not utilized today except for grazing; the area is eroded with bedrock exposed in places, and the soil appears to be exhausted.

Phase-by-Phase Site Size and Population Estimates:

Phase	Area (ha)	Low	High	Mean
V	1.35	14	34	24

SITE 50
Municipio: Santa Inés
UTM: E720800/N1723600
Environment: Low piedmont/1520 m
Site Size: 0.80 ha
Periodization: V
Condition: Poor (eroded)

Description: Sola 50 was located on the modern path from Santa Inés that passed Sola 49 and led into the mountains. A *barranca* was 250 m away. The site was cleared of vegetation, but not farmed at the time of the survey. Ceramics were identical to those at Sola 49, with fine paste brownwares and a gray jar body. No structures, terraces, or other artifacts were observed.

Phase-by-Phase Site Size and Population Estimates:

Phase	Area (ha)	Low	High	Mean
V	0.80	8	20	14

SITE 51
Municipio: Santa Inés
UTM: E720000/N1723900
Environment: Low piedmont/1460 m
Site Size: 0.43 ha
Periodization: V
Condition: Poor (eroded)

Description: Sola 51 was found at the foot of the piedmont zone, directly overlooking the alluvium. The site was cleared of vegetation. Water from a *barranca* was 100 m distant. The site and nearby lands are irrigated and farmed today. Many modern potsherds were on the surface; these included San Marcos wares and a medium thick orangeware reportedly common some 60 years ago. Other ceramics were Postclassic utilitarian brownwares similar to other sites near Santa Inés. No other artifacts were seen.

Phase-by-Phase Site Size and Population Estimates:

Phase	Area (ha)	Low	High	Mean
V	0.43	4	11	8

SITE 52
Municipio: Santa Inés
UTM: E720800/N1722900
Environment: Low piedmont/1440 m
Site Size: 0.01 ha
Periodization: Ic
Condition: Poor (eroded)

Description: Sola 52 was found 1 km southeast of Santa Inés along a modern path leading to the valley floor. The Río Sola was 500 m south. The site was cleared of vegetation, but not plowed at the time of the survey. Erosion was severe. A *barranca* was 150 m distant. Alluvial lands were nearby. Nearby hillsides had contemporary terraces and ceramics; rows of maguey were planted along these terraces. Prehispanic ceramics included a variant crenelated rim bowl, and a grayware jar; both had a fine, compacted clay body. No other artifacts were recovered. This site was probably out of context, with the ceramics washing down from surrounding hills.

Phase-by-Phase Site Size and Population Estimates:

Phase	Area (ha)	Low	High	Mean
Ic	0.01	5	10	8

SITE 53
Municipio: Santa Inés
UTM: E720600/N1722500
Environment: Low piedmont/1400 m
Site Size: 0.01 ha
Periodization: V
Condition: Poor (eroded/looted)

Description: Sola 53 was confined to a small depression that was possibly a looted tomb. The site was located near a *barranca*, and only 150 m from the Río Sola. A modern path leading down to the valley floor crossed this site. Highly productive alluvium was nearby. Ceramics included utilitarian brownwares, G.3M, and Huitzo Red-on-Cream. No other artifacts were found.

Phase-by-Phase Site Size and Population Estimates:

Phase	Area (ha)	Low	High	Mean
V	0.01	5	10	8

SITE 54
Municipio: Santa Inés
UTM: E720400/N1722500
Environment: Low Alluvium/1380 m
Site Size: 0.01 ha
Periodization: IIIb-IV
Condition: Poor (isolated find)

Description: Sola 54 was located adjacent to the Río Sola, in a plowed maize field. A single brownware urn fragment was recovered. No other artifacts or indications of settlement were seen. The alluvial deposits were deep, however, so other evidence may be buried.

Phase-by-Phase Site Size and Population Estimates:

Phase	Area (ha)	Low	High	Mean
IIIb-IV	0.01	5	10	8

SITE 55
Municipio: Santa Inés
UTM: E721900/N1724200
Environment: High piedmont/1800 m

Site Size: 0.24 ha
Periodization: IIIa, V
Condition: Good

Description: Sola 55 was an isolated, high density site overlooking Santa Inés and the southern part of the Sola Valley. Water was not readily available; the nearest *barranca* was 250 m distant, and more than 100 m down slope. Pine forest prevailed at this elevation. The site is not farmed today, but had been plowed in years past.

There were two small mounds and a plaza. The mounds were badly damaged by past plowing. The hilltop site was connected to the ridgeline by a narrow *montura*, and delimited by eight terraces and a defensive ditch (these features were in good condition). The slope below the terraces was extremely steep. Artifacts were limited to ceramics and an ax fragment. Ceramics were Period IIIa orange-brownwares and graywares, and a smaller Period V component that included G.3Ms.

There were many similarities between this site and Sola 40, located directly opposite on the western side of the valley. Each site, whose occupation dated from Period IIIa (possibly the II-IIIa Transition), was re-occupied in Period V and had defensive and boundary control functions. Population estimates were based on the terraced area.

Phase-by-Phase Site Size and Population Estimates:

Phase	Area (ha)	Low	High	Mean
IIIa	0.24	40	80	60
V	0.08	20	40	30

SITE 56
Municipio: Santa Inés
UTM: E722700/N1724000
Environment: High piedmont/1920 m
Site Size: 0.01 ha
Periodization: Not defined
Condition: Excellent

Description: Sola 56 was an isolated mound, with no artifacts or indications of settlement nearby. There was no modern use. Pine forest dominated, though the site was located in a small clearing. The nearest water source was 350 m distant. Sola 56 was 850 m southeast of Sola 55. The single mound was built on a broad, flat area just before an extremely steep ascent into the mountains. The site may have functioned as a boundary marker, similar to the lone mound at Sola 6. Nearby sites suggest that Sola 56 dates to either Period IIIa or V.

Phase-by-Phase Site Size and Population Estimates:

Phase	Area (ha)	Low	High	Mean
Not Defined	0.01	—	—	—

SITE 57
Municipio: Santa Inés
UTM: E720000/N1724400
Environment: Low piedmont/1520 m
Site Size: 0.20 ha
Periodization: IIIa, V
Condition: Fair (plowed)

Description: Sola 57 was located on a plowed and irrigated piedmont shelf. An isolated modern household was nearby. A *barranca* was 150 m distant. Much of the low piedmont near Santa Inés is irrigated today. The site sat immediately above the alluvium of the Río Sola. Ceramics included Period IIIa orange-brownwares, and a Period V import, possibly Yanhuitlán Red-on-Cream. A chert flake was recovered.

Phase-by-Phase Site Size and Population Estimates:

Phase	Area (ha)	Low	High	Mean
IIIa	0.20	5	10	8
V	0.20	5	10	8

SITE 58
Municipio: Santa Inés
UTM: E719500/N1723900
Environment: High alluvium/1400 m
Site Size: 0.25 ha
Periodization: II, IIIa, V
Condition: Poor (plowed/eroded)

Description: Sola 58 sat on an alluvial terrace 450 m from the Río Sola. A *barranca* and irrigation works were 50 m from the site. Ceramics included two C.11/C.12 creamwares with red paint (Period II); utilitarian orange-brownwares and graywares (Period IIIa, or II-IIIa); G.3M, Huitzo Red-on-Cream, and thin, gray jar bodies (Period V). No other artifacts were observed. Sola 58 may have been larger, but river channel action and plowing has eroded much of the site.

Phase-by-Phase Site Size and Population Estimates:

Phase	Area (ha)	Low	High	Mean
II	0.25	5	10	8
IIIa	0.25	5	10	8
V	0.25	5	10	8

SITE 59
Municipio: Santa Inés
UTM: E719100/N1724200
Environment: High alluvium/1420 m
Site Size: 3.50 ha
Periodization: V
Condition: Poor (eroded)

Description: Sola 59 sat on an alluvial terrace, recently under cultivation, but not plowed at the time of the survey. The site was cleared of vegetation, and heavily eroded. Several contemporary households were located nearby. A *barranca* was 150 m distant; the Río Sola was 600 m southwest. The area is irrigated today. Ceramics were Period V utilitarian graywares and brownwares. No other artifacts were recovered.

Phase-by-Phase Site Size and Population Estimates:

Phase	Area (ha)	Low	High	Mean
V	3.50	35	88	62

SITE 60
Municipio: Rancho Viejo
UTM: E726600/N1717500
Environment: Low piedmont/1560 m
Site Size: 4.46 ha
Periodization: Ic
Condition: Fair (plowed)

Description: Sola 60 was located on the flat summit of an extremely steep piedmont spur near the confluence of the Sola and Atoyac rivers. Lands here are deeply incised, with only a narrow (approximately 100 m wide) alluvium. The site was 260 m above the valley floor. Water was available from *barrancas* 50-150 m distant. The site was largely cleared for agriculture, though *pino* and *encino* grew nearby.

Several sets of house foundations were observed, but were too damaged from modern plowing to map. Ceramics included a G.12 and G.12 variant, a tan bowl with basal rim, and utilitarian wares with a compact clay body. Ax fragments were associated with the intact house. The site was situated in a highly defensible location, but there were no terraces or other defensive constructions. This site would have been the Late Formative twin or outlying barrio of the more populous Sola 61, located 1 km northwest on the opposite side of the river.

Phase-by-Phase Site Size and Population Estimates:

Phase	Area (ha)	Low	High	Mean
Ic	4.46	45	112	79

SITE 61
Municipio: Rancho Viejo
UTM: E726000/N1718400
Environment: Low piedmont/1460 m
Site Size: 13.22 ha
Periodization: Ic, IIIa, IIIb-IV, V
Condition: Fair (plowed)

Description: Sola 61 was one of the key Late Formative sites in the valley. It was located near the confluence of the Sola and Atoyac rivers, at the southeastern limit of the project area. The site was built around a pillar-shaped rock outcrop with extremely steep terrain; the location was defensible and inaccessible. The eastern limit of the site abutted the narrow, sandy alluvium of the Río Sola. Site elevation ranges from 1300-1460 m. There was no modern habitation of the area; the site's lower reaches were farmed, though not irrigated.

Five isolated mounds and associated platforms were distributed across the site. Mound organization suggests that initial construction began in the Late Formative—most of the later sites had mound groups with more formal and enclosed spaces. Mound 1 was located on the narrow summit of the rock outcrop, and was certainly the least accessible portion of the site. This summit contained several small terraces, and a high density of ceremonial ceramics (including Period IV spiked braziers). Mound 2 and 3 were associated with platforms, and probably supported elite households. Recent looting in the Mound 2 platform has revealed a stucco floor above multiple tombs. Period I pottery was found in the fill of this platform. Two *metate* fragments were associated with the Mound 3 platform. It is possible, however, that Mound 4 and its associated plaza date from the Early Classic. Mound 4 and the east-facing wall of Terrace 23 that measured 6 m high and supported the higher ground descending from Mound 3 defined the plaza. A *mano* was found on top of Mound 4. Mound 5 also had a partial platform, though plowing has damaged it.

West of the Mound 3 platform, a subterranean tunnel gave access to a narrow pathway that traveled alongside the rock outcrop and exited on the flat terrain near Mound 5. The entrance to this tunnel was stone faced, and associated with ceramics of multiple time periods. At the northern site limit, down slope from Mound 4, a looted cave was reported by informants to have had approximately twelve conch shells and many greenstone beads. One of these shells was photographed and included in Nicholas and Feinman's report (this volume).

Ceramic collections included Period Ic types G.12 (combed bottom), K.3, and sherds with C.2/C.4 paint. In addition to utilitarian wares, the Period IIIa component included two G.23s. Ceramics found near Mound 1 were coarse paste brownware *sahumador* and brazier fragments often with spiked appliqué on the exterior of the vessel. These probably date to late Period IIIb-IV. A small Period IIIb-IV component was located among the ruined terraces. The Period V collections had Huitzo Red-on-Cream, Yanhuitlán Red-on-Cream, and miscellaneous gray jar bodies. Other artifacts (in addition to the ground stone mentioned above) included a green obsidian blade found in the plaza, and a single chert flake found near Mound 5. The lithic collection was limited despite good surface visibility over much of the site.

Twenty-three terraces were formally mapped, though at least twice that number once existed. Modern agriculture has destroyed most of

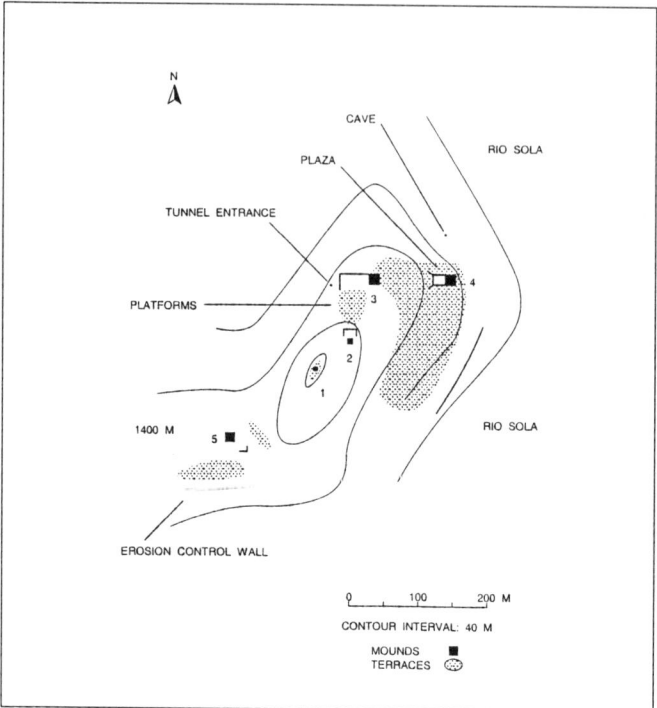

Figure A.19. Piedra de los Anticuados (S61).

the terraced area on the east side of the site. Population estimates use the approximate figure of 50 residential terraces for both the Ic and IIIa occupations. The site is known locally as "Piedra de los Anticuados."

Phase-by-Phase Site Size and Population Estimates:

Phase	Area (ha)	Low	High	Mean
Ic	13.22	142	498	320
IIIa	13.22	320	675	498
IIIb-IV	0.32	8	16	12
V	1.50	15	38	27

SITE 62
Municipio: Rancho Viejo
UTM: E726900/N1716000
Environment: Low piedmont/1480 m
Site Size: 1.27 ha
Periodization: Ic, IIIa, V
Condition: Excellent

Description: Sola 62 was situated at the southeastern limits of the project area, an extremely steep piedmont spur 200 m above the confluence of the Sola and Atoyac rivers. Land nearby was terraced, but these appeared to be modern constructions not related to the prehispanic site. The area was known locally as "Mogote Campesino."

Sola 62 had two low mounds and nine dispersed house mounds extending for 250 m. The mounds were dispersed, much like Sola 60 and 61, suggesting that construction dated in all three cases to the same period. Ceramic collections were taken in the vicinity of the mounds only; no surface artifacts were visible over the rest of the site. For this reason, identical site size and population estimates are given for all time periods represented.

Ceramics included a G.12 miniature; many Late Formative utilitarian wares similar in composition to the Sola 61 collections; Early

Classic utilitarian graywares and orange-brownwares; and Late Postclassic G.3Ms and gray jar bodies. No other artifacts were recovered. Sola 62 is one of the few instances where house foundations are intact, making it an excellent candidate for future excavations.

Phase-by-Phase Site Size and Population Estimates:

Phase	Area (ha)	Low	High	Mean
Ic	1.27	13	32	23
IIIa	1.27	13	32	23
V	1.27	13	32	23

SITE 63
Municipio: Rancho Viejo
UTM: E725500/N1716400
Environment: Low piedmont/1560 m
Site Size: 0.01 ha
Periodization: Ic
Condition: Good
Description: Sola 63 was located near the path from Rancho Viejo to San Vicente Coatlán. San Vicente is southeast of the project area, across the Atoyac river. Apart from foot transport, there is no modern use of the area. The site is located 100 m from the origin of two *barrancas*. Ceramics included many utilitarian brownwares and a burnished grayware bowl. The composition of these ceramics was identical to the Late Formative component at Sola 61. No other artifacts were recovered. Sola 61 was likely a single, isolated residence.

Phase-by-Phase Site Size and Population Estimates:

Phase	Area (ha)	Low	High	Mean
Ic	0.01	5	10	8

SITE 64
Municipio: Rancho Viejo
UTM: E723900/N1716500
Environment: Low piedmont/1660 m
Site Size: 0.45 ha
Periodization: Ic, V
Condition: Poor (modern use)
Description: Sola 64 was a single mound, badly damaged by modern settlement, and an associated ceramic scatter. Soils are generally poorer near Rancho Viejo than in other parts of the valley; nevertheless, several dispersed households have plowed fields in the sandy, rocky soil. The land is irrigated today. Proximity to Rancho Viejo and its irrigation facilities likely explains the concentration of modern settlement here. Ceramics included two G.12s. One gray jar body defined the Late Postclassic component. No other artifacts were recovered.

Phase-by-Phase Site Size and Population Estimates:

Phase	Area (ha)	Low	High	Mean
Ic	0.45	5	11	8
V	0.01	5	10	8

SITE 65
Municipio: Santos Niños
UTM: E721000/N1719900
Environment: Low piedmont/1440 m
Site Size: 38.61 ha
Periodization: Ic, IIIa, IIIb-IV, V
Condition: Fair (terraces plowed)

Description: Sola 65 was on a low eminence directly south of Santo Niño Mueve Corazones. The site limits extended into the high alluvium 200 m west of the Río Sola. Multiple *barrancas* run within the site limits. Several modern households occupy the site. Corn and a local cash crop are grown within the site limits. Both the *loma* and *bajío* are irrigated.

Three mound groups, five plazas, and two other individual mounds were dispersed across the site. The central architectural complex was the 4-mound group with ball court arrangement similar to Sola 10, 97, 104, and 111. The central complex was supported with large retention walls that gave the appearance of multi-level platforms supporting the structures. As argued in the text, this final architectural pattern likely dates to IIIb-IV. Sola 65's architecture and dispersed mound groups are highly comparable to the arrangement at Sola 97.

Ceramics included types G.12, G.35, and G.3M. Many utilitarian brownwares resembled IIIb-IV (G.35) grayware bowls. Other artifacts included a chert core, gray obsidian blade, and chert point found on the "platform" at the east side of Mound 9. An ax fragment was associated with a secondary mound group, west of the central complex. An exposed tomb was located among terraces near the *bajío*, away from any mound group. Finally, thin sheets of mica were seen approximately 50 m beyond the western site limit.

Multiple terraces extended across the length of *loma*, linking the separate mound groups. These, unfortunately, were so disturbed by modern farming that they could not be systematically mapped. It was not possible to count terrace fragments, so a higher density measure was used to estimate population in the terraced area.

Phase-by-Phase Site Size and Population Estimates:

Phase	Area (ha)	Low	High	Mean
Ic	0.50	5	13	9
IIIa	12.50	313	625	469
IIIb-IV	38.61	425	1169	797
V	1.36	14	34	24

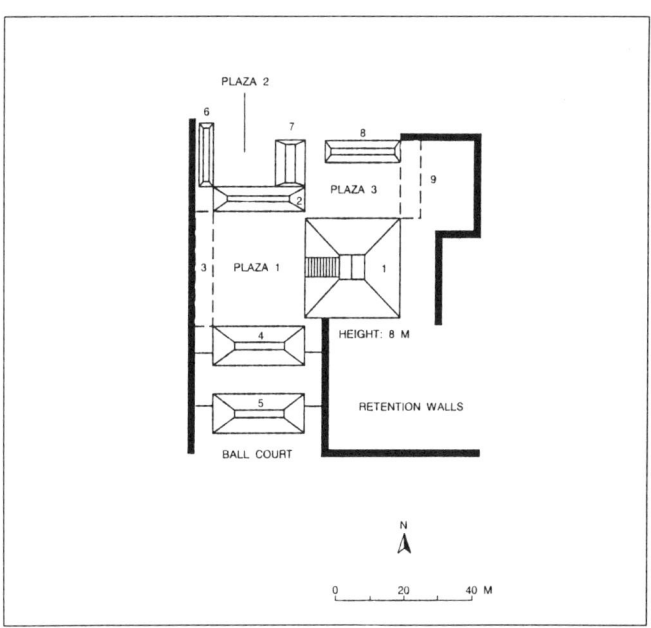

Figure A.20. Detail of the civic-ceremonial core at Santo Niño Mueve Corazones (S65).

SITE 66
Municipio: San Ildefonso
UTM: E719500/N1838200
Environment: High piedmont/1900 m
Site Size: 0.24 ha
Periodization: IIIb-IV, V
Condition: Fair (plowed)

Description: Sola 66 was a single isolated residence supported by a terrace. The site has been plowed in the past, but was not under cultivation at the time of the survey. A *barranca* was 75 m from the site. The ceramic collection consisted of thick, fine paste brownwares (IIIb-IV), a few graywares that could date to IV/V, and a G.3M miniature. A chert flake was recorded. Human cranial fragments were visible on the surface. Rock outcrops on the northern face of this hill had exposed chert veins and flakes, but evidence for quarrying was not found. This site was almost certainly single component, dating to either late IIIb-IV or early V.

Phase-by-Phase Site Size and Population Estimates:

Phase	Area (ha)	Low	High	Mean
IIIb-IV	0.24	5	10	8
V	0.24	5	10	8

SITE 67
Municipio: San Ildefonso
UTM: E720000/N1837400
Environment: Mountain/2100 m
Site Size: 22.25 ha
Periodization: IIIa, V
Condition: Excellent

Description: Sola 67 was the hilltop site known locally as "La Muchacha." Water was not readily available; the nearest *barranca* originated 140 m down slope. Terrain was extremely steep. The site was not plowed; terraces were intact, and housemounds visible. Pine forest covered the site.

Two mounds rested on the narrow summit of the site. Terraces extended down all sides of the hilltop. Defensive walls 5-m high and a 6-m wide ditch covered the most accessible approaches. Looters' pits revealed a tomb, stucco floors, and provided several good ceramic collections. Apart from the looting, surface visibility was extremely limited (the looting was not extensive). Artifacts included ceramics and a quartz hammer stone. Given the limited surface visibility, future work must assess whether additional periods were present.

Thirty-two terraces were mapped, forming the basis of the population estimates. The site size measures the entire area within the defensive features. Occupation did not extend beyond the terraced area, however, so the population estimate is based entirely on the terrace count.

Phase-by-Phase Site Size and Population Estimates:

Phase	Area (ha)	Low	High	Mean
IIIa	22.25	160	320	240
V	0.01	5	10	8

SITE 68
Municipio: San Francisco
UTM: E721800/N1834300
Environment: Mountain/2060 m
Site Size: 11.80 ha
Periodization: IIIb-IV, V
Condition: Poor (plowed)

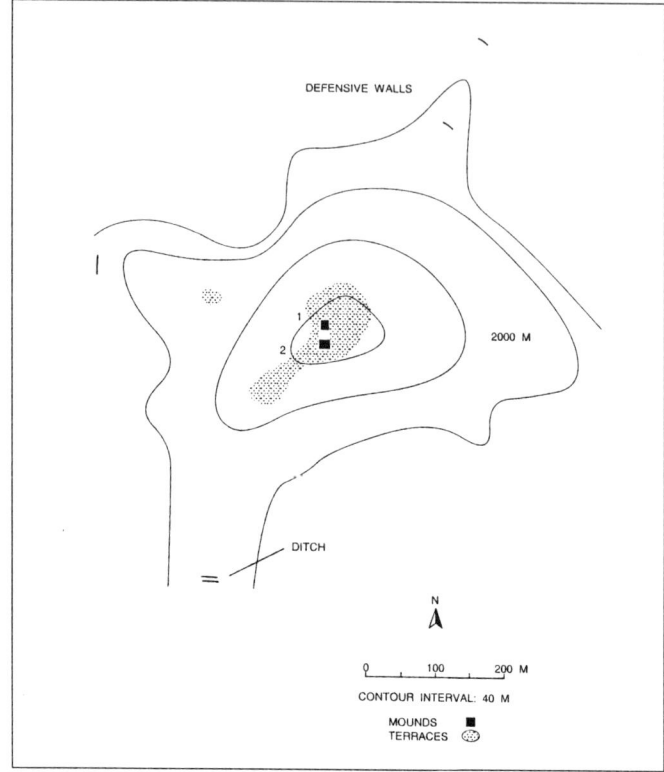

A.21. La Muchacha (S67).

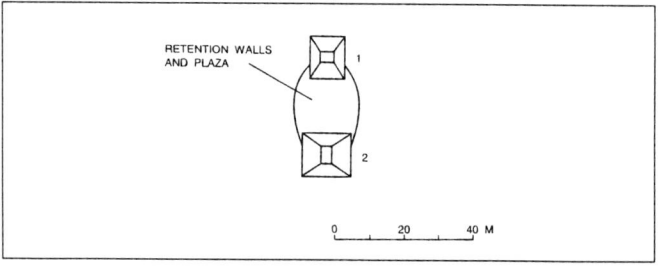

A.21a. Detail of civic-ceremonial core at La Muchacha (S67).

Description: Sola 68 was located in the high mountain pass north of the highway leading into the valley. Agriculture has heavily damaged the site, although no plowing has taken place for about 20 years (based on the estimated age of succeeding tree species). Surface visibility was poor. Nearest water source was 250 m distant.

Two dispersed mounds were located on successive high points of the loma. Mound 1 may have had a companion structure forming a small plaza, but the area was too damaged from plowing to be certain. Portions of the site were terraced, but these walls were destroyed by plowing and could not be measured. A ditch measuring 6 × 40 m guarded the southwest approach to the site. A small limestone quarry was found where building stone was extracted. Multiple stone piles were observed in separate locations on the site. The quarried stone was identical to that used in the mound construction. Ceramics were dominated by Late Postclassic brownwares and G.3Ms. There was one example of Huitzo Red-on-Cream. A smaller IIIb-IV component also was present, composed of utilitarian brownwares. Other artifacts included chert flakes, found below the terraced area at the northern site limit.

The dispersed nature of the mound construction and the many isolated houses is consistent with a Late Postclassic date for the main phase of occupation. Population estimates use a higher density figure for the area of ruined terraces.

Phase-by-Phase Site Size and Population Estimates:

Phase	Area (ha)	Low	High	Mean
IIIb-IV	4.40	65	150	108
V	11.80	163	370	267

SITE 69
Municipio: San Francisco
UTM: E722400/N1834400
Environment: High piedmont/1980 m
Site Size: 8.32 ha
Periodization: IIIb-IV, V
Condition: Excellent

Description: Sola 69 was located north of the highway on the *montura* between hilltops at Sola 68 and 70 (Cerro Yaco). The site was on a modern path that leads from San Andrés Zabache (southern Valley of Oaxaca) into the mountains north of the pass (and modern highway) leading into the Sola Valley. The site was not plowed at the time of the survey, but had been farmed in the recent past (much like Sola 68). A *barranca* forms adjacent to the site limits. Extraction of *cal* for lime production has taken place in historic times, with numerous small pits found. Three *cal* (or possibly *carbón*) ovens were seen. Modern ceramics were found on the site.

A low mound with looted tomb was associated with a terrace supporting two houses. These houses had Period V ceramics on the surface. This arrangement of low mound with adjacent terrace and twin houses also occurred at Sola 111. North of Mound 1 were two more low structures forming a plaza. This portion of the site was associated with IIIb-IV and V ceramics. Many intact houses were dispersed across the site, associated with Period V ceramics. These structures, houses, and terraces were all in excellent condition. Ceramics consisted of IIIb-IV and V utilitarian wares and Late Postclassic G.3Ms. There was a gray obsidian blade and chert flake collected.

Sola 69 started 200 m east of the Sola 68 site limits. Sola 68 and 69 could be considered part of the same dispersed settlement, especially during the Late Postclassic.

Phase-by-Phase Site Size and Population Estimates:

Phase	Area (ha)	Low	High	Mean
IIIb-IV	0.50	5	13	9
V	8.32	88	218	153

SITE 70
Municipio: San Francisco
UTM: E723500/N1834800
Environment: Mountain/2100 m
Site Size: 1.38 ha
Periodization: IIIb-IV, V
Condition: Good

Description: Sola 70 was located on the summit of Cerro Yaco. Three *barrancas* originated near the site, the nearest was 75 m distant. A modern path crossed the site, linking the southern limits of the Valley of Oaxaca to this ridgeline north of the highway. There was a modern house nearby and part of the site was plowed. The hilltop was cleared of vegetation and had outstanding views into the Valleys of Sola, Ejutla, and Oaxaca.

The site consisted of a single isolated residence associated with Period V ceramics. In a small plowed field nearby more ceramics were collected. These ceramics were IIIb-IV and V utilitarian brownwares (or perhaps entirely early V). There was also a chert flake and chert core in the collection.

Phase-by-Phase Site Size and Population Estimates:

Phase	Area (ha)	Low	High	Mean
IIIb-IV	0.45	5	11	8
V	0.90	9	23	16

SITE 71
Municipio: San Andrés
UTM: E726500/N1837000
Environment: High piedmont/1820 m
Site Size: 7.15 ha
Periodization: IIIb-IV, V
Condition: Fair (terraces plowed)

Description: Sola 71 was located on steeply sloping terrain along the ridgeline leading up to Cabo de Hacha. This is the beginning of the mountainous corridor separating the Valleys of Sola, Ejutla, and Oaxaca. Most vegetation had been cleared for agriculture, although *espino*, *tepeguaje*, and *encino* were present. The lowest reaches of the site above the highway were plowed at the time of the survey. The nearest *barranca* originates 150 m below the site on extremely steep terrain.

At the highest point of the site a low platform supported a mound; house foundations were visible on the mound. These structures dated to the Postclassic; this architectural arrangement was similar to Sola 111. Ceramics included a G.35, G.3Ms (one misfired), gray jar bodies, and utilitarian brownwares. Other artifacts were limited to three chert flakes and chert debitage.

Almost the entire site had been terraced; but the terraces were destroyed by modern agriculture. Since no terraces could be counted, a higher density figure was used for the terraced area in the population estimates. The ceramics suggest that this site was contemporary with Sola 111, whose main occupation was early Period V. Sola 71 and 111 straddled the entrance into the Sola Valley during this period.

Phase-by-Phase Site Size and Population Estimates:

Phase	Area (ha)	Low	High	Mean
IIIb-IV	0.15	5	10	8
V	7.15	169	341	255

SITE 72
Municipio: San Andrés
UTM: E726400/N1837200
Environment: High piedmont/1860 m
Site Size: 0.01
Periodization: V
Condition: Poor (eroded)

Description: Sola 72 was located 200 m upslope from Sola 71, and was probably an isolated house or houses associated with the larger site. The site had been cleared for agriculture and was badly eroding with bedrock exposed in places. The nearest water source was found 250 m below the site on extremely steep terrain. Ceramics were limited to a thin, gray jar body and utilitarian brownwares. This site could be considered part of Sola 71.

Phase-by-Phase Site Size and Population Estimates:

Phase	Area (ha)	Low	High	Mean
V	0.01	5	10	8

SITE 73
Municipio: San Andrés
UTM: E726100/N1838000
Environment: High piedmont/1900 m
Site Size: 0.06 ha
Periodization: V
Condition: Poor (eroded)
   Description: Sola 73 was another site found on the ascent of Cabo de Hacha. The site was situated on a narrow shelf approximately 200 m upslope from Sola 72. The site area was cleared of vegetation and badly eroded. Water was 250 m distant. Ceramics included thin, gray jar bodies and utilitarian brownwares. A green obsidian blade was found. This site was another isolate likely associated with Sola 71.

Phase-by-Phase Site Size and Population Estimates:

Phase	Area (ha)	Low	High	Mean
V	0.06	5	10	8

SITE 74
Municipio: San Martín
UTM: E726100/N1838800
Environment: Mountain/2240 m
Site Size: 0.02 ha
Periodization: IIIb-IV, V
Condition: Excellent
   Description: Sola 74 was located on the summit of Cabo de Hacha. A *mojonera* within the site forms the boundary between San Andrés Zabache, San Martín Lachila, and Santa María Ayoquezco. The area is forest covered; pine trees dominate. The site consisted of a small mound and defensive wall. Ceramics included a *sahumador*, three urn fragments, utilitarian brownwares, and thin, gray jar bodies and G.3Ms. The urn fragments were dated to IIIb-IV, but the site was probably single component dating to the IV/V boundary. Chert flakes were present.

Phase-by-Phase Site Size and Population Estimates:

Phase	Area (ha)	Low	High	Mean
IIIb-IV	0.02	5	10	8
V	0.02	5	10	8

SITE 75
Municipio: Ayoquezco
UTM: E726300/N1839000
Environment: Mountain/2240 m
Site Size: 16.88 ha
Periodization: IIIb-IV, V
Condition: Excellent
   Description: Sola 75 was located on the summit of Cabo de Hacha. The site was forest covered and had never been plowed. Tree species were dominated by *pino* and *encino*. A mountain stream had its origins within the site limits. Heavy forest litter limited surface visibility.
   Two mounds defined a small plaza, while a third mound, sunken patio groups, and several houses were widely dispersed across the site. An exposed tomb was associated with one of the sunken patio groups. Ceramics consisted of thick, utilitarian and finer paste graywares, and brownwares, but the collections were limited by surface conditions. No other artifacts were observed. Future work should reconsider the component sizes for this occupation.
   Sola 75 was one of the best preserved sites in the study region. The site would be an excellent candidate for excavation, although its remote mountain setting presents logistical difficulties.

Phase-by-Phase Site Size and Population Estimates:

Phase	Area (ha)	Low	High	Mean
IIIb-IV	16.88	169	422	296
V	8-12	125	175	150

SITE 76
Municipio: Ayoquezco
UTM: E726100/N1840400
Environment: Mountain/2160 m
Site Size: 0.06 ha
Periodization: V
Condition: Poor (isolated find)
   Description: Sola 76 was located in a clearing north of the summit of Cabo de Hacha. There was no immediately accessible water source. Pine forest was predominant. The site consisted of exposed chert nodules with a single utilitarian brownware sherd. High quality chert extraction may have occurred here, although no direct evidence of quarrying activities was found.

Phase-by-Phase Site Size and Population Estimates:

Phase	Area (ha)	Low	High	Mean
V	0.06	5	10	8

SITE 77
Municipio: San Ildefonso
UTM: E723500/N1837300
Environment: Low piedmont/1640 m
Site Size: 3.00 ha
Periodization: IIIb-IV, V
Condition: Poor (modern use)
   Description: Sola 77 was found in the low piedmont south of the road leading to San Sebastián de las Grutas. The site was located 50 m from the nearest *barranca*, and 250 m from the Río de las Grutas. The area is used today for *cal* production. Cut stone from the prehispanic site was stacked for lime extraction. The site was not plowed at the time of the survey. Surface visibility was poor.
   Prehispanic features were heavily damaged by the reuse of building stone and plowing. Three dispersed mounds and six terraces were mapped. The largest structure rested on a platform at the highest point on the site. The site's organization was reminiscent of other Late Postclassic sites in the study region. Ceramics included utilitarian brownwares along with gray jar bodies and a G.3M. No other artifacts were observed. Limited surface visibility complicated site size estimates. Future work should reassess the figures given here.

Phase-by-Phase Site Size and Population Estimates:

Phase	Area (ha)	Low	High	Mean
IIIb-IV	0.50	5	13	9
V	3.00	58	131	95

SITE 78
Municipio: San Ildefonso
UTM: E723600/N1837200
Environment: Low piedmont/1640 m
Site Size: 0.04 ha
Periodization: Not defined
Condition: Poor (plowed/eroded)
   Description: Sola 78 was in the low piedmont south of the highway leading to San Sebastián de las Grutas. Water was available from a *barranca* 250 m away, and from the Río de las Grutas 500 m distant.

A modern path leading into the mountains crossed Sola 78. The area was not plowed when surveyed. Surface visibility was poor.

Three heavily damaged mounds were arranged round a small plaza. No ceramics or other artifacts were visible on the surface. The architectural arrangement suggests a construction date of IIIa or IIIb-IV. The site size measures only the area encompassed by the mound group. Future work is needed to better define this site.

Phase-by-Phase Site Size and Population Estimates:

Phase	Area (ha)	Low	High	Mean
Not Defined	0.04	—	—	—

SITE 79
Municipio: Ayoquezco
UTM: E722800//N1839900
Environment: Low piedmont/1660 m
Site Size: 0.18 ha
Periodization: Ic, IIIa
Condition: Poor (modern use)

Description: Sola 79 was located in a plowed field, north of the highway leading to San Sebastián de las Grutas. A barranca provided water 100 m from the site; the Río de las Grutas was 450 m distant. The site had a modern household; the land was irrigated. No prehispanic structures were seen. Artifacts included modern, colonial, and prehispanic ceramics. A Late Formative component was defined with a K.3; Classic ceramics were composed of utilitarian graywares, brownwares, and an eroded G.23. A *mano* fragment was recorded.

Phase-by-Phase Site Size and Population Estimates:

Phase	Area (ha)	Low	High	Mean
Ic	0.01	5	10	8
IIIa	0.18	5	10	8

SITE 80
Municipio: Ayoquezco
UTM: E722900/N1839800
Environment: Low piedmont/1640 m
Site Size: 0.23 ha
Periodization: V
Condition: Good

Description: Sola 80 consisted of a single Period V house, still intact, with an associated ceramic scatter in an adjacent plowed field. The area was irrigated. The nearest water source was 500 m distant. Ceramics were utilitarian brownwares and gray jar bodies.

Phase-by-Phase Site Size and Population Estimates:

Phase	Area (ha)	Low	High	Mean
V	0.23	5	10	8

SITE 81/82
Municipio: Ayoquezco
UTM: E723400/N1838600
Environment: Low piedmont/1700 m
Site Size: 12.50 ha
Periodization: Ic, IIIa, V
Condition: Good

Description: Sola 81 and 82 have been combined. Sola 81 was a Late Postclassic occupation at the base of the hilltop; Sola 82 was the Classic period hilltop site. Sola 81/82 was located on an extremely steep hilltop 120 m above the Río de las Grutas, on the north side of the road leading to San Sebastián de las Grutas. The river was immediately adjacent to the site, while *barrancas* pass either side of the hilltop. The site had not been plowed; surface visibility was poor, although numerous looters' pits provided additional ceramic collections.

A four-mound group, sunken plaza, and adjacent ball court oriented 20 degrees east, were mapped on the hilltop. House foundations were visible on the mounds. Other houses were interspersed within the architectural core. A looted tomb was in the center of the plaza. Looting and erosion showed multiple construction episodes in the architectural core. Twenty-three hillside terraces were intact, also with house foundations. There was a soil retention wall, defensive wall, and ditch at the base of the hilltop on the northwest side. Despite the looting, there was no damage from agriculture and the site was in excellent condition.

Ceramics included many Period V diagnostics, including brownwares with mica temper, gray jar bodies, and G.3Ms. The Ic component had types G.12 (combed bottom) and K.3. Many graywares and brownwares belonged to the "Classic" period, but were not especially diagnostic. The architectural layout suggests Periods IIIa, IIIb-IV, or both; but these periods could not be distinguished based on the limited ceramic collections. The "Classic" ceramics were most similar to nearby Sola 67, a Period IIIa site.

A *mano* fragment and ax were associated with Mound 1; two *metate* fragments were recorded among the lower terraces on the northwest side of the hilltop. A relatively high density of chert debitage was found beyond the terraced area at the base of the hilltop. This was in a Period V residential context.

Site size and population estimates were hampered by the poor surface visibility and limited ceramic collections. Future work must reassess the figures given here. The occupied terrace count plus non-terraced area was used for these estimates.

Phase-by-Phase Site Size and Population Estimates:

Phase	Area (ha)	Low	High	Mean
Ic	6-10	129	226	178
IIIa	11.20	130	268	199
V	8.80	95	200	148

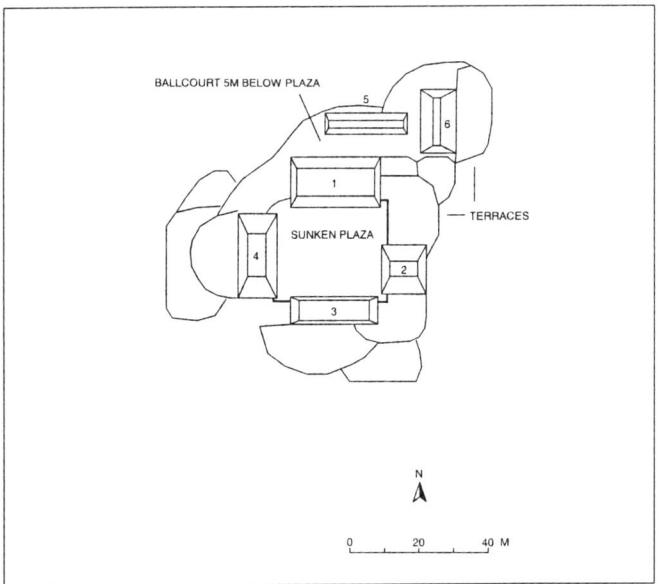

Figure A.22. Detail of civic-ceremonial core at Sola 81/82.

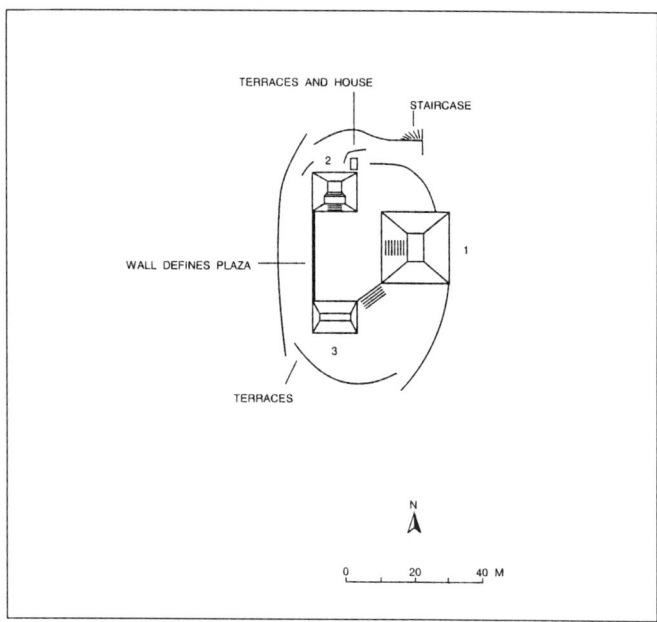

Figure A.23. Detail of the civic-ceremonial core at Cerro Orcón (S84).

SITE 83
Municipio: San Ildefonso
UTM: E716200/N1839100
Environment: High piedmont/1840 m
Site Size: 2.15 ha
Periodization: IIIb-IV, V
Condition: Fair (plowed)

Description: Sola 83 was found on a plowed hillside near San Sebastián de las Grutas (but land of another *municipio*). Water was available from a *barranca* 75 m distant. Vegetation was cleared for farming. The site was 1 km from the origin of the Río de las Grutas. Fields near the site were irrigated. Surface visibility was excellent.

Approximately 10 ruined terraces constituted the settlement. The terraces were completely destroyed by modern farming and could not be mapped. The site had a high density of chert flakes and debitage. Ceramics were primarily IIIb-IV thick, utilitarian orange brownwares (similar to G.35s); a smaller Period V component included Huitzo Red-on-Cream. The site was located on the same *loma* as Sola 84, and was associated with that larger settlement. Population estimates use a higher density figure for the terraced area.

Phase-by-Phase Site Size and Population Estimates:

Phase	Area (ha)	Low	High	Mean
IIIb-IV	2.15	44	91	68
V	0.50	13	25	19

SITE 84
Municipio: San Ild/Seb.
UTM: E715800/N1839500
Environment: High piedmont/1920 m
Site Size: 15.55 ha
Periodization: Ic, II, IIIa, IIIb-IV, V
Condition: Excellent

Description: Sola 84 was the hilltop site known locally as "Cerro Orcón." A *mojonera* at the site marked the boundary between San Sebastián de las Grutas and San Ildefonso Sola. Water was available from *barrancas* less than 100 m distant on the north and south sides of the site. The origin of the Río de las Grutas was 1 km east. The entrance to the large cave at San Sebastián was 200 m north. The hilltop was not plowed; *pino* and *encino* trees covered the site. Surface visibility was poor.

A three-mound group and plaza was mapped on the summit of Cerro Orcón. Forty-nine residential terraces, and an additional area of ruined terraces, were constructed on the hillside. A fourth mound built over a platform was located on a lower level of the site. A low wall defined the west side of the plaza. An erosion control wall on the east side of the site extended for nearly 200 m. Ceramics were recovered from several small looters' pits on the site. Diagnostic ceramics included types G.12 (combed bottom), and K.3; C.11/C.12 and C.20; a G.23, possibly misfired, in a yellow (*amarillo*) clay body; thick orange brownware bowls (an analog G.35); and Huitzo Red-on-Cream. A small lithic collection had chert flakes and debitage.

Surface visibility was limited to backdirt from the looters' pits. Diagnostic ceramics from Ic-V were present; their precise distribution, however, was unclear. The architectural complex and site layout suggest a "Classic" period date for the main phase of occupation. Surface sherds seen among recently plowed, ruined terraces at the base of the site had only Period IIIa ceramics. Site size and population estimates need future revision.

Phase-by-Phase Site Size and Population Estimates:

Phase	Area (ha)	Low	High	Mean
Ic	6-10	162	362	262
II	2-6	100	200	150
IIIa	15.55	308	615	462
IIIb-IV	2-6	100	200	150
V	1-2	38	75	57

SITE 85
Municipio: San Ildefonso
UTM: E717300/N1839100
Environment: Low piedmont/1740 m
Site Size: 0.40 ha
Periodization: Not defined
Condition: Good

Description: Sola 85 was located on an eminence above the highly productive alluvium near San Sebastián de las Grutas. The Río de las Grutas was 250 m distant. The land was cleared of vegetation and plowed; a modern household occupied the site. Primary reduction of chert cobbles took place here; chert cobbles and flakes were on the surface, and two chert tools were recovered. In the recently plowed field, surface visibility was excellent; still, no ceramics were seen. Sola 85 most likely dated to Period V (see nearby Sola 86 and 87 below).

Phase-by-Phase Site Size and Population Estimates:

Phase	Area (ha)	Low	High	Mean
Not Defined	0.40	—	—	—

SITE 86
Municipio: San Ildefonso
UTM: E717700/N1838700
Environment: Low piedmont/1740 m
Site Size: 0.09 ha
Periodization: V
Condition: Good

Description: Sola 86 was located near the alluvium south of San Sebastián de las Grutas. A *barranca* was 150 m distant; the Río de las

Grutas, 700 m. The area was overgrown; the surface covered with pine needles. Beans were planted in the nearby *bajío*. There was a single, isolated prehispanic house associated with Period V ceramics and lithic debris. The lithics included a tested chert cobble, chert flakes, and a tool. The sherd distribution covered an area of 30 × 30 m; the full distribution of exposed chert veins was 30 × 300 m, and had evidence of intermittent exploitation (shatter and small flakes).

Phase-by-Phase Site Size and Population Estimates:

Phase	Area (ha)	Low	High	Mean
V	0.09	5	10	8

SITE 87
Municipio: San Ildefonso
UTM: E717200/N1839000
Environment: Low piedmont/1720 m
Site Size: 0.09 ha
Periodization: V
Condition: Good

Description: Sola 87 was located on a low eminence above the alluvium south of San Sebastián de las Grutas. A *barranca* was 100 m west; the Río de las Grutas 300 m distant. A ruined and abandoned modern house was on the site. Pine and oak trees were the predominant vegetation. Surface visibility was poor.

The site had a low platform and mound, supported by a terrace wall. Period V ceramics were associated with this structure. This arrangement conforms to other Late Postclassic mound/platform architecture in Sola. Natural chert outcrops described for Sola 86 extended to the limits of this site. Sola 87 may have been larger, but poor surface visibility restricted observations to the mound and platform. Sola 86 and 87 occupied the same *loma*; they were likely part of the same dispersed Late Postclassic settlement.

Phase-by-Phase Site Size and Population Estimates:

Phase	Area (ha)	Low	High	Mean
V	0.09	5	10	8

SITE 88
Municipio: San Ildefonso
UTM: E715700/N1838700
Environment: High piedmont/1960 m
Site Size: 1.69 ha
Periodization: IIIb-IV, V
Condition: Fair (eroded/looted)

Description: Sola 88 was a hilltop site 2.5 km southwest of San Sebastián de las Grutas. Water from a barranca was 250 m distant. The piedmont lands west of the Sola 88 ridgeline were irrigated at the time of the survey. The site was located on the steeply sloping ridgeline between central places at Sola 23 and 84. Sola 88 was overgrown and covered in pine trees when surveyed; surface visibility was poor. Good ceramic collections were available, however, from several looters' pits.

A low mound was situated atop one of the twin peaks at the site, associated with Period V pottery on the unplowed surface. On the east flank of the ridgeline below the mound, four to six badly eroded terraces were constructed. These terraces were used in the population estimates given below. Exposed surfaces and looters' pits revealed IIIb-IV and V ceramics. Chert flakes were present. Future work should reassess the site size estimates, given the limited surface visibility.

Phase-by-Phase Site Size and Population Estimates:

Phase	Area (ha)	Low	High	Mean
IIIb-IV	1.69	45	88	67
V	1.69	45	88	67

SITE 89
Municipio: San Ildefonso
UTM: E715000/N1839400
Environment: High piedmont/1920 m
Site Size: 0.01 ha
Periodization: Not defined
Condition: Poor (isolated find)

Description: Sola 89 was located 300 m west of Sola 84, in a plowed field. The site was located along the path that connects San Sebastián de las Grutas to the piedmont zone west of the El Obispo ridgeline. *Barrancas* provided water 100 m from the site. A modern household was nearby. One undiagnostic grayware was found. The sherd was worn on the edges and may have been a tool (possibly for ceramic production). A chert flake also was collected. This site probably dated earlier than the Postclassic, but is otherwise undatable based on current data.

Phase-by-Phase Site Size and Population Estimates:

Phase	Area (ha)	Low	High	Mean
Not Defined	0.01	—	—	—

SITE 90
Municipio: San Sebastián
UTM: E715900/N1840000
Environment: High piedmont/1900 m
Site Size: 4.00 ha
Periodization: IIIa, IIIb-IV, V
Condition: Poor (eroded)

Description: Sola 90 was found on the flat, piedmont shelf immediately above the cave entrance at San Sebastián de las Grutas. The Río de las Grutas is said to originate at this point (*ojo de agua*). The site was not plowed when surveyed; surface visibility was poor.

Two low mounds aligned E/W were found on top of the *loma*; 13 terraces extended past the road to the southeast. The mounds, built over bedrock outcrops, were in poor condition; no plaza was formed between the structures. These rude structures may have been a shrine or boundary marker placed atop a ritually important cave.

Ceramics were not especially diagnostic, though most of the orange brownwares pertained to a long "Classic" period. Period IIIa and IIIb-IV were lumped together in the site size and population estimates given below. A smaller Period V component was present; but its true distribution was difficult to gauge on the unplowed surface. A chert flake was collected. Both "Classic" and Period V ceramics were found at the cave mouth.

Future work should reassess the extent of these occupations. The great cave at San Sebastián also should receive further attention. It is a wet cave, with soils and other debris continually being deposited; excavations would provide much needed data on cave use in prehispanic times.

Phase-by-Phase Site Size and Population Estimates:

Phase	Area (ha)	Low	High	Mean
IIIa	4.00	85	180	133
IIIb-IV	4.00	85	180	133
V	2-4	30	75	53

SITE 91
Municipio: San Andrés
UTM: E726300/N1836000
Environment: Low piedmont/1540 m
Site Size: 0.16 ha
Periodization: V
Condition: Poor (plowed)

Description: Sola 91 was found on the piedmont shelf adjacent to the highway, near the pass separating the Sola and Oaxaca Valleys. Water was available from *barrancas* on either side of the *loma*, 200 m distant. The site was not plowed when surveyed; an isolated modern household was on the premises. Heavy secondary growth (scrub and xerophytic vegetation) covered the surface.

A low mound, heavily damaged by past plowing, was mapped. A single terrace, 2 m above the level of the mound, supported one or more house foundations now destroyed by plowing. G.3M and Period V brownwares were collected. The location of the site and its lone mound also suggest a Late Postclassic date. No other artifacts were observed. The site may have been larger; poor surface visibility has obscured the original site dimensions.

Phase-by-Phase Site Size and Population Estimates:

Phase	Area (ha)	Low	High	Mean
V	0.16	5	10	8

SITE 92
Municipio: San Andrés
UTM: E726000/N1836100
Environment: Low piedmont/1540 m
Site Size: 0.09 ha
Periodization: V
Condition: Poor (plowed)

Description: Sola 92 was located on the piedmont shelf immediately south of the highway. The site was not plowed and overgrown with heavy secondary growth. A *barranca* provided water 100 m from the site. There was a mound, or possibly mound on a low platform, greatly disturbed by past plowing. Period V utilitarian brownwares were in evidence. A chert tool was collected. The site may have been larger; but heavy undergrowth limited surface observations.

Phase-by-Phase Site Size and Population Estimates:

Phase	Area (ha)	Low	High	Mean
V	0.09	5	10	8

SITE 93
Municipio: San Andrés
UTM: E727000/N1835000
Environment: Low piedmont/1640 m
Site Size: 0.50 ha
Periodization: V
Condition: Poor (modern use)

Description: Sola 93 was found at the edge of the piedmont shelf that extends from Cabo de Hacha directly overlooking the pass separating the Sola and Oaxaca Valleys. The highway runs immediately north of the site; the historic *camino real* passed on the site's south side. At the base of the *loma*, 220 m below the site, the Río de las Grutas joined the Río Atoyac. The nearest water source was a *barranca* 250 m distant. The site was not plowed; scrub and xerophytic vegetation covered the area. A telephone relay tower occupied the *loma*. Ceramics were Period V utilitarian brownwares. No other artifacts were observed.

Phase-by-Phase Site Size and Population Estimates:

Phase	Area (ha)	Low	High	Mean
V	0.50	5	13	9

SITE 94
Municipio: San Francisco
UTM: E717100/N1827200
Environment: Low piedmont/1540 m
Site Size: 0.80 ha
Periodization: IIIa, V
Condition: Fair (plowed)

Description: Sola 94 was located in a plowed, irrigated field on the *lomas* above modern San Francisco Sola. Surface visibility was excellent. The site was located 750 m east of the modern cemetery. A *barranca* was located 100 m distant. There was either a small mound or house on the site, but plowing destroyed the structure. Ceramics were orange brownwares and a G.35, all from Period IIIa; a small Period V occupation was in evidence as well. Other artifacts included a *mano*; a gray obsidian blade; and chert flakes.

Phase-by-Phase Site Size and Population Estimates:

Phase	Area (ha)	Low	High	Mean
IIIa	0.80	8	20	14
V	0.01	5	10	8

SITE 95
Municipio: San Francisco
UTM: E717700/N1827400
Environment: Low piedmont/1560 m
Site Size: 0.25 ha
Periodization: IIIa
Condition: Poor (plowed)

Description: Sola 95 was located on a plowed, irrigated field in the hills east of San Francisco Sola. A *barranca* was 75 m distant. Surface visibility was excellent. Several large, prehispanic cut stones were strewn about the site; plowing has destroyed the house or other structure that once stood here. Ceramics were all orange brownwares, dating to Period IIIa. No other artifacts were seen.

Phase-by-Phase Site Size and Population Estimates:

Phase	Area (ha)	Low	High	Mean
IIIa	0.25	5	10	8

SITE 96
Municipio: San Francisco
UTM: E717900/N1826700
Environment: Low piedmont/1560 m
Site Size: 0.50 ha
Periodization: IIIa, V
Condition: Good

Description: Sola 96 was found on the flat summit of steeply sloping piedmont overlooking the alluvium of the Río Sola. Water was not readily available on site; the nearest *barranca* was 250 m distant, and 100 m down slope. Modern ceramics were found on the surface, though no contemporary houses were nearby. The site has not been plowed in recent years, but surface visibility was still good. Prehispanic house foundations remained intact, associated with Period V ceramics. A smaller Period IIIa component was present. No other artifacts were found.

Phase-by-Phase Site Size and Population Estimates:

Phase	Area (ha)	Low	High	Mean
IIIa	0.08	5	10	8
V	0.50	5	13	9

SITE 97
Municipio: San Francisco
UTM: E718500/N1724700
Environment: High alluvium/1440 m
Site Size: 54.20 ha
Periodization: IIIa, IIIb-IV, V
Condition: Good

Description: Sola 97 was located in the *bajío* 4 km southeast of San Francisco Sola. The site—known locally as "Shilegua"—bordered the east bank of the Río Sola, adjacent to highly productive low alluvium under cultivation today. The area was irrigated; two *barrancas* were joined within the site limits on their way to the river. The area was cleared of vegetation. Several dispersed modern households occupied the site. A road linking San Francisco and Santa Inés passed through the site.

Four dispersed mound groups were mapped. The architectural core, Mounds 1-9, had three plazas and a ball court. This arrangement was reminiscent of other IIIb-IV sites in the region (Sola 10, 104, and 111). Eight plazas altogether were mapped; the unusually large Plaza 5 (38 × 86 m) linked Mounds 1-9 with Mounds 12-16. A small proportion of the site was terraced; the terraces were ruined by modern plowing, however, and could not be formally mapped. Numerous house foundations, in varying states of disrepair, were recorded. The best preserved of these were three houses round a small patio located on a small eminence west of Mounds 10 and 11. This final structure formed Plaza 8, defined by a wall on the west side. Ceramics were generally composed of IIIb-IV orange brownwares and G.35 bowls. A possible imitation plumbate hemispherical bowl with incised designs was associated with Mound 17. Small Period IIIa and V components were present as well. No lithics were observed. Several *manos* and *metates* were recorded. Finally, a carved stone was set into the facade of the church at Santa Inés Sola; Sola 97 was the nearest large site and the likely point of origin for this carved stone.

Although portions of the site were plowed when surveyed, good ceramic collections were not always available; in some instances this was likely due to past episodes of soil deposition. Future work should reconsider the true dimensions of the respective components, particularly for Period IIIa.

Phase-by-Phase Site Size and Population Estimates:

Phase	Area (ha)	Low	High	Mean
IIIa	0.24	5	10	8
IIIb-IV	54.20	545	1360	953
V	0.01	5	10	8

SITE 98
Municipio: San Francisco
UTM: E717900/N1826000
Environment: High alluvium/1400 m
Site Size: 0.01 ha
Periodization: IIIb-IV
Condition: Good

Description: Sola 98 was found in a plowed field southeast of San Francisco Sola. *Barrancas* flowed within 100 m of the site; the Río Sola was 450 m southwest. These lands are irrigated today. A G.35 was recovered. There was also a *mano* fragment. Deep alluvial deposits likely obscured other prehispanic remains; the true site size, therefore, was probably larger.

Phase-by-Phase Site Size and Population Estimates:

Phase	Area (ha)	Low	High	Mean
IIIb-IV	0.01	5	10	8

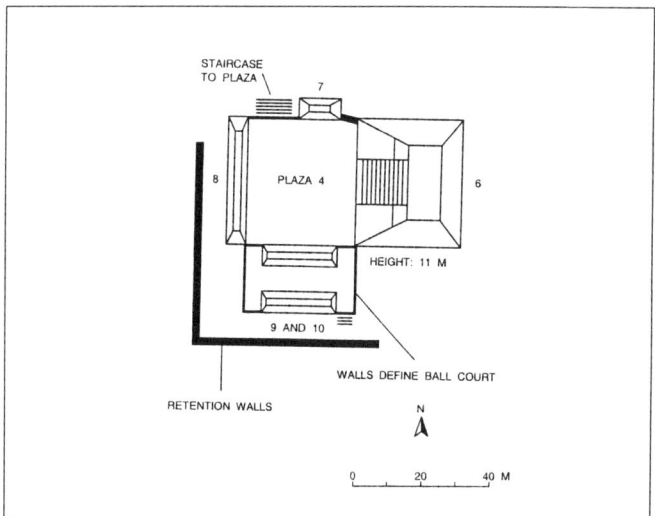

Figure A.24. Detail of the civic-ceremonial core at Shilegua (S97).

SITE 99
Municipio: San Francisco
UTM: E717600/N1724400
Environment: High alluvium/1400 m
Site Size: 0.01 ha
Periodization: V
Condition: Fair (plowed)

Description: Sola 99 was a lone Period V house on the valley floor. The Río Sola was 300 m southwest. The land was under cultivation when surveyed. Period V ceramics and a gray obsidian blade were found.

Phase-by-Phase Site Size and Population Estimates:

Phase	Area (ha)	Low	High	Mean
V	0.01	5	10	8

SITE 100
Municipio: San Francisco
UTM: E717900/N1725100
Environment: High alluvium/1420 m
Site Size: 0.02 ha
Periodization: V
Condition: Good

Description: Sola 100 was found in a plowed field 400 m east of the Río Sola. A prehispanic terrace wall supported two house foundations. Period V pottery was associated with the houses. A *mano* fragment, two obsidian blades, and a chert flake were recorded.

Phase-by-Phase Site Size and Population Estimates:

Phase	Area (ha)	Low	High	Mean
V	0.02	5	10	8

SITE 101
Municipio: San Francisco
UTM: E718400/N1725200
Environment: Low piedmont/1460 m
Site Size: 0.01 ha
Periodization: IIIa
Condition: Fair (plowed)

Description: Sola 101 was found in the low hills directly overlooking the alluvium 750 m east of the Río Sola. These lands were plowed and irrigated. Dispersed modern households were located in the vicinity. A *barranca* was 50 m from the site. The site consisted of an isolated house associated with Period IIIa grayware and orange brownware sherds. No other artifacts were recorded.

Phase-by-Phase Site Size and Population Estimates:

Phase	Area (ha)	Low	High	Mean
IIIa	0.01	5	10	8

SITE 102
Municipio: San Francisco
UTM: E718100/N1826200
Environment: Low piedmont/1520 m
Site Size: 1.50 ha
Periodization: Ic, IIIa
Condition: Poor (plowed)

Description: Sola 102 was found in the low hills overlooking the alluvium, 2 km southeast of San Francisco Sola. This land was irrigated, but not plowed when surveyed. A *barranca* was 50 m from the site. The site is known locally as "La Loma de Zibachi," and "Sitio de las Ruinitas."

A low mound, nearly plowed away, was mapped. Four terraces supported the mound and several houses that have been plowed away. The site's defining characteristic was its multi-room structure, with cut stone foundations and adobe walls still intact, that has remained partially exposed. According to local informants, the structure had been "excavated" in the 1950s by the former owner. The exposed portion of the structure—with interconnected room blocks and 1 × 1 m "storage cells"—occupied an area of 20 × 20 m. Unfortunately, heavy secondary growth prevented detailed mapping. The structure continued into the side of the *loma*.

A variety of artifacts were found on the surface, though not directly associated with the multi-room structure. Ceramics included a G.12, K.3, and two brownware sherds with eccentric rims. There was a small Period IIIa component; it appeared that the room blocks dated to Period Ic and were then buried in eroding sediments while the mound and terraces dated later in time. A green obsidian blade, chert and quartz flakes, basalt hammerstone, and ax fragment were recovered.

Phase-by-Phase Site Size and Population Estimates:

Phase	Area (ha)	Low	High	Mean
Ic	1.50	15	38	27
IIIa	0.06	5	10	8

SITE 103
Municipio: San Francisco
UTM: E717200/N1826000
Environment: High alluvium/1380 m
Site Size: 0.02 ha
Periodization: IIIb-IV
Condition: Good

Description: Sola 103 was an isolated prehispanic house 1.25 km southeast of San Francisco Sola. A *barranca* was 50 m away, and the Río Sola 250 m distant. The site was plowed; a modern house was nearby. The prehispanic remains consisted of stone foundations and utilitarian ceramics. No other artifacts were recovered.

Phase-by-Phase Site Size and Population Estimates:

Phase	Area (ha)	Low	High	Mean
IIIb-IV	0.02	5	10	8

SITE 104
Municipio: San Francisco
UTM: E716500/N1826100
Environment: High alluvium/1400 m
Site Size: 10.10 ha
Periodization: IIIb-IV, V
Condition: Poor (plowed/modern use)

Description: Sola 104 was found on the southern limits of San Francisco Sola, and the east bank of the Río Sola. There were modern households within the site limits. The land was plowed and irrigated. The prehispanic remains have severe damage from the modern occupation.

An integrated complex of mounds, plazas, and a ball court were constructed on a low eminence at the river's edge. The complex was oriented 320 degrees west. Significantly, the architectural cores of key IIIb-IV sites at Sola 10 and 97 were aligned through Sola 104. Terrace walls supported the monumental architecture, but not, apparently, prehispanic houses. These soil retention walls gave the appearance of a "platform" over which the mounds were constructed. Ceramics included G.35 bowls, their brownware analogs, and G.3Ms. The majority of the ceramics probably pertained to late Period IIIb-IV.

A second, smaller mound group (probably two mounds with plaza) was located 40 m north; but the prehispanic remains there had become so integrated with a modern household it was impossible to map.

Phase-by-Phase Site Size and Population Estimates:

Phase	Area (ha)	Low	High	Mean
IIIb-IV	10.10	101	253	177
V	0.45	5	11	8

SITE 105
Municipio: San Miguel
UTM: E718000/N1830900
Environment: High piedmont/1820 m
Site Size: 0.30 ha
Periodization: IIIb-IV, V
Condition: Good

Description: Sola 105 was located on the ridgeline leading up to Cerro El Obispo, immediately south of Highway 131, and 4.5 km NE of San Miguel Sola de Vega. This location marks the pass descending into the Sola Valley. The nearest water source was a barranca 80 m down slope and 350 m distant. The site was plowed; maize had recently been cultivated. Modern households were located nearby.

A low mound and platform were aligned E/W, forming a plaza between them; two houses rested atop the platform. Period IIIb-IV ceramics were associated with the houses. These structures were heavily damaged by modern agriculture and looting. Ceramics at the site included a G.35, several brownware analogs to the G.35, and a G.3M. These ceramics were probably contemporary, existing on the IV/V horizon. Chert flakes were present.

Phase-by-Phase Site Size and Population Estimates:

Phase	Area (ha)	Low	High	Mean
IIIb-IV	0.30	5	10	8
V	0.01	5	10	8

SITE 106
Municipio: San Miguel
UTM: E718400/N1830800
Environment: High piedmont/1840 m
Site Size: 0.01 ha
Periodization: IIIb-IV
Condition: Fair (plowed)

Description: Sola 106 was located 100 m east of the Sola 105 site limits. A *barranca* was 120 m down slope and 250 m distant. The site had been plowed in the past, but not when surveyed. A single, isolated prehispanic house was associated with Period IIIb-IV ceramics. No other artifacts were seen. Sites 105 and 106 were certainly associated, and might be considered a single occupation during IIIb-IV times. The ceramic distribution was not continuous between the two, however, and Sola 106 was situated at a higher elevation.

Phase-by-Phase Site Size and Population Estimates:

Phase	Area (ha)	Low	High	Mean
IIIb-IV	0.01	5	10	8

SITE 107
Municipio: San Miguel
UTM: E717000/N1830300
Environment: Low piedmont/1640 m
Site Size: 0.80 ha
Periodization: IIIb-IV, V
Condition: Poor (plowed)

Description: Sola 107 was found on a flat shelf of the steeply sloping piedmont 2.5 km NE of San Miguel Sola de Vega. *Barrancas* were accessible on either side of the *loma*, 150 m distant. The surface was plowed when surveyed, and had been planted with maize; modern households used the irrigation facilities located nearby. The historic *camino real* passed through Sola 107; this path was still walked from modern San Miguel and San Francisco to El Obispo on the east side of the ridgeline.

Two low mounds, badly damaged by the plow, were dispersed on the *loma*. Mound 1, supported by a platform, had two house foundations at its summit. Mound 2 was associated with a low wall defining a patio. Ceramics included G.3M and polychrome. A smaller IIIb-IV component also was present. Chert flakes were found on the platform. Sola 107 could be significant to understanding the relationship between Sola's two Late Postclassic petty kingdoms, given its location on the transport corridor between the two.

Phase-by-Phase Site Size and Population Estimates:

Phase	Area (ha)	Low	High	Mean
IIIb-IV	0.20	5	10	8
V	0.80	8	20	14

SITE 108
Municipio: San Miguel
UTM: E716400/N1830000
Environment: Low piedmont/1580 m
Site Size: 0.01
Periodization: Ic
Condition: Good

Description: Sola 108 was recorded on a low piedmont shelf east of Highway 131, and 2.75 km NE of San Miguel Sola de Vega. *Barrancas* provided water on either side of the *loma*, 250 m distant. Nearby lands were irrigated; but the site was not plowed when surveyed. The site was covered with many large *enebro* trees. The site likely represented a single, isolated house dating to Late Formative times. Ceramics included a G.12 (combed bottom) and utilitarian brownwares. Sola 107 was one of the sites that followed the transportation route across the Sola region, linking highlands and coast.

Phase-by-Phase Site Size and Population Estimates:

Phase	Area (ha)	Low	High	Mean
Ic	0.01	5	10	8

SITE 109
Municipio: San Miguel
UTM: E716500/N1827300
Environment: Low piedmont/1500 m
Site Size: 1.00 ha
Periodization: IIIa
Condition: Fair (eroded)

Description: Sola 109 was found in the low hills above San Miguel Sola de Vega, 750 m NE of the church. The site was located on the historic path between San Miguel/San Francisco and the east side of the El Obispo ridgeline. A *barranca* provided water 100 m away. The land had a slight slope, was plowed in the recent past and eroded in places. The area was cleared of trees, though not plowed when surveyed, and overgrown with short grass.

Archaeological remains consisted of a small mound and two dispersed houses. An erosion control wall supported the mound. Artifacts included orange brownwares and a chert flake. The ceramics were few and somewhat ambiguous, but suggested at least a Period IIIa occupation. Future work should determine if other occupations were present.

Phase-by-Phase Site Size and Population Estimates:

Phase	Area (ha)	Low	High	Mean
IIIa	1.00	10	25	18

SITE 110
Municipio: San Miguel
UTM: E717500/N1829300
Environment: High piedmont/1820 m
Site Size: 1.00 ha
Periodization: IIIa, V
Condition: Poor (plowed/looted)

Description: Sola 110 was found on a flat shelf on the steeply sloping hills in the El Obispo range east of Highway 131. The historic path crossing this range into the Sola Valley passed near this site. The site was not plowed, though had been in the past, and was covered with heavy secondary growth. The most accessible water source was 150 m distant. The site was near the source of four *barrancas*. A modern household was nearby.

The site had a low, crudely constructed mound, now badly damaged by looting and the plow. Period IIIa utilitarian wares and Period V thin, gray storage jars were present; no other artifacts were seen. The site location would have served as an excellent observation point.

Phase-by-Phase Site Size and Population Estimates:

Phase	Area (ha)	Low	High	Mean
IIIa	1.00	10	25	18
V	0.02	5	10	8

SITE 111
Municipio: San Francisco
UTM: E723500/N1831200
Environment: Mountain/2080 m
Site Size: 89.20 ha
Periodization: IIIa, IIIb-IV, V
Condition: Good

Description: Sola 111 was the largest site in the Sola survey region, found 1.25 km east of the Agencia El Obispo, on lands controlled by San Francisco Sola. Highway 131 passes 2.25 km north of the site. The Río Atoyac flows 1.5 km from the eastern site limit. East of the Atoyac the land belongs to the *Distrito* of Ejutla. A major *barranca* originates within the site limits. Isolated modern households

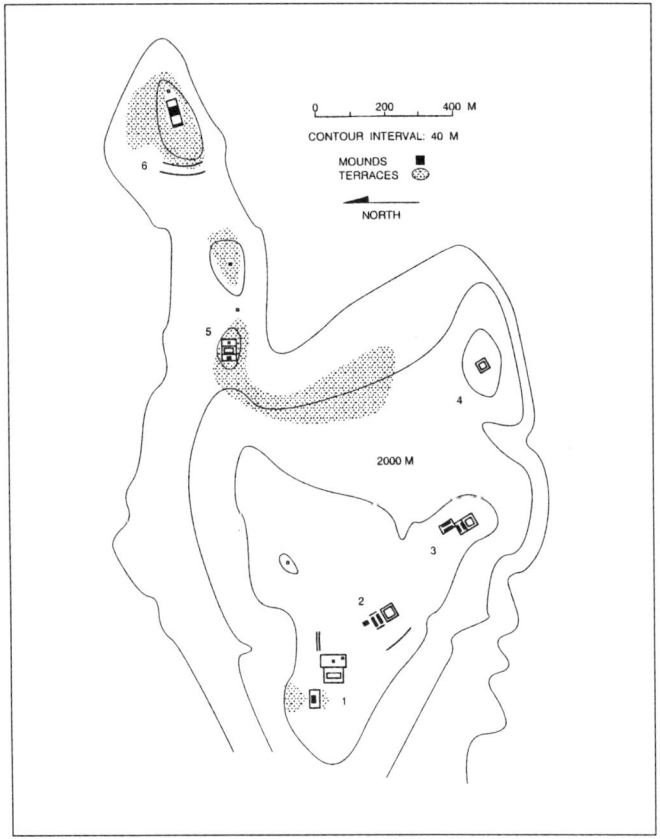

Figure A.25. Los Paderones (S111).

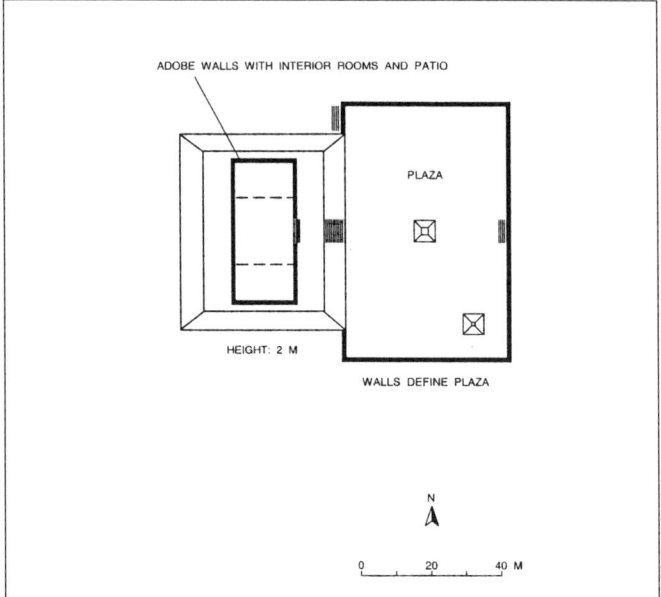

Figure A.26. Detail of the civic-ceremonial core at Los Paderones.

were dispersed across the site; large portions were plowed when surveyed. Surface visibility was excellent. Despite the modern agriculture, most of the site was intact. The site was located adjacent to the historical transportation route leading into the Sola Valley.

The site had five major architectural complexes, spread across a branching series of *lomas*. Complex 1 had a low mound and platform; adjacent residential terraces; erosion control walls; and a large platform supporting a "palace" structure with standing adobe walls and interior rooms. A staircase led down to a sunken plaza surrounded by walls on all sides. An altar and secondary mound were located within the plaza. Borrow pits had been excavated near the platform. Period V ceramics were associated with this complex. Ceramics included examples of Huitzo Red-on-Cream, G.3Ms (two were misfired), and polychrome.

Complex 2, 75 m southeast, had a ball court, small mound supporting a house, and a large central plaza surrounded on all sides by room blocks or patio groups—house foundations set on low earthen platforms tightly clustered round small interior patios. An erosion control wall supported these components. Further along this same branch of the *loma*, Complex 3 had two ball courts—set perpendicular to each other—and adjacent to another large plaza surrounded on all sides by patio groups. Complex 4, located at the furthest extent of another branch of the *loma*, had a smaller and less ornate set of connected patio groups. Both Complexes 3 and 4 were associated with Period V pottery, including more G.3Ms (one misfired) and Huitzo Red-on-Cream. A *mano* was found near Complex 4; a *metate* was among the ruined terraces between Complexes 4 and 5. The landscape was extremely steep south of Complexes 3 and 4, making this portion of the site naturally defensible. Complex 4 had both IIIb-IV and V pottery on the surface.

The eastern arm of the *loma* had Complexes 5 and 6. This branch extended toward the Río Atoyac, and provided an observation point into the adjacent Valleys of Ejutla and Oaxaca. Complex 5 was a second "palace" structure with adjacent plaza and mound. It too had standing adobe walls, but was in poorer condition than the Complex 1 "palace". A *metate* was seen among the ruined terraces of Complex 5. Complex 6 was densely terraced, had a series of 5 m high defensive walls closing the accessible portion of the site, and had a large mound supported by a platform and plaza on its high point. This portion of the site had IIIa, IIIb-IV, and V pottery on the surface. The architecture conforms with Classic period stylistic canons for the Sola region, and likely was the site center during this time. There was still a significant Period V component in this portion of the site; ceramics included G.3Ms, Graphite-on-Orange, Huitzo Red-on-Cream, and a G.3M snake support.

Occupation was continuous between all major complexes, with heavy ceramic densities on the plowed surface. Most of the terraces on the site were ruined; a higher density figure, therefore, was used for the population estimate over the terraced area. Curiously, despite excellent surface visibility, no obsidian was seen. Chert flakes and tools were found, however, associated with the various residential patio groups.

Sola 111 was one of the key IIIb-IV sites in the region; by Period V it was the seat of a Late Postclassic petty kingdom whose boundaries extended into the Ejutla and Oaxaca Valleys. The carved stones from the church of San Francisco Sola are reported to have come from here. See Berlin (1951) for his account of this site.

Phase-by-Phase Site Size and Population Estimates:

Phase	Area (ha)	Low	High	Mean
IIIa	12.50	313	625	469
IIIb-IV	53.00	555	1500	1028
V	89.20	1162	2680	1921

SITE 112
Municipio: San Francisco
UTM: E721700/N1831500
Environment: Mountain/2020 m
Site Size: 2.20 ha
Periodization: V
Condition: Poor (modern use)

Description: Sola 112 was located immediately east of the Agencia of El Obispo, along the ridgeline leading to Sola 111, the region's major Late Postclassic site. The site and its mounds were completely integrated with a modern household, and were therefore in extremely poor condition. The surface beyond the contemporary house was plowed; surface visibility was excellent. Multiple barrancas were accessible, from 75-150 m distant. The historic transportation route connecting the Sola, Ejutla, and Oaxaca regions passed within the site limits.

The site had a platform, approximately 20 m square, supporting a low mound. Two other mounds were located on the platform's west side, forming a plaza. Terraces extended a short distance on north and south sides of the platforms. These features could not be formally measured, due to the degree of plow damage and modern reuse of building material. Ceramics were all Period V.

Sola 112 clearly had strong functional relations with the nearby center, and could be considered one of the dispersed complexes associated with that site. Surface material, however, was not continuous between sites 111 and 112. Population estimates used a higher density figure for the terraced area.

Phase-by-Phase Site Size and Population Estimates:

Phase	Area (ha)	Low	High	Mean
V	2.20	25	60	43

SITE 113
Municipio: San Francisco
UTM: E719200/N1830200
Environment: Mountain/2240 m
Site Size: 1.60 ha
Periodization: V
Condition: Fair (looted)

Description: Sola 113 was located near the summit of the El Obispo ridgeline, and straddled the historic *camino real* as it crossed its highest point before descending into the Sola Valley. Colonial coins have been found in the vicinity. The pass is still crossed today by travelers between San Francisco Sola and El Obispo.

The site was not plowed when surveyed; pine trees covered the ridgeline. Surface visibility was poor. The site had a steep slope. The nearest water source was 250 m distant, and 140 m down slope. Considerable looting has damaged the architecture.

A low mound and platform was aligned with the ridgeline at the northern site limit. South of this point the *camino real* passed along a *montura*, and the site continued upslope, south to a second low mound also aligned with the ridgeline. A series of eight terraces supporting houses continued upslope to the southern site limit. Population estimates relied on the terrace count only, since steepness of slope prevented settlement on non-terraced areas.

Phase-by-Phase Site Size and Population Estimates:

Phase	Area (ha)	Low	High	Mean
V	1.60	40	80	60

SITE 114/115
Municipio: San Francisco
UTM: E719700/N1829400
Environment: Mountain/2320 m
Site Size: 1.40 ha
Periodization: IIIa, IIIb-IV, V
Condition: Fair (looted)

Description: Sites 114 and 115 have been combined. Sola 114/115 was found at the summit of the El Obispo ridgeline, 350 m north of Cerro El Obispo. The nearest water was a *barranca* 50 m distant. The site has not been plowed, but the mounds were looted. Pine forest covered the site, limiting surface visibility. The site was located on very steep terrain.

The southeastern portion of the site—originally the Sola 114 component—had a small mound and four terraces. Ceramics and two *metate* fragments were associated with the terraces. To the northwest—originally considered Sola 115—the terrain was very steep, with a succession of three ditches cutting access to the ridgetop that at one point narrowed to just 15 m wide. Another small mound with a patio was placed at the last high point. This mound had the distinction of being the only such structure in the Sola region that was not looted.

Site size estimates were difficult do to intermittent surface visibility, but periods IIIa-V were present. It was not possible to determine the construction phase for the mounds or defensive features. The majority of the ceramics did, however, date to Periods IIIa and IIIb-IV. Population estimates considered only the terrace count—the rest of the site was far to steep to support occupation without terracing.

Phase-by-Phase Site Size and Population Estimates:

Phase	Area (ha)	Low	High	Mean
IIIa	1.40	20	40	30
IIIb-IV	1.40	20	40	30
V	1.40	20	40	30

SITE 116
Municipio: San Francisco
UTM: E720800/N1829200
Environment: Mountain/2340 m
Site Size: 0.50 ha
Periodization: V
Condition: Good

Description: Sola 116 was located at the highest point of the El Obispo ridgeline, east of Cerro El Obispo. A secondary access path across the mountains and into Sola Valley crossed the site. The site had a commanding view into the Ejutla and Oaxaca Valleys. The nearest water source was a *barranca* 200 m distant, and 80 m down slope. Ruined fences from a recent encampment for grazing were located within the site limits. Pine forest covered the site; surface visibility was limited. Two low, dispersed mounds were mapped on the ridgeline. A small ceramic collection was made from the area between the mounds. No other artifacts were seen.

Phase-by-Phase Site Size and Population Estimates:

Phase	Area (ha)	Low	High	Mean
V	0.50	5	13	9

SITE 117
Municipio: San Francisco
UTM: E721200/N1828400
Environment: Mountain/2280 m
Site Size: 0.30 ha
Periodization: V
Condition: Good

Description: Sola 117 was a dispersed Late Postclassic site located on a slightly lower level from Sola 116 on the same ridgeline. The area was pine forest covered and not plowed, though some modern lime extraction has taken place. The nearest water source was a *barranca* 200 m distant, and 140 m down slope. The site consisted of four houses and associated ceramics. The site was undoubtedly associated with the nearby Sola 116, and might be considered part of the same dispersed settlement. Population estimates used the house count only.

Phase-by-Phase Site Size and Population Estimates:

Phase	Area (ha)	Low	High	Mean
V	0.30	20	40	30

SITE 118
Municipio: San Francisco
UTM: E721500/N1829600
Environment: Mountain/2180 m
Site Size: 0.02 ha
Periodization: V
Condition: Good

Description: Sola 118 was an isolated Late Postclassic house. The area was pine forest covered and not utilized at present. The nearest water source was a *barranca* 50 m from the site. House foundations and associated ceramics were recorded.

Phase-by-Phase Site Size and Population Estimates:

Phase	Area (ha)	Low	High	Mean
V	0.02	5	10	8

SITE 119
Municipio: San Miguel
UTM: E718600/N1833300
Environment: High piedmont/1840 m
Site Size: 0.02 ha
Periodization: V
Condition: Poor (plowed)

Description: Sola 119 was found in a plowed field on steep terrain just south of Highway 131. A *barranca* was 150 m distant; nearby lands were irrigated. There was a modern household near the site. Given the steep terrain, the site was probably terraced but modern plowing has erased any such indications. Period V ceramics included a G.3M. No other artifacts were seen. The prehispanic site was probably a single, isolated house.

Phase-by-Phase Site Size and Population Estimates:

Phase	Area (ha)	Low	High	Mean
V	0.02	5	10	8

SITE 120
Municipio: San Miguel
UTM: E719800/N1832800
Environment: High piedmont/1980 m
Site Size: 0.50 ha
Periodization: IIIa, V
Condition: Poor (plowed/eroded)

Description: Sola 120 was found in a plowed field in the high piedmont leading into the El Obispo range, south of Highway 131 near Tierra Colorada. There was a modern household nearby; the site area was cleared of vegetation, though the pine forest begins slightly further upslope. Erosion was severe in places. The nearest water source was a *barranca* 200 m distant. Three remnant terraces remained, but these could not be mapped due to the modern disturbance. Population estimates for the IIIa site used the terrace count along with the non-terraced area. The Period V occupation was not terraced; it included a G.3M. There was also a Postclassic-style chert point.

Phase-by-Phase Site Size and Population Estimates:

Phase	Area (ha)	Low	High	Mean
IIIa	0.50	20	33	27
V	0.04	5	10	8

Appendix B

Structures and Measures

Site	Structure	Base (m)	Top (m)	Height (m)	Phase
Sola 1	Mound 1	22 × 21	11 × 7	9	III-IV
	Mound 2	11 × 30	2 × 24	5	III-IV
	Mound 3	21 × 9	18 × 3.5	2	III-IV
	Mound 4	9 × 16	3 × 14	1.7	III-IV
	Adoratorio	4 × 6			III-IV
	Plaza 1	46 × 38			III-IV
	Plaza 2	16 × 30			III-IV
	Platform 1	8 × 12			III-IV
	Mound 5	14 × 16	7 × 8	5	III-IV
	Mound 6	13 × 13			IV-V
	Sunken Pat.	12 × 10		1	IV-V
	Mound 7	26 × 6	21 × 2.5	6	III-IV
	Mound 8	26 × 6	21 × 2.5	6	III-IV
	Ball Court	38 × 10			III-IV
	Defen. Wall	110			III-IV
Sola 3	Mound 1	19 × 18	6 × 5	7	III-V
	Mound 2	26 × 28	20 × 23	2	III-V
	Mound 3	15 × 8		2.5	III-V
	Platform 1	24 × 26			III-V
Sola 5	Mound 1	8 × 6	4 × 3	1.5	IIIa
Sola 6	Mound 1	12 × 11		1	IIIb-IV
Sola 8	Mound 1	38 × 21	9 × 4	8	IIIb-IV
	Mound 2	43 × 20	24 × 2	5	IIIb-IV
	Plaza 1	38 × 23			IIIb-IV
Sola 10	Mound 1	30 × 30	23 × 30	3.5	III-V
Sola 10	Mound 2	21 × 21	5 × 7	6	III-IV
	Adoratorio				III-IV
	Plaza 1	35 × 26			III-IV
	Mound 3	2 × 33	1 × 22	3	III-IV
	Mound 4	4 × 14	2 × 13		III-IV
	Ball Court	11 × 45			III-V
	Mound 5	18 × 15	4 × 3	6	III-IV
	Mound 6	25 × 15	6 × 4	7.5	IIIb-IV
Mound 7	29 ¥ 22	29 × 22	2	IIIb-IV	
	Mound 8	16 × 15	5 × 6	3	IIIb-IV
Sola 12	Mound 1	38 × 12	16 × 8	4.5	IIIb-IV
	Mound 2	12 × 7.5		2	IIIb-IV
Sola 13	Mound 1	13 × 11	4 × 3	3.5	IIIb-IV
Sola 16	Mound 1	14 × 22	5 × 10	3.5	IIIa

159

Site	Structure	Base (m)	Top (m)	Height (m)	Phase
	Mound 2	19 × 12	11 × 4	2.5	IIIa
	Mound 3	8 × 21		2	IIIa
	Mound 4	22 × 9	10 × 4	2.5	IIIa
	Plaza	25 × 26			IIIa
Sola 18	Mound 1	8 × 8		2.5	V
Site	Structure	Base (m)	Top (m)	Height (m)	Phase
Sola 20	Mound 1	16 × 10	9 × 4	0.80	V
	Mound 2	10 × 20	5 × 15	0.50	V
	Mound 3	12 × 20	6 × 13	1.50	V
	Mound 4	42 × 22	29 × 16	3	V
	Mound 5	20 × 35	8 × 22	1.50	V
	Mound 6	20 × 35	8 × 22	1.50	V
Sola 20	Mound 7	32 × 22	29 × 16	3	V
	Plaza				V
Sola 21	Mound 1	46 × 8		3.5	V
	Mound 2	6 × 18	1 × 15	2.5	V
	Ball Court	58 × 15			V
Sola 22	Mound 1	22 × 6	17 × 2	2	V
Sola 23	Mound 1	14 × 12	9 × 5	3	IIIa
	Mound 2	11 × 12	5 × 6	2	IIIa
	Mound 3	25 × 18	13 × 11	2	IIIa
	Mound 4	11 × 4			IIIa
	Plaza 1	7 × 8			IIIa
	Plaza 2	7.5 × 8			IIIa
	Mound 5	11 × 7	5 × 2	2	IIIa
	Mound 6	8 × 12	2 × 6	0.5	IIIa
	Platform 1	5 × 11			IIIa
	Mound 7	22 × 10	18 × 2	4	IIIa
	Mound 8	22 × 10	18 × 2	4	IIIa
	Ball Court	38 × 8			IIIa
	Platform 2	14 × 24	12 × 19	6.5	IIIa
	Mound 9	7 × 21	1.5 × 16	4.5	IIIa
	Plaza 3	15 × 23			IIIa
	Mound 10	23 × 22	4 × 8	7.5	IIIa
	Mound 11	25 × 19			IIIa
	Mound 12				IIIa
	Mound 13	12 × 12	5 × 6	1	IIIa
Sola 23	Mound 14	10 × 12	4 × 4	3	IIIa
	Sunken Pat.	14 × 12		1.5	IV/V
	Plaza 4	10 × 12			IIIa
	Platform 3	40 × 25			IIIa
	Mound 15	4 × 14	2 × 10	1.5	IIIa
	Platform 4	35 × 15		1.5	IIIa
	Mound 16	13 × 16	4 × 8	2	IIIa
	Plaza 5	16 × 23			IIIa
	Mound 17	20 × 23	5 × 8	5.5	IIIa
	Plaza 6	12 × 10			IIIa
	Mound 18	10 × 10	4 × 5	1.5	IIIa
	Mound 19	4 × 10		2	IIIa
	Plaza 7	10 × 10			IIIa
	Mound 20	11 × 12	6 × 6	2	IIIa
	Mound 21	16 × 14	10 × 8	2	IIIa
	Plaza 8	4 × 14			IIIa
	Mound 22	18 × 16	5 × 8	6	IIIa
	Plaza 9	15 × 18			IIIa
	Mound 23	14 × 14	4 × 10	5	IIIa
	Mound 24	6 × 4	2 × 2	1.5	IIIa
	Mound 25	10 × 10			IIIa
Sola 24	Mound 1	12 × 9		1.5	V
Sola 28	Mound 1	10 × 8			IIIa
	Mound 2	4 × 11			IIIa

Appendix B: Structures and Measures 161

Site	Structure	Base (m)	Top (m)	Height (m)	Phase
	Plaza 1	10 × 10			IIIa
Sola 32	Mound 1	10 × 10	5 × 7	2	III-V
	Plaza 1	14 × 12			III-V
	Mound 2	10 × 10		2	III-V
Sola 33	Mound 1	17 × 14	5 × 4		I
Sola 35	Mound 1	9 × 14	3 × 5	1.75	IIIa
	Platform 1	16 × 20			IIIa
Sola 36	Mound 1	13 × 14	8 × 7	2.25	III-IV
	Mound 2	8 × 18			III-IV
	Plaza 1	14 × 23			III-IV
Sola 39	Mound 1	9 × 12	8 × 7	1.50	II-V
	Mound 2	46 × 42	12 × 6	20	II-IV
	Mound 3	12 × 53	2 × 49	2.5	II-IV
	Mound 4	26 × 21	11 × 6	11	I-IV
	Mound 5	38 × 21	31 × 4.5	5.5	I-IV
	Mound 6	10 × 45	2 × 40	4	II-IV
	Plaza 1	46 × 64			II-IV
	Adoratorio	12 × 12	6 × 6	2.5	III-IV
	Mound 7	19 × 26	10 × 9	3	III-IV
	Mound 8				III-IV
	Platform 1	35 × 104		2.5	II-IV
	Mound 9	38 × 16	28 × 4.5	2.5	II-IV
	Mound 10	15 × 47.5	2 × 22	5.5	II-IV
	Mound 11	15 × 47.5	2 × 22	5.5	II-IV
	Mound 12	38 × 16	28 × 4.5	2.5	II-IV
	Ball Court	5 × 55			II-IV
Sola 39	Mound 13	20 × 19	4 × 2	5	III-IV
	Mound 14	15 × 13			III-IV
	Sunken Pat.	23.5 × 23		2	IV-V
	Platform 2			1	I-IV
	Platform 3			5	I-IV
	Platform 4			5.5	I-IV
	Mound 15	17 × 8		2	IV/V
	Mound 16	18 × 17	6 × 6	3	IV/V
	Mound 17	18 × 15			IV/V
	Plaza 2	15 × 15			I-IV
	Mound 18	6 × 20			II-IV
	Mound 19	23 × 5.5	20 × 3	5	II-IV
	Mound 20	23 × 5.5	20 × 3	5	II-IV
	Ball Court	41 × 5			II-IV
	Mound 21	24 × 65	3 × 36	4	II
	Mound 22	26 × 25	13 × 11	5	II
	Plaza 3	16 × 25			II
	Sunken Pat.	16 × 15			IV/V
	Mound 23	14 × 20		0.80	IV/V
	Mound 24	29 × 25		12	III-IV
Sola 40	Mound 1	12 × 11	7 × 5	1	III-V
	Platform 1	10 × 16			III-V
	Def. Wall	60			III-V
Sola 47	Mound 1	20 × 13	4 × 2	3	I-V
	Mound 2	23 × 14	12 × 2	5.5	I-V
Sola 47	Mound 3	17 × 16		4	I-V
	Plaza 1	23 × 9			I-V
	Plaza 2	24 × 16			I-V
Sola 55	Mound 1	14 × 13	4 × 3	1.5	III-V
	Mound 2	15 × 10	7 × 4	0.5	III-V
	Plaza 1	17 × 11			III-V
Sola 56	Mound 1	10 × 7	4 × 3	1.5	III-V
Sola 61	Mound 1	4 × 3			IV
	Mound 2	10 × 8	5 × 3	2.5	Ic
	Platform 1	12 × 25			Ic
	Platform 2	7 × 9			Ic

Site	Structure	Base (m)	Top (m)	Height (m)	Phase
	Platform 3	15 × 5			I-V
	Platform 4	5 × 11			IV-V
	Platform 5	12 × 12			IV-V
	Mound 3	16 × 15	8 × 8	2.5	III-V
	Mound 4	17 × 16	5 × 5	3	III-IV
	Plaza 1	17 × 14			III-IV
	Mound 5	12 × 12	4 × 3	2.5	IV-V
	Platform 6	16 × 8			IV-V
Sola 62	Mound 1	14 × 7		0.5	V
	Mound 2	12 × 12	6 × 6	1.5	V
	Plaza 1	14 × 10			V
Sola 64	Mound 1	16 × 15		3	Ic
Sola 65	Mound 1	27 × 29	7 × 4	8	III-IV
	Mound 2	7 × 27	1.5 × 18	4	III-IV
Sola 65	Plaza 1	14 × 25			III-IV
	Mound 3				III-IV
	Mound 4	11 × 24	2 × 14	4	III-IV
	Mound 5	11 × 24	2 × 14	4	III-IV
	Ball Court	8 × 36			III-IV
	Mound 6	17 × 4	15 × 3	2.5	III-IV
	Mound 7	13 × 9	11 × 3	3.5	III-IV
	Platform 1	18 × 6			III-IV
	Plaza 2	15 × 18			III-IV
	Mound 8	7 × 13	2 × 10	1.5	III-IV
	Mound 9	25 × 6		1.5	III-IV
	Plaza 3	21 × 28			III-IV
	Platform 2	17 × 16			III-IV
	Mound 10	24 × 21	7 × 4	4	III-IV
	Platform 3	11 × 28			IIIb-IV
	Mound 11	50 × 16		2	IIIb-IV
	Mound 12	34 × 7		4	IIIb-IV
	Plaza 4	50 × 40			IIIb-IV
	Platform 4	25 × 25			IIIb-IV
	Mound 13	21 × 18	9 × 6	4	IIIb-IV
Sola 67	Mound 1	12 × 10	3 × 4	3	IIIa
	Mound 2	12 × 14	5 × 3	2	IIIa
	Plaza 1	14 × 18			IIIa
Sola 68	Mound 1	9 × 25	4 × 19	2	IV-V
	Mound 2	7 × 15	4 × 10	1	IV-V
Sola 69	Mound 1	6 × 3.5		0.5	V
	Mound 2	6 × 5	2.5 × 2.5	1.5	V
	Mound 3	5 × 5	1.5 × 1.5	2	V
	Plaza 1	6 × 3.5			V
Sola 71	Platform 1	22 × 16		0.5	V
	Mound 1	7 × 24			V
Sola 74	Mound 1	3 × 4		1	V
Sola 75	Mound 1	12 × 12	4 × 4	2	IIIb-IV
	Mound 2	8 × 17	6 × 12	1.5	IIIb-IV
	Mound 3	17 × 17	7 × 9	3.5	IIIb-IV
	Plaza 1	16 × 16			IIIb-IV
	Sunken Pat.	9 × 12			IV-V
	Sunken Pat.	9 × 12			IV-V
	Sunken Pat.	9 × 12			IV-V
Sola 77	Mound 1	4 × 4			V
	Mound 2	7 × 7			V
	Mound 3	20 × 20			IV-V
	Platform 1				IV-V
Sola 78	Mound 1	4 × 9			
	Mound 2	9 × 3			
	Mound 3	10 × 4			
	Plaza 1	10 × 13			
Sola 82	Mound 1	26 × 14	25 × 8	2.5	I-III
	Mound 2	14 × 12	5 × 8	3	I-III
	Mound 3	8 × 25	6 × 20	2	I-III

Appendix B: Structures and Measures

Site	Structure	Base (m)	Top (m)	Height (m)	Phase
Sola 82	Mound 4	23 × 11	12 × 5	1.5	I-III
	Plaza 1	20 × 20			I-V
	Mound 5	6 × 22	3 × 24	1.5	III-V
	Mound 6	18 × 10	12 × 2	1.5	III-V
	Ball Court	5 × 37			III-V
	Platform 1	20 × 12			III-V
	Defen. Wall	20			I-V
Sola 84	Mound 1	20 × 20	8 × 5	4	I-IV
	Mound 2	13 × 11	4 × 3	4.5	I-IV
	Mound 3	9 × 15	2 × 9	2.5	I-IV
	Plaza 1	20 × 20			I-IV
	Mound 4	13 × 16	2 × 6	1.5	III-IV
	Platform 1	20 × 18			III-IV
Sola 87	Mound 1	10 × 5	4 × 4		V
	Platform 1	25 × 20			V
Sola 88	Mound 1	12 × 12	5 × 5	1.25	IV-V
Sola 90	Mound 1	7 × 9	5 × 6	1.5	V
	Mound 2	7 × 11	4 × 6	2.5	V
Sola 91	Mound 1	6 × 6	2 × 2	0.5	V
Sola 92	Mound 1	8 × 8		1	V
Sola 97	Mound 1	11 × 8	4 × 3	2	IIIb-IV
	Mound 2	42 × 30	5 × 4	5	IIIb-IV
	Plaza 1	22 × 15			IIIb-IV
	Mound 3	22 × 24	20 × 3	1	IIIb-IV
	Mound 4	12 × 8	10 × 6	1.5	IIIb-IV
	Plaza 2	22 × 12			IIIb-IV
	Mound 5	17 × 6	15 × 3	2	IIIb-IV
	Plaza 3	38 × 86			IIIb-IV
	Mound 6	36 × 31	8 × 5	11	IIIb-IV
	Mound 7	6 × 18	2 × 10	4	IIIb-IV
	Mound 8	32 × 6	28 × 2.5	2	IIIb-IV
	Plaza 4	36 × 32			IIIb-IV
	Mound 9	6 × 23	2 × 19	8	IIIb-IV
	Mound 10	6 × 23	2 × 19	8	IIIb-IV
	Ball Court	7 × 32			IIIb-IV
	Mound 11	11 × 22	4 × 17	4	IIIb-IV
	Mound 12	22 × 21	5 × 6	4	IIIb-IV
	Plaza 5	12 × 22			IIIb-IV
	Mound 13	18 × 18	8 × 8	4	IIIb-IV
	Plaza 6	22 × 18			
Sola 102	Mound 1	8 × 8		1.5	Ic
Sola 104	Mound 1	6 × 42	4 × 32	4	IIIb-IV
	Mound 2	20 × 2	18 × 0.5	3	IIIb-IV
	Mound 3				IIIb-IV
	Mound 4				IIIb-IV
	Plaza 1	40 × 40			IIIb-IV
	Mound 5	6 × 32	1.5 × 21	3.5	IIIb-IV
	Mound 6				IIIb-IV
	Ball Court	? × 40			IIIb-IV
	Mound 7				IIIb-IV
	Mound 8				IIIb-IV
	Plaza 2	20 × 50			IIIb-IV
Sola 105	Mound 1	15 × 17	9 × 12		IIIb-IV
	Platform 1				IIIb-IV
	Plaza 1	25 × 16			IIIb-IV
Sola 109	Mound 1	20 × 20	8 × 8	4	IIIa
Sola 110	Mound 1	4 × 4		1	IIIa
Sola 111	Mound 1	9 × 18	4 × 9	0.75	V
	Platform 1	31 × 50		0.5	V
	Platform 2	54 × 48	45 × 35	2	V
	Adobe Walls	42 × 18		2.5	V
	Plaza 1	71 × 46			V
	Adoratorio	6 × 6	2 × 2	1.5	V
	Mound 2	6 × 6	1 × 1	1.5	V

Site	Structure	Base (m)	Top (m)	Height (m)	Phase
	Plaza 2	35 × 35			V
	Mound 3	31 × 10	21 × 1	3	V
Sola 111	Mound 4	31 × 10	21 × 1	3	V
	Ball Court	40 × 7			V
	Mound 5	10 × 14	7 × 3	1.8	V
	Mound 6	27 × 18	23 × 3	4	IV-V
	Mound 7	27 × 18	23 × 3	4	IV-V
	Ball Court	40 × 7			IV-V
	Mound 8	21 × 14	14 × 1	4	IV-V
	Mound 9	21 × 14	14 × 1	4	IV-V
	Ball Court	38 × 7			IV-V
	Plaza 3	21 × 21			IV-V
	Sunken Pat.				IV-V
	Platform 3	42 × 23	38 × 19	6	IV-V
	Adobe Walls	26 × 11		1	IV-V
	Mound 10				IV V
	Plaza 4	42 × 26			IV-V
	Plaza 5	42 × 18			IV-V
	Sunken Pat.				IV-V
	Mound 11	14 × 8	12 × 3	0.4	III-V
	Mound 12	29 × 25	9 × 7	5	III-V
	Plaza 6	31 × 20			III-V
	Sunken Pat.				IV-V
Sola 112	Mound 1				V
	Platform 1	20 × 20			V
	Mound 2				V
	Mound 3				V
	Plaza 1	15 × 20			V
Sola 113	Mound 1	11 × 11		3	V
	Mound 2	6 × 7	2 × 3	1	V
Sola 114	Mound 1	11 × 11	5 × 4	3	III-V
Sola 115	Mound 1	12 × 14	6 × 6	2	III-V
Sola 116	Mound 1	7 × 7	4.5 × 4.5	2	V
	Mound 2	8 × 7	3.5 × 3	1	V

Appendix C

Site Summaries by Phase

TABLE C.1. Ic Phase Sites in the Sola Valley

Site	Municipio	UTM	Grid	Environment	Elevation	Site Size (ha)	Population	Rank
17	San Miguel	E715100/N1826000	S4W1	Low Piedmont	1480 m	0.01	8	3
30	Sn Ildefonso	E720500/N1835000	S2E2	Mountain	2160 m	0.01	8	3
33	San Miguel	E718400/N1831800	S2E1	High Piedmont	1820 m	4.33	108	2
39	Santa María	E610600/N1833300	S2W2	Low Piedmont	1520 m	14.81	360	1
42	Santos Reyes	E715100/N1723900	S4W1	Low Piedmont	1640 m	1.50	27	3
44	Santos Reyes	E715000/N1724900	S4W1	Low Piedmont	1540 m	0.01	8	3
47	Santos Reyes	E716300/N1725000	S4E1	Low Piedmont	1460 m	4.65	82	2
52	Santa Inés	E720800/N1722900	S5E2	Low Piedmont	1440 m	0.01	8	3
60	Rancho Viejo	E726600/N1717500	S6E3	Low Piedmont	1560 m	4.46	79	2
61	Rancho Viejo	E726000/N1718400	S6E3	Low Piedmont	1460 m	13.22	320	1
62	Rancho Viejo	E726900/N1716000	S6E3	Low Piedmont	1480 m	1.27	23	3
63	Rancho Viejo	E725500/N1716400	S6E3	Low Piedmont	1560 m	0.01	8	3
64	Rancho Viejo	E723900/N1716500	S6E2	Low Piedmont	1660 m	0.45	8	3
65	Santos Niños	E721000/N1719900	S5E2	Low Piedmont	1440 m	0.50	9	3
79	Ayoquezco	E722800/N1839900	S1E2	Low Piedmont	1660 m	0.01	8	3
82	Ayoquezco	E723400/N1838600	S1E2	Low Piedmont	1700 m	6-10	178	2
84	Sn Ildef/Seb	E715800/N1839500	S1W1	High Piedmont	1920 m	6-10	262	1
102	Sn Francisco	E718100/N1826200	S4E1	Low Piedmont	1520 m	1.50	27	3
108	San Miguel	E716400/N1830000	S3E1	Low Piedmont	1580 m	0.01	8	3

TABLE C.2. Period II Sites in the Sola Valley

Site	Municipio	UTM	Grid	Environment	Elevation	Site Size (ha)	Population	Rank
3	San Juan	E613500/N1827800	S4W1	Low Piedmont	1580 m	1.12	42	3
8	San Juan	E714200/N1828600	S3W1	Low Piedmont	1520 m	0.20	8	3
10	Sn Juan/Ild	E714000/N1827000	S4W1	Low Piedmont	1540 m	1.24	22	3
15	San Juan	E613000/N1829100	S3W1	Low Piedmont	1520 m	5.44	95	3
23	Sn María/Ild	E717000/N1834600	S2E1	Mountain	2300 m	1.65	29	2
32	Sn Ildefonso	E718100/N1836500	S1E1	High Piedmont	1920 m	0.62	11	3
34	San Juan	E715000/N1831100	S3W1	Low Piedmont	1520 m	0.01	8	3
39	Santa María	E610600/N1833300	S2W2	Low Piedmont	1520 m	19.94	440	1
47	Santos Reyes	E716300/N1725000	S4E1	Low Piedmont	1460 m	1.10	20	3
58	Santa Inés	E719500/N1723900	S5E1	High Alluvium	1400 m	0.25	8	3
84	San Ild/Seb	E715800/N1839500	S1W1	High Piedmont	1920 m	2-6	150	2

TABLE C.3. Period IIIa Sites in the Sola Valley

Site	Municipio	UTM	Grid	Environment	Elevation	Site Size (ha)	Population	Rank
1	San Juan	E612000/N1827400	S4W1	High Piedmont	1800 m	8.50	304	2
3	San Juan	E613500/N1827800	S4W1	Low Piedmont	1580 m	12.00	450	2
4	San Juan	E714300/N1828000	S4W1	Low Piedmont	1520 m	1.66	30	4
5	San Juan	E612100/N1826000	S4W1	Mountain	2100 m	3.17	109	3
7	San Juan	E612100/N1827300	S4W1	High Piedmont	1820 m	0.20	8	5
9	San Juan	E714600/N1828200	S3W1	Low Piedmont	1500 m	0.15	8	5
10	San Juan/Ild	E714000/N1827000	S4W1	Low Piedmont	1540 m	12.80	224	3
11	San Juan	E714000/N1827300	S4W1	High Alluvium	1520 m	1.27	23	5
14	San Juan	E613000/N1829200	S3W1	Low Piedmont	1560 m	6.20	109	3
16	Santa María	E613500/N1831600	S3W1	Low Piedmont	1520 m	5.07	89	3
17	San Miguel	E715100/N1826000	S4W1	Low Piedmont	1480 m	0.75	14	5
18	San Miguel	E714000/N1826000	S4W1	Low Piedmont	1700 m	7.80	157	3
19	San Miguel	E714700/N1725800	S4W1	Low Piedmont	1500 m	1.38	25	4
20	San Juan	E610200/N1829000	S3W2	Mountain	2400 m	1-5	53	4
21	San Miguel	E714000/N1826500	S4W1	Low Piedmont	1680 m	3.06	110	3
23	Sn María/Ild	E717000/N1834600	S2E1	Mountain	2300 m	71.08	1915	1
23A	Sn María/Ild	E717000/N1834600	S1E1	High Piedmont	1960 m	0.63	17	5
25	San Ildefonso	E719500/N1836000	S1E1	Mountain	2200 m	0.40	8	5
28	San Ildefonso	E717500/N1836200	S1E1	High Piedmont	1940 m	3.72	65	4
32	San Ildefonso	E718100/N1836500	S1E1	High Piedmont	1920 m	8.44	148	3
34	San Juan	E715000/N1831100	S3W1	Low Piedmont	1520 m	2.28	40	4
35	Santa María	E716000/N1835100	S2W1	High Piedmont	1920 m	2.39	42	4
37	Santa María	E610100/N1833200	S2W2	High Alluvium	1480 m	0.02	8	5
39	Santa María	E610600/N1833300	S2W2	Low Piedmont	1520 m	31.06	713	2
40	Santos Reyes	E714700/N1721800	S5W1	Mountain	2180 m	4.12	162	3
41	Santos Reyes	E715100/N1723900	S4W1	Low Piedmont	1640 m	0.20	8	5
45	Santos Reyes	E715000/N1724800	S4W1	Low Piedmont	1500 m	3.00	53	4
47	Santos Reyes	E716300/N1725000	S4E1	Low Piedmont	1460 m	4.00	70	4
48	Santa Inés	E720000/N1724200	S4E1	Low Piedmont	1460 m	0.01	8	5
55	Santa Inés	E721900/N1724200	S4E2	High Piedmont	1800 m	0.24	60	4
57	Santa Inés	E720000/N1724400	S4E1	Low Piedmont	1520 m	0.20	8	5
58	Santa Inés	E719500/N1723900	S5E1	High Alluvium	1400 m	0.25	8	5
61	Rancho Viejo	E726000/N1718400	S6E3	Low Piedmont	1460 m	13.22	498	2
62	Rancho Viejo	E726900/N1716000	S6E3	Low Piedmont	1480 m	1.27	23	5
65	Santos Niños	E721000/N1719900	S5E2	Low Piedmont	1440 m	12.50	469	2
67	San Ildefonso	E720000/N1837400	S1E2	Mountain	2100 m	22.25	240	3
79	Ayoquezco	E722800/N1839900	S1E2	Low Piedmont	1660 m	0.18	8	5
82	Ayoquezco	E723400/N1838600	S1E2	Low Piedmont	1700 m	11.20	199	3
84	San Ild/Seb	E715800/N1839500	S1W1	High Piedmont	1920 m	15.55	462	2

Appendix C: Site Summaries by Phase

Table C.3 continued

Site	Municipio	UTM	Grid	Environment	Elevation	Site Size (ha)	Population	Rank
90	San Sebastián	E715900/N1840000	S1W1	High Piedmont	1900 m	4.00	133	3
94	San Francisco	E717100/N1827200	S4E1	Low Piedmont	1540 m	0.80	14	5
95	San Francisco	E717700/N1827400	S4E1	Low Piedmont	1560 m	0.25	8	5
96	San Francisco	E717900/N1826700	S4E1	Low Piedmont	1560 m	0.08	8	5
97	San Francisco	E718500/N1724700	S4E1	High Alluvium	1440 m	0.24	9	5
101	San Francisco	E718400/N1725200	S4E1	Low Piedmont	1460 m	0.01	8	5
102	San Francisco	E718100/N1826200	S4E1	Low Piedmont	1520 m	0.06	8	5
109	San Miguel	E716500/N1827300	S4E1	Low Piedmont	1500 m	1.00	18	5
110	San Miguel	E717500/N1829300	S3E1	High Piedmont	1820 m	1.00	18	5
111	San Francisco	E723500/N1831200	S3E2	Mountain	2080 m	12.50	469	2
114/115	San Francisco	E719700/N1829400	S3E1	Mountain	2320 m	1.40	30	4
120	San Miguel	E719800/N1832800	S2E1	High Piedmont	1980 m	0.50	27	4

TABLE C.4. Period IIIb-IV Sites in the Sola Valley

Site	Municipio	UTM	Grid	Environment	Elevation	Site Size (ha)	Population	Rank
1	San Juan	E612000/N1827400	S4W1	High Piedmont	1800 m	8.50	304	2
3	San Juan	E613500/N1827800	S4W1	Low Piedmont	1580 m	12.00	250	2
6	San Juan	E611500/N1826300	S4W1	Mountain	2040 m	3.84	98	3
7	San Juan	E612100/N1827300	S4W1	High Piedmont	1820 m	0.20	8	4
8	San Juan	E714200/N1828600	S3W1	Low Piedmont	1520 m	6.37	112	3
10	San Juan/Ild	E714000/N1827000	S4W1	Low Piedmont	1540 m	29.62	519	2
12	San Juan	E613600/N1830000	S3W1	High Alluvium	1460 m	16.21	284	2
13	San Juan	E613500/N1829700	S3W1	High Alluvium	1440 m	4.11	72	3
23	Sn María/Ild	E717000/N1834600	S2E1	Mountain	2300 m	19.22	475	2
24	San Ildefonso	E717900/N1835400	S2E1	High Piedmont	1980 m	3.50	62	3
32	San Ildefonso	E718100/N1836500	S1E1	High Piedmont	1920 m	2.78	49	4
38	Santa María	E612200/N1832000	S2W1	Low Alluvium	1420 m	0.48	9	5
39	Santa María	E610600/N1833300	S2W2	Low Piedmont	1520 m	31.06	713	1
45	Santos Reyes	E715000/N1724800	S4W1	Low Piedmont	1500 m	3.00	53	3
47	Santos Reyes	E716300/N1725000	S4E1	Low Piedmont	1460 m	8.05	141	3
54	Santa Inés	E720400/N1722500	S5E2	Low Alluvium	1380 m	0.01	8	4
61	Rancho Viejo	E726000/N1718400	S6E3	Low Piedmont	1460 m	0.32	12	4
65	Santos Niños	E721000/N1719900	S5E2	Low Piedmont	1440 m	38.61	797	1
66	San Ildefonso	E719500/N1838200	S1E1	High Piedmont	1900 m	0.24	8	4
68	San Francisco	E721800/N1834300	S2E2	Mountain	2060 m	4.40	108	3
69	San Francisco	E722400/N1834400	S2E2	High Piedmont	1980 m	0.50	9	4
70	San Francisco	E723500/N1834800	S2E2	Mountain	2100 m	0.45	8	4
71	San Andrés	E726500/N1837000	S1E3	High Piedmont	1820 m	0.15	8	4
74	San Martín	E726100/N1838800	S1E3	Mountain	2240 m	0.02	8	4
75	Ayoquezco	E726300/N1839000	S1E3	Mountain	2240 m	16.88	296	2
77	San Ildefonso	E726100/N1840400	N1E3	Mountain	2160 m	0.50	9	4
83	San Ildefonso	E716200/N1839100	S1E1	High Piedmont	1840 m	2.15	68	3
84	San Ild/Seb	E715800/N1839500	S1W1	High Piedmont	1920 m	2-6	150	3
88	San Ildefonso	E715700/N1838700	S1W1	High Piedmont	1960 m	1.69	67	3
90	San Sebastián	E715900/N1840000	S1W1	High Piedmont	1900 m	4.00	133	3
97	San Francisco	E718500/N1724700	S4E1	High Alluvium	1440 m	54.20	953	1
98	San Francisco	E717900/N1826000	S4E1	High Alluvium	1400 m	0.01	8	4
103	San Francisco	E717200/N1826000	S4E1	High Alluvium	1380 m	0.02	8	4
104	San Francisco	E716500/N1826100	S4E1	High Alluvium	1400 m	10.10	177	3
105	San Miguel	E718000/N1830900	S3E1	High Piedmont	1820 m	0.30	8	4
106	San Miguel	E718400/N1830800	S3E1	High Piedmont	1840 m	0.01	8	4
107	San Miguel	E717000/N1830300	S3E1	Low Piedmont	1640 m	0.20	8	4
111	San Francisco	E723500/N1831200	S3E2	Mountain	2080 m	53.00	1028	1
114	San Francisco	E719700/N1829400	S3E1	Mountain	2320 m	1.40	30	4

TABLE C.5. Period V Sites in the Sola Valley

Site	Municipio	UTM	Grid	Environment	Elevation	Site Size (ha)	Population	Rank
1	San Juan	E612000/N1827400	S4W1	High Piedmont	1800 m	1.20	21	5
2	San Juan	E612800/N1827400	S4W1	Low Piedmont	1620 m	0.02	8	5
3	San Juan	E613500/N1827800	S4W1	Low Piedmont	1580 m	20.47	584	2
4	San Juan	E714300/N1828000	S4W1	Low Piedmont	1520 m	0.02	8	5
5	San Juan	E612100/N1826000	S4W1	Mountain	2100 m	0.01	8	5
6	San Juan	E611500/N1826300	S4W1	Mountain	2040 m	0.01	8	5
7	San Juan	E612100/N1827300	S4W1	High Piedmont	1820 m	0.69	12	5
10	San Juan/Ild	E714000/N1827000	S4W1	Low Piedmont	1540 m	11.71	205	3
11	San Juan	E714000/N1827300	S4W1	High Alluvium	1520 m	0.96	17	5
17	San Miguel	E715100/N1826000	S4W1	Low Piedmont	1480 m	0.75	14	5
18	San Miguel	E714000/N1826000	S4W1	Low Piedmont	1700 m	23.19	426	2
19	San Miguel	E714700/N1725800	S4W1	Low Piedmont	1500 m	0.25	8	5
20	San Juan	E610200/N1829000	S3W2	Mountain	2400 m	30.19	663	2
21	San Miguel	E714000/N1826500	S4W1	Low Piedmont	1680 m	20.20	538	2
22	San Ildefonso	E715300/N1827900	S4W1	Low Piedmont	1460 m	4.64	81	4
23(3)	Sn María/Idel	E717000/N1834600	S2E1	Mountain	2300 m	13.41	272	3
24	San Ildefonso	E717900/N1835400	S2E1	High Piedmont	1980 m	5.09	89	4
25	San Ildefonso	E719500/N1836000	S1E1	Mountain	2200 m	1.88	83	4
26	San Ildefonso	E719500/N1836200	S1E1	Mountain	2180 m	0.01	8	5
27	San Ildefonso	E719400/N1834700	S2E1	Mountain	2100 m	4.66	82	4
29	San Ildefonso	E720000/N1835900	S2E1	Mountain	2120 m	6.37	163	3
30	San Ildefonso	E720500/N1835000	S2E2	Mountain	2160 m	0.01	8	5
31	San Ildefonso	E719000/N1834000	S2E1	Mountain	2220 m	50.30	1534	1
32	San Ildefonso	E718100/N1836500	S1E1	High Piedmont	1920 m	2.49	44	4
39	Santa María	E610600/N1833300	S2W2	Low Piedmont	1520 m	1.58	63	4
40	Santos Reyes	E714700/N1721800	S5W1	Mountain	2180 m	4.12	162	3
41/42	Santos Reyes	E715100/N1723900	S4W1	Low Piedmont	1640 m	1.50	27	4
45	Santos Reyes	E715000/N1724800	S4W1	Low Piedmont	1500 m	3.76	66	4
46	Santos Reyes	E715000/N1722800	S5W1	Low Piedmont	1720 m	0.03	8	5
47	Santos Reyes	E716300/N1725000	S4E1	Low Piedmont	1460 m	8.05	141	3
49	Santa Inés	E720200/N1723300	S5E2	Low Piedmont	1500 m	1.35	24	5
50	Santa Inés	E720800/N1723600	S5E2	Low Piedmont	1520 m	0.80	14	5
51	Santa Inés	E720000/N1723900	S5E2	Low Piedmont	1460 m	0.43	8	5
53	Santa Inés	E720600/N1722500	S5E2	Low Piedmont	1400 m	0.01	8	5
55	Santa Inés	E721900/N1724200	S4E2	High Piedmont	1800 m	0.08	30	4
57	Santa Inés	E720000/N1724400	S4E1	Low Piedmont	1520 m	0.20	8	5
58	Santa Inés	E719500/N1723900	S5E1	High Alluvium	1400 m	0.25	8	5
59	Santa Inés	E719100/N1724200	S4E1	High Alluvium	1420 m	3.50	62	4
61	Rancho Viejo	E726000/N1718400	S6E3	Low Piedment	1460 m	1.50	27	4
62	Rancho Viejo	E726900/N1716000	S6E3	Low Piedmont	1480 m	1.27	23	5
64	Rancho Viejo	E723900/N1716500	S6E2	Low Piedmont	1660 m	0.01	8	5
65	Santos Niños	E721000/N1719900	S5E2	Low Piedmont	1440 m	1.36	24	4
66	San Ildefonso	E719500/N1838200	S1E1	High Piedmont	1900 m	0.24	8	5
67	San Ildefonso	E720000/N1837400	S1E2	Mountain	2100 m	0.01	8	5
68	San Francisco	E721800/N1834300	S2E2	Mountain	2060 m	11.80	267	3
69	San Francisco	E722400/N1834400	S2E2	High Piedmont	1980 m	8.32	153	3
70	San Francisco	E723500/N1834800	S2E2	Mountain	2100 m	0.90	16	5
71	San Andrés	E726500/N1837000	S1E3	High Piedmont	1820 m	7.15	255	3
72	San Andrés	E726400/N1837200	S1E3	High Piedmont	1860 m	0.01	8	5
73	San Andrés	E726100/N1838000	S1E3	High Piedmont	1900 m	0.06	8	5
74	San Martín	E726100/N1838800	S1E3	Mountain	2240 m	0.02	8	5
75	Ayoquezco	E726300/N1839000	S1E3	Mountain	2240 m	8-12	150	3
76	Ayoquezco	E726100/N1840400	N1E3	Mountain	2160 m	0.06	8	5
77	San Ildefonso	E723500/N1837300	S1E2	Low Piedmont	1640 m	3.00	95	4
80	Ayoquezco	E722900/N1839800	S1E2	Low Piedmont	1640 m	0.23	8	5
82	Ayoquezco	E723400/N1838600	S1E2	Low Piedmont	1700 m	8.80	148	3
83	San Ildefonso	E716200/N1839100	S1E1	High Piedmont	1840 m	0.50	19	5
84	San Ild/Seb	E715800/N1839500	S1W1	High Piedmont	1920 m	1-2	57	4
86	San Ildefonso	E717700/N1838700	S1E1	Low Piedmont	1740 m	0.09	8	5
87	San Ildefonso	E717200/N1839000	S1E1	Low Piedmont	1720 m	0.09	8	5

Table C.5 continued

Site	Municipio	UTM	Grid	Environment	Elevation	Site Size (ha)	Population	Rank
88	San Ildefonso	E715700/N1838700	S1W1	High Piedmont	1960 m	1.69	67	4
90	San Sebastián	E715900/N1840000	S1W1	High Piedmont	1900 m	2-4	53	4
91	San Andrés	E726300/N1836000	S1E3	Low Piedmont	1540 m	0.16	8	5
92	San Andrés	E726000/N1836100	S1E3	Low Piedmont	1540 m	0.09	8	5
93	San Andrés	E727000/N1835000	S2E3	Low Piedmont	1640 m	0.50	9	5
94	San Francisco	E717100/N1827200	S4E1	Low Piedmont	1540 m	0.01	8	5
96	San Francisco	E717900/N1826700	S4E1	Low Piedmont	1560 m	0.50	9	5
97	San Francisco	E718500/N1724700	S4E1	High Alluvium	1440 m	0.01	8	5
99	San Francisco	E717600/N1724400	S4E1	High Alluvium	1400 m	0.01	8	5
100	San Francisco	E717900/N1725100	S4E1	High Alluvium	1420 m	0.02	8	5
104	San Francisco	E716500/N1826100	S4E1	High Alluvium	1400 m	0.45	8	5
105	San Miguel	E718000/N1830900	S3E1	High Piedmont	1820 m	0.01	8	5
107	San Miguel	E717000/N1830300	S3E1	Low Piedmont	1640 m	0.80	14	5
110	San Miguel	E717500/N1829300	S3E1	High Piedmont	1820 m	0.02	8	5
111	San Francisco	E723500/N1831200	S3E2	Mountain	2080 m	89.20	1921	1
112	San Francisco	E721700/N1831500	S3E2	Mountain	2020 m	2.20	43	4
113	San Francisco	E719200/N1830200	S3E1	Mountain	2240 m	1.60	60	4
114/115	San Francisco	E719700/N1829400	S3E1	Mountain	2320 m	1.40	30	4
116	San Francisco	E720800/N1829200	S2E2	Mountain	2340 m	0.50	9	5
117	San Francisco	E721200/N1828400	S2E2	Mountain	2280 m	0.30	30	4
118	San Francisco	E721500/N1829600	S2E2	Mountain	2180 m	0.02	8	5
119	San Miguel	E718600/N1833300	S2E1	High Piedmont	1840 m	0.02	8	5
120	San Miguel	E719800/N1832800	S2E1	High Piedmont	1980 m	0.04	8	5

Appendix D

Productive Potentials by Phase

TABLE D.1. Productive Potentials of Occupied Grid Squares in the Sola Valley during the Ic Phase

Grid Square	Total Surveyed (Hectares)	Type I	Type II	Type III 100%	Type III 10%	Resource-Based Potential Population	Labor-Based Potential Population	Archaeo-logical Population (# Sites)	Surplus/Deficit Potential
S1E1+	1618	117	22	553	926	1556	669	262 (1)	255%
S1E2	1600	—	51	124	1425	599	359	186 (2)	193%
S2E2	1600	—	—	—	1600	272	1	8 (1)	13%
S2W2	1228	235	—	128	865	1161	1010	360 (1)	281%
S3E1	1600	—	—	20	1580	302	50	116 (2)	43%
S4E1	1600	302	—	565	733	2110	370	109 (2)	339%
S4W1	1600	120	—	370	1110	1224	146	43 (3)	340%
S5E2	1600	160	—	203	1237	1097	58	17 (2)	341%
S6E2	1600	25	—	153	1422	577	27	8 (1)	338%
S6E3	1375	—	—	25	1350	272	111	430 (4)	26%
Total	15,371	959	73	2141	12,198	9170	2801	1539 (19)	182%

TABLE D.2. Productive Potentials of Occupied Grid Squares in the Sola Valley during Period II

Grid Square	Total Surveyed (Hectares)	Type I	Type II	Type III 100%	Type III 10%	Resource-Based Potential Population	Labor-Based Potential Population	Archaeo-logical Population (# Sites)	Surplus/Deficit Potential
S1E1+	1618	117	22	553	926	1809	655	161 (2)	407%
S2E1	1600	—	141	112	1347	956	98	29 (1)	338%
S2W2	1228	235	—	128	865	1384	1231	440 (1)	280%
S3W1	1600	358	—	785	457	3085	458	111 (3)	413%
S4E1	1600	302	—	565	733	2485	82	20 (1)	410%
S4W1	1600	120	—	370	1110	1428	235	64 (2)	367%
S5E1	1600	158	—	450	992	1715	33	8 (1)	413%
Total	10,846	1290	163	2963	6430	12,862	2792	833 (11)	335%

Appendix D: Productive Potentials by Phase

TABLE D.3. Productive Potentials of Occupied Grid Squares in the Sola Valley during Period IIIa

Grid Square	Total Surveyed (Hectares)	Type I	Type II	Type III 100%	Type III 10%	Resource-Based Potential Population	Labor-Based Potential Population	Archaeo-logical Population (# Sites)	Surplus/Deficit Potential
S1E1+	1618	117	22	553	926	2189	2189	2656 (6)	82%
S1E2	1600	—	51	124	1425	842	562	447 (3)	126%
S1E3	1093	—	39	—	1054	406	31	8 (1)	388%
S2E1	1600	—	141	112	1347	1144	735	219 (2)	196%
S2W1	1560	5	—	160	1395	749	135	51 (2)	265%
S2W2	1228	235	—	128	865	1601	1479	721 (2)	205%
S3E1	1600	—	—	20	1580	432	55	48 (2)	115%
S3E2	1340	—	—	—	1340	325	114	469 (1)	24%
S3W1	1600	358	—	785	457	3661	631	137 (3)	461%
S3W2	1123	—	—	20	1103	316	56	53 (1)	106%
S4E1	1600	302	—	565	733	2941	696	151 (9)	461%
S4E2	1523	—	—	10	1513	391	36	60 (1)	60%
S4W1	1600	120	—	370	1110	1719	1698	1515 (13)	113%
S5E1	1600	158	—	450	992	2057	37	8 (1)	463%
S5E2	1600	160	—	203	1237	1528	1254	469 (1)	267%
S5W1	1473	—	—	—	1473	357	41	170 (2)	24%
S6E3	1375	—	—	25	1350	388	181	521 (2)	35%
Total	25,133	1455	253	3525	19,900	21,046	9930	7703 (52)	129%

TABLE D.4. Productive Potentials of Occupied Grid Squares in the Sola Valley during Period IIIb-IV

Grid Square	Total Surveyed (Hectares)	Type I	Type II	Type III 100%	Type III 10%	Resource-Based Potential Population	Labor-Based Potential Population	Archaeo-logical Population (# Sites)	Surplus/Deficit Potential
S1E1+	1618	117	22	553	926	2889	2678	950 (7)	282%
S1E2	1600	—	51	124	1425	1109	48	9 (1)	533%
S1E3	1093	—	39	—	1054	539	293	312 (3)	94%
S2E1	1600	—	141	112	1347	1529	331	62 (1)	534%
S2E2	1600	—	—	—	1600	504	39	125 (3)	31%
S2W1	1560	5	—	160	1395	976	44	9 (1)	489%
S2W2	1228	235	—	128	865	2156	1994	713 (1)	280%
S3E1	1600	—	—	20	1580	561	74	54 (4)	137%
S3E2	1340	—	—	—	1340	422	324	1028 (1)	32%
S3W1	1600	358	—	785	457	4872	2602	468 (3)	556%
S4E1	1600	302	—	565	733	3919	3820	1287 (5)	297%
S4W1	1600	120	—	370	1110	2273	2157	1232 (6)	175%
S5E2	1600	160	—	203	1237	2037	1821	805 (2)	225%
S6E3	1375	—	—	25	1350	504	38	12 (1)	317%
Total	21,014	1297	253	3045	16,419	24,290	16,263	7066	230%

TABLE D.5. Productive Potentials of Occupied Grid Squares in the Sola Valley during Period V

Grid Square	Total Surveyed (Hectares)	Type I	Type II	Type III 100%	Type III 10%	Resource-Based Potential Population	Labor-Based Potential Population	Archaeological Population (# Sites)	Surplus/Deficit Potential
N1E3	476	—	—	—	476	196	3	8 (1)	38%
S1E1+	1618	117	22	553	926	3740	3091	537 (12)	576%
S1E2	1600	—	51	124	1425	1428	876	259 (4)	338%
S1E3	1093	—	39	—	1054	688	421	445 (7)	95%
S2E1	1600	—	141	112	1347	1939	1939	1974 (7)	98%
S2E2	1600	—	—	—	1600	659	183	491 (7)	37%
S2E3	1251	—	93	—	1158	1083	59	9 (1)	656%
S2W2	1228	235	—	128	865	2762	504	63 (1)	800%
S3E1	1600	—	—	20	1580	734	124	120 (5)	103%
S3E2	1340	—	—	—	1340	552	552	1964 (2)	28%
S3W2	1123	—	—	20	1103	537	347	663 (1)	52%
S4E1	1600	303	—	565	732	5051	2080	260 (9)	800%
S4E2	1523	—	—	10	1513	665	49	30 (1)	163%
S4W1	1600	120	—	370	1110	2943	2943	2031 (16)	145%
S5E1	1600	158	—	450	992	3524	64	8 (1)	800%
S5E2	1600	160	—	203	1237	2625	624	78 (5)	800%
S6E2	1600	25	—	153	1422	1394	64	8 (1)	800%
S6E3	1375	—	—	25	1350	659	113	50 (2)	226%
Total	23,827	1118	346	2733	21,230	31,179	14,036	8998 (83)	156%

References Cited

Acosta, Jorge R.
1965 Preclassic and Classic architecture of Oaxaca. In: Handbook of Middle American Indians, edited by Robert Wauchope and Gordon R. Willey, vol. 3, pp. 814-36. Austin: University of Texas Press.

Acosta, Jorge R., and Javier Romero
1992 Exploraciones en Monte Negro, Oaxaca: 1937-1938, 1938-1939 y 1939-1940. México: Instituto Nacional de Antropología e Historia.

Adams, Robert McC.
1966 The Evolution of Urban Society. Chicago: Aldine-Atherton.
1978 Strategies of maximization, stability, and resilience in Mesopotamian society, settlement, and agriculture. Proceedings of the American Philosophical Society 122:329-35.
1981 Heartland of Cities: Surveys of Ancient Settlement and Land Use on the Central Floodplain of the Euphrates. Chicago: University of Chicago Press.

Appel, Jill
1982 A summary of the ethnohistoric information relevant to the interpretation of Late Postclassic settlement pattern data, the central and Valle Grande survey zones. In: Monte Albán's Hinterland, Part I: The Prehispanic Settlement Patterns of the Central and Southern Parts of the Valley of Oaxaca, Mexico, by Richard E. Blanton, Stephen Kowalewski, Gary Feinman, and Jill Appel, pp. 139-48. Memoirs of the University of Michigan Museum of Anthropology, no. 15. Ann Arbor.

Balkansky, Andrew K.
1997a Archaeological Settlement Patterns of the Sola Valley, Oaxaca, Mexico. Ph.D. dissertation, University of Wisconsin, Madison. Ann Arbor: University Microfilms.
1997b Archaeological settlement patterns of the Sola Valley, Oaxaca, Mexico. Mexicon 19:12-18.
1998a Urbanism and early state formation in the Huamelulpan Valley of southern Mexico. Latin American Antiquity 9:37-67.
1998b Origin and collapse of complex societies in Oaxaca (Mexico): evaluating the era from 1965 to the present. Journal of World Prehistory 12:451-93.
1998c Marshall H. Saville's Excavations at Xoxocotlán, Oaxaca. Manuscript.
1999 Settlement pattern studies in the Mixteca Alta, Oaxaca, 1966-1996. In: Settlement Pattern Studies in the Americas: Fifty Years since Virú, edited by Brian R. Billman and Gary M. Feinman, pp. 191-202. Washington, D.C.: Smithsonian Institution Press.
2001 On emerging patterns in Oaxaca archaeology. Current Anthropology 42(4):559-61.

Balkansky, Andrew K., Gary M. Feinman, and Linda M. Nicholas
1997 Pottery kilns of ancient Ejutla, Oaxaca, Mexico. Journal of Field Archaeology 24:139-60.

Balkansky, Andrew K., Stephen A. Kowalewski, Verónica Pérez Rodríguez, Thomas J. Pluckhahn, Charlotte A. Smith, Laura R. Stiver, Dmitri Beliaev, John F. Chamblee, Verenice Y. Heredia Espinoza, and Roberto Santos Pérez
2000 Archaeological survey in the Mixteca Alta of Oaxaca, Mexico. Journal of Field Archaeology 27:365-89.

Ball, Hugh G., and Donald L. Brockington
1978 Trade and travel in prehispanic Oaxaca. In: Mesoamerican Communication Routes and Cultural Contacts, edited by Thomas A. Lee, Jr. and Carlos Navarrete, pp. 107-14. Provo, Utah: Papers of the New World Archaeological Foundation.

Beals, Ralph L.
1969 Southern Mexican highlands and adjacent coastal regions: introduction. In: Handbook of Middle American Indians, vol. 7, edited by Robert Wauchope and Evon Z. Vogt, pp. 315-28. Austin: University of Texas Press.

Berdan, Frances F., and Patricia Rieff Anawalt (editors)
1992 The Codex Mendoza. 4 vols. Berkeley: University of California Press.

Berdan, Frances F., Richard E. Blanton, Elizabeth H. Boone, Mary G. Hodge, Michael E. Smith, and Emily Umberger
1996 Aztec Imperial Strategies. Washington, D.C.: Dumbarton Oaks.

Berlin, Heinrich
1946 Three Zapotec Stones. Notes on Middle American Archaeology and Ethnology 66. Washington, D.C.: Carnegie Institution of Washington Division of Historical Research.

1951 A survey of the Sola region in Oaxaca, Mexico. Ethnos 16:1-17.
1957 Las antiguas creencias en San Miguel Sola, Oaxaca, México. In: Idolatría y Superstición entre los Indios de Oaxaca, pp. 7-89. México: Ediciones Toledo.

Bernal, Ignacio
1949 Exploraciones en Coixtlahuaca, Oax. Revista Mexicana de Estudios Antropológicos 10:5-76.
1958 Exploraciones en Cuilapan de Guerrero, 1902-1954. Informe 7. México: Instituto Nacional de Antropología e Historia.
1965 Archaeological synthesis of Oaxaca. In: Handbook of Middle American Indians, edited by Robert Wauchope and Gordon R. Willey, vol. 3, pp. 788-813. Austin: University of Texas Press.
1966 The Mixtecs in the archaeology of the Valley of Oaxaca. In: Ancient Oaxaca: Discoveries in Mexican Archaeology and History, edited by John Paddock, pp. 345-66. Stanford: Stanford University Press.
1980 A History of Mexican Archaeology: The Vanished Civilizations of Middle America. New York: Thames and Hudson.
1983 The effect of settlement pattern studies on the archaeology of Central Mexico. In: Prehistoric Settlement Patterns: Essays in Honor of Gordon R. Willey, edited by Evon Z. Vogt and Richard M. Leventhal, pp. 389-98. Albuquerque: University of New Mexico Press.

Bernal, Ignacio, and Lorenzo Gamio
1974 Yagul, el palacio de los seis patios. Serie Antropológica 16. México: Instituto de Investigaciones Antropológicas Universidad Nacional Autónoma de México.

Billman, Brian R., and Gary M. Feinman (editors)
1999 Settlement pattern Studies in the Americas: Fifty Years since Virú. Washington, D.C.: Smithsonian Institution Press.

Blanton, Richard E.
1972 Prehispanic Settlement Patterns of the Ixtapalapa Peninsula Region, Mexico. Occasional Papers no. 6. University Park: Department of Anthropology, Pennsylvania State University.
1976 The origins of Monte Albán. In: Cultural Change and Continuity: Essays in Honor of James Bennett Griffin, edited by Charles E. Cleland, pp. 223-32. New York: Academic Press.
1978 Monte Albán: Settlement Patterns at the Ancient Zapotec Capital. New York: Academic Press.
1983 The founding of Monte Albán. In: The Cloud People: Divergent Evolution of the Zapotec and Mixtec Civilizations, edited by Kent V. Flannery and Joyce Marcus, pp. 83-87. New York: Academic Press.
1990 Theory and practice in Mesoamerican archaeology: a comparison of two modes of scientific inquiry. In: Debating Oaxaca Archaeology, edited by Joyce Marcus, pp. 1-16. Anthropological Papers of the University of Michigan Museum of Anthropology, no. 84. Ann Arbor.

Blanton, Richard E. and Gary M. Feinman
1984 The Mesoamerican world-system: a comparative perspective. American Anthropologist 86:673-82.

Blanton, Richard E., Gary M. Feinman, Stephen A. Kowalewski, and Linda M. Nicholas
1999 Ancient Oaxaca: The Monte Albán State. Cambridge: Cambridge University Press.

Blanton, Richard E., Gary M. Feinman, Stephen A. Kowalewski, and Peter N. Peregrine
1996 A dual-processual theory for the evolution of Mesoamerican civilization. Current Anthropology 37:1-14.

Blanton, Richard E., Stephen A. Kowalewski, Gary M. Feinman, and Jill Appel
1981 Ancient Mesoamerica: A Comparison of Change in Three Regions. Cambridge: Cambridge University Press.
1982 Monte Albán's Hinterland, Part I: The Prehispanic Settlement Patterns of the Central and Southern Parts of the Valley of Oaxaca, Mexico. Memoirs of the University of Michigan Museum of Anthropology, no. 15. Ann Arbor.

Blanton, Richard E., Stephen A. Kowalewski, Gary M. Feinman, and Laura M. Finsten
1993 Ancient Mesoamerica: A Comparison of Change in Three Regions. Cambridge: Cambridge University Press.

Bourdieu, Pierre
1977 Outline of a Theory of Practice. Cambridge: Cambridge University Press.

Bradomín, José M.
1992 Toponimia de Oaxaca: crítica etimológica. Oaxaca.

Brockington, Donald L.
1973 Archaeological Investigations at Miahuatlán, Oaxaca. Vanderbilt University Publications in Anthropology, no. 7. Nashville, Tennessee.

Brumfiel, Elizabeth M.
1992 Breaking and entering the ecosystem: gender, class, and faction steal the show. American Anthropologist 94:551-67.

Byland, Bruce E.
1980 Political and Economic Evolution in the Tamazulapan Valley, Mixteca Alta, Oaxaca, Mexico: A Regional Approach. Ph.D. dissertation, Pennsylvania State University, University Park. Ann Arbor: University Microfilms.

Byland, Bruce E., and John M. D. Pohl
1994 In the Realm of 8 Deer: The Archaeology of the Mixtec Codices. Norman: University of Oklahoma Press.

Carmagnani, Marcello
1988 El regreso de los dioses: el proceso de reconstitución de la identidad étnica en Oaxaca, siglos XVII y XVIII. México: Fondo de Cultura Económica.

Carneiro, Robert L.
1970 A theory of the origin of the state. Science 169:733-38.

Carta de efectos climáticos
1980 Oaxaca: INEGI.

Carta geológica
1980 Oaxaca: INEGI.

Caso, Alfonso
1928 Las estelas zapotecas. México: Secretaría de Educación Pública.

1938 Exploraciones en Oaxaca, quinta y sexta temporadas, 1936-1937. Publicación no. 34. México: Instituto Panamericano de Geografía e Historia.
1939 Culturas mixteca y zapoteca. Ediciones Encuadernables del Nacional.
1942 Resumen del informe de las exploraciones en Oaxaca durante la 7a y la 8a temporadas, 1937-1938 y 1938-1939. México: Actas del XXVII Congreso Internacional de Americanistas, 1939, 2:159-87.
1947 Calendario y escritura de las antiguas culturas de Monte Albán. In: Obras completas de Miguel Othón de Mendizábal, vol. 1 (México).
1949 El mapa de Teozacoalco. Cuadernos Americanos 8:145-81.
1965a Zapotec writing and calendar. In: Handbook of Middle American Indians, edited by Robert Wauchope and Gordon R. Willey, vol. 3, pp. 931-47. Austin: University of Texas Press.
1965b Mixtec writing and calendar. In: Handbook of Middle American Indians, edited by Robert Wauchope and Gordon R. Willey, vol. 3, pp. 948-61. Austin: University of Texas Press.

Caso, Alfonso, and Ignacio Bernal
1965 Ceramics of Oaxaca. In: Handbook of Middle American Indians, edited by Robert Wauchope and Gordon R. Willey, vol. 3, pp. 871-95. Austin: University of Texas Press.

Caso, Alfonso, Ignacio Bernal, and Jorge R. Acosta
1967 La cerámica de Monte Albán. Memorias XIII. México: Instituto Nacional de Antropología e Historia.

Childe, V. Gordon
1951 Social Evolution. London: Watts & Co.

Cowgill, George L.
1975 On the causes and consequences of ancient and modern population changes. American Anthropologist 77:505-25.
1993 Beyond criticizing new archaeology. American Anthropologist 95:551-73.

Córdova, fray Juan de
1578a Vocabulario en lengua zapoteca. México: Pedro Charte and Antonio Ricardo. (Reprinted in 1942)
1578b Arte del idioma zapoteca. México: Pedro Balli. (Reprinted in 1886)

de Balsalobre, Gonzalo
1988 Relación auténtica de las idolatrías, supersticiones, y vanas
[1656] observaciones de los indios del Obispado de Oaxaca. In: Idolatría y superstición entre los indios de Oaxaca, pp. 91-135. México: Ediciones Toledo.

de Burgoa, Francisco
1989 Geográfica descripción. 2 vols. México: Editorial Porrúa.
[1674]

de Cicco, Gabriel, and Donald Brockington
1956 Reconocimiento arqueológico en el suroeste de Oaxaca. Informe 6. México: Dirección de Monumentos Prehispánicos, Instituto Nacional de Antropología e Historia.

del Paso y Troncoso, Francisco (editor)
1905 Relaciones geográficas de Oaxaca. Papeles de Nueva España. Segunda serie, geografía y estadística, vol. IV. Madrid: Tipográfico "Sucesores de Rivadeneyra."

DeMarrais, Elizabeth, Luis Jaime Castillo, and Timothy Earle
1996 Ideology, materialization, and power strategies. Current Anthropology 37:15-31.

de Montmollin, Olivier
1997 A regional study of Classic Maya ballcourts from the Upper Grijalva Basin, Chiapas, Mexico. Ancient Mesoamerica 8:23-41.

Dennis, Philip A.
1987 Intervillage Conflict in Oaxaca. New Brunswick, New Jersey: Rutgers University Press.

Drennan, Robert D.
1976 Fábrica San José and Middle Formative Society in the Valley of Oaxaca. Memoirs of the University of Michigan Museum of Anthropology, no. 8. Ann Arbor.
1983 Radiocarbon dates for the Oaxaca region. In: The Cloud People: Divergent Evolution of the Zapotec and Mixtec Civilizations, edited by Kent V. Flannery and Joyce Marcus, pp. 363-70. New York: Academic Press.
1984 Long-distance transport costs in pre-Hispanic Mesoamerica. American Anthropologist 86:105-12.
1989 The mountains north of the Valley. In: Monte Albán's Hinterland, Part II: Pre-Hispanic Settlement Patterns in Tlacolula, Etla, and Ocotlán, the Valley of Oaxaca, Mexico, by Stephen A. Kowalewski, Gary M. Feinman, Laura Finsten, Richard E. Blanton, and Linda M. Nicholas, pp. 367-84. Memoirs of the University of Michigan Museum of Anthropology, no. 23. Ann Arbor.

Ekholm, Kajsa, and Jonathan Friedman
1985 Towards a global archaeology. Critique of Anthropology 5:97-119.

Elam, J. Michael
1989 Defensible and fortified sites. In: Monte Albán's Hinterland, Part II: Prehispanic Settlement Patterns in Tlacolula, Etla, and Ocotlán, the Valley of Oaxaca, Mexico, by Stephen A. Kowalewski, Gary M. Feinman, Laura Finsten, Richard E. Blanton, and Linda M. Nicholas, pp. 385-407. Memoirs of the University of Michigan Museum of Anthropology, no. 23. Ann Arbor.

Falconer, Steven E., and Stephen H. Savage
1995 Heartlands and hinterlands: alternative trajectories of early urbanization in Mesopotamia and the southern Levant. American Antiquity 60:37-58.

Feinman, Gary M.
1982 Patterns of ceramic production and distribution: periods Early I through V. In: Monte Albán's Hinterland, Part I: The Prehispanic Settlement Patterns of the Central and Southern Parts of the Valley of Oaxaca, Mexico, by Richard E. Blanton, Stephen A. Kowalewski, Gary M. Feinman, and Jill Appel, pp. 181-206. Memoirs of the University of Michigan Museum of Anthropology, no. 15. Ann Arbor.

Feinman, Gary M., Stephen A. Kowalewski, Laura Finsten, Richard E. Blanton, and Linda Nicholas
1985 Long-term demographic change: a perspective from the Valley of Oaxaca. Journal of Field Archaeology 12:333-62.

Feinman, Gary M., and Joyce Marcus (editors)
1998 Archaic States. Santa Fe, New Mexico: School of American Research Press.

Feinman, Gary M., and Linda M. Nicholas
1988 The prehispanic settlement history of the Ejutla Valley, Mexico: a preliminary perspective. Mexicon 10:5-13.
1990a At the margins of the Monte Albán state: settlement patterns in the Ejutla Valley, Oaxaca, Mexico. Latin American Antiquity 1:216-46.
1990b Settlement and land use in ancient Oaxaca. In: Debating Oaxaca Archaeology, edited by Joyce Marcus, pp. 71-113. Anthropological Papers of the University of Michigan Museum of Anthropology, no. 84. Ann Arbor.
1992 Pre-Hispanic interregional interaction in southern Mexico: the Valley of Oaxaca and the Ejutla Valley. In: Resources, Power, and Interregional Interaction, edited by Edward M. Schortman and Patricia A. Urban, pp. 75-116. New York: Plenum Press.
1993 Shell-ornament production in Ejutla: implications for highland-coastal interaction in ancient Oaxaca. Ancient Mesoamerica 4:103-19.
1995 Household craft specialization and shell ornament manufacture in Ejutla, Mexico. Expedition 37:14-24.
1996 Defining the Eastern Limits of the Monte Albán State: Systematic Settlement Pattern Survey in the Guirún Area, Oaxaca, Mexico. Mexicon 18:91-97.
1997 Ejutla Valley survey data.

Feinman, Gary M., Linda M. Nicholas, and William D. Middleton
1993 Craft activities at the prehispanic Ejutla site, Oaxaca, Mexico. Mexicon 15:33-41.

Fernández de Miranda, María Teresa, Mauricio Swadesh, and Roberto J. Weitlaner
1960 El panorama etno-lingüístico de Oaxaca y el istmo. Revista Mexicana de Estudios Antropológicos 16:137-57.

Finsten, Laura
1983 The Classic-Postclassic Transition in the Valley of Oaxaca, Mexico: A Regional Analysis of the Process of Political Decentralization in a Prehistoric Complex Society. Ph.D. dissertation, Purdue University. Ann Arbor: University Microfilms.
1996 Frontier and periphery in southern Mexico: the Mixtec sierra in highland Oaxaca. In: Pre-Columbian World Systems, edited by Peter N. Peregrine and Gary M. Feinman, pp. 77-95. Madison, Wisconsin: Prehistory Press.

Finsten, Laura, and Stephen A. Kowalewski
1991 The Peñoles project: results. Paper presented at the 90th annual meeting of the American Anthropological Association, Chicago.
1999 Spatial scales and process: in and around the Valley of Oaxaca. In: Settlement Pattern Studies in the Americas: Fifty Years since Virú, edited by Brian R. Billman and Gary M. Feinman, pp. 22-35. Washington, D.C.: Smithsonian Institution Press.

Finsten, Laura, Stephen A. Kowalewski, Charlotte A. Smith, Mark D. Borland, and Richard D. Garvin
1996 Circular architecture and symbolic boundaries in the Mixtec sierra, Oaxaca. Ancient Mesoamerica 7:19-36.

Flannery, Kent V.
1972 The cultural evolution of civilizations. Annual Review of Ecology and Systematics 3:399-426.
1976 The trouble with regional sampling. In: The Early Mesoamerican Village, edited by Kent V. Flannery, pp. 159-60. New York: Academic Press.
1983 Major Monte Albán V sites: Zaachila, Xoxocotlán, Cuilapan, Yagul, and Abasolo. In: The Cloud People: Divergent Evolution of the Zapotec and Mixtec Civilizations, edited by Kent V. Flannery and Joyce Marcus, pp. 290-95. New York: Academic Press.
1986 A visit to the master. In: Guilá Naquitz: Archaic Foraging and Early Agriculture in Oaxaca, Mexico, edited by Kent V. Flannery, pp. 511-19. New York: Academic Press.
1995 Prehistoric social evolution. In: Research Frontiers in Anthropology, edited by C. Ember and M. Ember, pp. 1-26. Englewood Cliffs, New Jersey: Prentice-Hall.
1999 Process and agency in early state formation. Cambridge Archaeological Journal 9:3-21.

Flannery, Kent V. (editor)
1976 The Early Mesoamerican Village. New York: Academic Press.
1986 Guilá Naquitz: Archaic Foraging and Early Agriculture in Oaxaca, Mexico. New York: Academic Press.

Flannery, Kent V., Anne V. T. Kirkby, Michael J. Kirkby, and Aubrey Williams, Jr.
1967 Farming systems and political growth in ancient Oaxaca. Science 158:445-54.

Flannery, Kent V. and Joyce Marcus
1976 Evolution of the public building in Formative Oaxaca. In: Cultural Change and Continuity: Essays in Honor of James Bennett Griffin, edited by Charles E. Cleland, pp. 205-21. New York: Academic Press.
1983a The earliest public buildings, tombs, and monuments at Monte Albán, with notes on the internal chronology of Period I. In: The Cloud People: Divergent Evolution of the Zapotec and Mixtec Civilizations, edited by Kent V. Flannery and Joyce Marcus, pp. 87-91. New York: Academic Press.
1983b The origins of the state in Oaxaca. In: The Cloud People: Divergent Evolution of the Zapotec and Mixtec Civilizations, edited by Kent V. Flannery and Joyce Marcus, pp. 79-83. New York: Academic Press.
1983c Urban Mitla and its rural hinterland. In: The Cloud People: Divergent Evolution of the Zapotec and Mixtec Civilizations, edited by Kent V. Flannery and Joyce Marcus, pp. 295-300. New York: Academic Press.
1983d An editorial opinion on the Mixtec impact. In: The Cloud People: Divergent Evolution of the Zapotec and Mixtec Civilizations, edited by Kent V. Flannery and Joyce Marcus, pp. 277-79. New York: Academic Press.
1994 Early Formative Pottery of the Valley of Oaxaca, Mexico. Memoirs of the University of Michigan Museum of Anthropology, no. 27. Ann Arbor.

Flannery, Kent V., and Joyce Marcus (editors)
1983 The Cloud People: Divergent Evolution of the Zapotec and Mixtec Civilizations. New York: Academic Press.

Frank, Andre Gunder
1967 Capitalism and Underdevelopment in Latin America: Historical Studies of Chile and Brazil. New York: Monthly Review Press.
1993 Bronze Age World System Cycles. Current Anthropology 34:383-429.

Fried, Morton
1967 The Evolution of Political Society. New York: Random House.

Garzón, Domingo
1994 Santa María Lachixio, Sola de Vega. In: Relaciones
[1777] geográficas de Oaxaca 1777- 1778, edited by Manuel Esparza, pp. 178-89. México: CIESAS.

Gaxiola González, Margarita
1984 Huamelulpan. Un centro urbano de la Mixteca Alta. México: Instituto Nacional de Antropología e Historia.

Gerhard, Peter
1972 A Guide to the Historical Geography of New Spain. Cambridge: Cambridge University Press.

Giddens, Anthony
1984 The Constitution of Society: Outline of the Theory of Structuration. Berkeley: University of California Press.

Gould, Stephen Jay
1996 Full House: The Spread of Excellence from Plato to Darwin. New York: Harmony Books.

Guzmán, Eulalia
1934 Exploración arqueológico en la Mixteca Alta. Anales del Museo Nacional de Arqueología, Historia, y Etnografía 5:17-42.

Hall, Thomas D., and Christopher Chase-Dunn
1993 The world-systems perspective and archaeology: forward into the past. Journal of Archaeological Research 1:121-43.

Hassan, Fekri A.
1981 Demographic Archaeology. New York: Academic Press.

Hirth, Kenneth G.
1980 The Teotihuacan Classic: A Regional Perspective from Eastern Morelos. Vanderbilt University Publications in Anthropology, no. 25. Nashville, Tennessee.
1989 Militarism and social organization at Xochicalco, Morelos. In: Mesoamerica After the Collapse of Teotihuacan A.D. 700-900, edited by Richard A. Diehl and Janet Catherine Berlo, pp. 69-81. Washington, D.C.: Dumbarton Oaks Research Library and Collection.
1995 Urbanism, militarism, and architectural design: an analysis of Epiclassic sociopolitical structure at Xochicalco. Ancient Mesoamerica 6:237-50.

Hodder, Ian
1986 Reading the Past: Current Approaches to Interpretation in Archaeology. Cambridge: Cambridge University Press.

Hodge, Mary G.
1998 Archaeological views of Aztec culture. Journal of Archaeological Research 6:197-238.

Hunt, Eva
1972 Irrigation and the socio-political organization of the Cuicatec cacicazgos. In: The Prehistory of the Tehuacán Valley, vol. 4: Chronology and Irrigation, edited by Frederick Johnson, pp. 162-248. Austin: University of Texas Press.

Jansen, Maarten
1998 Monte Albán y Zaachila en los Códices Mixtecos. In: The Shadow of Monte Albán: Politics and Historiography in Postclassic Oaxaca, Mexico, by Maarten Jansen, Peter Kröfges, and Michel R. Oudijk, pp. 67-122. Leiden: Research School CNWS.

Jansen, Maarten, Peter Kröfges, and Michel R. Oudijk
1998 The Shadow of Monte Albán: Politics and Historiography in Postclassic Oaxaca, Mexico. Leiden: Research School CNWS.

Johnson, Gregory A.
1977 Aspects of regional analysis in archaeology. Annual Review of Anthropology 6:479-508.
1980 Rank-size convexity and system integration: a view from archaeology. Economic Geography 56:234-47.
1981 Monitoring complex system integration and boundary phenomena with settlement size data. In: Archaeological Approaches to the Study of Complexity, edited by S. E. van der Leeuw, pp. 143-88. Amsterdam: University of Amsterdam.
1987 The changing organization of Uruk administration on the Susiana Plain. In: The Archaeology of Western Iran: Settlement and Society from Prehistory to the Islamic Conquest, edited by Frank Hole, pp. 107-40. Washington, D.C.: Smithsonian Institution Press.

Joyce, Arthur A.
1993a Interregional interaction and social development on the Oaxaca coast. Ancient Mesoamerica 4:67-84.
1993b The Interregional Impact of State Formation in Oaxaca. Report submitted on research activities performed as a 1992-93 Kalbfleisch Fellow, American Museum of Natural History, New York.

Joyce, Arthur A., and Marcus Winter
1996 Ideology, power, and urban society in pre-Hispanic Oaxaca. Current Anthropology 37:33-47.

Joyce, Arthur A., Marcus Winter, and Raymond G. Mueller
1998 Arqueología de la Costa de Oaxaca: Asentamientos del Periodo Formativo en el Valle del Río Verde Inferior. Oaxaca: Centro INAH.

Kirkby, Anne V. T.
1973 The Use of Land and Water Resources in the Past and Present Valley of Oaxaca. Memoirs of the University of Michigan Museum of Anthropology, no. 5. Ann Arbor.

Kohl, Philip L.
1987 The use and abuse of world systems theory: the case for the pristine west Asian state. In: Advances in Archaeological Method and Theory, edited by Michael B. Schiffer, vol. 11, pp. 1-35. New York: Academic Press.

Kowalewski, Stephen A.
1976 Prehispanic Settlement Patterns of the Central Part of the Valley of Oaxaca, Mexico. Ph.D. dissertation, University of Arizona. Ann Arbor: University Microfilms.
1980 Population-resource balances in Period I of Oaxaca, Mexico. American Antiquity 45:151-65.
1982a Population and agricultural potential: Early I through V. In: Monte Albán's Hinterland, Part I: The Prehispanic Settlement Patterns of the Central and Southern Parts of the Valley of Oaxaca, Mexico, by Richard E. Blanton, Stephen Kowalewski, Gary Feinman, and Jill Appel, pp. 149-80. Memoirs of the University of Michigan Museum of Anthropology, no. 15. Ann Arbor.
1982b The evolution of primate regional systems. Comparative Urban Research 9:60-78.
1983 The archaeological evidence for Sa'a Yucu. In: The Cloud People: Divergent Evolution of the Zapotec and Mixtec Civilizations, edited by Kent V. Flannery and Joyce Marcus, p. 289. New York: Academic Press.
1990a The evolution of complexity in the Valley of Oaxaca. Annual Review of Anthropology 19:39-58.
1990b Merits of full-coverage survey: examples from the Valley of Oaxaca, Mexico. In: The Archaeology of Regions, edited by Stephen A. Kowalewski and Suzanne K. Fish, pp. 33-85. Washington, D.C.: Smithsonian Institution Press.
1990c Scale and complexity: issues in the archaeology of the Valley of Oaxaca. In: Debating Oaxaca Archaeology, edited by Joyce Marcus, pp. 207-70. Anthropological Papers of the University of Michigan Museum of Anthropology, no. 84. Ann Arbor.
1994 Internal subdivisions of communities in the prehispanic Valley of Oaxaca. In: Factional Competition and Political Development in the New World, edited by Elizabeth M. Brumfiel and John W. Fox, pp. 127-37. Cambridge: Cambridge University Press.

Kowalewski, Stephen A., Andrew K. Balkansky, Dmitri Beliaev, John F. Chamblee, Verenice Y. Heredia Espinoza, Verónica Pérez Rodríguez, Thomas J. Pluckhahn, Roberto Santos Pérez, Charlotte A. Smith, and Laura R. Stiver
1999 Informe técnico final. Recorrido regional en la Mixteca Alta, Oaxaca. Manuscript on file, Instituto Nacional de Antropología e Historia, Centro Regional de Oaxaca, México.

Kowalewski, Stephen A., Richard E. Blanton, Gary M. Feinman, and Laura Finsten
1983 Boundaries, scale, and internal organization. Journal of Anthropological Archaeology 2:32-56.

Kowalewski, Stephen A., Gary M. Feinman, Laura Finsten, and Richard E. Blanton
1991 Pre-Hispanic ballcourts from the Valley of Oaxaca, Mexico. In: The Mesoamerican Ballgame, edited by Vernon L. Scarborough and David R. Wilcox, pp. 25-44. Tucson: University of Arizona Press.

Kowalewski, Stephen A., Gary M. Feinman, Laura Finsten, Richard E. Blanton, and Linda M. Nicholas
1989 Monte Albán's Hinterland, Part II: Prehispanic Settlement Patterns in Tlacolula, Etla, and Ocotlán, the Valley of Oaxaca, Mexico. Memoirs of the University of Michigan Museum of Anthropology, no. 23. Ann Arbor.

Kowalewski, Stephen A., Charles Spencer, and Elsa Redmond
1978 Description of ceramic categories. In: Monte Albán: Settlement Patterns at the Ancient Zapotec Capital, by Richard E. Blanton, pp. 167-93. New York: Academic Press.

Kuhn, Thomas S.
1962 The Structure of Scientific Revolutions. Chicago: University of Chicago Press.

Lenski, Gerhard
1976 History and social change. American Journal of Sociology 82:548-64.

Lind, Michael
1987 The Sociocultural Dimensions of Mixtec Ceramics. Vanderbilt University Publications in Anthropology, no. 33. Nashville, Tennessee.

Lorenzo, José Luis
1960 Aspectos físicos del Valle de Oaxaca. Revista Mexicana de Estudios Antropológicos 16:49-65.

MacNeish, Richard S., Frederick A. Peterson, and Kent V. Flannery
1970 The Prehistory of the Tehuacán Valley, vol. 3: Ceramics. Austin: University of Texas Press.

Marcus, Joyce
1974 The iconography of power among the Classic Maya. World Archaeology 6:83-94.
1976 The iconography of militarism at Monte Albán and neighboring sites in the Valley of Oaxaca. In: The Origins of Religious Art and Iconography in Preclassic Mesoamerica, edited by Henry B. Nicholson, pp. 123-39. Latin American Center, University of California at Los Angeles.
1980 Zapotec writing. Scientific American 242:50-64.
1983a The conquest slabs of Building J, Monte Albán. In: The Cloud People: Divergent Evolution of the Zapotec and Mixtec Civilizations, edited by Kent V. Flannery and Joyce Marcus, pp. 106-8. New York: Academic Press.
1983b The genetic model and the linguistic divergence of the Otomangueans. In: The Cloud People: Divergent Evolution of the Zapotec and Mixtec Civilizations, edited by Kent V. Flannery and Joyce Marcus, pp. 4-12. New York: Academic Press.
1983c Changing patterns of stone monuments after the fall of Monte Albán, A.D. 600-900. In: The Cloud People: Divergent Evolution of the Zapotec and Mixtec Civilizations, edited by Kent V. Flannery and Joyce Marcus, pp. 191-97. New York: Academic Press.
1983d Teotihuacán visitors on Monte Albán monuments and murals. In: The Cloud People: Divergent Evolution of the Zapotec and Mixtec Civilizations, edited by Kent V. Flannery and Joyce Marcus, pp. 175-81. New York: Academic Press.
1989 From centralized systems to city-states: possible models for the Epiclassic. In: Mesoamerica After the Decline of Teotihuacan A.D. 700-900, edited by Richard A. Diehl and Janet Catherine Berlo, pp. 201-8. Washington, D.C.: Dumbarton Oaks.

1992a Dynamic cycles of Mesoamerican states. National Geographic Research & Exploration 8:392-411.
1992b Mesoamerican Writing Systems: Propaganda, Myth, and History in Four Ancient Civilizations. Princeton, New Jersey: Princeton University Press.

Marcus, Joyce (editor)
1990 Debating Oaxaca Archaeology. Anthropological Papers of the University of Michigan Museum of Anthropology, no. 84. Ann Arbor.

Marcus, Joyce, and Kent V. Flannery
1983 An introduction to the Late Postclassic. In: The Cloud People: Divergent Evolution of the Zapotec and Mixtec Civilizations, edited by Kent V. Flannery and Joyce Marcus, pp. 217-26. New York: Academic Press.
1990 Science and science fiction in Postclassic Oaxaca: or, yes, Virginia, there is a Monte Albán IV. In: Debating Oaxaca Archaeology, edited by Joyce Marcus, pp. 191-205. Anthropological Papers of the University of Michigan Museum of Anthropology, no. 84. Ann Arbor.
1996 Zapotec Civilization: How Urban Society Evolved in Mexico's Oaxaca Valley. London: Thames and Hudson.

Markman, Charles W.
1981 Prehispanic Settlement Dynamics in Central Oaxaca, Mexico: A View from the Miahuatlán Valley. Vanderbilt University Publications in Anthropology, no. 26. Nashville, Tennessee.

Martínez López, Cira, Robert Markens, Marcus Winter, and Michael D. Lind
2000 Cerámica de la Fase Xoo (Época Monte Albán IIIb-IV) del Valle de Oaxaca. Oaxaca: Centro INAH.

Matadamas Díaz, Raúl
1998 Informe técnico del proyecto arqueológico: Bocana del Río Copalita, Huatulco, Oaxaca. Primera fase de la primera temporada, de enero a abril de 1998. Oaxaca: Centro INAH.

Mayr, Ernst
1997 This is Biology: The Science of the Living World. Cambridge: Harvard University Press.

McAndrews, Timothy L., Juan Albarracin-Jordan, and Marc Bermann
1997 Regional settlement patterns in the Tiwanaku Valley of Bolivia. Journal of Field Archaeology 24:67-83.

Middleton, William Drummond
1998 Craft Specialization at Ejutla, Oaxaca, Mexico: An Archaeometric Study of the Organization of Household Craft Production. Ph.D. dissertation, University of Wisconsin, Madison. Ann Arbor: University Microfilms.

Monaghan, John
1994 Irrigation and ecological complementarity in Mixtec cacicazgos. In: Caciques and Their People: A Volume in Honor of Ronald Spores, edited by Joyce Marcus and Judith Francis Zeitlin, pp. 143-61. Anthropological Papers of the University of Michigan Museum of Anthropology, no. 89. Ann Arbor.

Murphy, Arthur D. and Alex Stepick
1991 Social Inequality in Oaxaca: A History of Resistance and Change. Philadelphia: Temple University Press.

Nicholas, Linda M.
1989 Land use in prehispanic Oaxaca. In: Monte Albán's Hinterland, Part II: Prehispanic Settlement Patterns in Tlacolula, Etla, and Ocotlán, the Valley of Oaxaca, Mexico, by Stephen A. Kowalewski, Gary M. Feinman, Laura Finsten, Richard E. Blanton, and Linda M. Nicholas, pp. 449-505. Memoirs of the University of Michigan Museum of Anthropology, no. 23. Ann Arbor.

Nicholas, Linda M., Gary M. Feinman, Stephen A. Kowalewski, Richard E. Blanton, and Laura Finsten
1986 Prehispanic colonization of the Valley of Oaxaca, Mexico. Human Ecology 14:131-62.

Oudijk, Michel R.
1998 The genealogy of Zaachila. In: The Shadow of Monte Albán: Politics and Historiography in Postclassic Oaxaca, Mexico, by Maarten Jansen, Peter Kröfges, and Michel R. Oudijk, pp. 13-36. Leiden: Research School CNWS.

Paddock, John
1966 Oaxaca in ancient Mesoamerica. In: Ancient Oaxaca: Discoveries in Mexican Archaeology and History, edited by John Paddock, pp. 83-242. Stanford: Stanford University Press.
1983 The Oaxaca barrio at Teotihuacán. In: The Cloud People: Divergent Evolution of the Zapotec and Mixtec Civilizations, edited by Kent V. Flannery and Joyce Marcus, pp. 170-75. New York: Academic Press.

Paddock, John, Joseph R. Mogor, and Michael D. Lind
1968 Lambityeco Tomb 2: a preliminary report. Boletín de Estudios Oaxaqueños 25:1-24.

Parry, William J.
1987 Chipped Stone Tools in Formative Oaxaca, Mexico: Their Procurement, Production, and Use. Memoirs of the University of Michigan Museum of Anthropology, no. 20. Ann Arbor.

Parsons, Jeffrey R.
1971 Prehistoric Settlement Patterns of the Texcoco Region, Mexico. Memoirs of the University of Michigan Museum of Anthropology, no. 3. Ann Arbor.
1972 Archaeological settlement patterns. Annual Review of Anthropology 1:127-50.

Parsons, Jeffrey R., Charles M. Hastings, and Ramiro Matos M.
1997 Rebuilding the state in highland Peru: herder-cultivator interaction during the Late Intermediate period in the Tarama-Chinchaycocha region. Latin American Antiquity 8:317-41.

Paynter, Robert
1983 Expanding the scope of settlement analysis. In: Archaeological Hammers and Theories, edited by James A. Moore and Arthur S. Keene, pp. 233-75. New York: Academic Press.

Peregrine, Peter
1996 Introduction: world-systems theory and archaeology. In: Pre-Columbian World Systems, edited by Peter N. Peregrine and Gary M. Feinman, pp. 1-11. Madison, Wisconsin: Prehistory Press.

Plog, Stephen, Fred Plog, and Walter Wait
1978 Decision making in modern surveys. In: Advances in Archaeological Method and Theory, edited by Michael B. Schiffer, vol. 1, pp. 383-421. New York: Academic Press.

Plunket, Patricia S.
1983 An Intensive Survey in the Yucuita Sector of the Nochixtlán Valley, Oaxaca, Mexico. Ph.D. dissertation, Tulane University, New Orleans. Ann Arbor: University Microfilms.

Pohl, John M. D., John Monaghan, and Laura R. Stiver
1997 Religion, economy, and factionalism in Mixtec boundary zones. In: Códices y documentos sobre México: Segundo simposio, edited by Salvador Rueda Smithers, Constanza Vega Soza, and Rodrigo Martínez Baracs, pp. 205-32. México: Instituto Nacional de Antropología e Historia and Dirección General de Publicaciones del Consejo Nacional para la Cultura y las Artes.

Pohl, Mary E. D., and John M. D. Pohl
1994 Cycles of conflict: political factionalism in the Maya Lowlands. In: Factional Competition and Political Development in the New World, edited by Elizabeth M. Brumfiel and John W. Fox, pp. 138-57. Cambridge: Cambridge University Press.

Redmond, Elsa M.
1983 A Fuego y Sangre: Early Zapotec Imperialism in the Cuicatlán Cañada, Oaxaca, Mexico. Memoirs of the University of Michigan Museum of Anthropology, no. 16. Ann Arbor.

Región sierra sur. Oaxaca.
1993 México: INEGI.

Rendón, Juan José
1967 Relaciones internas de las lenguas de la familia zapoteco-chatino. Anales de Antropología 4:187-90.
1975 Estudio de los factores sociales en la diversificación del zapoteco. Anales de Antropología 12:283-318.

Renfrew, Colin
1972 The Emergence of Civilization. London: Methuen.

Sanders, William T.
1965 The Cultural Ecology of the Teotihuacan Valley: A Preliminary Report of the Results of the Teotihuacan Valley Project. Ms. on file, Department of Sociology and Anthropology, Pennsylvania State University, University Park.
1970 The population of the Teotihuacan Valley, the Basin of Mexico and the Central Mexican symbiotic region in the 16th century. In: The Teotihuacan Valley Project Final Report, vol. 1. Occasional Papers in Anthropology, no. 3. University Park: The Pennsylvania State University.
1972 Population, Agricultural History, and Societal Evolution in Mesoamerica. In: Population Growth: Anthropological Implications, edited by Brian Spooner, pp. 101-53. Cambridge: MIT Press.

Sanders, William T., and Deborah L. Nichols
1988 Ecological theory and cultural evolution in the Valley of Oaxaca. Current Anthropology 29:33-80.

Sanders, William T., Jeffrey R. Parsons, and Robert S. Santley
1979 The Basin of Mexico: Ecological Processes in the Evolution of a Civilization. New York: Academic Press.

Sanders, William T., and Robert S. Santley
1978 Review of Monte Albán: settlement patterns at the ancient Zapotec capital. Science 202:303-4.

Sanders, William T., and David L. Webster
1978 Unilinealism, multilinealism, and the evolution of complex societies. In: Social Archaeology: Beyond Subsistence and Dating, edited by Charles Redman, pp. 249-302. New York: Academic Press.

Sanderson, Stephen K.
1990 Social Evolutionism: A Critical History. Oxford: Basil Blackwell.

Santley, Robert S.
1980 Disembedded capitals reconsidered. American Antiquity 45:132-45.
1983 Ancient population at Monte Albán: a reconsideration of methodology and culture history. Haliksa'i, University of New Mexico Contributions to Anthropology 2:64-84.
1992 Debating Oaxaca archaeology. Journal of Field Archaeology 19:100-105.

Santley, Robert S., and Rani T. Alexander
1992 The political economy of core-periphery systems. In: Resources, Power, and Interregional Interaction, edited by Edward M. Schortman and Patricia A. Urban, pp. 23-50. New York: Plenum Publishing.

Saville, Marshall H.
1898 Unpublished archives (accession number 30/6980-6986). American Museum of Natural History, New York.

Schortman, Edward M. and Patricia A. Urban
1992 Current trends in interaction research. In: Resources, Power, and Interregional Interaction, edited by Edward M. Schortman and Patricia A. Urban, pp. 235-56. New York: Plenum Publishing.

Service, Elman R.
1962 Primitive Social Organization: An Evolutionary Perspective. New York: Random House.
1975 The Origins of the State and Civilization: The Process of Cultural Evolution. New York: W.W. Norton.

Sewell, William H., Jr.
1992 A theory of structure: duality, agency, and transformation. American Journal of Sociology 98:1-29.

Shanks, Michael, and Christopher Tilley
1988 Social Theory and Archaeology. Albuquerque: University of New Mexico Press.

Shepard, Anna
1967 Preliminary notes on the paste composition of Monte Albán pottery. In: La cerámica de Monte Albán, by Alfonso Caso, Ignacio Bernal, and Jorge R. Acosta, pp. 477-84. Memorias XIII. México: Instituto Nacional de Antropología e Historia.

Smith, Carol
1976 Regional Analysis. New York: Academic Press.

Smith, C. Earle, and Joseph W. Hopkins III
1983 Environmental contrasts in the Otomanguean region. In: The Cloud People: Divergent Evolution of the Zapotec and Mixtec Civilizations, edited by Kent V. Flannery and Joyce Marcus, pp. 13-18. New York: Academic Press.

Smith, Michael E., and Mary G. Hodge
1994 An introduction to Late Postclassic economies and polities. In: Economies and Polities in the Aztec Realm, edited by Mary G. Hodge and Michael E. Smith, pp. 1-42. Albany: Institute for Mesoamerican Studies SUNY.

Spencer, Charles S.
1982 The Cuicatlán Cañada and Monte Albán: A Study of Primary State Formation. New York: Academic Press.
1988 Comment on Ecological Theory and Cultural Evolution in the Valley of Oaxaca, by William T. Sanders and Deborah L. Nichols. Current Anthropology 29:65-66.
1990 On tempo and mode of state formation: neoevolutionism reconsidered. Journal of Anthropological Archaeology 9:1-30.
1993 Human agency, biased transmission, and the cultural evolution of chiefly authority. Journal of Anthropological Archaeology 12:41-74.
1998 A mathematical model of primary state formation. Cultural Dynamics 10:5-20.

Spencer, Charles S., and Elsa M. Redmond
1997 Archaeology of the Cañada de Cuicatlán, Oaxaca. Anthropological Papers of the American Museum of Natural History, no. 80. New York.
2001 Multilevel selection and political evolution in the Valley of Oaxaca, 500-100 B.C. Journal of Anthropological Archaeology 20:195-229.

Spores, Ronald
1965 The Zapotec and Mixtec at Spanish Contact. In: Handbook of Middle American Indians, edited by Robert Wauchope and Gordon R. Willey, vol. 3, pp. 962-87. Austin: University of Texas Press.
1967 The Mixtec Kings and Their People. Norman: University of Oklahoma Press.
1969 Settlement, farming technology, and environment in the Nochixtlán Valley. Science 166:557-69.
1972 An Archaeological Settlement Survey of the Nochixtlán Valley, Oaxaca. Vanderbilt University Publications in Anthropology, no. 1. Nashville, Tennessee.
1974 Marital alliance in the political integration of Mixtec kingdoms. American Anthropologist 76:297-311.
1983a Ramos phase urbanization in the Mixteca Alta. In: The Cloud People: Divergent Evolution of the Zapotec and Mixtec Civilizations, edited by Kent V. Flannery and Joyce Marcus, pp. 120-23. New York: Academic Press.
1983b Postclassic Mixtec kingdoms: ethnohistoric and archaeological evidence. In: The Cloud People: Divergent Evolution of the Zapotec and Mixtec Civilizations, edited by Kent V. Flannery and Joyce Marcus, pp. 255-60. New York: Academic Press.
1983c Las Flores phase settlement patterns in the Nochixtlán Valley. In: The Cloud People: Divergent Evolution of the Zapotec and Mixtec Civilizations, edited by Kent V. Flannery and Joyce Marcus, pp. 152-55. New York: Academic Press.
1984 The Mixtecs in Ancient and Colonial Times. Norman: University of Oklahoma Press.
1993 Tututepec: a Postclassic-period Mixtec conquest state. Ancient Mesoamerica 4:167-74.

Stein, Gil
1998 World systems theory and alternative modes of interaction in the archaeology of culture contact. In: Studies in Culture Contact: Interaction, Culture Change, and Archaeology, edited by J. Cusick, pp. 220-55. Carbondale: Southern Illinois University Press.

Stern, Steve J.
1988 Feudalism, capitalism, and the world-system in the perspective of Latin America and the Caribbean. The American Historical Review 93:829-72.

Steward, Julian H.
1955 Theory of Culture Change: The Methodology of Multilinear Evolution. Urbana: University of Illinois Press.

Stiver, Laura R.
2001 Prehispanic Mixtec Settlement and State in the Teposcolula Valley of Oaxaca, Mexico. Ph.D. dissertation, Vanderbilt University, Nashville. Ann Arbor: University Microfilms.

Swadesh, Morris
1967 Lexicostatistic classification. In: Handbook of Middle American Indians, edited by Robert Wauchope and Norman A. McQuown, vol. 5, pp. 79-115. Austin: University of Texas Press.

Taylor, William
1972 Landlord and Peasant in Colonial Oaxaca. Stanford: Stanford University Press.

Urcid, Javier
1993 The Pacific coast of Oaxaca and Guerrero: the westernmost extent of Zapotec script. Ancient Mesoamerica 4:141-65.
2001 Zapotec Hieroglyphic Writing. Washington, D.C.: Dumbarton Oaks.

Wallerstein, Immanuel
1974 The Modern World System: Capitalist Agriculture and the Origins of the European World-Economy in the 16th Century. New York: Academic Press.

Warner, John C.
1976 Survey of the market system in the Nochixtlán Valley and the Mixteca Alta. In: Markets in Oaxaca, edited by Scott Cook and Martin Diskin, pp. 107-31. Austin: University of Texas Press.

Whalen, Michael E.
1981 Excavations at Santo Domingo Tomaltepec: Evolution of a Formative Community in the Valley of Oaxaca, Mexico. Memoirs of the University of Michigan Museum of Anthropology, no. 11. Ann Arbor.
1986 Sources of the Guilá Naquitz chipped stone. In: Guilá Naquitz: Archaic Foraging and Early Agriculture in Oaxaca, Mexico, edited by Kent V. Flannery, pp. 141-46. New York: Academic Press.

Whalen, Michael E., and Paul E. Minnis
1996 Ball courts and political centralization in the Casas Grandes region. American Antiquity 61:732-46.

White, Leslie
1959 The Evolution of Culture. New York: McGraw-Hill.

Whitecotton, Joseph W.
1977 The Zapotecs: Princes, Priests, and Peasants. Norman: University of Oklahoma Press.
1992 Culture and exchange in Postclassic Oaxaca: a world-system perspective. In: Resources, Power, and Interregional Interaction, edited by Edward M. Schortman and Patricia A. Urban, pp. 51-74. New York: Plenum Publishing.

Winter, Marcus (editor)
1994 Monte Albán: estudios recientes. Oaxaca: Centro INAH.

Wolf, Eric R.
1982 Europe and the People without History. Berkeley: University of California Press.

Workinger, Andrew, and Arthur A. Joyce
1997 Boundary dynamics on the coast of Oaxaca, Mexico. Paper presented at the 62nd annual meeting of the Society for American Archaeology, Nashville.

Wright, Henry T.
1987 The Susiana hinterlands during the era of primary state formation. In: The Archaeology of Western Iran: Settlement and Society from Prehistory to the Islamic Conquest, edited by Frank Hole, pp. 141-55. Washington, D.C.: Smithsonian Institution Press.

Yoffee, Norman, and George L. Cowgill (editors)
1988 The Collapse of Ancient States and Civilizations. Tucson: University of Arizona Press.

Zagarell, Allen
1975 An archaeological survey in the northeast Baxtiari Mountains. Proceedings of the 3rd Annual Symposium on Archaeological Research in Iran 3:145-56. Tehran: Iranian Centre for Archaeological Research.

Zeitlin, Judith Francis
1978 Changing patterns of resource exploitation, settlement distribution, and demography on the southern isthmus of Tehuantepec, Mexico. In: Prehistoric Coastal Adaptations: The Economy and Ecology of Maritime Middle America, edited by Barbara L. Stark and Barbara Voorhies, pp. 151-78. New York: Academic Press.
1993 The politics of Classic-Period ritual interaction: iconography of the ballgame cult in coastal Oaxaca. Ancient Mesoamerica 4:121-40.

Zeitlin, Robert N.
1990 The isthmus and the Valley of Oaxaca: questions about Zapotec imperialism in Formative Period Mesoamerica. American Antiquity 55:250-61.
1993 Pacific coastal Laguna Zope: a regional center in the Terminal Formative hinterlands of Monte Albán. Ancient Mesoamerica 4:85-101.

Zeitlin, Robert N., and Arthur A. Joyce
1999 The Zapotec-imperialism argument: insights from the Oaxaca coast. Current Anthropology 40:383-92.